E
E
E
E
D
C

Arne Jacobsen
Designing Denmark

Trapholt
Aarhus University Press
Yale University Press

Exhibition and catalogue is supported by:

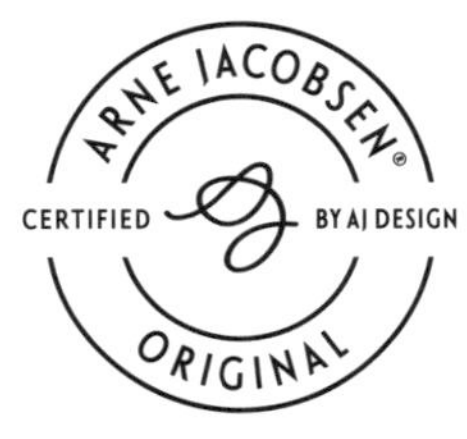

Arne Jacobsen Design I/S

FRITZ HANSEN

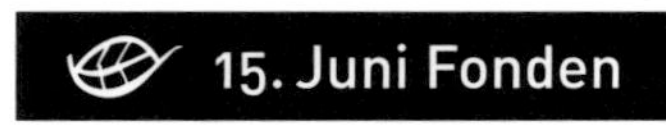

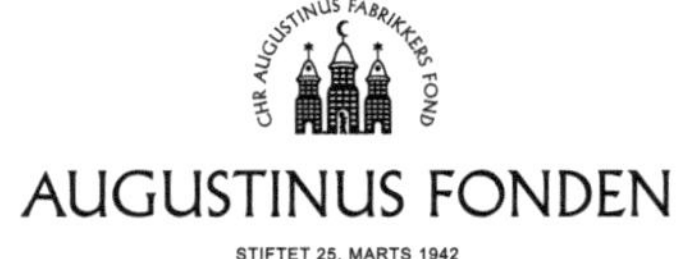

BESTLES FOND

Knud Højgaards Fond

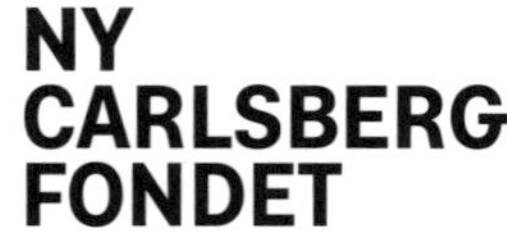

William Demant | Fonden

Arne Jacobsen

Designing Denmark

Arne Jacobsen on the patio of his home on Strandvejen

Photo: Egon Engmann/Ritzau Scanpix

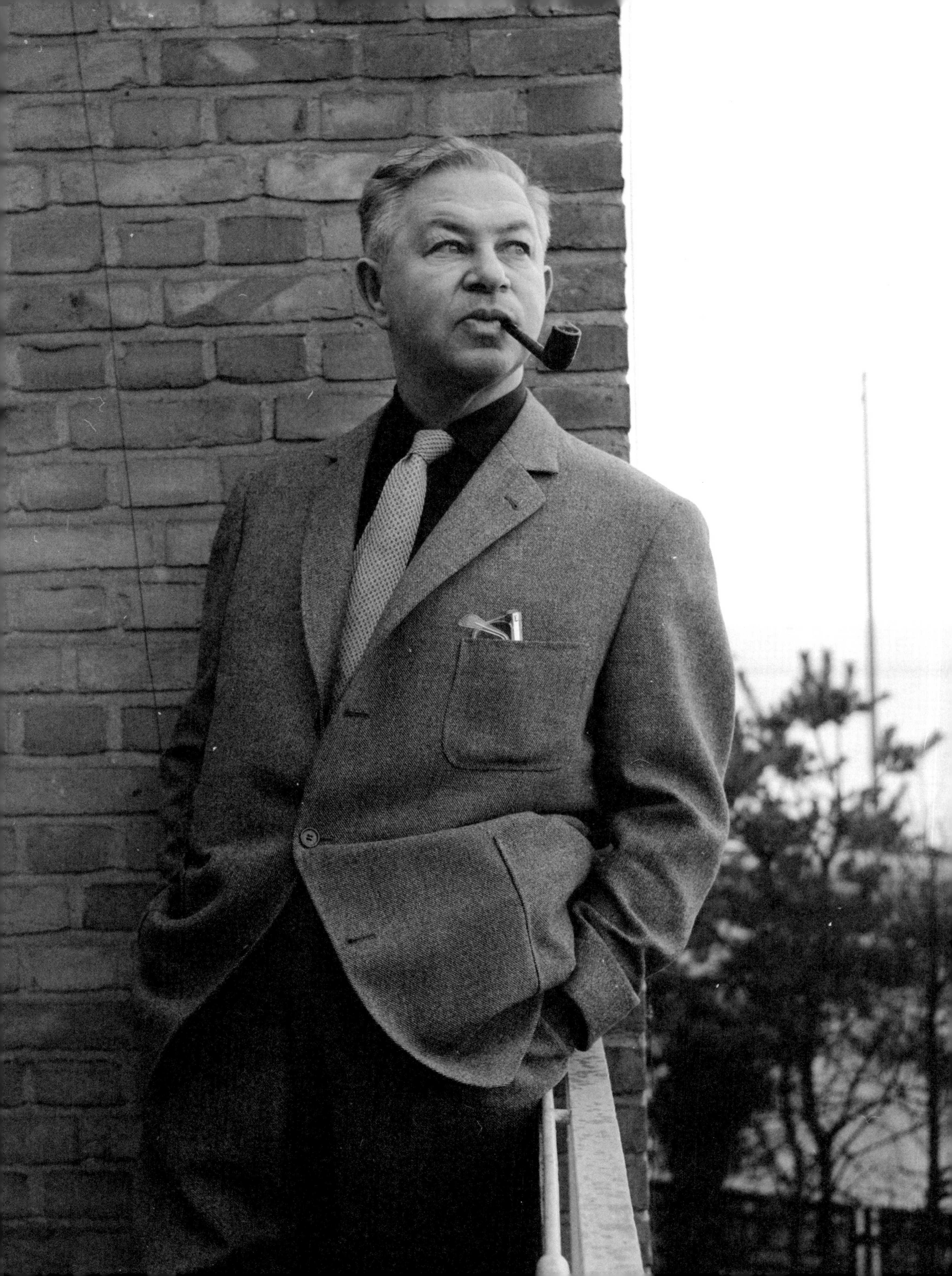

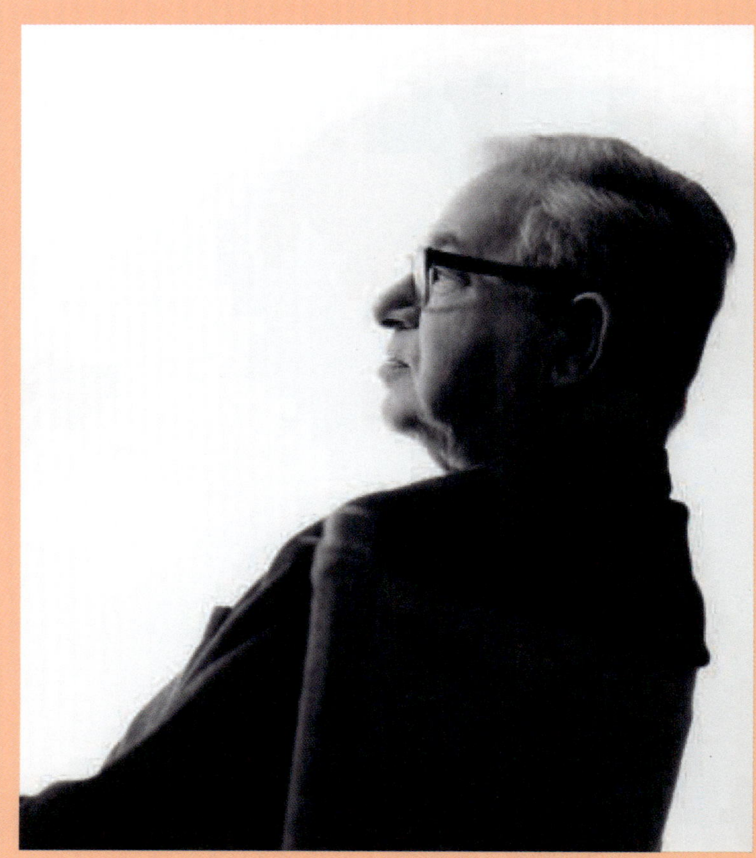

130

Art was in his blood

Arne Jacobsen's pursuit of aesthetic cohesiveness

Katrine Stenum Poulsen

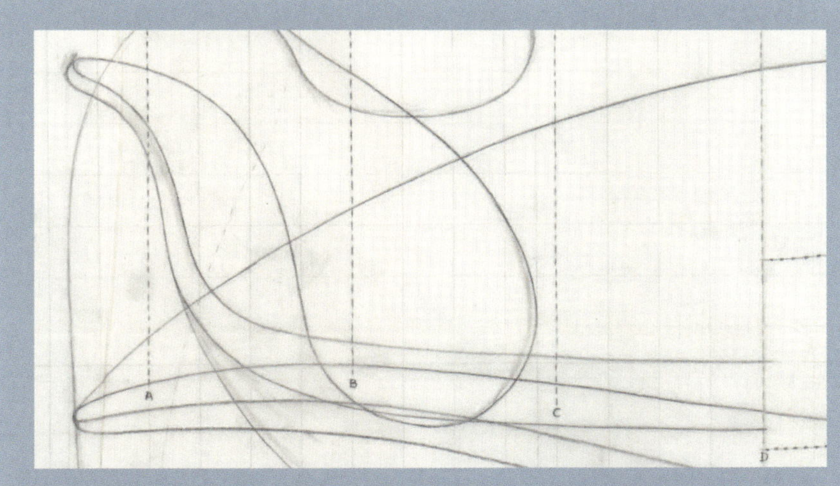

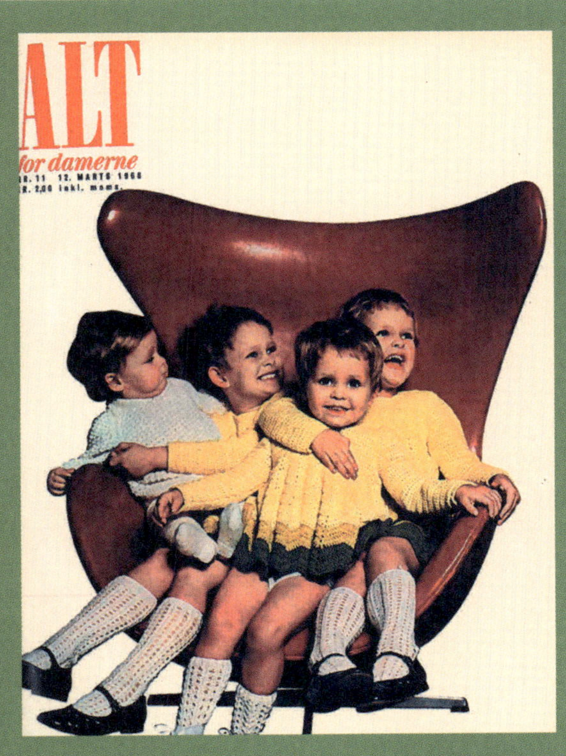
ALT
for damerne

Preface

Karen Grøn
Director

Contemporary relevance is a central issue every time we plan a major project at Trapholt. When carrying out our preparations, we always ask ourselves one question: what makes this particular topic interesting today? This time, our immediate present has rather overtaken our projections: this exhibition on Arne Jacobsen examines the role played by Danish Design within the wider, fundamental connection between the Danish people and the welfare society to which we all contribute. A welfare society whose importance has since been repeatedly emphasised in the efforts made to mitigate the effects of the COVID-19 pandemic.

In the wake of World War II, Denmark built the society that we know today. Danish architects and designers helped develop the visual side of the welfare state through new public buildings and furniture for public spaces. Børge Mogensen, Finn Juhl, Hans J. Wegner, Poul Henningsen and Arne Jacobsen created an aesthetic that still holds sway today in communal areas such as libraries, townhouses, schools, offices and hospitals. One may see such interiors as places that are not only functional, but also aesthetically communicative and accessible. The aesthetic shores up a national self-image which insists that aesthetically pleasing functionality is not the sole reserve of the rich, but a common good to which we all have access due to the redistribution of financial resources in the community.

Arne Jacobsen was one of the most influential designers in the overall development of Danish society. Everywhere you looked, you would see Arne Jacobsen's furniture, textiles and lamps – and the same still holds true today. In his major total designs – where he created everything from the architecture of the building to the smallest details – Arne Jacobsen also had a clear vision about the art to be incorporated in the totality. The results were unified aesthetic expressions of the Danish welfare state, a set-up which in principle benefits all Danes. This universal applicability is evidenced by the fact that in Denmark, unlike many of our European neighbours, there is a general consensus on the fact that aesthetics, form and materials are important for our well-being in shared and private spaces alike.

Arne Jacobsen brought international currents to Denmark, which would at times promt fierce debate. Today many believe that his work is a clear example of Danish design. It is interesting to note how what was once thought foreign becomes part of a shared self-understanding. The narrative claiming Arne Jacobsen's design as distinctly Danish shows how a conglomerate of objects, events and contexts can take root locally over time. This begs the question: can anything truly be called authentically Danish? Perhaps the essence of 'Danishness' is in fact constantly changing and evolving?

Arne Jacobsen – Designing Denmark is the most comprehensive exhibition and catalogue on the danish designer to date. It showcases the full range of his textiles, design, art and architecture from his earliest career up until his death, and also features a section on the afterlife of his designs up to the present day. His work reached far beyond the well-known classics, and one of the primary purposes of the exhibition is to demonstrate the rich scope of his endeavours.

The exhibition was created by curator Katrine Stenum Poulsen, who collaborated with Annika Skaarup Larsen, art historian and registrar at Arne Jacobsen Design I/S, and Nan Dahlkild, associate professor at the Department of Communication, University of Copenhagen, on the research and curation underpinning the project.

The publication opens with an introduction to Arne Jacobsen, exploring his life and work through five chronological themes: From student to studio owner, Winning the hearts of the Danes, Arne Jacobsen – Designing Denmark, International fame, and the legacy of Arne Jacobsen.

Katrine Stenum Poulsen's article then goes on to examine the crucial importance of Arne Jacobsen's keen interest in art for the preparation – and our contemporary understanding – of his architectural total designs. Stenum Poulsen delves into his original dream of becoming an artist, his own persistent practice as an artist, his artistic approach to working processes, and his insistence on controlling which art should be included in his projects, for example at Rødovre City Hall. The article also unpacks Arne Jacobsen's relationship with the art scene and his specific connection to the European post-war avant-garde evidenced by his signing of the manifesto of 'Le Groupe Espace'.

In her article, co-curator Annika Skaarup Larsen breaks the mould established by the classic narrative about the young Arne Jacobsen as a Modernist rebel. Instead, Skaarup Larsen describes him as a creative innovator who transforms well-known formats and practices through a constant creative and intuitive exchange with the materials chosen, an exchange involving processes that are not predetermined. The article argues that we can promote creativity in our society by focusing more on artistic approaches in schools, moving away from an overly one-sided focus on mathematical and cognitive subjects.

Associate professor Nan Dahlkild from the Department of Communication at the University of Copenhagen describes how the development of Danish welfare society involved a pervasive insistence that material growth should be followed by cultural growth and aesthetics. Dahlkild describes how a diverse range of cultural and cooperative forces, manufacturers, media and businesses interacted with and supported the political visions concerning the Danish welfare state's cultural and aesthetic tasks: for example, a minimalist interior in a city hall could signal a less lofty, more democratic approach to administration and politics, bridging the gap between the public and the private.

Arne Jacobsen – Designing Denmark was made possible by the kind support and funding from 15. Juni Fonden, Augustinus Fonden, Bestles Fond, Knud Højgaards Fond, Ny Carlsbergfondet and William Demant Fonden.

Trapholt is grateful to all the partners involved, without whom this project would not have existed: &Tradition, Borås Tapeter, Dansk Møbelkunst, Designmuseum Denmark, Dissing+Weitling, Fritz Hansen, Georg Jensen Damask, HOWE, Louis Poulsen, the Munkegård School, Nationalmuseum Stockholm, Novo Nordisk History Collection, the Royal Danish Library - Danish National Art Library, Royal Institute of British Architects, Rudersdal City Hall, Rødovre Kommune Lokalhistorisk Samling, Rødovre Library, St. Catherine's College, Stelton, VOLA and Aarhus City Hall.

Trapholt would also like to extend warm thanks to all private lenders for their generosity and cooperation. A big thank you goes out to Mathias Bøgeholdt for professional insights and advice. Special thanks are due to scholar and associate professor Nan Dahlkild from the University of Copenhagen. Special thanks also go out to Arne Jacobsen Design I/S for their unwavering support for the project. Most importantly, Trapholt would like to thank the Jacobsen, Holmblad and Magnussen families and the exhibition's curators, Katrine Stenum Poulsen and Annika Skaarup Larsen.

Arne Jacobsen Designing Denmark

Introduction 01

Katrine Stenum Poulsen
Annika Skaarup Larsen

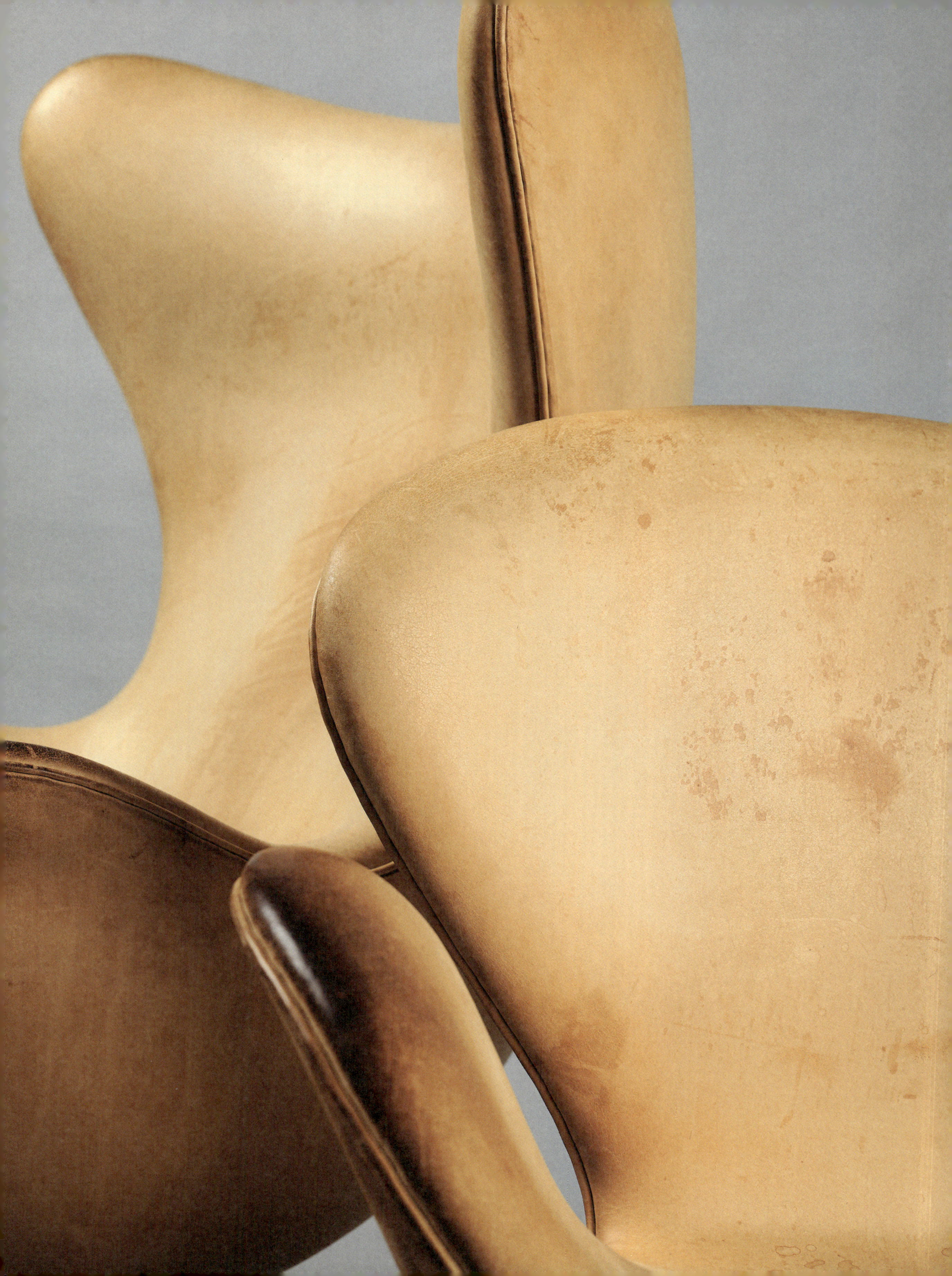

'The time of ornaments is over. Now it is rhythm that matters, rhythm and proportion.'

– Arne Jacobsen, 1954

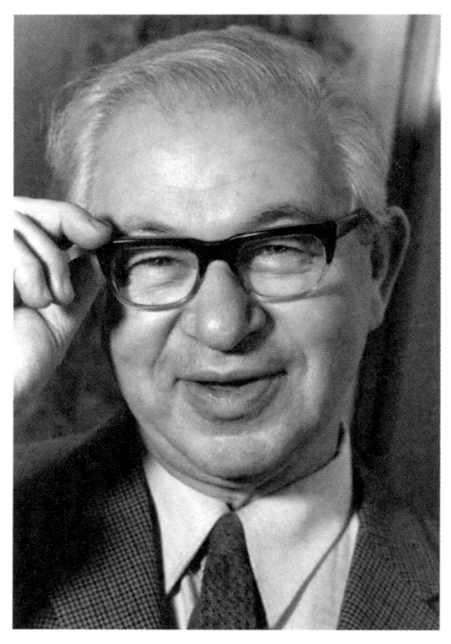

Architect and designer Arne Jacobsen
Photo: Mogens Berger/Ritzau Scanpix

Arne Jacobsen (1902–1971) was one of the most influential architects and designers in Danish design history. His elegant, distinctive and easily recognisable furniture played a major role in Denmark's evolution as a design nation, and today, 50 years after his death, his furniture is still often featured in modern homes and widely used in public settings as an exponent of good Danish design.

Arne Jacobsen was unusual, in that he worked both as an architect and as a designer. In his large public and private buildings such as the Aarhus City Hall (1942), the Munkegård School (1957) and the famous SAS Royal Hotel (1960), Arne Jacobsen created total designs – *Gesamtkunstwerks* – that featured both freestanding and built-in furniture, lamps, door handles, textiles, planting and artistic decoration, all combined clearly and concisely to convey his minimalist aesthetic to the people of Denmark. As indicated in the quote above (Bostrup, 1954), his aesthetic was informed by rhythm and proportion, rejecting the ornament and decoration of the past.

During the six decades of Arne Jacobsen's career, Danish society evolved from a society of shortage and relative poverty into a modern industrialised nation and a welfare society. Housing redevelopments, expansions of infrastructure and major social reforms all changed the face of Denmark, giving Arne Jacobsen and his colleagues plenty to do. Arne Jacobsen was particularly busy in the Copenhagen area and in the suburban municipalities of Gentofte and Rødovre, making his mark on urban spaces with large public projects, commissions for private companies and several residential buildings.

During this period, Denmark achieved increased prosperity, and the furniture manufacturers took great interest in raising the standard of living, both materially and culturally. The new welfare state made its physical mark in the form of new public spaces and public institutions furnished with Danish furniture by designers such as Arne Jacobsen, Poul Henningsen and Hans J. Wegner. Today we still move in and among these spaces, which shape and govern our physical and sensory understanding of Denmark's welfare society

Throughout his life, Arne Jacobsen had a keen eye for the latest currents and movements, observing and responding to society's expectations and new needs. Consequently, his life was all about creativity, innovation and a way of working, which remains extremely relevant today – a time when the world is once again facing major challenges and upheavals. Arne Jacobsen's work reminds us of how shape, colour and materials affect our perception and experience of the world we inhabit.

From student to studio owner

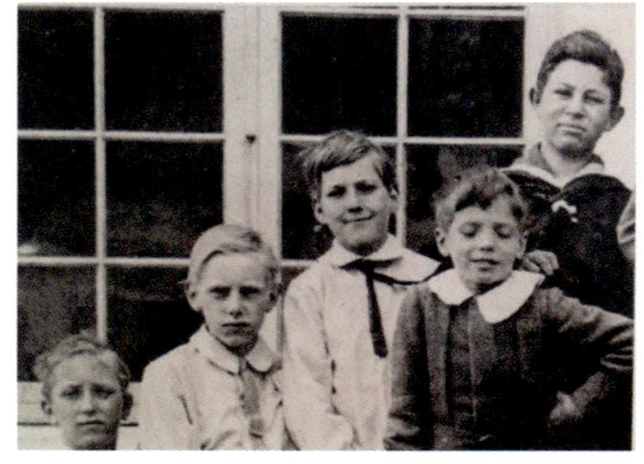

Arne Jacobsen (at the back, on the right) at boarding school. The other boys in the photo include the brothers Mogens and Flemming Lassen (extreme left), who were to play a major role in Arne Jacobsen's career

Photo: Private photo

Arne Emil Jacobsen was born on 11 February 1902. His father was a wholesaler who imported safety pins, snap fasteners and similar items for large department stores. His mother was a trained bank clerk and, in her spare time, a passionate flower painter. Restless in school, Arne Jacobsen was sent away to a boarding school in Nærum at the age of eleven. Here a teacher spotted a special talent for drawing in her young pupil and encouraged him to hone his skills in the fields of both drawing and painting. Arne Jacobsen started dreaming of becoming a painter, but his father had other plans for his son, insisting on a proper, sensible education. Prompted by his schoolmate Flemming Lassen, Arne Jacobsen chose architecture, where his interest in drawing would stand him in good stead. He soon enrolled in the building, construction and architecture classes at a technical school and spent his summers as a mason's apprentice, also spending some time in Germany.

Having graduated from technical school in 1924, he was admitted to the Royal Danish Academy of Fine Art's School of Architecture, studying under the architects and professors Kay Fisker, Ivar Bentsen and Kaj Gottlob. The teaching centred on the study of classical and ancient architecture. On study trips

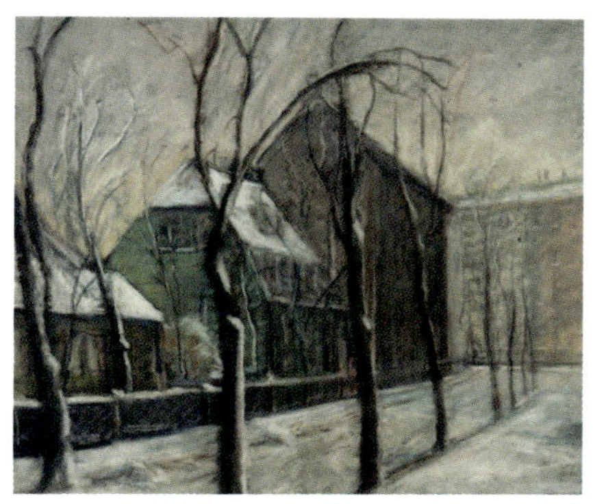

Painting of Classensgade, where Arne Jacobsen lived as a child. The painting is supposedly the work of the 14- or 16-year-old Arne Jacobsen

Photo: Private photo

and in Kaj Gottlob's 'temple class', the students acquired an understanding of the classical concept of beauty by sketching old buildings and plaster casts. Here, the young Arne made good use of his remarkable talent for drawing and enjoyed great success with his beautiful, artistic watercolours. In 1927, Arne Jacobsen married Marie Jelstrup Holm, whom he met while studying at technical school. In 1927, Arne Jacobsen also graduated from the Royal Danish Academy of Fine Arts and embarked on his career as an architect.

The 1920s marked a dramatic period in Danish architecture, with modern currents from Europe challenging established building traditions. As part of the industrialisation process, large parts of Denmark's population moved from the country to the big towns and cities. This movement created a new social structure with a large working class living in cramped conditions in the dilapidated backyards of the city. Similar social developments were witnessed abroad, prompting a design revolution. Its most radical expression occurred at the German Bauhaus school, which rejected the decorated house façades of the middle classes and their expensive, elaborate cabinetry in favour of architecture and design that focused on functionality and reflected the rational, pure aesthetic of new industry. Towards the end of the decade, Arne Jacobsen became part of the vanguard that brought the new modernist currents to Denmark.

As early as 1927, while still a student, Arne Jacobsen designed his first detached houses in the Copenhagen area. That same year he got a job at 'Københavns Stadsarkitekt' – the municipal architectural office of the City of Copenhagen – where he designed his first public project for the Enghaveparken residential area in Vesterbro. In his

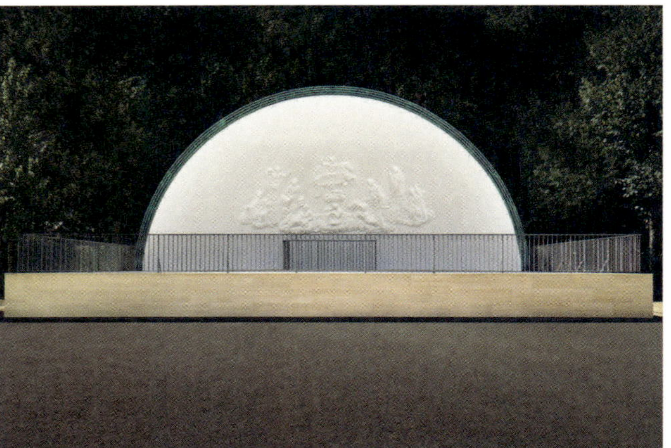

The buildings in the Enghave Park were Arne Jacobsen's first public-sector commission and a rare example of his use of the neoclassical style

Photo: Einar Kornerup A/S

first projects, Arne Jacobsen continued to work within a neoclassical aesthetic, adhering to the reinterpretation of the antiquity's ideals of beauty, which were still prevalent at the Academy. In 1929, however, European Modernism made its breakthrough in Denmark, giving rise to what is known in Danish contexts as Functionalism or its nickname 'Funkis'. His breakthrough came at a major housing and construction fair held in Forum in 1929, where Arne Jacobsen and Flemming Lassen presented 'The House of the Future'. With its white, spiral-shaped exterior and open, functional interior, the house was an interpretation of new ideas that the young architects had discovered in the works of the architect Le Corbusier in France and the Bauhaus school in Germany. The spectacular round house stole all the media attention, and overnight Arne Jacobsen became a household name in Denmark. That same year he set up his own design studio, which quickly gained solid financial footing from the many houses he designed in the wake of the House of the Future success. 'From that point on, every schoolteacher in Denmark wanted an Arne Jacobsen house' said the architect Erik Møller, who worked at the design studio at the time (Thau & Vindum, 1998, p. 77).

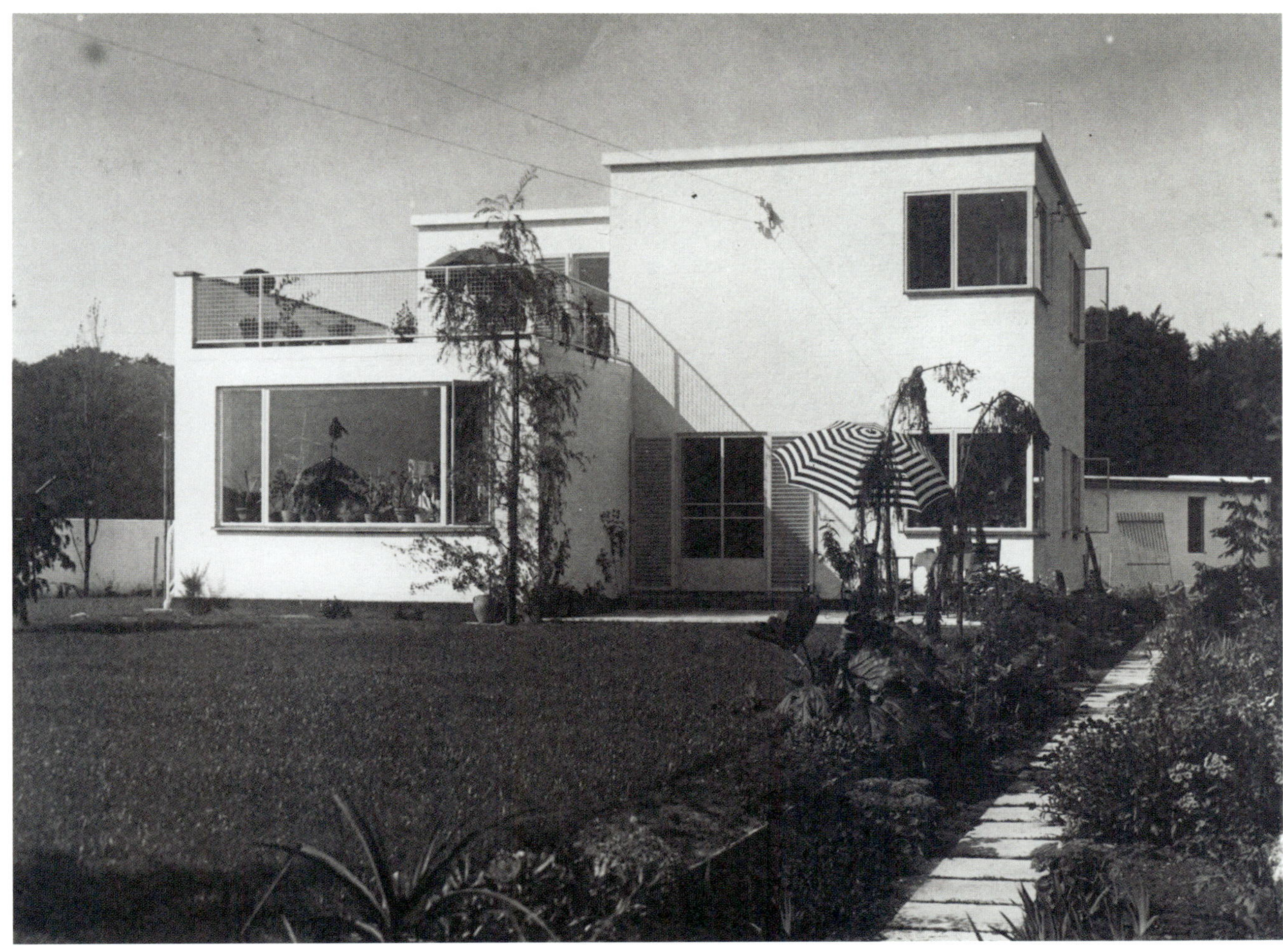

Arne Jacobsen's private villa in Ordrup, designed in 1929. With its white, cubist exterior the house is an example of the Functionalist style of the era, known as 'Funkis', but the construction itself is a traditional brick house

Photo: The Royal Danish Library

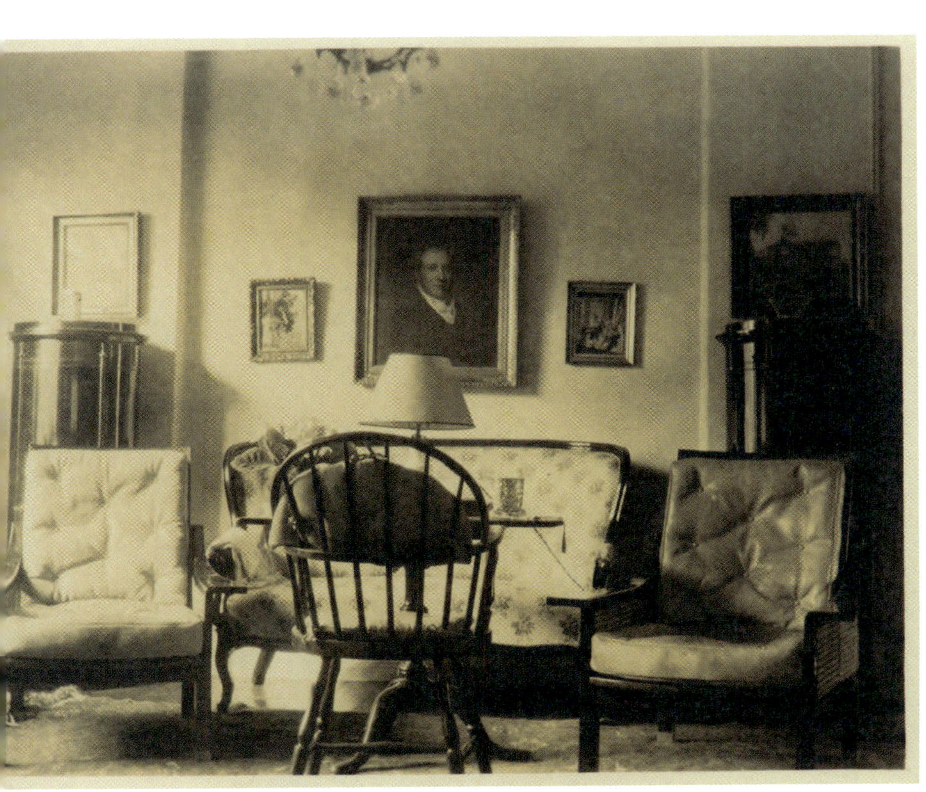

Arne Jacobsen's living room at his home in Ordrup

Photo: Private photo

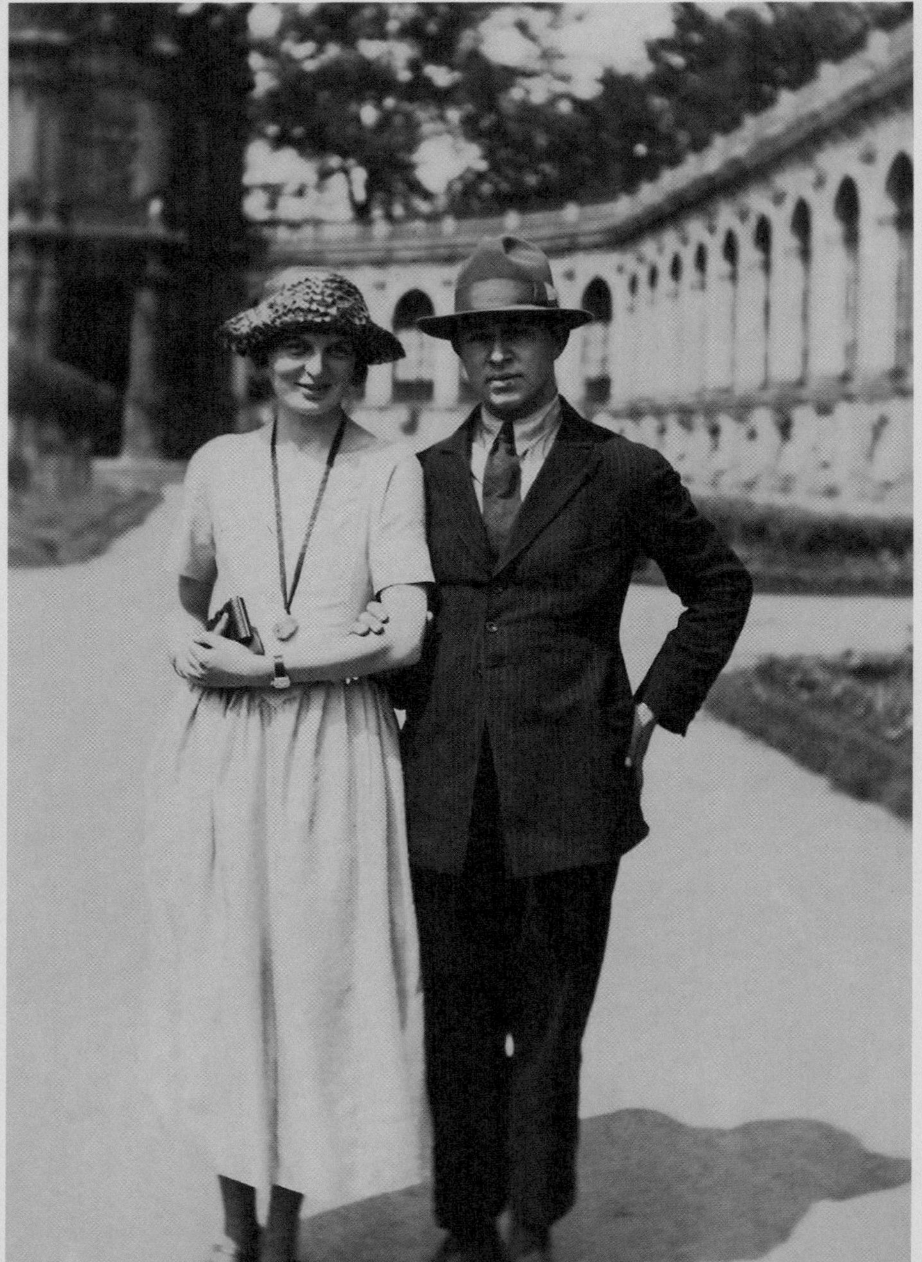

Arne and Marie Jacobsen on their honeymoon in the late 1920s

Photo: Private photo

Arne and Marie had two sons: Johan and Niels Kevin

Photo: Private photo

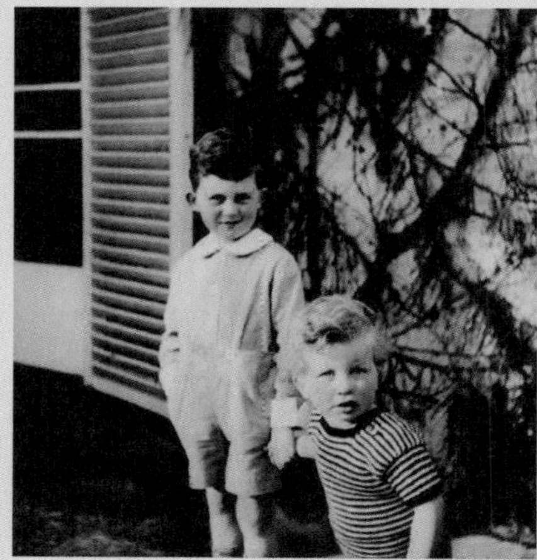

Arne and Marie

The match between Arne Jacobsen and Marie Jelstrup Holm may be described as a case of opposites attract. The young Faroese woman was part of the radical cultural scene in Denmark and had many ideas that ran counter to those of the conservatively-raised Arne Jacobsen. They honeymooned in Germany and Italy, where Arne Jacobsen spent time exploring the arts of photography and watercolour. During her years in Copenhagen, Marie was involved in the world of the arts, moving in social circles that included artists and poets. She was also a close friend of the architect and public debater Poul Henningsen and the poet Otto Gelsted, who often visited the young couple's home. Arne and Marie had two sons, Johan and Niels Kevin. Their marriage lasted until the early 1940s, at which point they separated.

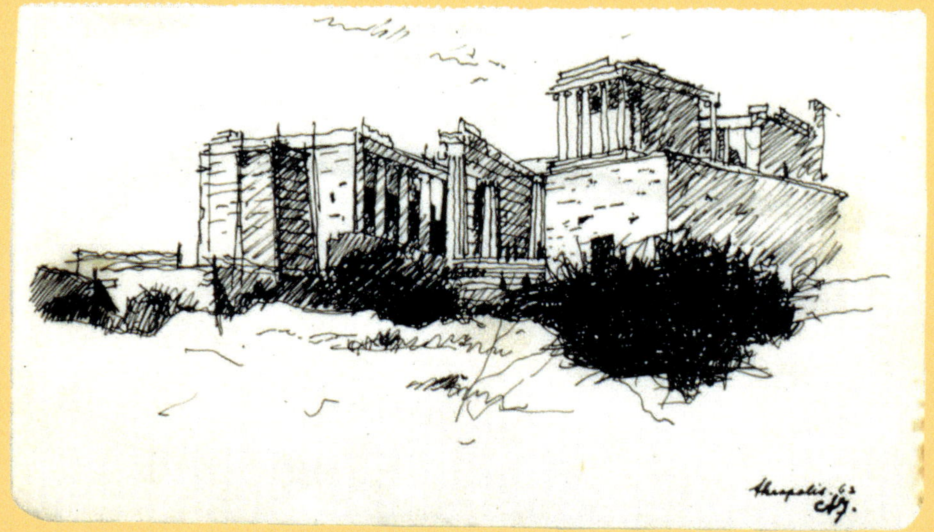

Pages from Arne Jacobsen's sketchbooks, which he used particularly when travelling

Photo: Private photo

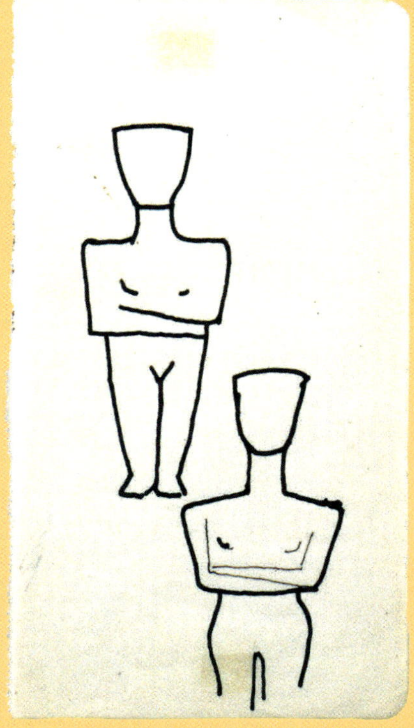

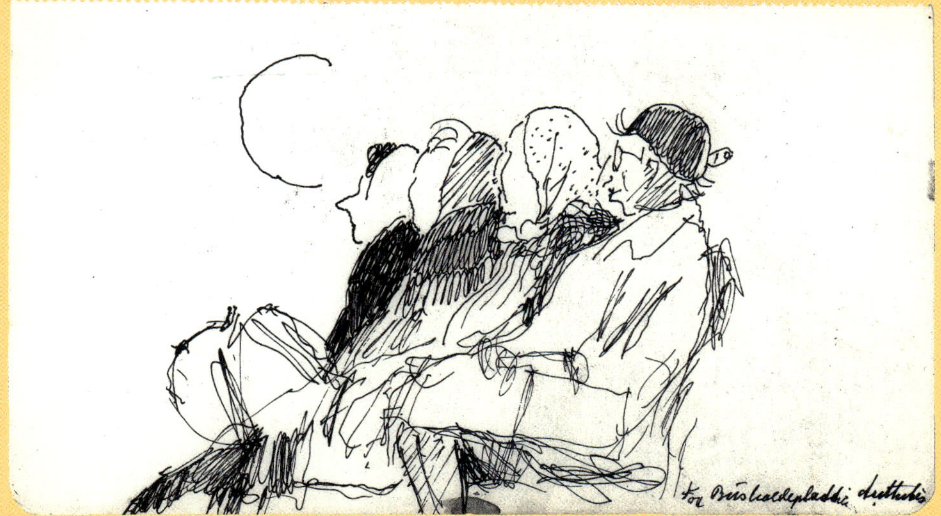

Arne Jacobsen and the arts

Throughout his life, Arne Jacobsen was an avid photographer and painter. On his various trips and holidays, he made extensive use of his camera and film camera. Shot in a montage style, his footage testifies to a keen sense of curiosity and awareness of the details and aesthetics of his surroundings. Architecture, nature studies and landscapes were favourite subjects in his photographs, films and watercolours. On several occasions, he would translate the subjects originally captured with camera and brush, reshaping them into patterns used in his textile and design work.

Arne Jacobsen's sketchbooks served as a diary of his life. They contained notes, sketches of people, buildings and patterns. At home he drew inspiration from the garden, studying many different plant species in his watercolours. He often spent hours outside, while the employees at his studio, located in the basement floor of his house, worked on the designs and drawings for the company's current construction projects.

Arne Jacobsen gradually built a private art collection featuring some of Denmark's greatest artists such as Asger Jorn, Richard Mortensen and Preben Hornung. Arne Jacobsen's international outlook was also evident in the collection, which contained works by the French painters Victor Vasarely, Jean Dewasne and Charles Lapicque.

A watercolour rendition by Arne Jacobsen and Flemming Lassen of the House of the Future with its distinctive, spiral-shaped floor plan

Photo: The Royal Danish Library – The Danish National Art Library

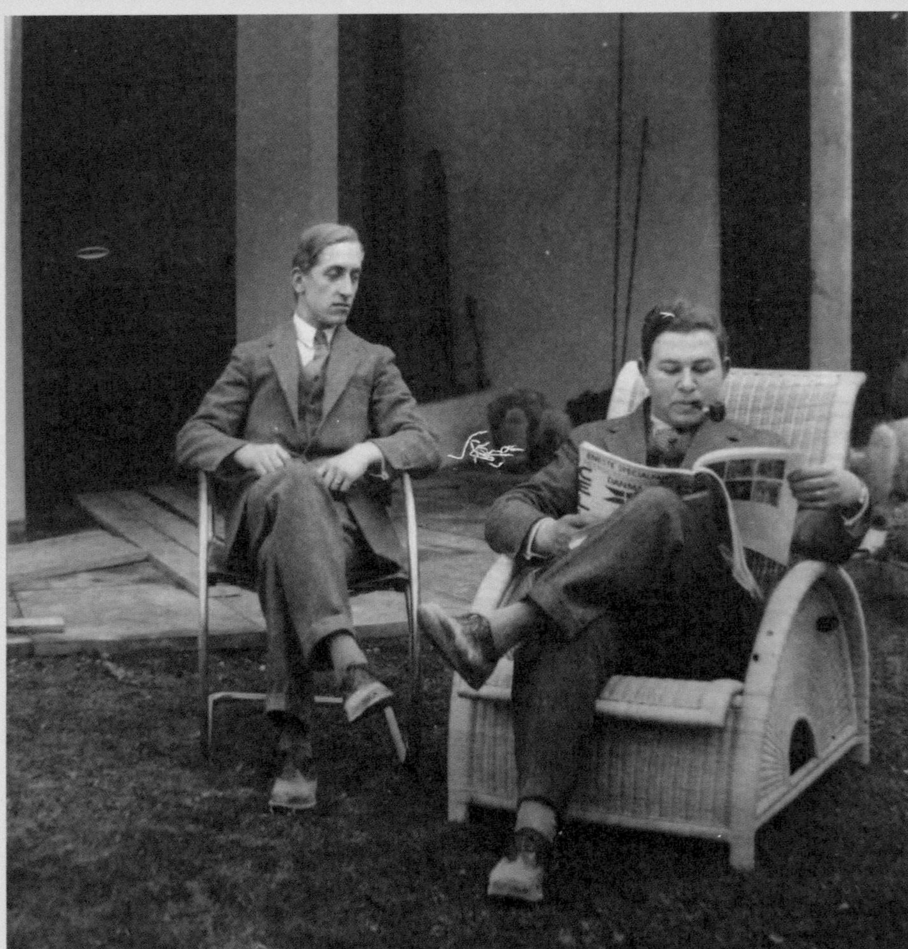

Arne Jacobsen and Flemming Lassen in front of the House of the Future. Flemming Lassen (on the left) is sitting in Mies van der Rohe's MR chair and Arne Jacobsen in his own Forest Snail chair

Photo: & Tradition/ByLassen

The House of the Future

Arne Jacobsen got his big breakthrough in Denmark in 1929 with the House of the Future. He designed the house in collaboration with Flemming Lassen for the Danish Architects' Housing and Construction Exhibition in Forum in 1929, where it was showcased as the two young architects submission for the Danish Association of Architects' competition for a 'House of the Future' which, according to the competition rules, should disregard any obstacles 'posed by any shortcomings in our present-day technology and legislation' (Thau & Vindum, 1998, p. 216). They won the competition, prompting a great deal of attention from the industry and in the Danish press.

The house was the two architects' take on the White Modernism, which was rapidly gaining ground in Europe at the time. With its spiral-shaped floor plan, spectacular technical solutions, two garages (one for a speedboat, the other for a car) and a helipad on the roof, the house also embodied the optimistic outlook of the 1920s. Featuring electric underfloor heating, the house was also equipped with a pneumatic tube system connected to the local post office, tables that automatically transport cigars and other items to diners, and a doormat with a built-in vacuum cleaner that automatically cleaned your shoes. The house was decorated with brightly-coloured walls, ceilings and floors, and was furnished with Mies van der Rohe's modern steel furniture, alongside Arne Jacobsen's new wicker chair known as the Paris chair (1929), its streamlined contours reflecting the spiral shape of the house.

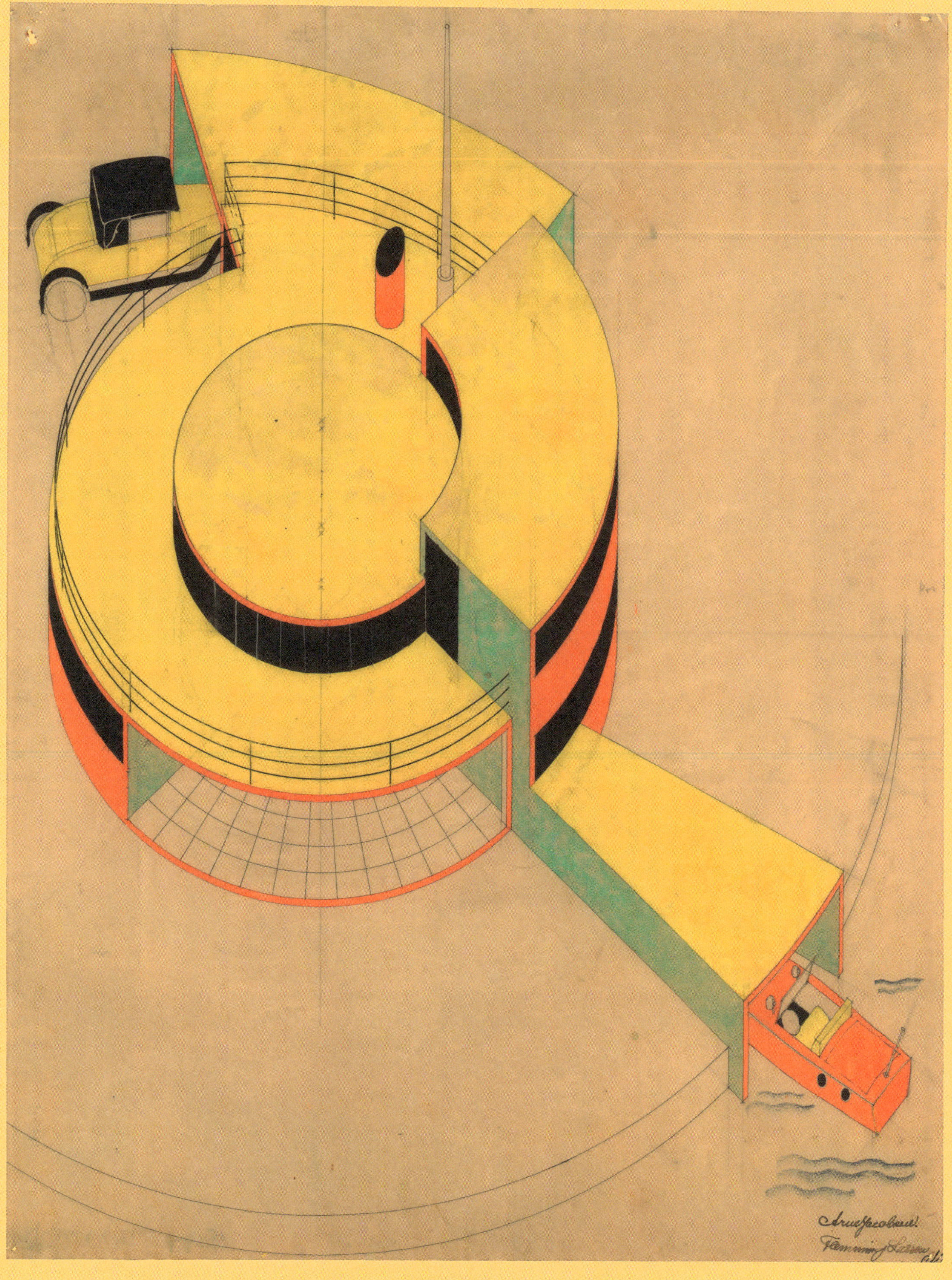

Winning the hearts of the Danes

Aarhus City Hall. Arne Jacobsen and Erik Møller's first proposal was a sober administration building without a tower. However, in the press, the people of the city expressed a desire for a more traditional, monumental town hall. Accordingly, the architects made various alterations to the plans and added the tower

Photo: Jens Kirkeby/Ritzau Scanpix

From the mid-1930s, Arne Jacobsen made his mark on the face of Denmark with a number of prominent public buildings, corporate offices and several private homes north of Copenhagen. In the early 1930s, Arne Jacobsen designed no less than two public beach bathing facilities: one at Dragør Sydstrand (1933); the other at Bellevue north of Copenhagen (1932). While the beach bathing facility in Dragør was subsequently demolished, the Bellevue project evolved into one of Arne Jacobsen's major works, featuring the residential project Bellavista (1934), Bellevue Theatre (1937) and the famous petrol station at Skovshoved (1937). The large public beach bathing facilities and the bright flats in the Bellavista building reflected the Vitalist movement of the era, in which outdoor life, physical activity and healthy living conditions took centre stage in the concept of the good life and figured in the work of the artists and architects of the day.

During this period, Arne Jacobsen made his first public *Gesamtkunstwerk*, designing every aspect of his interiors. From the mid-1930s, visitors to the Bellevue Theatre, the Landmandsbanken bank and the Stellings Farvehandel paint shop on Skindergade in Copenhagen could enjoy Arne Jacobsen's modern aesthetics in meticulously planned spaces with customised fixtures and furnishings.

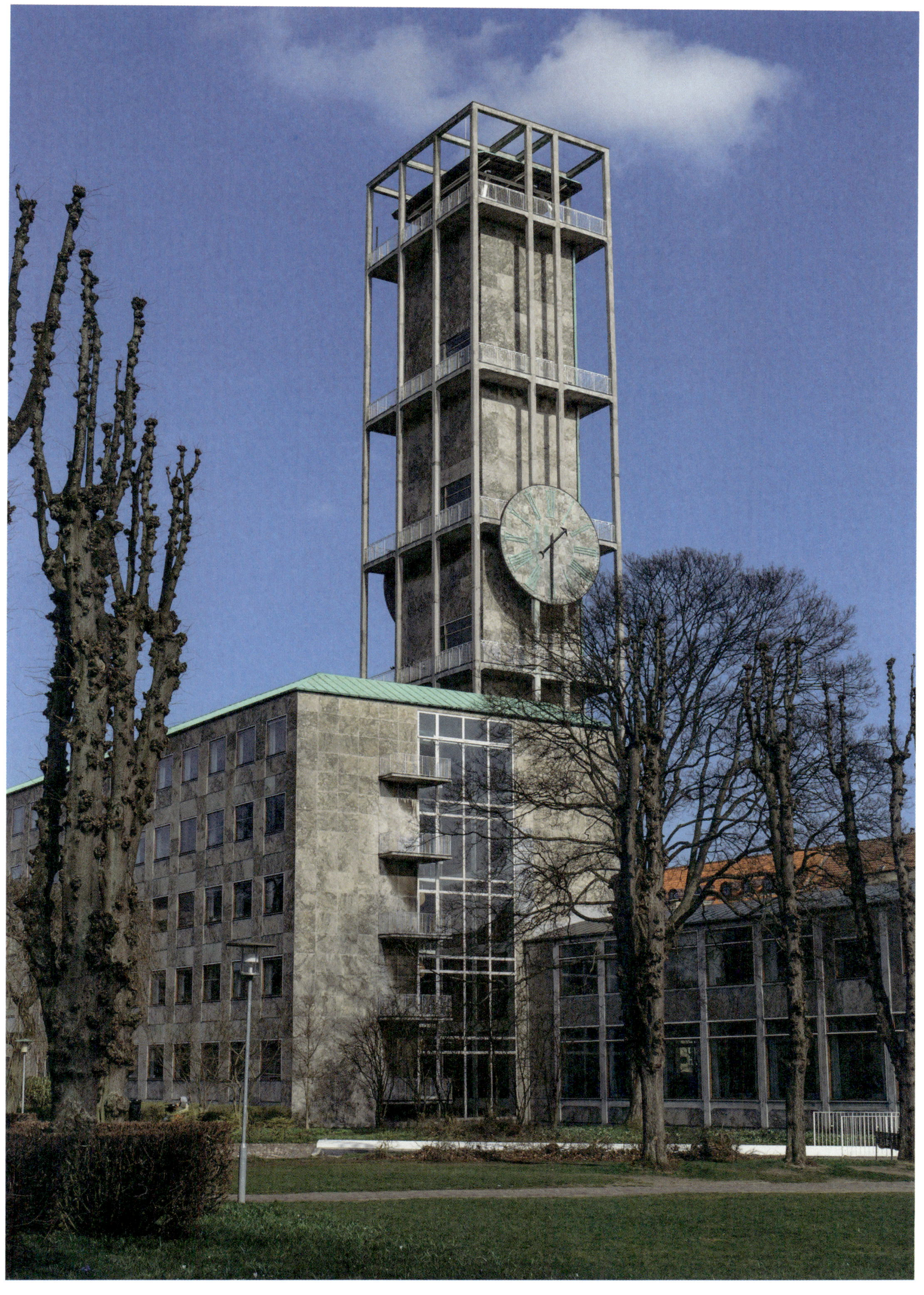

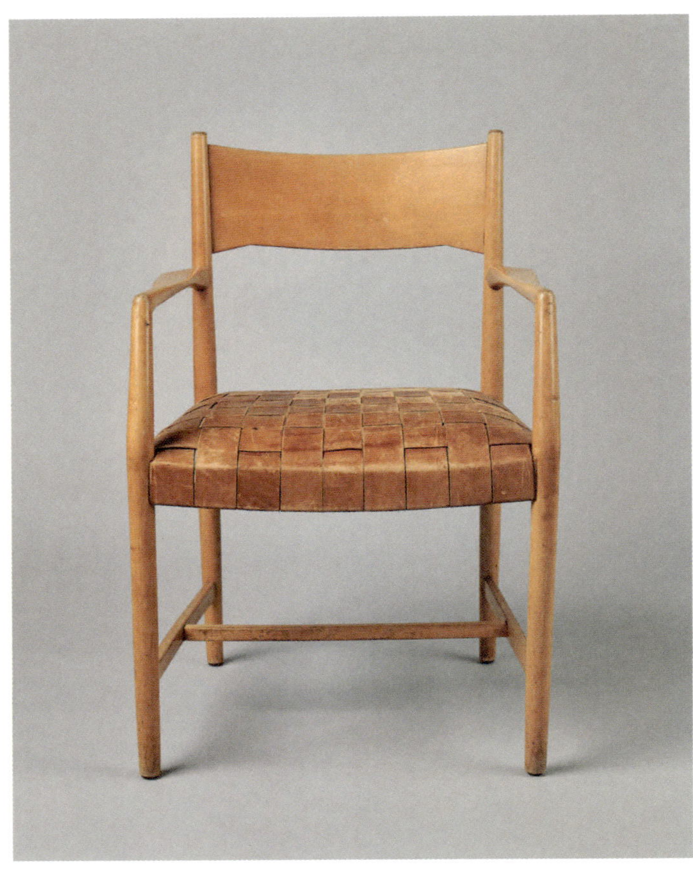

The meeting chair was part of the architect's total design for Aarhus City Hall. Hans J. Wegner, at the time a recent architecture graduate and an employee at the design studio, was given the job of designing the many items of furniture for the city hall

The 1940s were to be a crucial decade for Arne Jacobsen. In 1942, he completed two projects that were highlights of his career so far: Aarhus City Hall, designed in collaboration with Erik Møller; and Søllerød City Hall, designed in collaboration with Flemming Lassen. In both buildings the architects designed and orchestrated everything from architecture to furniture, lighting, and even special typefaces for each building. In Søllerød, Arne Jacobsen was also involved in the design of the fabrics for the building. It is in the context of this work that he met his second wife, the textile printer Jonna Møller. The following year, the couple were forced to flee to Sweden, fearing Nazi prosecution on account of Arne Jacobsen's Jewish roots. There was not much work for architects during the war. As soon as Denmark was free again, the couple returned to Copenhagen where Arne Jacobsen wasted no time in resuming work at his design studio.

Telephone desk and desk lamp; part of Arne Jacobsen and Flemming Lassen's total design for Søllerød City Hall, today Rudersdal City Hall

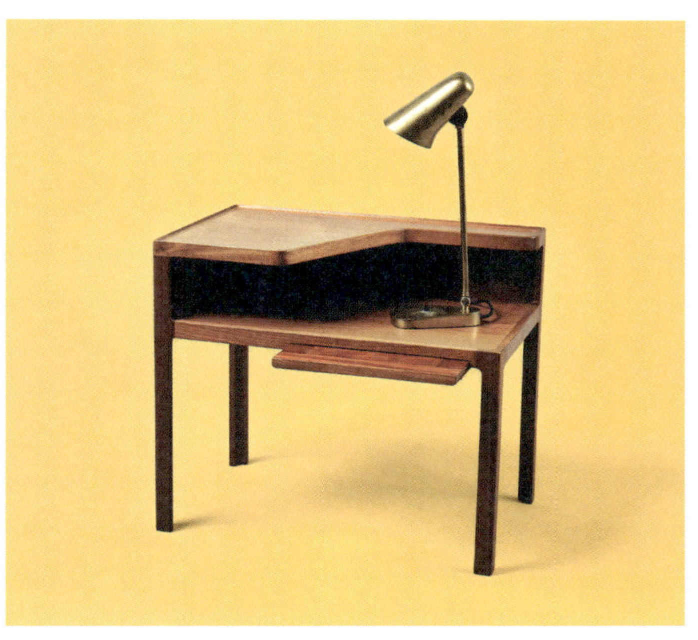

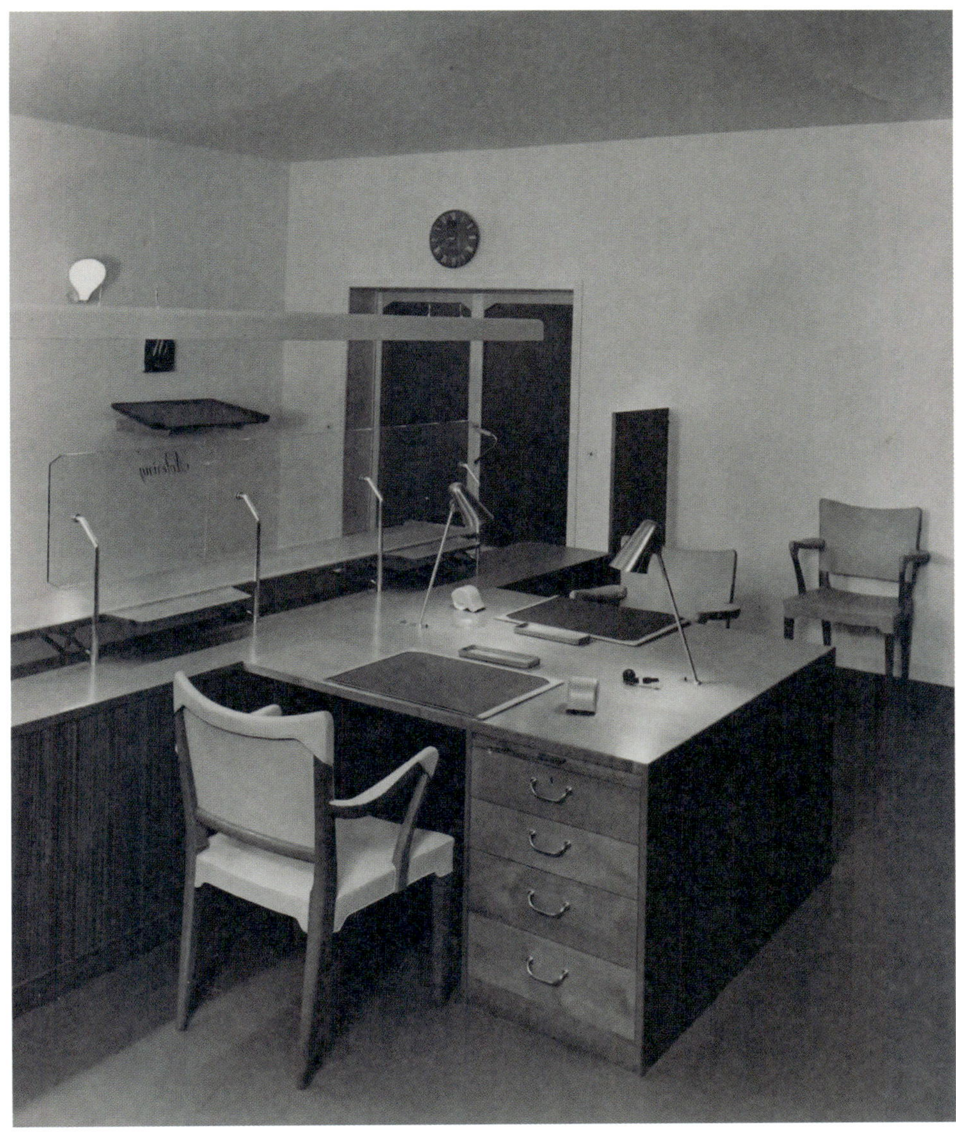

Søllerød Town Hall, now known as Rudersdal Town Hall, around the time of its opening in 1942

Photo: Aage Strüwing © Jørgen Strüwing

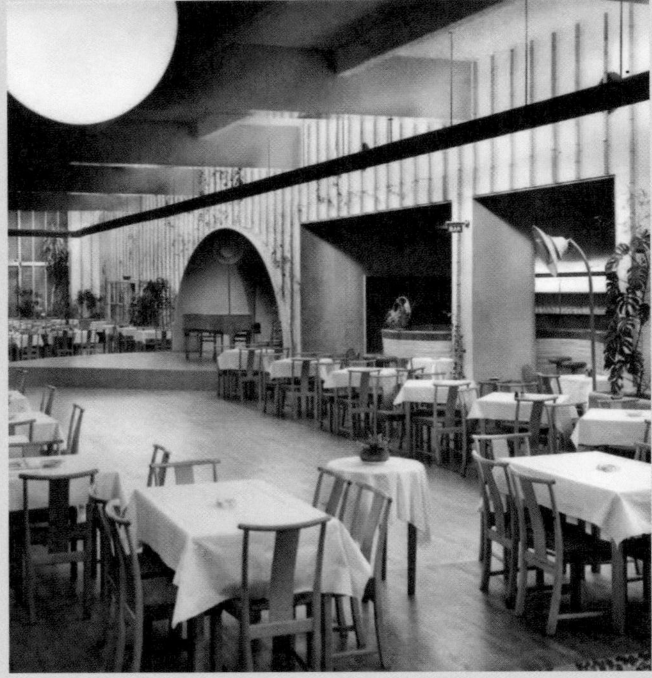

The Bellevue Theatre restaurant around the time of its opening in 1937

Photo: Aage Strüwing © Jørgen Strüwing

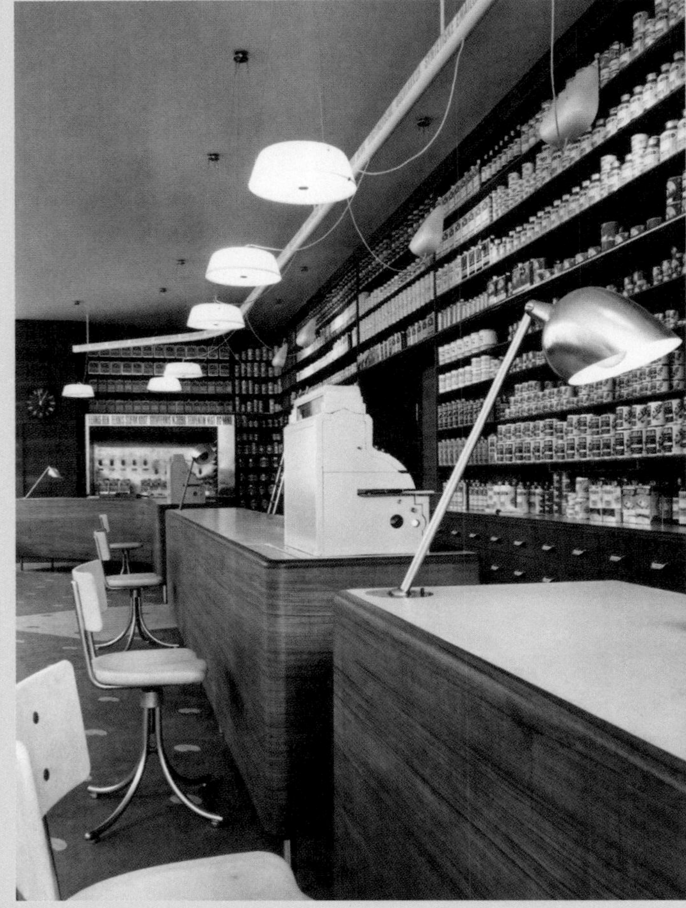

The head office and flagship store of the Stellings Farvehandel paint company around the time of its opening in 1937. Arne Jacobsen designed not only the building, but also all the furniture and fixtures and fittings

Photo: Aage Strüwing © Jørgen Strüwing

His first furniture

The earliest known furniture attributed to Arne Jacobsen dates from the mid-1920s, designed while the young Arne was still a student. At the 1925 Exposition Universelle in Paris he was awarded a silver medal for a chair design that has subsequently been lost, and two years later, in 1927, he had his debut at Charlottenborg in Copenhagen, presenting library furniture designed for the bookseller Fergo. These early pieces of furniture revealed clear signs of the influence of professor Kaare Klint, the great reformer of Danish furniture at the time, whose classes on furniture design Arne Jacobsen attended at the Royal Danish Academy of Fine Arts.

In the late 1920s, Arne Jacobsen embarked on extensive experiments with new shapes and materials. Examples included the wicker chair known as the Paris chair (1929), a bar stool crafted out of steel pipes for the Stellings Farvehandel paint shop (1937) and a chair with a back in bent wood for the Bellevue Theatre (1937). In 1932, together with Flemming Lassen, he designed a 'gentleman's room' or study for the master carpenter N. C. Christoffersen, featuring cubist armchairs upholstered in white washable material suitable for the practical, modern home. Arne Jacobsen also designed several armchairs, which, with their simple organic aesthetic, presaged his future success as a furniture designer in the 1950s. While he designed his famous shell-type chairs and furniture for the SAS Royal Hotel with industrial mass production in mind, he created the earlier pieces of furniture in collaboration with cabinetmakers, which was entirely in keeping with the prevailing craftsmanship tradition of the day.

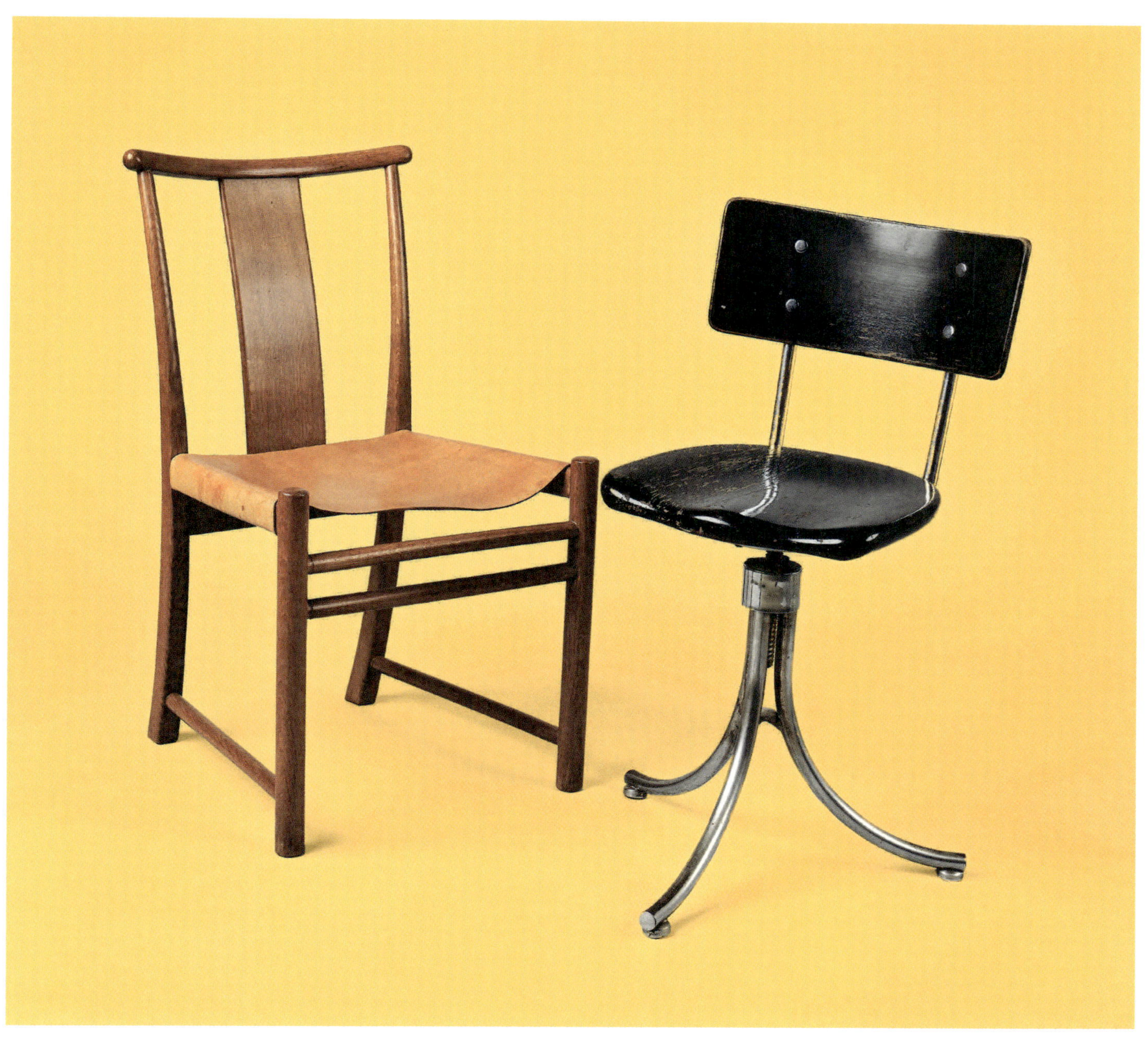

Chair for the Bellevue Theatre restaurant (left) and chair from the mid-1930s, which Arne Jacobsen used in his design for the Stellings Farvehandel paint shop (right)

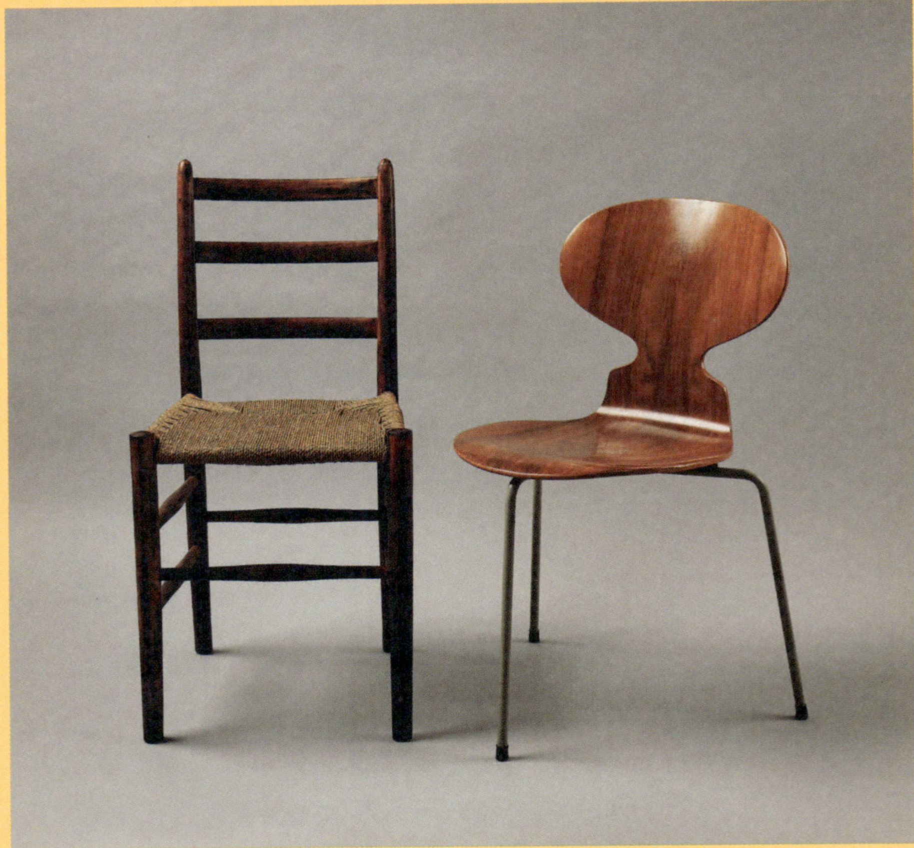

Chair designed for Novo Terapeutisk Laboratorium in 1935 and the Ant chair from 1952, both designed by Arne Jacobsen

Trapholt Collection

Arne Jacobsen and Novo – a lifelong partnership

The partnership between Arne Jacobsen and the pharmaceutical company Novo Terapeutisk Laboratorium (Novo Therapeutic Laboratory), now known as Novo Nordisk, was a special chapter in the story of his life. In the early 1930s, Arne Jacobsen designed homes for the founders of Novo Terapeutisk Laboratorium, the brothers Harald and Thorvald Pedersen, and two years later a new, modern factory building – known as Fuglebakken – for the company, situated in Frederiksberg. This commission marked the beginning of a partnership, in which Jacobsen became permanently affiliated with the company. The relationship would last throughout Arne Jacobsen's lifetime and involved a range of factories and office buildings, first in Denmark and later in Germany and France too. The projects for Novo allowed Arne Jacobsen to explore a more industrial aspect of his aesthetic, one that would come to infuse his architecture in general.

Jacobsen's collaboration with Novo also gave rise to the development of new furniture, the first example in connection with the Fuglebakken factory in 1935, where Arne Jacobsen designed customised furniture for the staff rooms and offices.

A better-known anecdote dates from the first years of the 1950s, when Arne Jacobsen was commissioned to design a canteen for the company, and grabbed the opportunity to promote his new shell-type chair, the Ant. In fact, Arne Jacobsen had been having difficulties in getting Fritz Hansen to put the small, three-legged chair into production. Only when he was able to present them with an order of 200 chairs for Novo's new canteen was Fritz Hansen persuaded to begin production of what was to become one of the most important furniture designs of the 20th century.

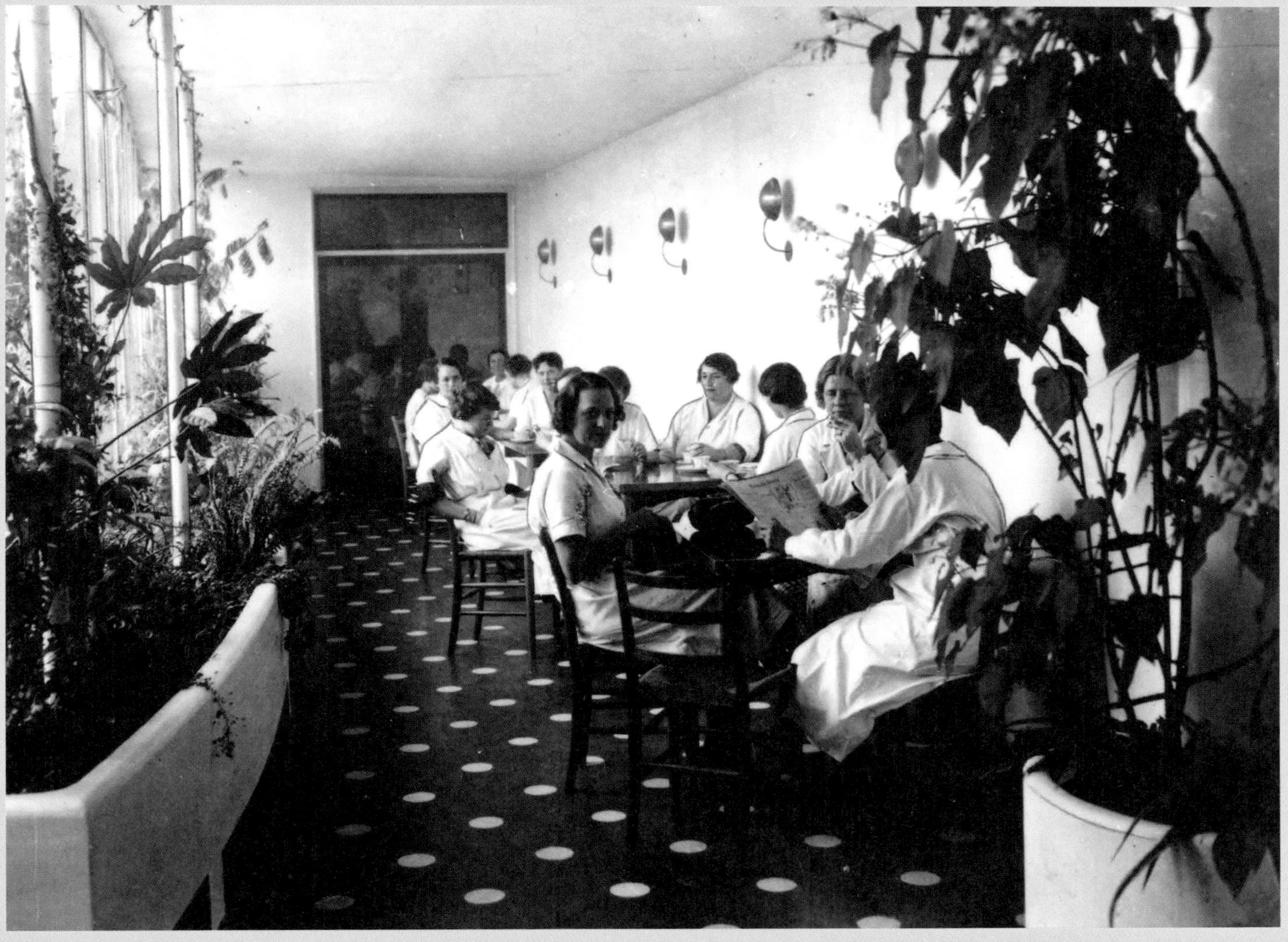

The canteen at Novo Terapeutisk Laboratorium, whose new factory Arne Jacobsen designed in 1935. He designed customised furniture for the canteen

Photo: Novo Nordisk History Collection

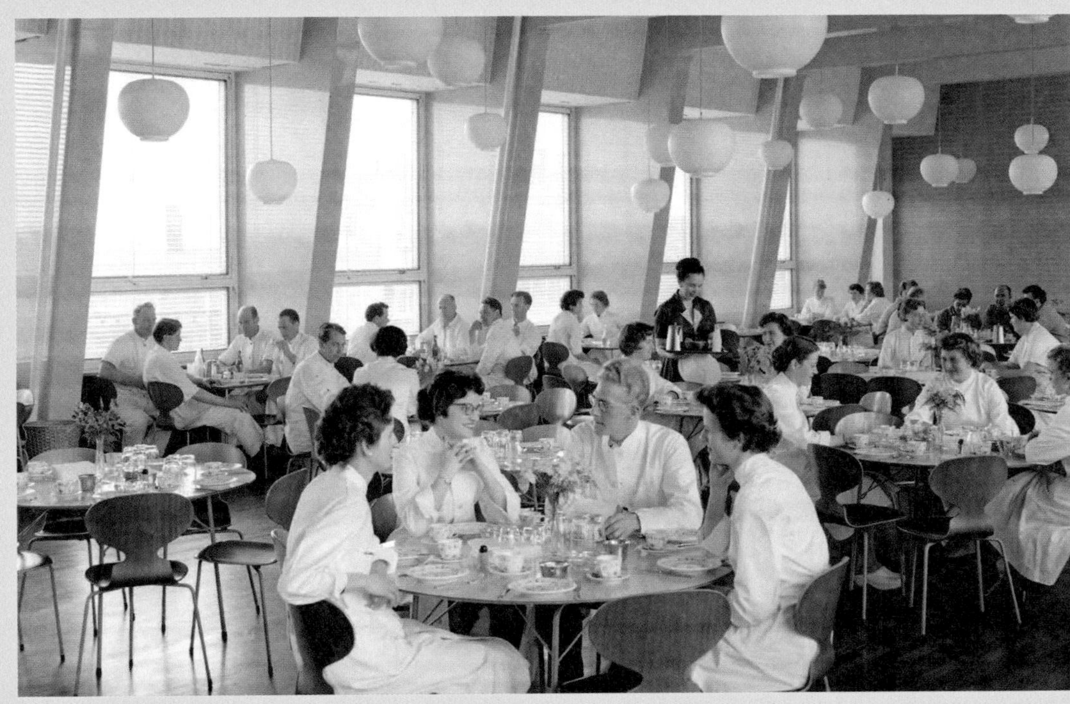

In the early 1950s, the company's new canteen was refurbished with Arne Jacobsen furniture, including his entirely new shell-type chair known as the Ant

Photo: Novo Nordisk History Collection

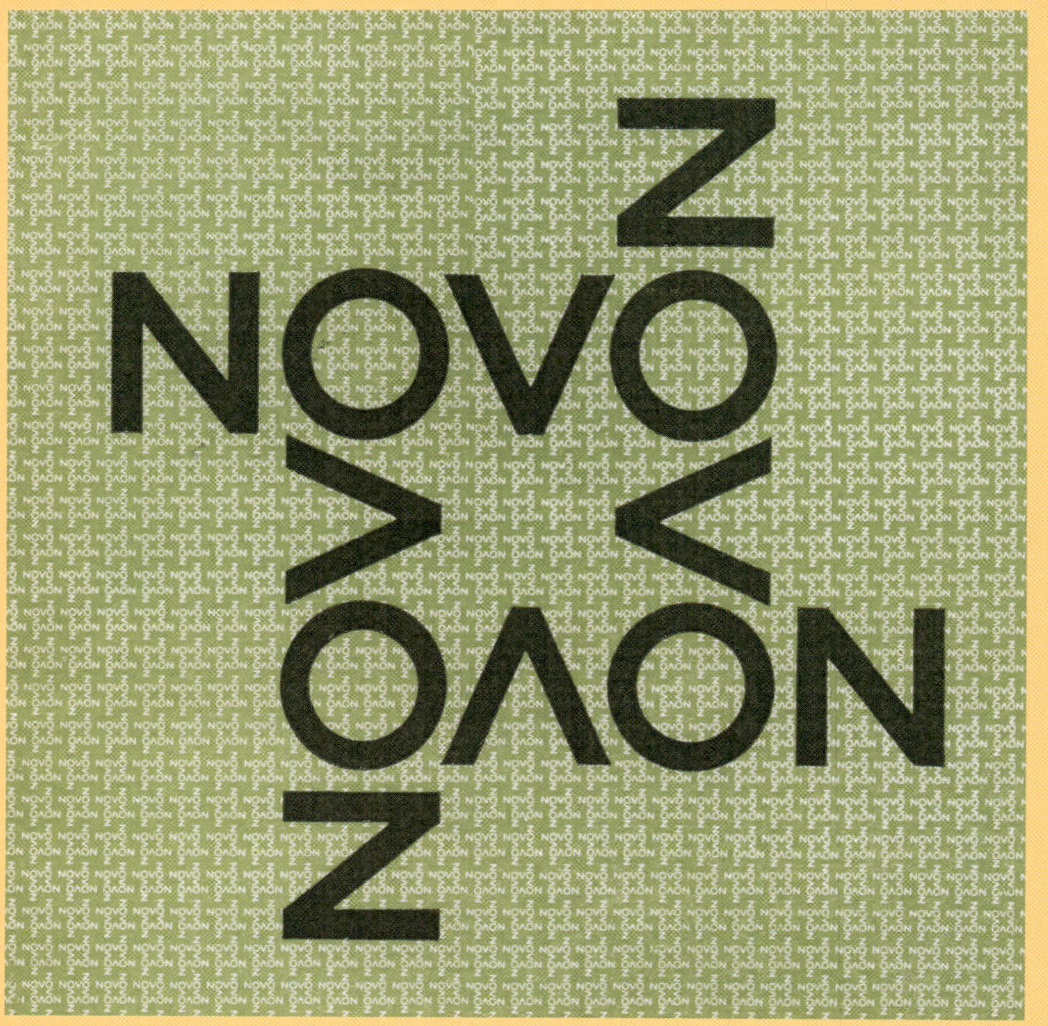

Logo designed by Arne Jacobsen in the 1960s

Photo: Novo Nordisk History Collection

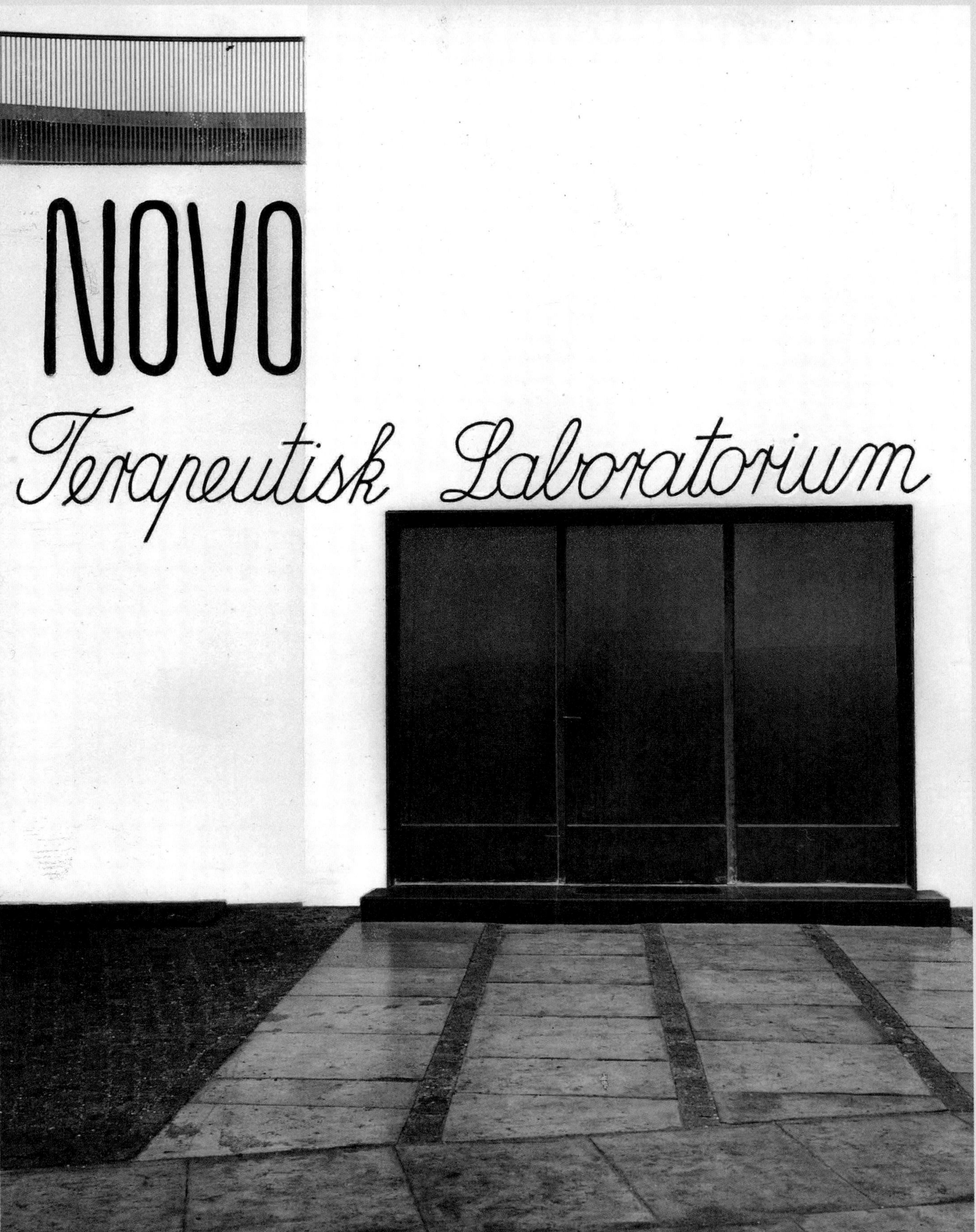

Arne Jacobsen also designed the sign for the façade of the factory at Fuglebakken (1935)

Photo: Novo Nordisk History Collection

Wallpaper featuring the 'Bio-Bio' pattern (c. 1950)

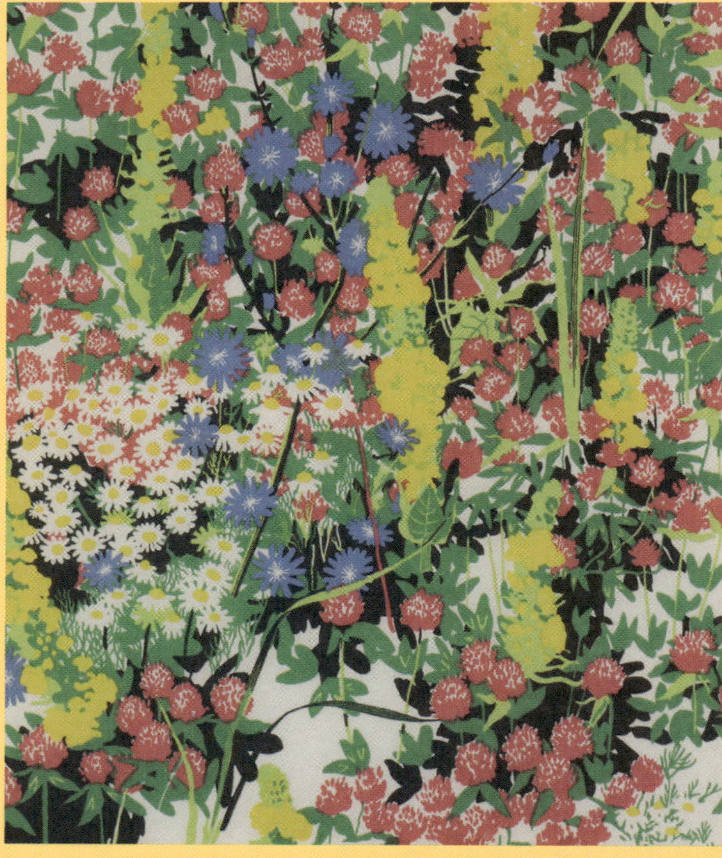

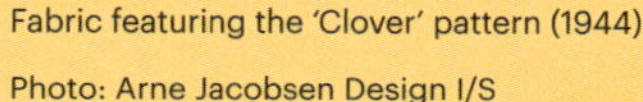

Fabric featuring the 'Clover' pattern (1944)

Photo: Arne Jacobsen Design I/S

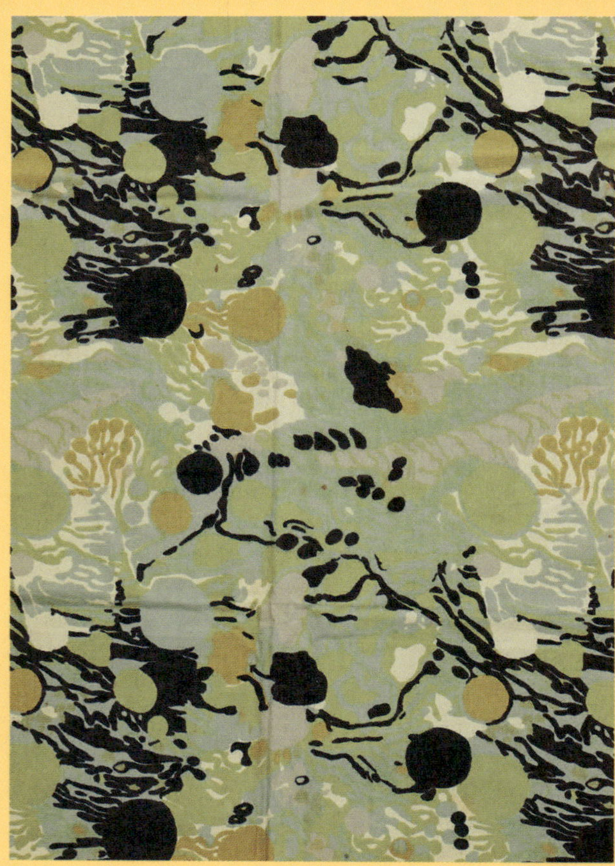

Fabric featuring the 'Sea' pattern (1950s)

Photo: Arne Jacobsen Design I/S

Arne Jacobsen and textiles

Arne Jacobsen's second wife, Jonna Møller, was a trained textile printer, and when the two met in the early 1940s they started creating textile and wallpaper designs together. In 1943, the couple were forced to flee to Sweden. Arne Jacobsen was of Jewish descent, so staying in Denmark during the German occupation would put him at risk. They escaped by rowing a boat across the Sound along with their friends, Inger and Poul Henningsen.

During their time in Sweden, Arne Jacobsen and Jonna Møller were forced to reinvent their working lives as there was scant work for an architect during a time of war. Jonna helped transform Arne Jacobsen's many watercolours and plant studies into textile patterns, and soon they were being produced, enjoying great success in Denmark, Sweden and the USA.

The textile and wallpaper patterns Arne Jacobsen designed in the 1940s featured minute detail and colourful plants. They looked rather like the watercolours he used to paint in his garden, arranged to facilitate the repetition of a wallpaper pattern. In the late 1950s and up through the 1960s, Arne Jacobsen was increasingly inspired by the concrete and abstract trends of painting and his patterns started to move in a more geometric direction.

Arne Jacobsen Designing Denmark

In the decades following World War II, Danish society underwent major changes. From the mid-1950s onwards, funded by taxes and growing overall prosperity, the Danish welfare society evolved. In addition to universal old-age pension and an expanded social security system, the Danes now had access to a number of new public institutions that influenced most aspects of life, including creches, nursing homes for the elderly and public libraries.

Arne Jacobsen was one of the architects who helped embody the new society aesthetically. During his career, he made his mark on many aspects of Denmark's public spaces, designing city halls, schools, a library and corporate offices. Not only did he determine the overall design of the buildings; he was also responsible for the minutest details. In institutions such as the Munkegård School in Vangede (1957) and Rødovre Town Hall (1956), the people of Denmark encountered Arne Jacobsen's aesthetics in undiluted form. In these vast, total interiors, the architect himself designed every last detail and chose every single colour.

Post-war modernist architecture and design continued to build on the ideas of the Bauhaus school and others, using new materials and production

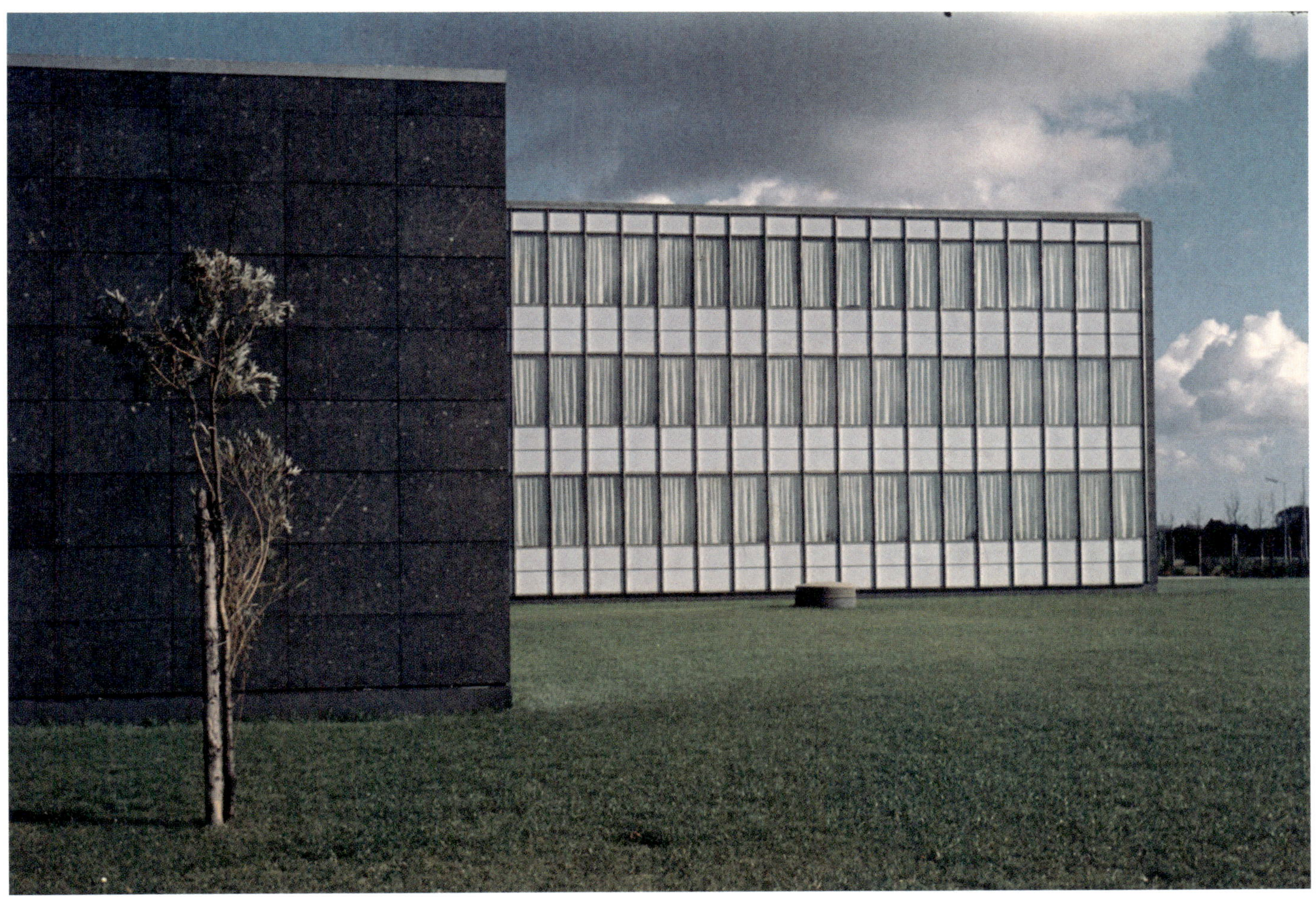

Rødovre Town Hall opened in 1956 - a modern administration building in steel and glass

Photo: Arne Jacobsen. The original can be found in: The Royal Danish Library – The Danish National Art Library

methods to democratise access to good design. In his own lifetime, Arne Jacobsen became acclaimed as the country's great Modernist, and much of his furniture expressed his fascination with the precise production aesthetics of industry. While many, such as Poul Henningsen, focused on the social aspects of the style, Arne Jacobsen did not share such views in public, but he emphasised the importance of making well-made and, in his eyes, beautiful furniture available to as many people as possible.

With the launch, in 1952, of the shell-type chair known as the Ant, created in collaboration with the furniture manufacturer Fritz Hansen, Arne Jacobsen made a firm name for himself as a furniture designer in Denmark and abroad. The chair and its descendants – especially the Series 7 chair (1955) – enjoyed

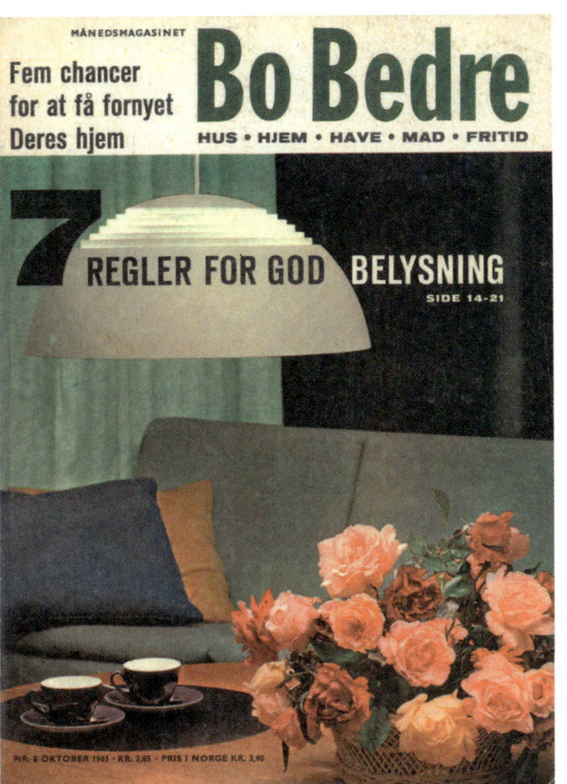

The shell chairs was used in private companies and public spaces throughout the country. This is the dining room of Aarhus County Hospital, furnished with Munkegård chairs

Photo: Fritz Hansen's archives

1961 saw the launch of the magazine *Bo Bedre*. It became an important channel for promoting Danish design vis-à-vis the people of Denmark. This is one of the first issues, featuring Arne Jacobsen's Royal pendant lamp

Photo: *Bo Bedre* No. 8, October 1961

great commercial success, featuring in many Danish homes, canteens, offices and lecture halls across the country.

Posterity's notions and narratives about Danish design or 'Danish Modern' were to a great extent based on the dream of the good life. Marketing by manufacturers emphasised the functionality, good craftsmanship and durability of the furniture. They also referred to a specifically Scandinavian way of life, and on several occasions the furniture was described as 'democratic' (Hansen, 2006). Here, the furniture was given a layer of additional significance closely related to the times and the new society of which they were originally part. The new minimalism heralded a time of fewer differences between social classes, and in the many public administrations it signalled a democratic relationship between citizen and state. Today, the Danes remain as enthusiastic about these furniture designs as they were then.

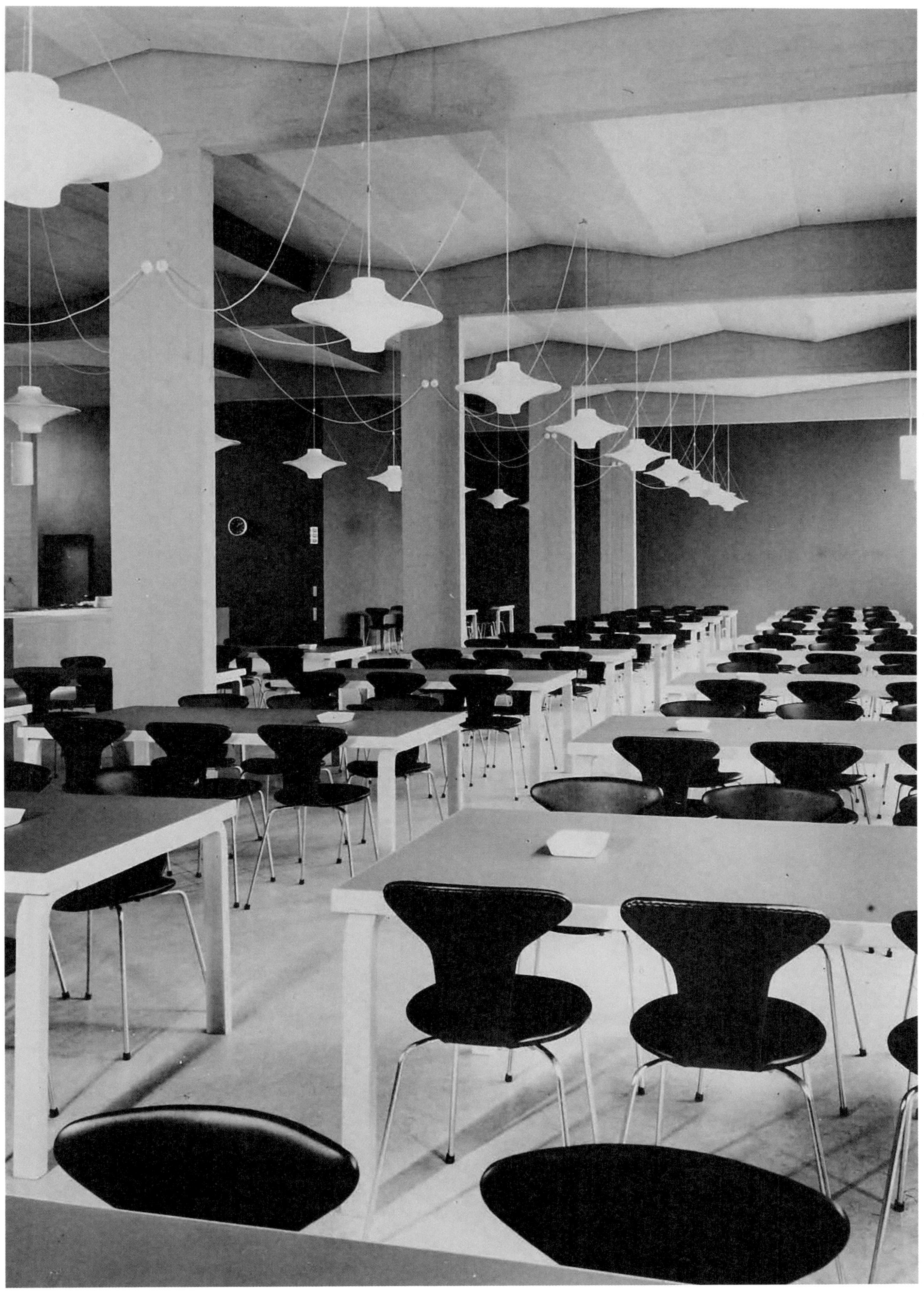

The lifeguard's tower at Bellevue Beach, featuring the distinctive blue stripes

Photo: Sandra Gonon/ Arkitekturbilleder.dk

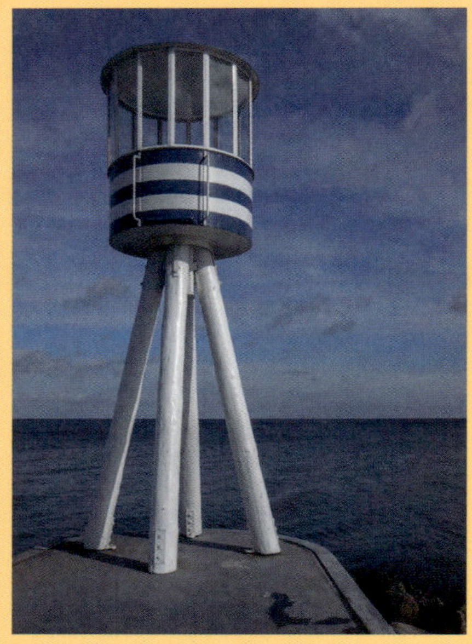

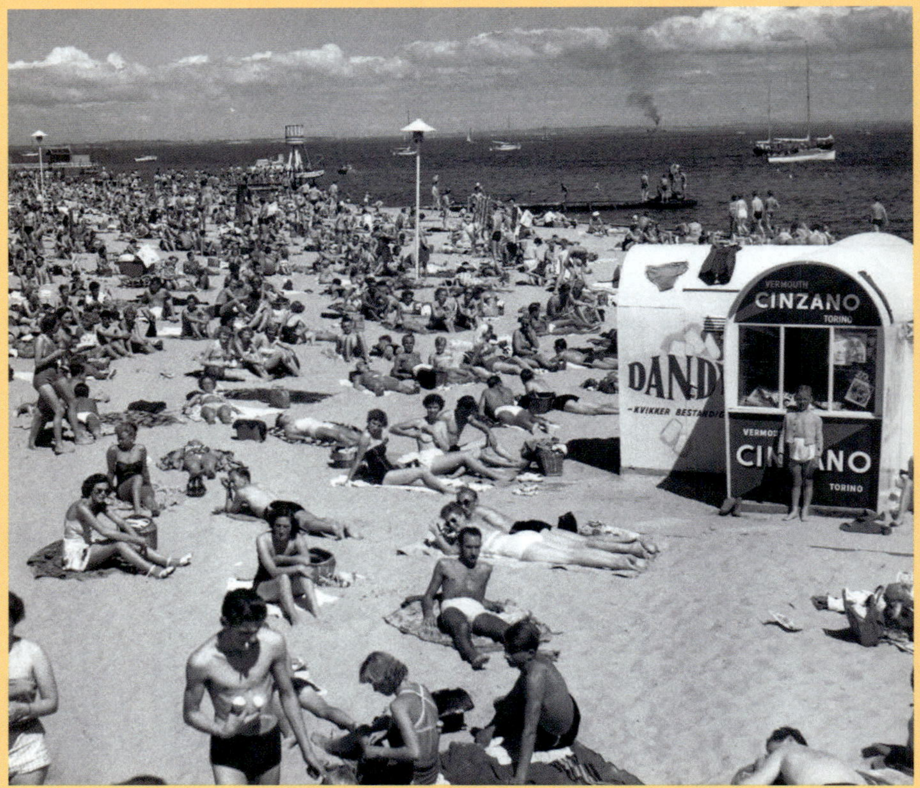

From 1932, Danes could visit Arne Jacobsen's 'white town' at Bellevue, north of Copenhagen. Here is the beach park in 1951 with Arne Jacobsen's kiosk building and the lifeguard tower in the background

Photo: Olaf Ibsen/Ritzau Scanpix

Arne Jacobsen in Gentofte

In terms of geographical areas, Gentofte, Denmark is more visibly and prominently permeated by Arne Jacobsen's legacy than anywhere else. This municipality – home to Jacobsen himself throughout his adult life – was where his career began in the late 1920s, designing private homes for the area's affluent citizens. In the following decade he designed the famous Bellevue area along Strandvejen, which soon acquired the moniker 'The White Town' because of the beach area, the Bellavista residential building, the Bellevue Theatre and the famous petrol station all built in the white 'Funkis' style of the period. Here Arne Jacobsen not only acted as an architect. He created a total design for the theatre and its restaurant complete with customised furniture and lamps, and he was in charge of the graphic design on elements such as the tickets for the beach bathing facility, ice-cream cups and the lifeguard's tower. All this was in keeping with the era's Vitalistic ideals of health, physicality, beauty and strength.

One of Arne Jacobsen's most important projects in Gentofte Municipality was the Munkegård School in Vangede. Completed in 1957, the school is a single-storey structure with wings that combine to form a grid structure, allowing each classroom to have its own private courtyard. In his total design for the school, Arne Jacobsen blended aesthetics and learning. He decorated the gardens with plants arranged in sophisticated patterns, adding plaster casts of reliefs and sculptures from art history. For the classrooms he designed two new chairs, the Tongue and the Munkegård chair, which, like the school desks that accompanied them, came in three sizes to suit the various age groups at the school. The extensive interior also included customised speakers, the Munkegård lamp and an artistic stage curtain featuring an Arne Jacobsen pattern.

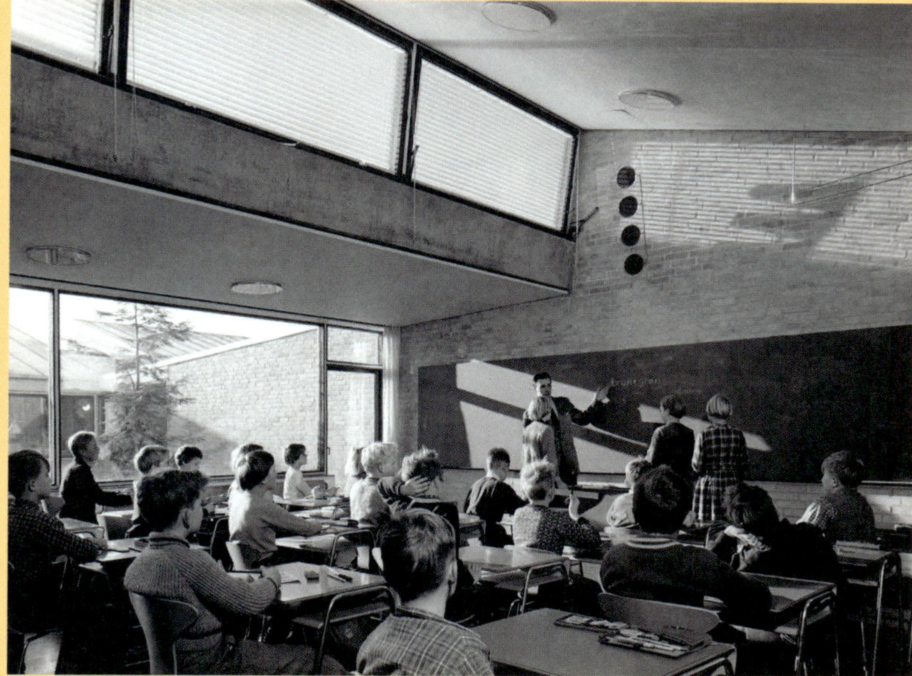

The Munkegård School (1957) is an example of how Arne Jacobsen designed his buildings in their entirety. In the classroom, the pupils are sitting on customised children's furniture

Photo: Aage Strüwing © Jørgen Strüwing

Interior of the Munkegård School around the time of the school's opening in 1957

Photo: Arne Jacobsen. The original can be found in: The Royal Danish Library – The Danish National Art Library

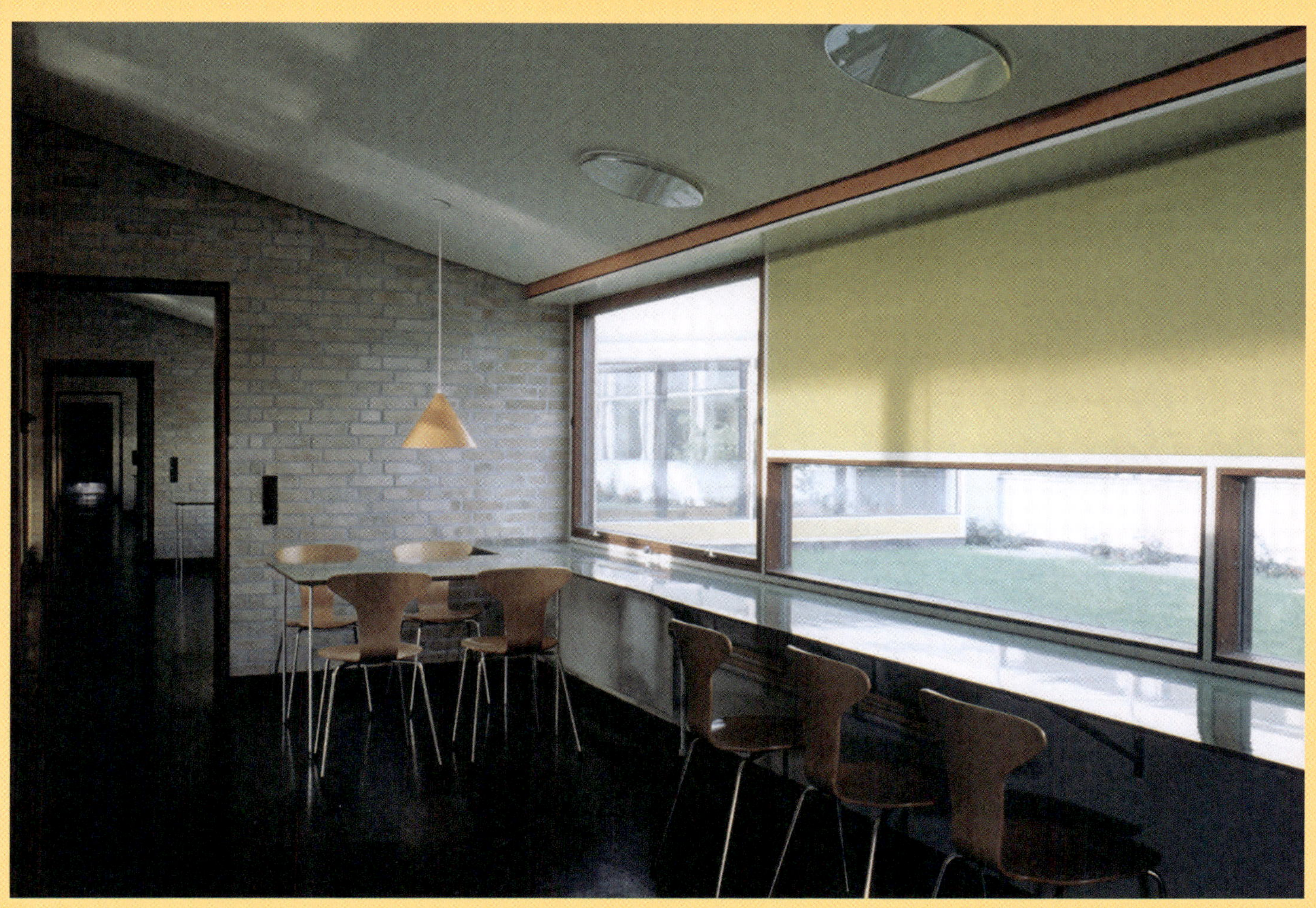

The Munkegård School
with its inner courtyards

Photo: Aage Strüwing ©
Jørgen Strüwing

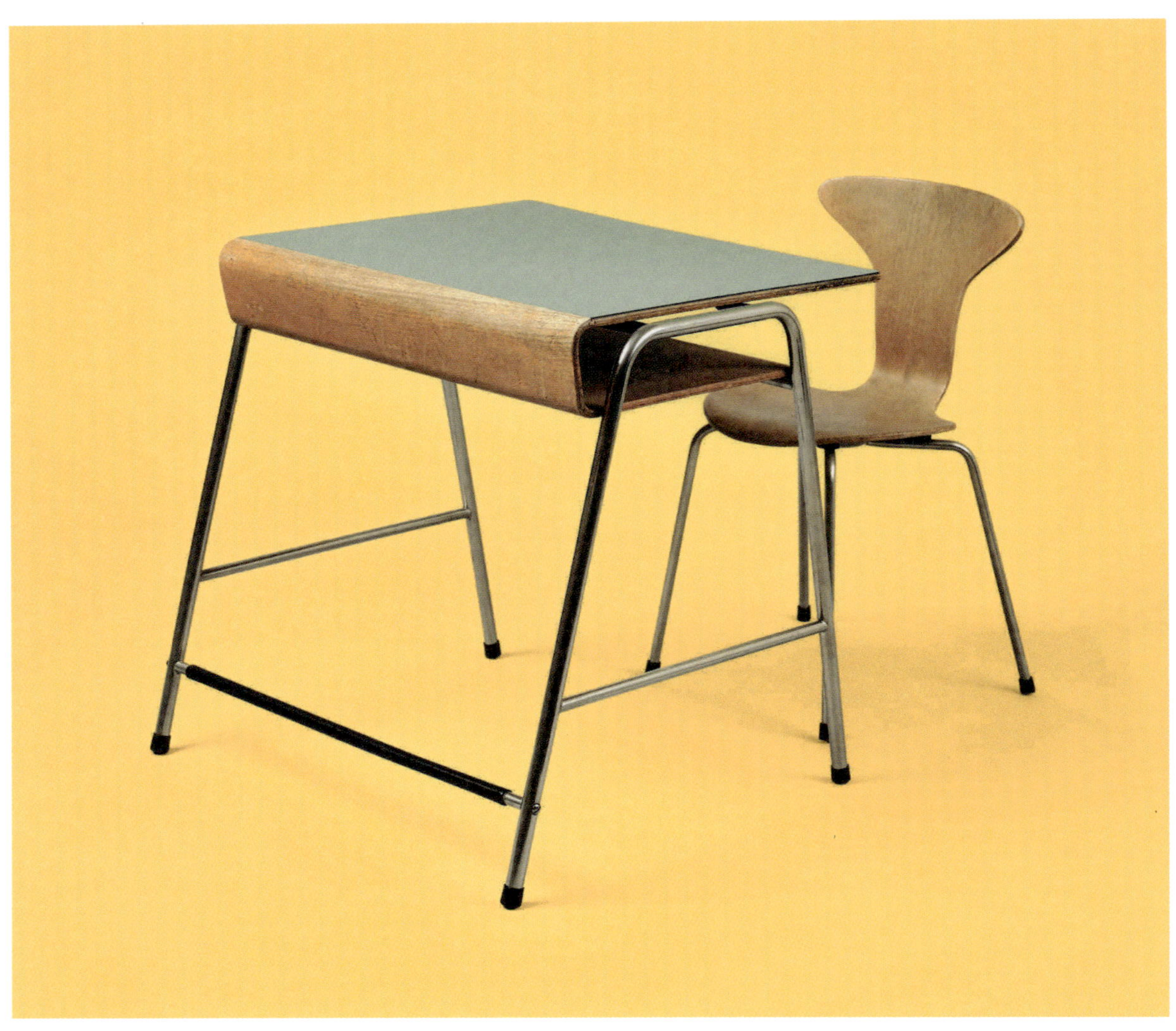

School desk and chair for
the Munkegård School

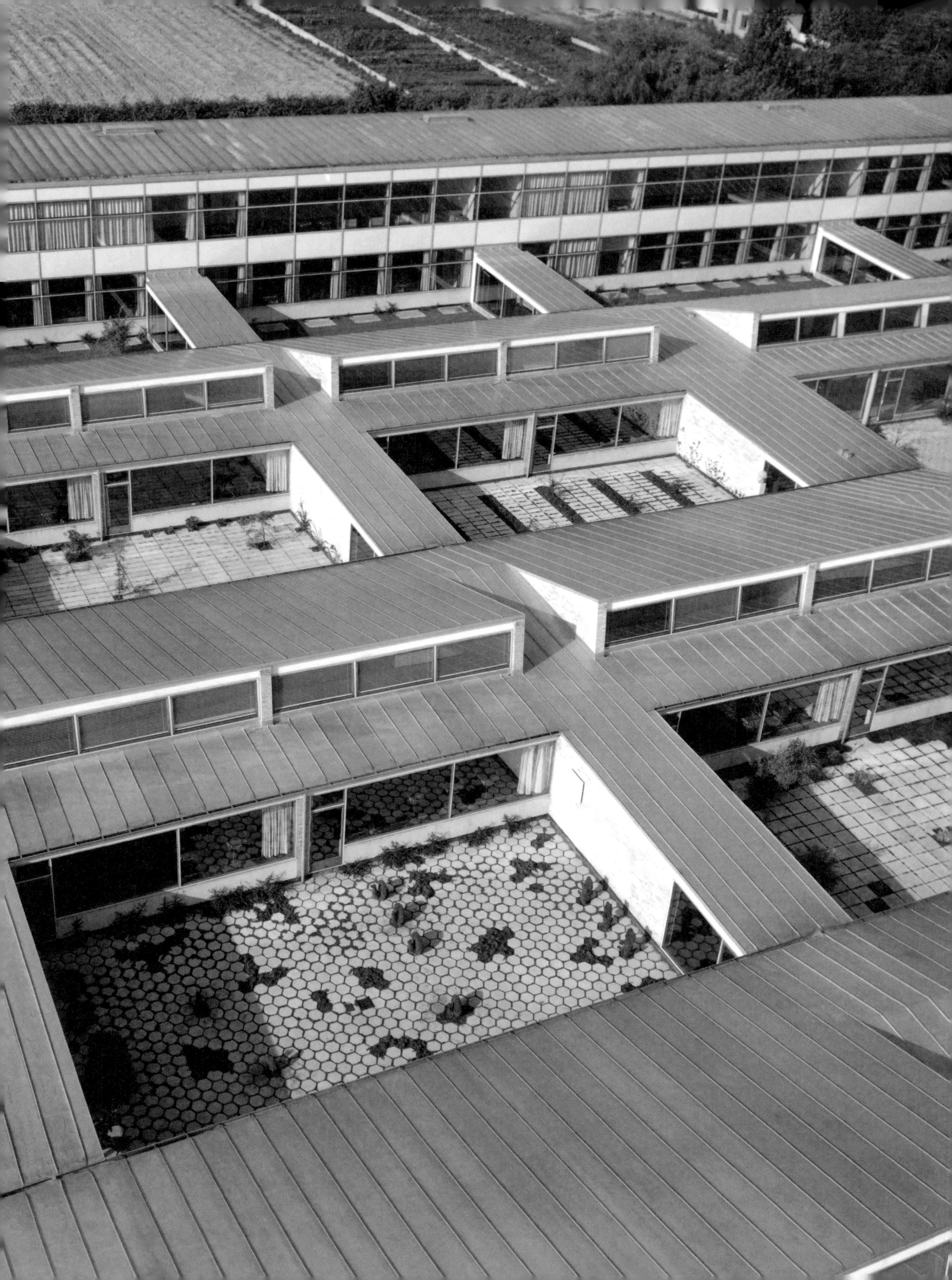

The graphic, glass-and-steel staircase in Rødovre Town Hall is an example of the functionalism that characterised the new public spaces, reflecting the modern welfare society and a breaking down of class divisions

Photo: Arne Jacobsen. The original can be found in: The Royal Danish Library – The Danish National Art Library

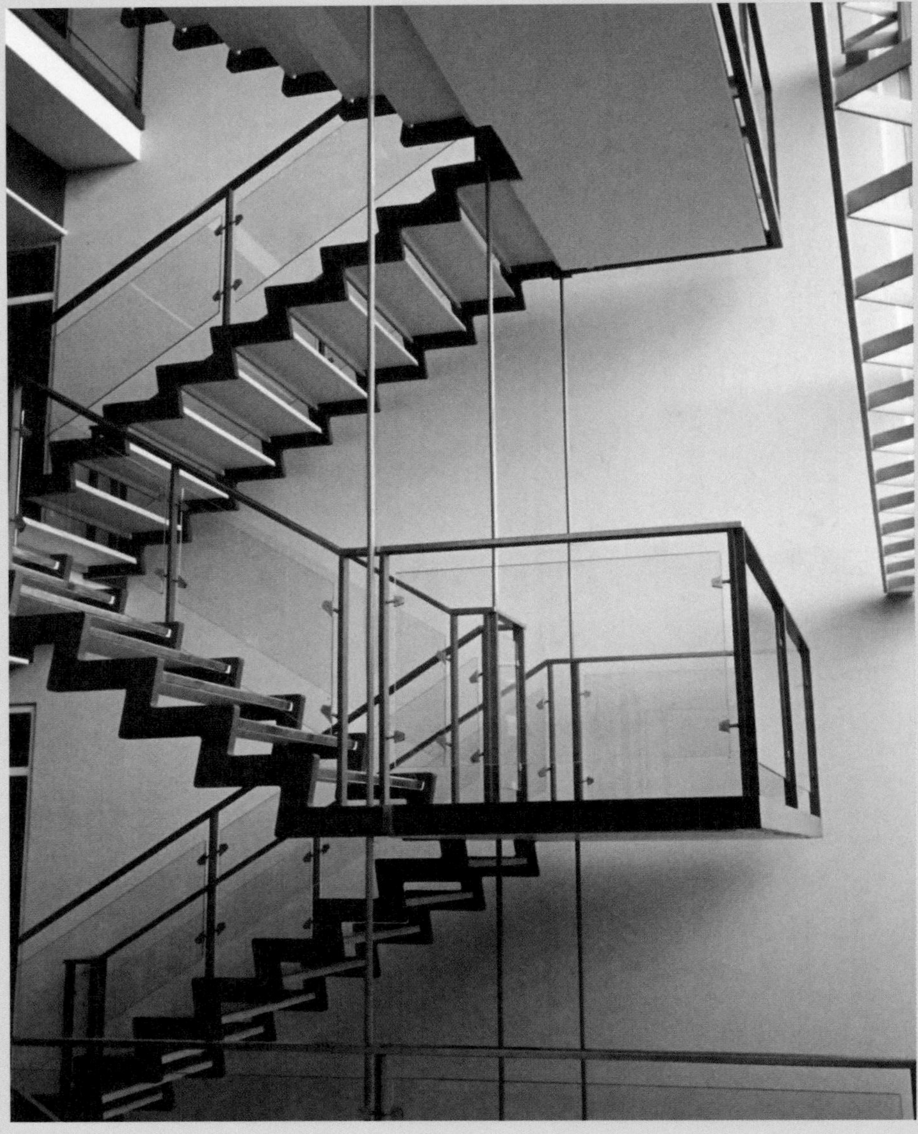

Welfare architecture and design for a new Denmark

In Rødovre, the urban planning seen in the decades after World War II was informed by the gradual construction of Denmark's welfare society and by a general wish to facilitate the good life in the suburbs, a haven where the skies were open and the homes larger than in inner-city Copenhagen. During this period, Arne Jacobsen made his mark on the area by designing a number of residential buildings and public institutions.

In 1948, he was one of the architects behind the plan for the residential area of Carlsro, a project that shortly afterwards led to a commission to design the new Rødovre Town Hall. Located in the town's main central square and officially inaugurated in 1956, the new city hall was a state-of-the-art administration building made of glass and steel and furnished with Arne Jacobsen's functional furniture. In the council's assembly hall, the politicians sat on Series 7 chairs at specially designed tables, while Dot stools and series 3300 sofas in the various public areas of the building welcomed visitors.

The town hall would later go on to be the centre of a major urban planning project, for which Arne Jacobsen also designed the adjacent Rødovre Library and a residential block east of the Town Hall. Together they formed an 'axis of democracy' that extended from the seat of official authority (the Town Hall) to the seat of public edification and information (the library) and into private homes, emphasising the close ties between politicians and the people. The 1969 library was a late major work in Arne Jacobsen's career, and here he created another total design to match that of the town hall. The interior included the Lily chair and the Dot stool in new, child-sized versions, along with bookcases, book carts and a mobile turntable, all designed by the architect himself. Nyager School (1964) was also designed by Arne Jacobsen and furnished with child-sized versions of his T chair.

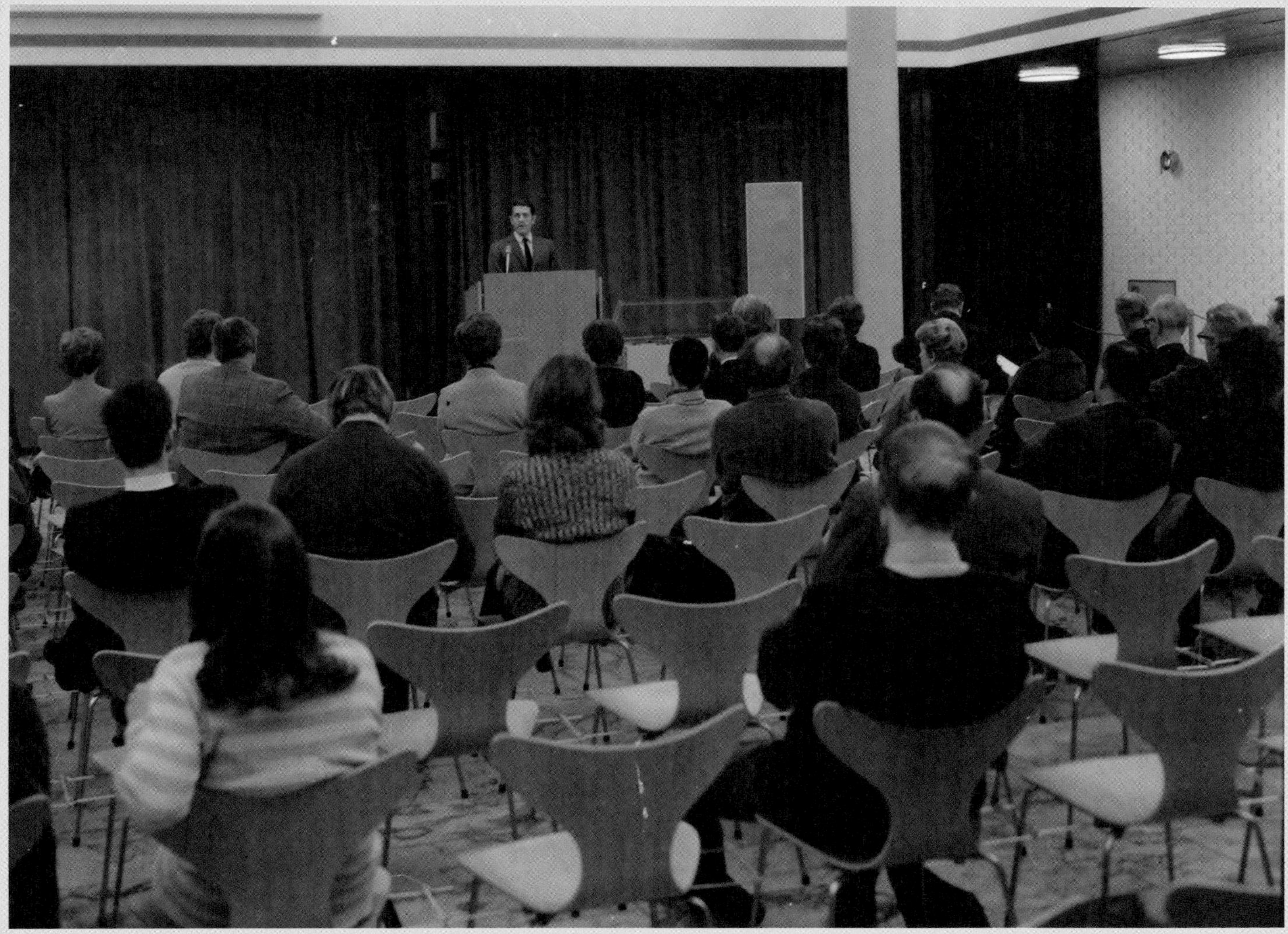

For the interior of Rødovre Library (1969) Arne Jacobsen's fixtures and fittings included the Lily, in both an adult and a children's version

Photo: Eigil Malmer

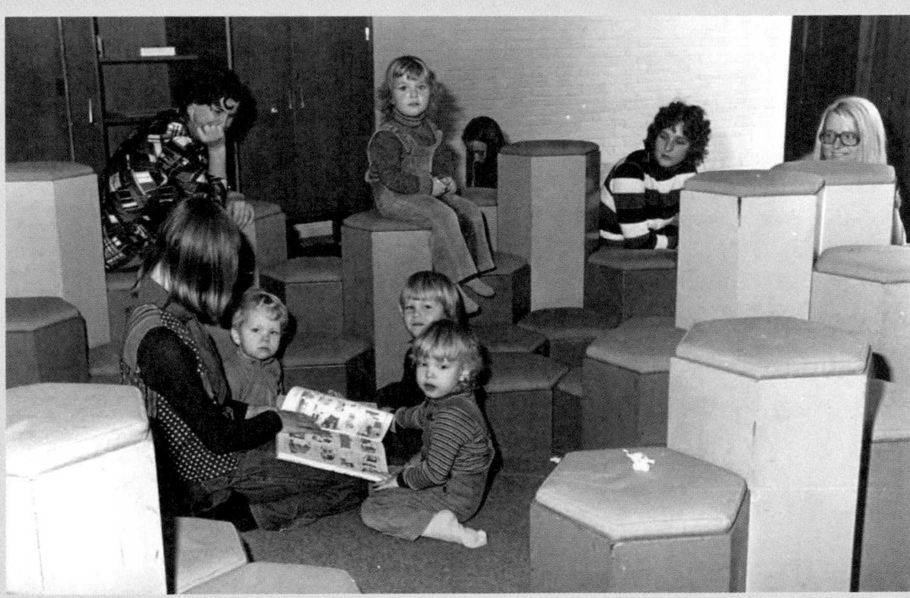

The children's section at Rødovre Library, for which Arne Jacobsen developed a range of new designs – including a child-sized version of the Lily chair

Photo: Eigil Malmer

The evolution of the shell chairs from 1952 to 1970. From the left: Ant, Tongue, Munkegård chair, Series 7, Series 7 with armrests, T chair, Lily and Lily with armrests

Photo: TOPFOTO/Scanpix Denmark

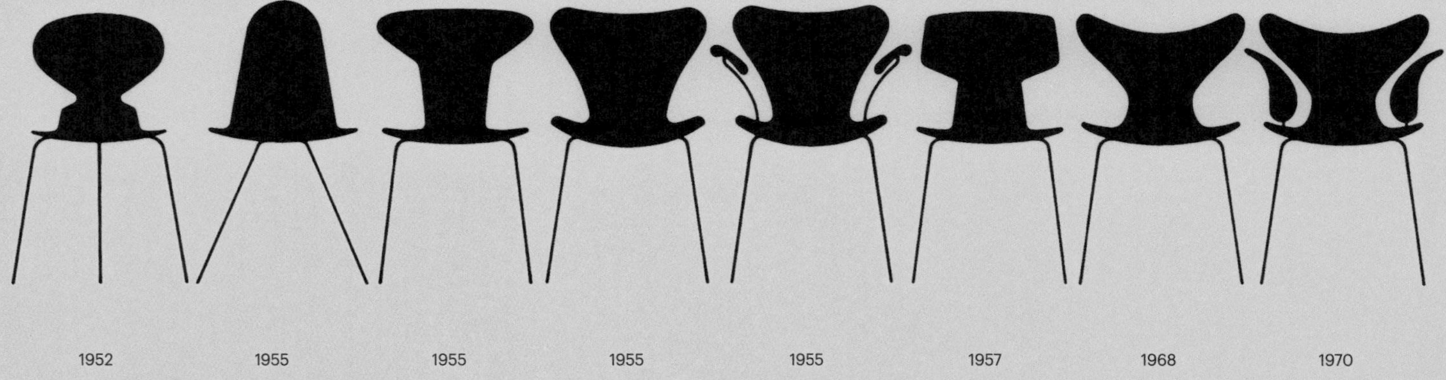

1952 1955 1955 1955 1955 1957 1968 1970

Shell-type chairs

In the winter of 1952, Arne Jacobsen and Fritz Hansen made design history when, to celebrate the company's 80th anniversary, they launched the Ant chair. The small, three-legged chair was created in response to the growing demand for a chair that would fit into the small dining kitchens and corporate canteens of the day. The major innovation was the fact that the back and seat were made out of a single plywood shell, moulded to curve in two directions. During the long development phase – which Arne Jacobsen said lasted an entire year – Arne Jacobsen and the Fritz Hansen engineers came up with ways of pushing the wood to its limits in order to create a chair that was not only solid and modern, with its stringently sober appearance, but also affordable, given that the chair could be manufactured industrially.

From the outset, the Ant was a huge success, and over the course of the next few years Arne Jacobsen and Fritz Hansen launched a wide range of shell-type chairs that may be regarded as variations on the first. The Tongue and the Munkegård chair were designed for the Munkegård School in 1955. That same year the partners also launched Series 7, which became the most popular design of them all, and continues to be sold by the million worldwide. It was followed by the Grand Prix chair and the T chair in 1957 and finally the Lily (1968), which was used at Nationalbanken, the central bank of Denmark, and at Rødovre Library. These chair designs have proved to be strikingly viable through the years despite changing tastes, and many of the models have remained in production ever since their initial launch, while others have been relaunched within the last ten years (2020).

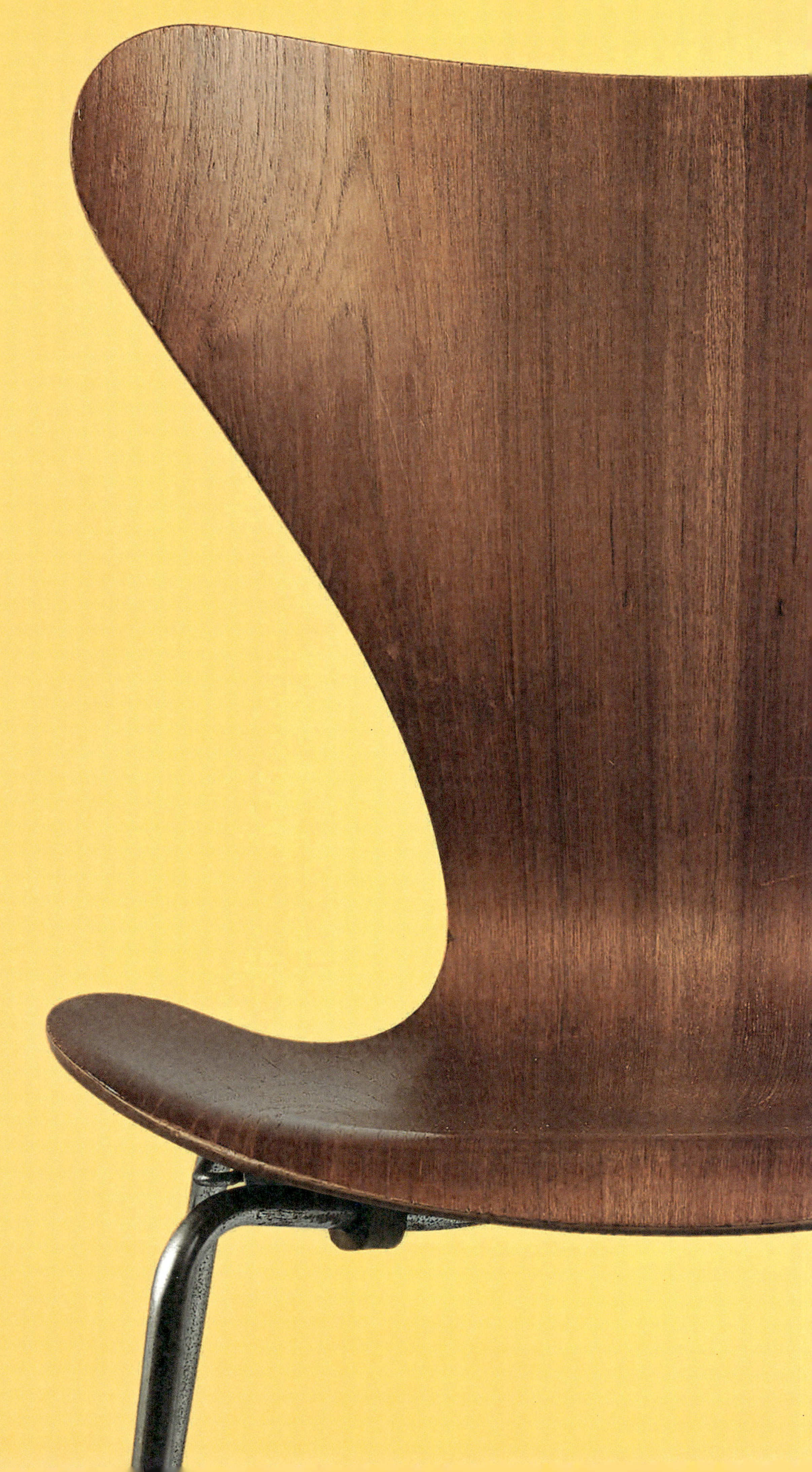

The Series 7 was first launched in 1955. From 1956 the Danes could see the design at Rødovre Town Hall

Trapholt Collection

International fame

SAS Royal Hotel in the 1960s

Photo: Ca Peterson Cap/TT/ Ritzau Scanpix

During the 1950s, Danish furniture design became internationally renowned, and Arne Jacobsen's furniture enjoyed huge export sales. In the 1960s, the aesthetics of Arne Jacobsen's designs changed. Based on a desire for flexibility and modular systems, he developed a number of designs based on repetitions of identical modules. Only a few of these, such as the VOLA series of taps and fixtures (1969) and the Cylinda Line range of homeware for Stelton (1967), were well received by the market. The tables and chairs designed in accordance with these principles did not become major sales successes or part of the grand narrative of Danish Modern.

The last thirteen years of Arne Jacobsen's career included major high-profile projects in Denmark and abroad. 1960 saw the opening of the SAS Royal Hotel in Copenhagen, Denmark's first skyscraper and a symbol of prosperity, travel and an international outlook. The hotel was Arne Jacobsen's undisputed magnum opus, designed and decorated down to the smallest detail, creating a totality that included everything from furniture and lamps to textiles, cutlery, vases – even the finials on the curtain rods. The chairs from the hotel became a huge success throughout the world, and today, the organic lines of the Swan and Egg chairs remain emblematic of the very finest that furniture design has to offer.

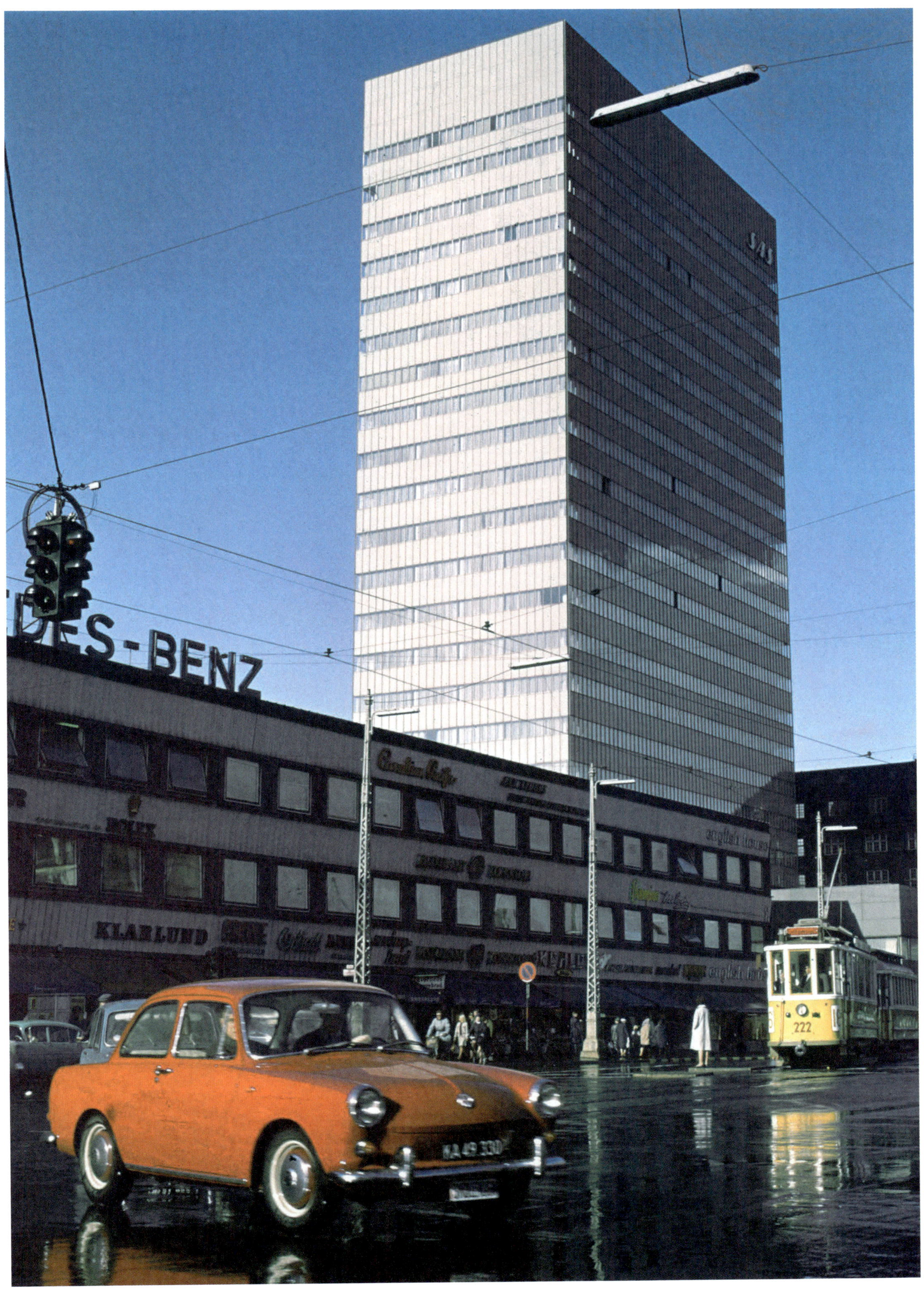
SAS
KLARLUND
222

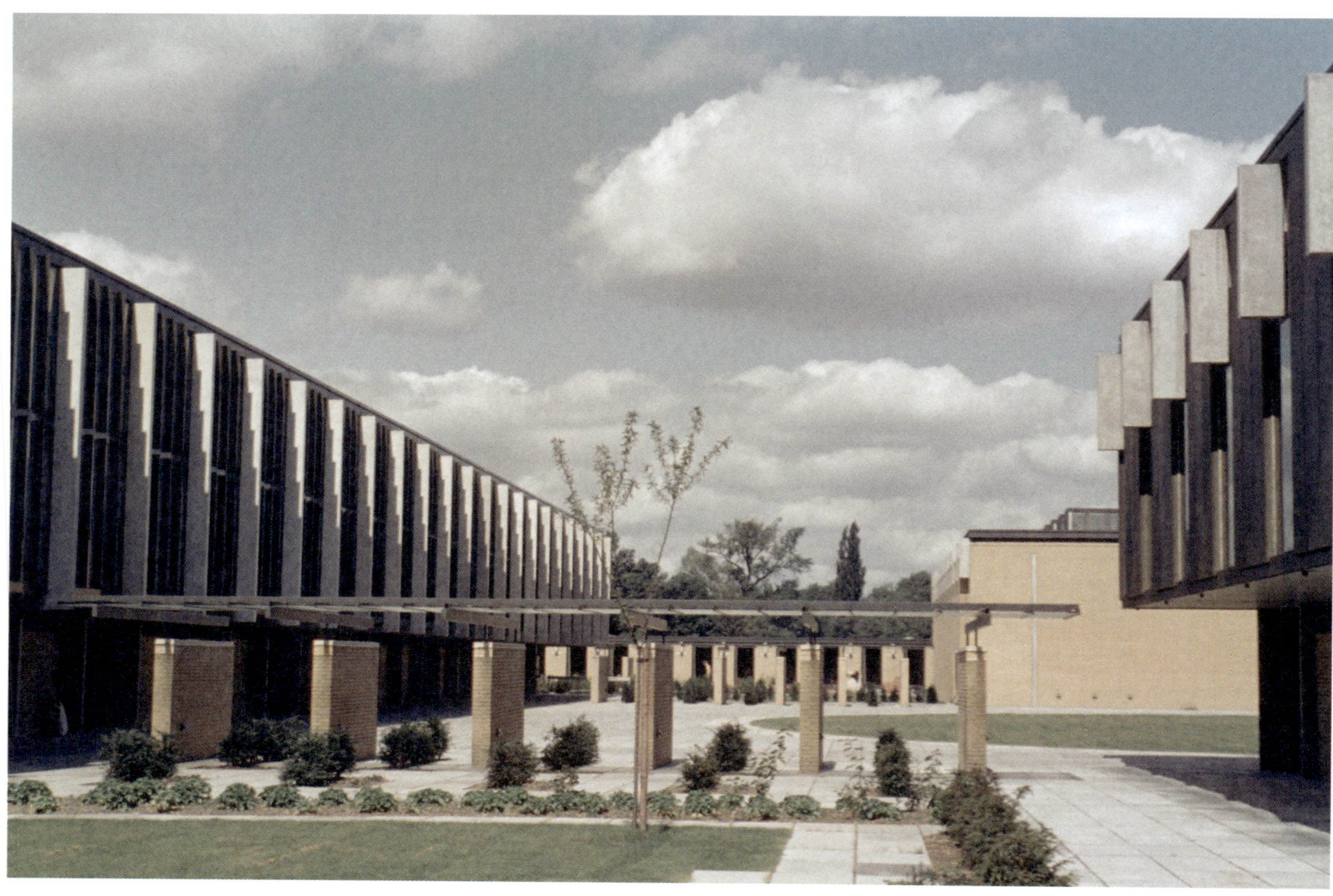

St. Catherine's College at the University of Oxford was Arne Jacobsen's first major project abroad

Photo: Arne Jacobsen. The original can be found in: The Royal Danish Library – The Danish National Art Library

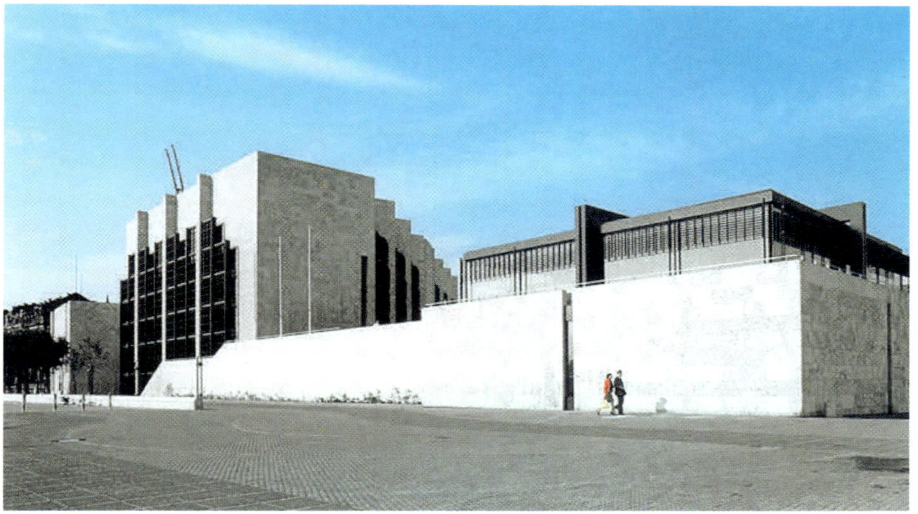

Mainz City Hall. The proposal was devised by Arne Jacobsen and Otto Weitling in 1968, while the building was constructed by Dissing+Weitling in 1975-76

Photo: Dissing+Weitling

During the same period, under intense media scrutiny in Denmark and England, Arne Jacobsen began working on St. Catherine's College, Oxford. His designs for the college, which awarded him an honorary doctorate in 1966, included what was known at the time as the 'Professor' chair. It went on to achieve considerable success as a conference and office chair under the name of the Oxford chair. The college was the first of a number of major projects abroad over the next two decades. The majority of those projects were in Germany, in collaboration with his partners Hans Dissing and Otto Weitling.

From the middle of the decade, the studio also focused intensively on another of Arne Jacobsen's major masterpieces, Danmarks Nationalbank, the central bank of Denmark, the first phase of which was completed in 1971.

Arne Jacobsen did not get to witness the completion of all the major projects launched by his studio during the 1960s. On March 24, 1971, he died unexpectedly at home, having just returned from his design studio. He was 69 years old and left behind a Denmark that looked very different from when he set up his design studio in 1929.

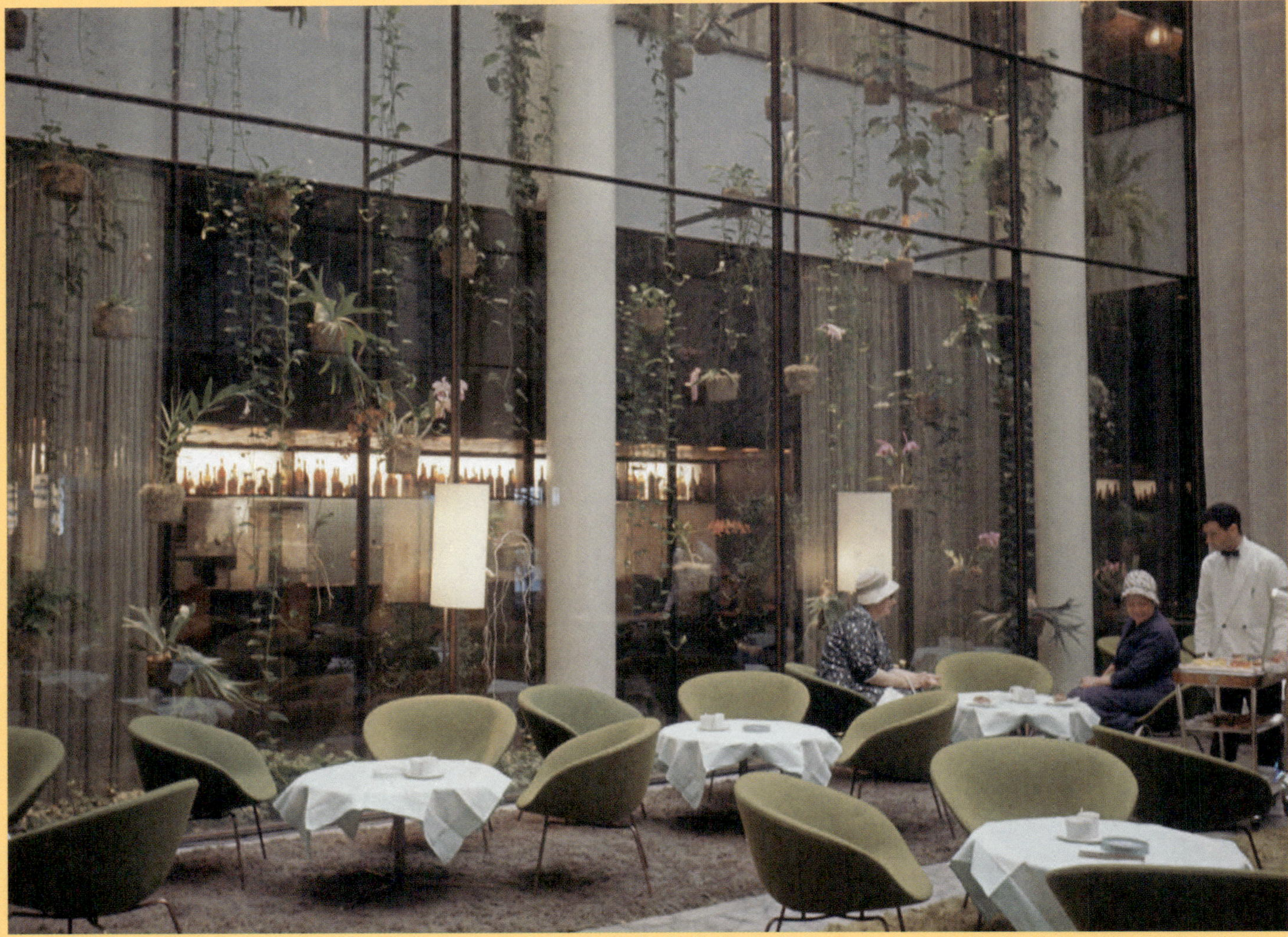

The winter garden at SAS Royal Hotel in the 1960s, featuring custom-designed furniture, including the Pot

Photo: Arne Jacobsen. The original can be found in: The Royal Danish Library – The Danish National Art Library

Furnishing the SAS Royal Hotel

Arne Jacobsen's furniture and interiors for the SAS Royal Hotel constituted a major masterpiece in Danish design history. In 1956, he was commissioned to design a hotel and an airport terminal for the airline SAS. Four years later, Copenhagen had its first skyscraper – one whose exterior and interior were the very quintessence of Arne Jacobsen's modern aesthetic.

At the airport terminal, completed in 1959, airline tourists could check in and wait in a state-of-the-art setting, seated in Arne Jacobsen's Series 3300 sofas (nicknamed the Airport sofa) before one of SAS's own buses took them directly to their planes. The hotel opened the following year. Arne Jacobsen designed every last detail, leaving nothing to chance. The doors were fitted with his AJ door handle, while in the restaurant guests ate with cutlery and drank from glasses specifically designed for the hotel. Even the carpets featured patterns designed by Arne Jacobsen. A few years prior to the creation of the hotel, the Fritz Hansen company secured the rights to a new production method that made it possible for furniture to be moulded out of polystyrene. This meant that the shapes created were no longer restricted by the technical limitations of wood. Working like a sculptor, Arne Jacobsen proceeded to design the Egg, Swan, Giraffe, Pot and Drop chairs, which became defining features of the hotel's interior.

From the outset, the Swan and the Egg, launched in 1958, attracted a great deal of media attention. The same year they were presented in Paris at the *Formes Scandinaves* exhibition. Ever since, they have upheld their status as highlights of Danish and international furniture design.

For the SAS Royal Hotel, Arne Jacobsen designed two versions of the Giraffe: one for the restaurant, upholstered in green textile and with wooden legs; the other for the Royal Suites on a swivel base

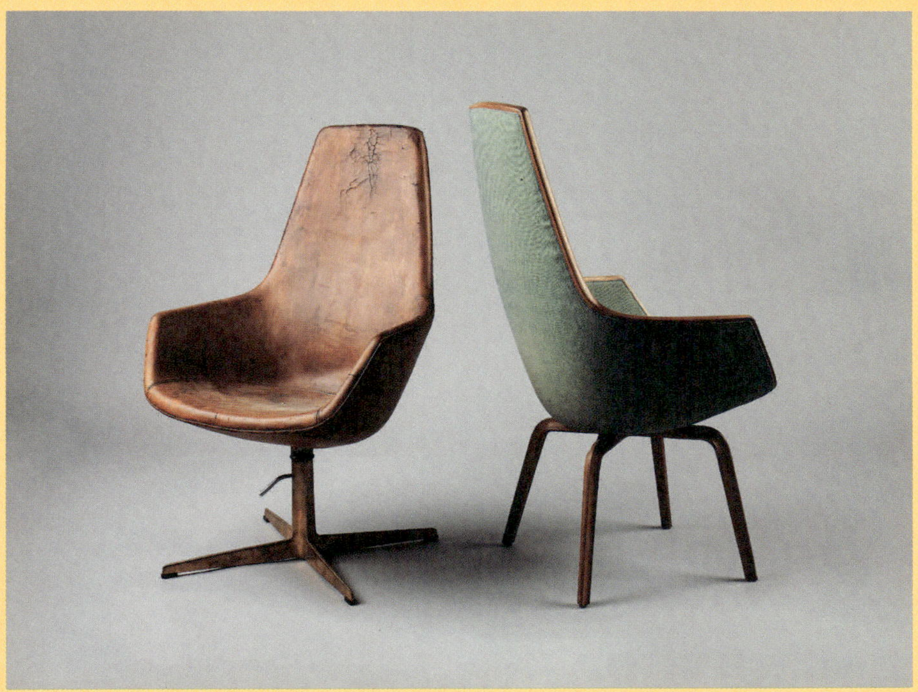

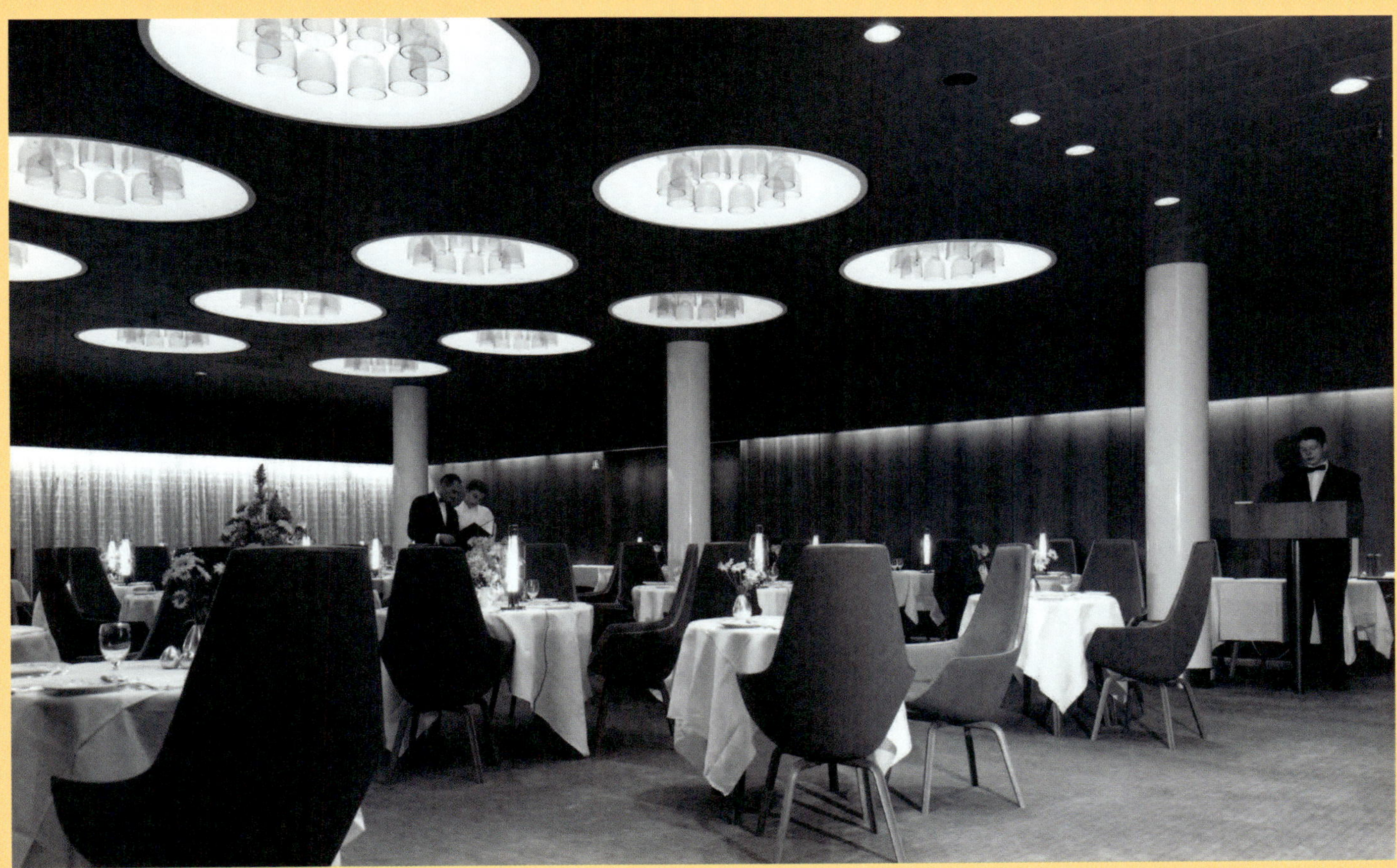

The SAS Royal Hotel restaurant around the time of its opening in 1960

Photo: Aage Strüwing © Jørgen Strüwing

The airport terminal at the SAS Royal Hotel opened in 1959, one year before the hotel. Here, airline tourists could check in and wait for their flights in a state-of-the-art setting

Photo: Arne Jacobsen. The original can be found in: The Royal Danish Library – The Danish National Art Library

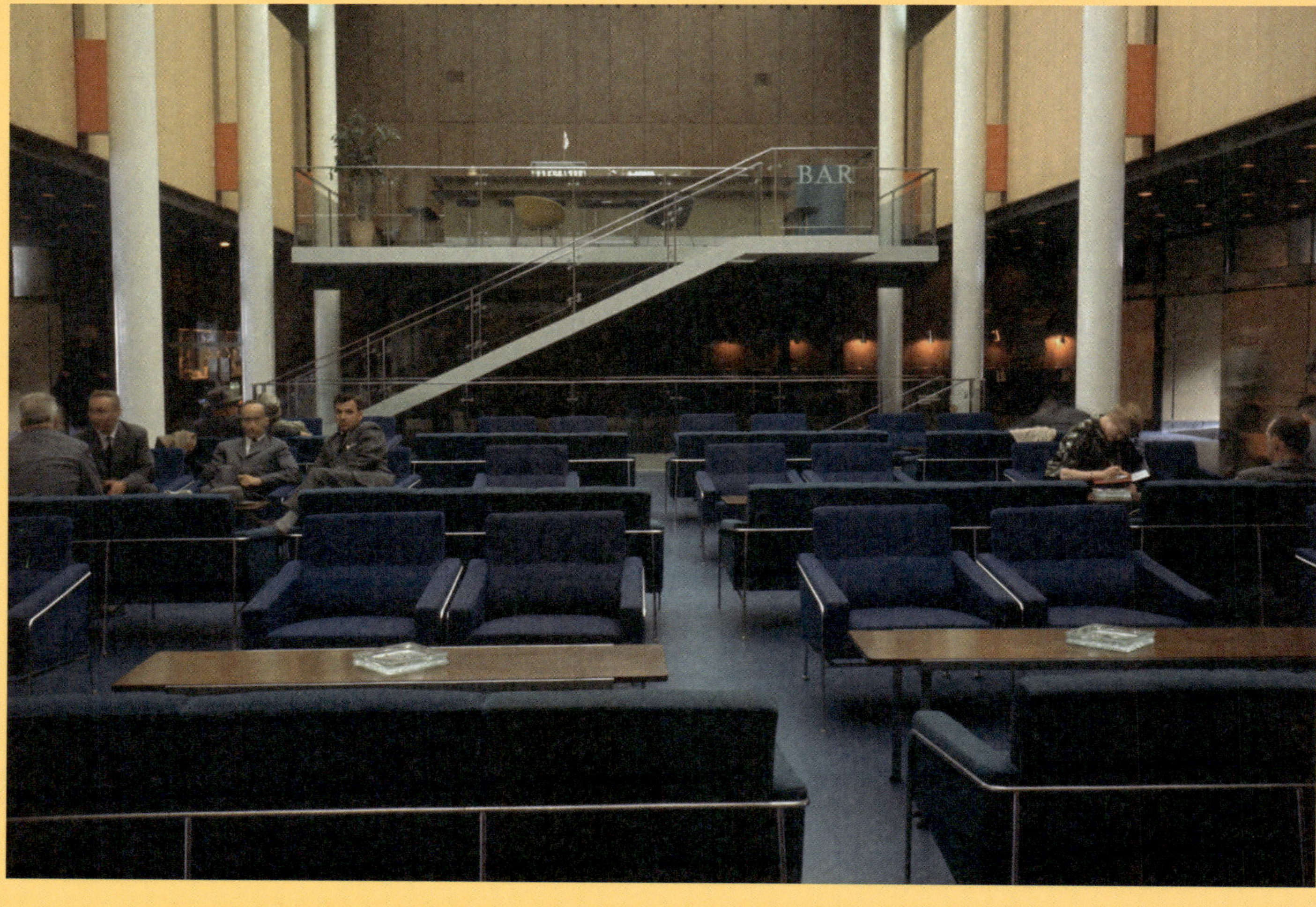

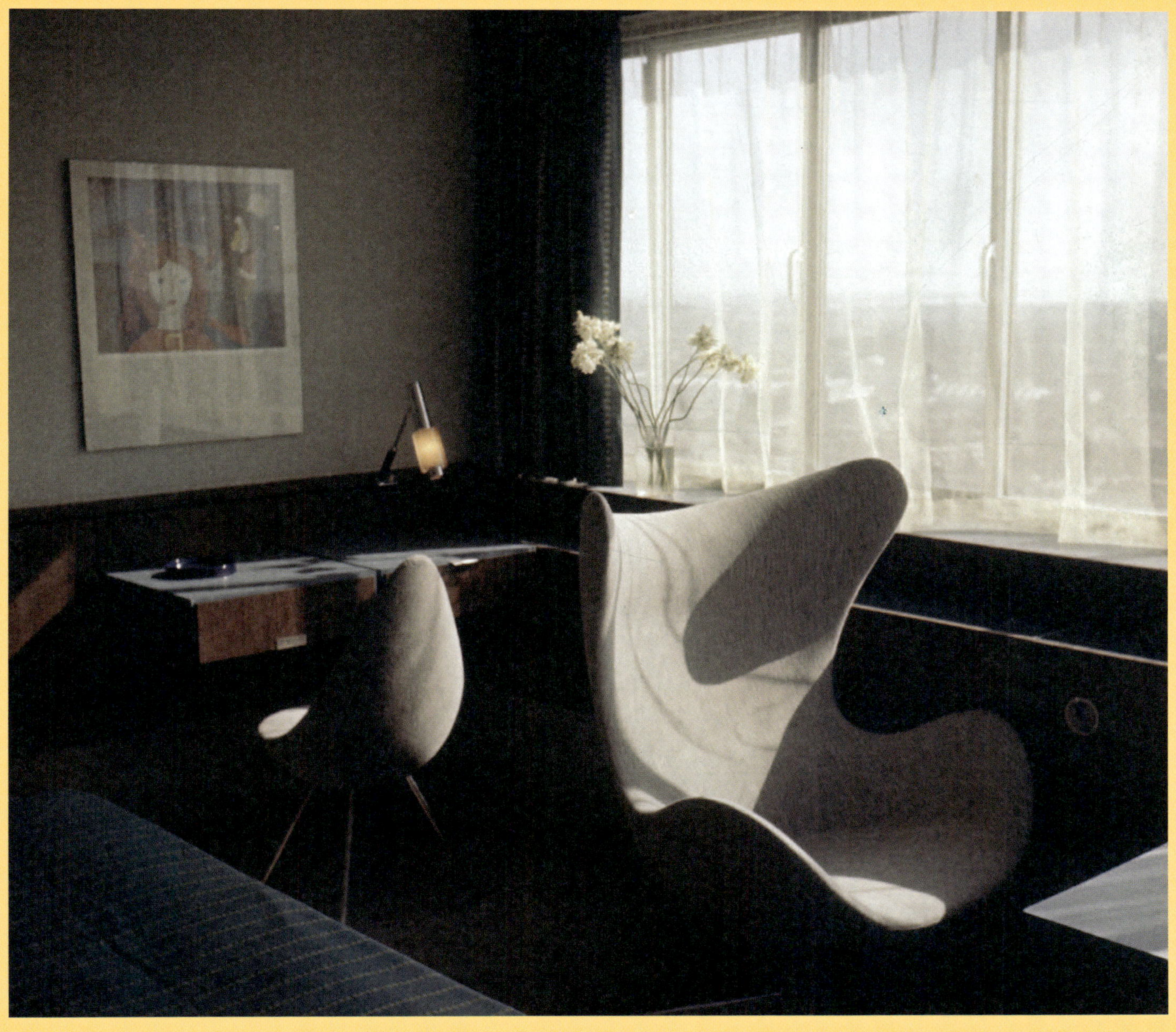

One of the SAS Royal Hotel's rooms around the time of its opening in 1960. It features the new chairs known as the Egg and the Drop. The Egg was made commercially available in 1958

Photo: Arne Jacobsen. The original can be found in: The Royal Danish Library – The Danish National Art Library

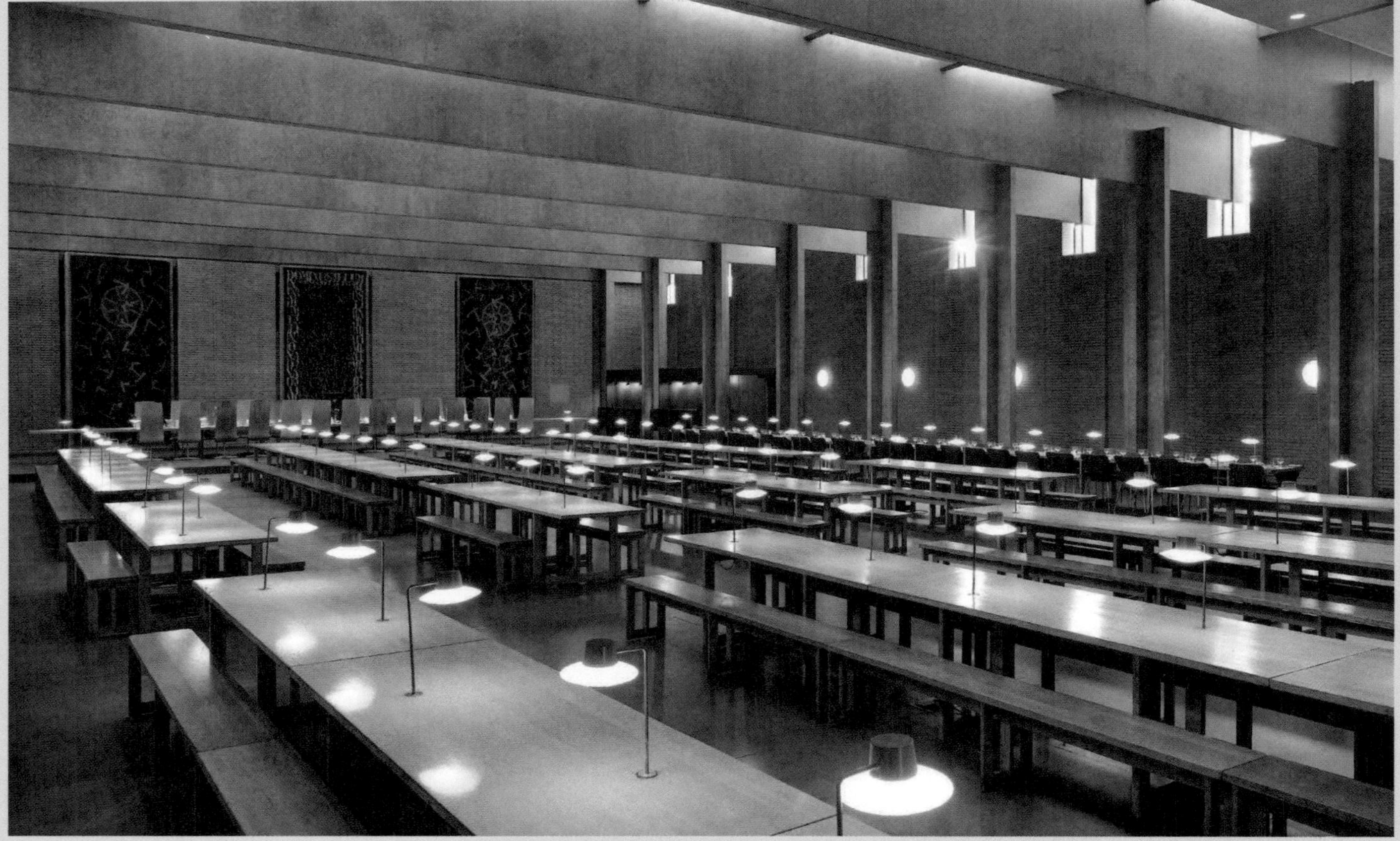

The dining hall at St. Catherine's College. Arne Jacobsen designed tables and benches for students, while the fellows sat on high-backed chairs at high table

Photo: Arcaid / Universal Images Group via Getty Images

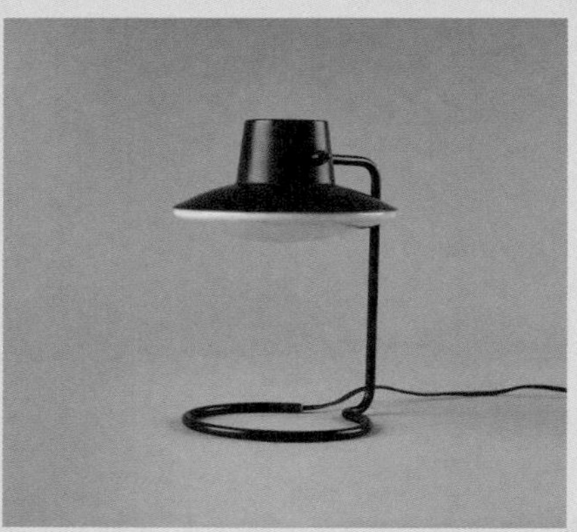

The Oxford lamp, designed for St. Catherine's College

Furnishing St. Catherine's College

Like the SAS Royal Hotel, both inside and out St. Catherine's College, Oxford is infused by Arne Jacobsen's aesthetic. Completed in 1964, the college was furnished with his already famous designs: the Swan, Series 3300, the Eklipta wall lamp and the AJ lamp. He also designed a new range of furniture for the college, some items of which became design classics, while others never became known outside of Oxford. For the students' rooms, Arne Jacobsen designed a built-in bed, the upholstered St. Catherine's armchair and footstool, and the Etude desk chair – all made of laminated oak. In the dining room, students were seated on benches, while the fellows sat at their own table on a plinth at one end of the room. With this interior, Arne Jacobsen ensured that students and fellows ate together – an important college tradition. At the same time, the high-backed Oxford chairs created the illusion of a confined space around the fellows' table. On the tables stood Oxford lamps – sometimes affectionately known as 'Sailor's caps'. While the furniture for the SAS Royal Hotel remains famous throughout the world today, the pieces created for St. Catherine's College in Oxford never became major commercial successes.

The Oxford chair shown with a high or low back. The high-backed model was designed for the fellows' table in the dining hall

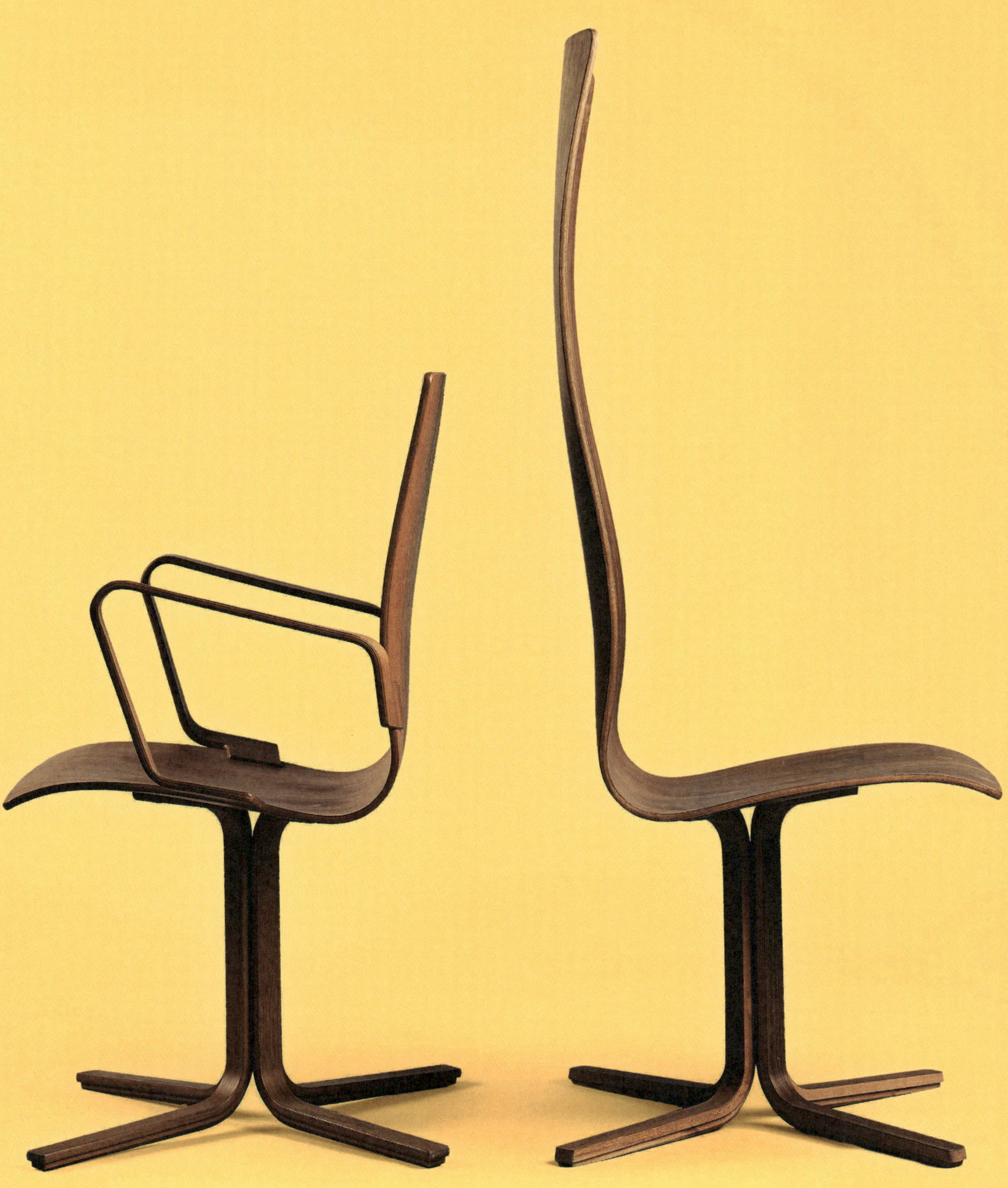

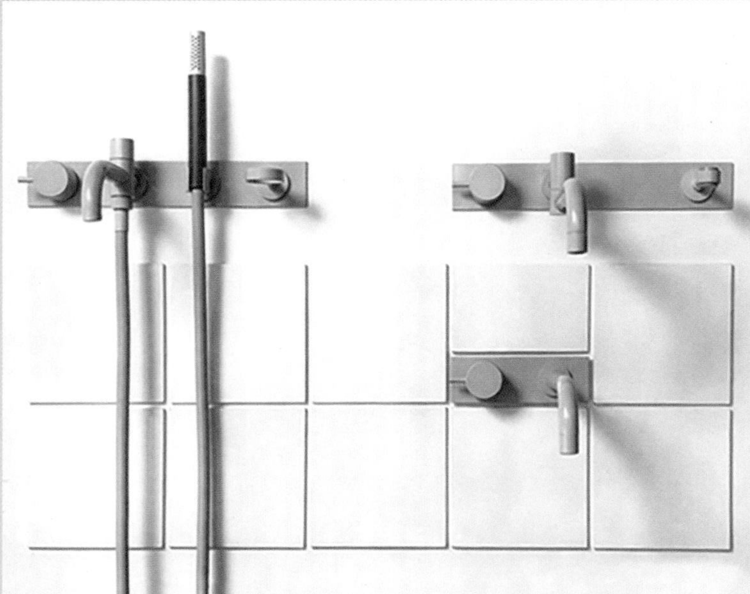

The VOLA faucet was developed in 1969, inspired by the manufacturer Verner Overgaard's idea of making a faucet that could be built into the wall, leaving only the handle and tap visible

Photo: VOLA

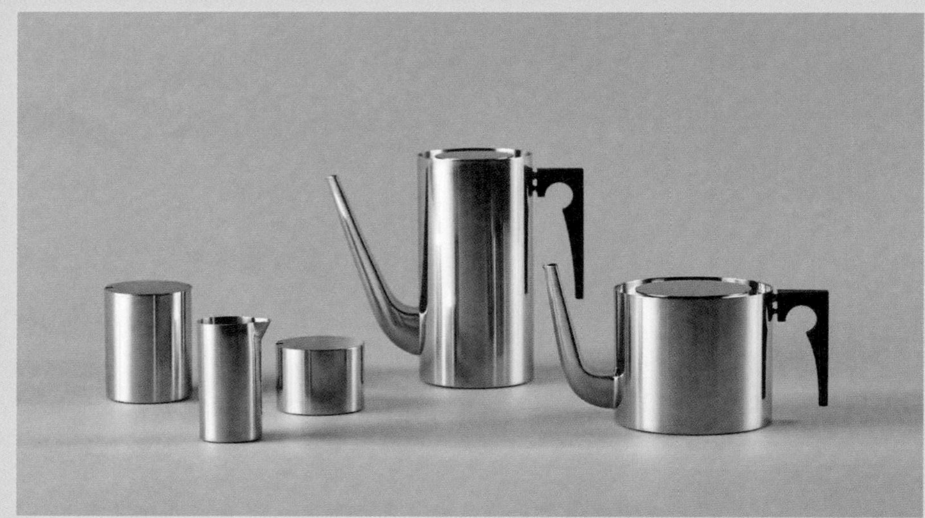

The idea behind the Cylinda Line (1967) was to use standard steel pipes as the basis for modern, affordable homeware to compete with traditional silverware

Trapholt Collection

A systematic approach

Arne Jacobsen remained innovative throughout his career. During the 1960s, he adopted a new approach, creating design systems based on standardised basic elements, which could be combined in different ways, forming the basis for individually tailored solutions. The trend found its clearest expression in the Kvadraflex and Kubeflex prefabricated houses, introduced in 1970. The houses never entered production, and the only Kubeflex house ever built can now be viewed at the Trapholt Museum in Kolding, where it is presented with its original interior.

The system approach is also evident in Arne Jacobsen's product designs from this period. The VOLA faucet series and the Series 3400 modular sofa (1971) directly reflect the idea of creating a design that can be adapted to the user's needs. The system elements were often based on basic geometric shapes such as the cube, circle and cylinder. For example, the popular Cylinda Line of home accessories from Stelton evolved from the idea of producing inexpensive homeware by using standard steel pipes – a production method which did not, however, prove feasible in practice. The safari chair known as Rover (1968) could be dismantled and reassembled by the user, a feature clearly reflected in the design itself, which emphasises the individual elements used in the chair's construction and how they fit together. These pieces were forerunners of trends later developed by companies such as IKEA. Arne Jacobsen never got to be part of this development. He died in 1971, and several of the visionary designs he developed towards the end of his life have since been largely forgotten.

Rover (1968)

Trapholt Collection

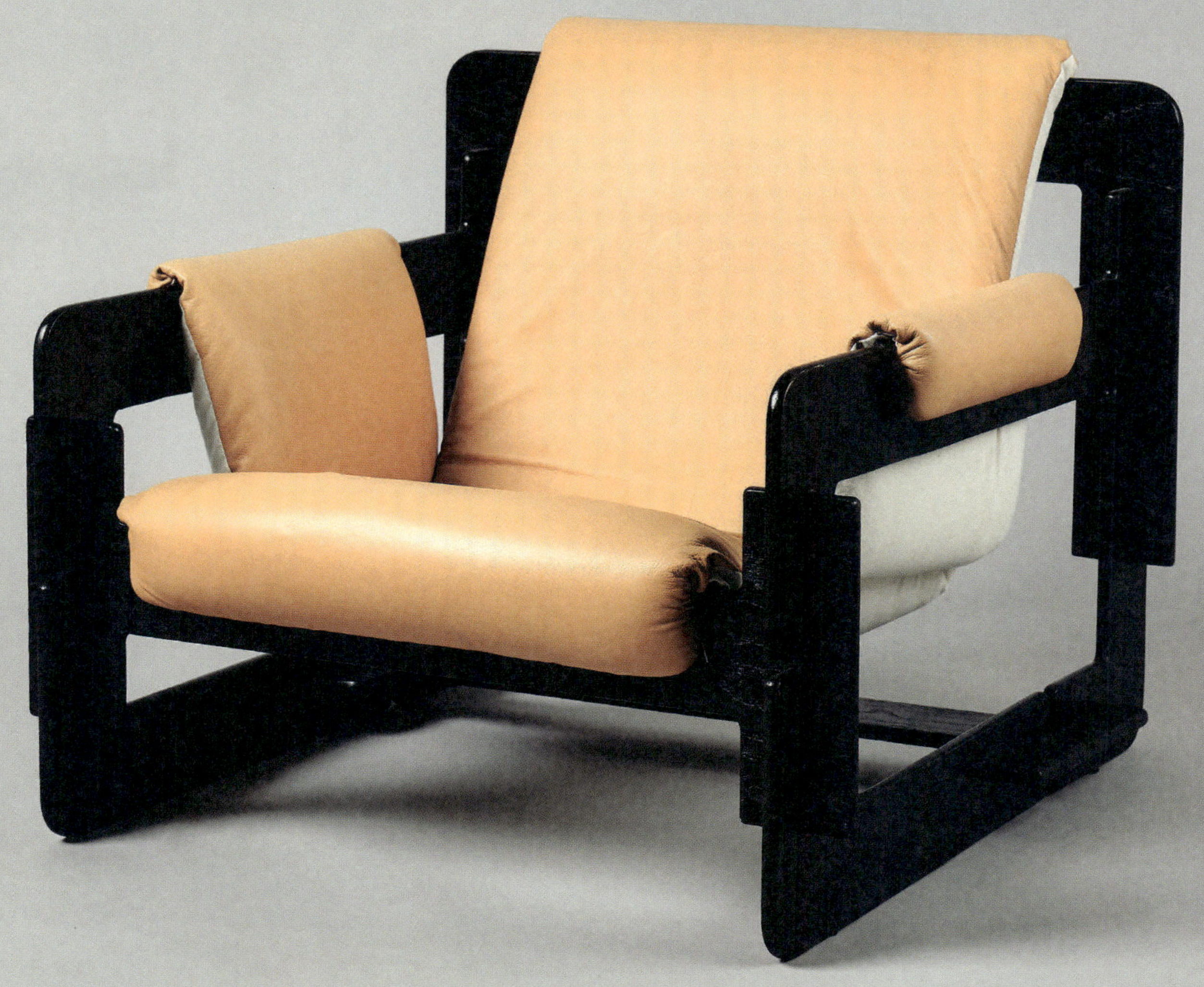

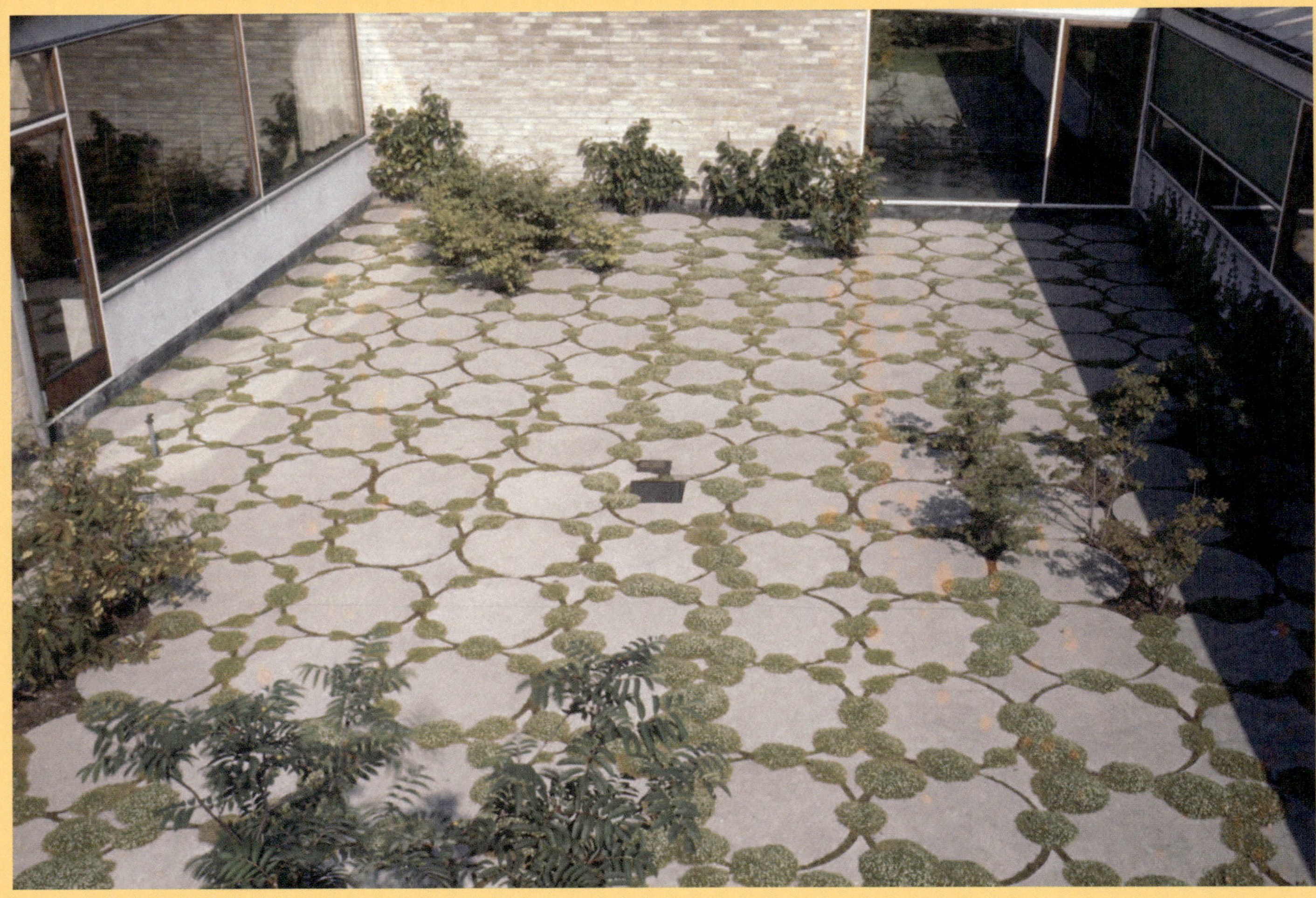

Courtyard at the Munkegård School

Photo: Arne Jacobsen. The original can be found in: The Royal Danish Library – The Danish National Art Library

The botanist

'If I have another life, I want to be a gardener' (Thau & Vindum, 1998, p. 123). With these words, Arne Jacobsen succinctly captured his lifelong interest in nature. At his home at 413 Strandvejen, he created his own botanical garden, featuring a wealth of plants that he brought home from his travels abroad. The garden was his haven, a place to escape from work – but also a place of inspiration. His lush textile patterns and the organic forms of designs such as the Swan chair clearly demonstrate how his studies of nature influenced his aesthetic.

As an architect, he deployed his interest in landscape and nature to expand his projects to include the landscape around the building: for example, when working on St. Catherine's College (1964), where he also designed the college park. Of particular note were his courtyards, which blurred the distinction between nature, art and design. When designing the courtyard gardens of Munkegård School in 1955, he filled them with selected plants and a special species of moss that grew between the tiles to form an abstract pattern. Some of the plants were pruned, turning them into topiary animals, alluding more to the ancient sculptures that Arne Jacobsen also placed in the school's courtyard than to wild nature. A similar approach was evident in his plan for one of the inner courtyards at Denmark's National Bank, its geometric stringency reminiscent of an abstract painting.

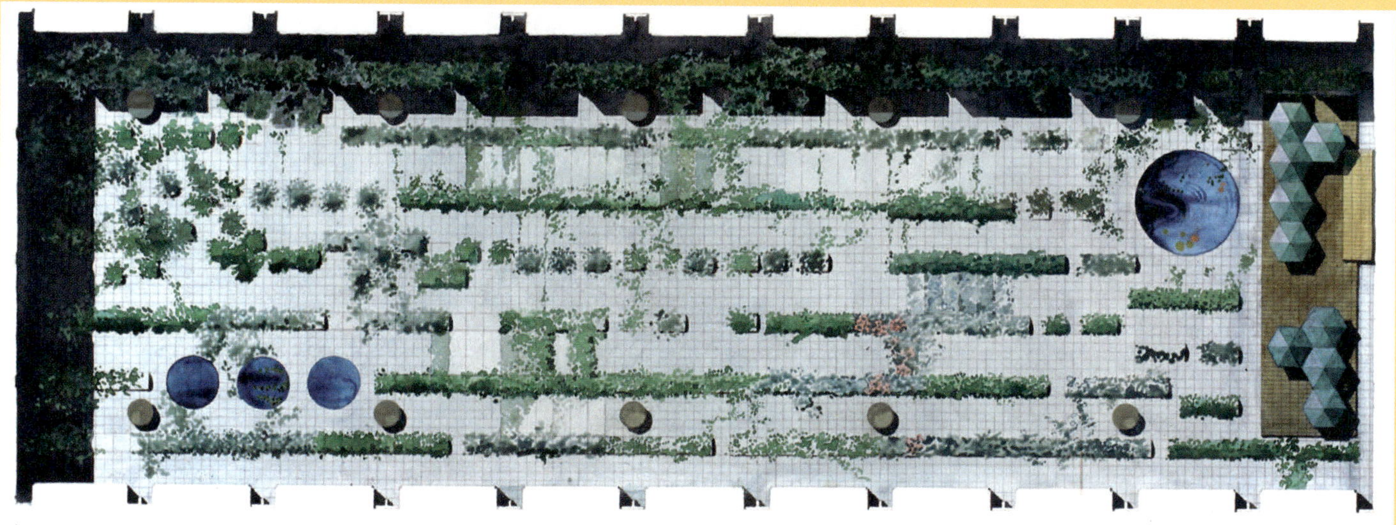

Garden design for the inner courtyard at the National Bank of Denmark

Photo: Dissing+Weitling

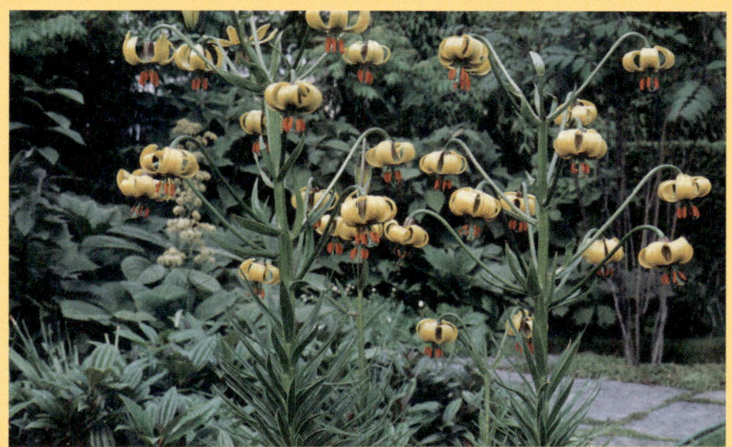

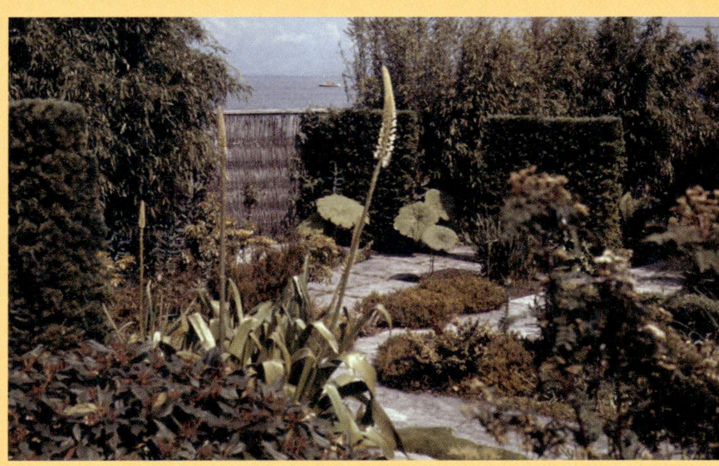

Arne Jacobsen's own photos from his garden at 413 Strandvejen

Photo: Arne Jacobsen. The original can be found in: The Royal Danish Library – The Danish National Art Library

The legacy of Arne Jacobsen

When Arne Jacobsen died in 1971, Hans Dissing and Otto Weitling, Arne Jacobsen's partners at the studio, took over and completed the ongoing projects, including Denmark's National Bank and the Danish embassy in London. The studio continued under their leadership and was renamed Dissing+Weitling. Still active today (2020), the studio upholds Arne Jacobsen's international outlook and ideas on architectural simplicity.

Despite the efforts of manufacturers to maintain the general enthusiasm for Danish design and Arne Jacobsen, in the 1970s post-war furniture and the 'Danish Modern' narrative began to encounter resistance. The new generation was shaped by the oil crisis, the war in Vietnam, the women's movement and anti-materialism. The young generation cast doubts on the picture of Denmark established by their parents with nuclear families, detached houses and designer furniture set snugly within the framework of the welfare state. Anti-authoritarian in spirit, the young built their own furniture out of old wooden crates and recycled pallets. For the first time in many years, Danish furniture manufacturers witnessed a decline in sales.

During the 1990s and 2000s, several attempts were made to invest Arne Jacobsen's designs with renewed relevance: for example, through new

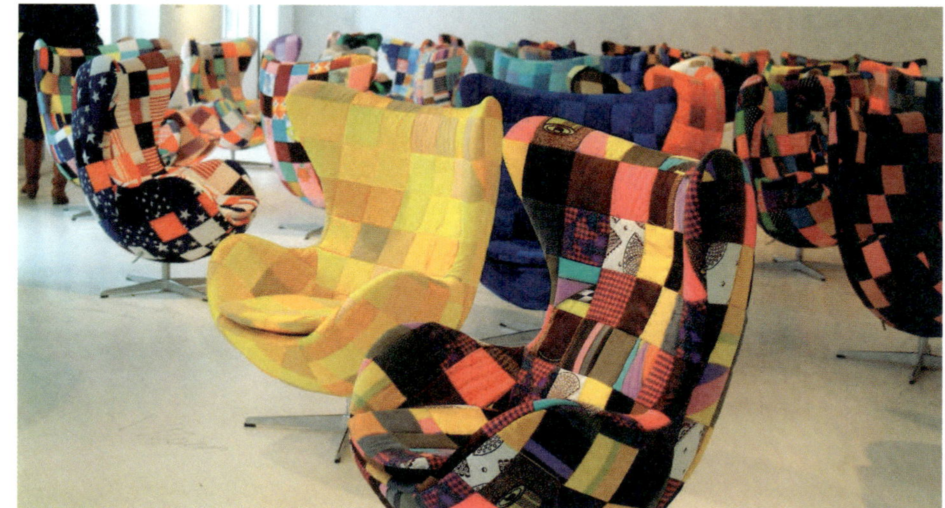

In 2008 the Danish artist Tal R creates a series featuring the Egg chair upholstered in multi-coloured patchwork on the occasion of the chair's 50th anniversary

Photo: Vittorio Zunino Celotto/ Getty Images

collaborations with living artists and designers. In 2008, to mark the occasion of the Egg chair's 50th anniversary, the Danish artist Tal R created a series of Egg chairs upholstered in multicoloured patchwork, while in 2015 Fritz Hansen launched a new colour range for the Series 7, created by the same artist. Today we are more interested in 1950s Danish design than ever before. Rediscovered designs by figures such as Børge Mogensen, Poul Henningsen, Hans J. Wegner and Arne Jacobsen are being relaunched or put into production for the first time. They appeal to all generations, prompting many people to decorate their homes with Danish furniture classics. Considering the ups and downs that have occurred through history, the question is: will this state of affairs continue?

Arne Jacobsen was not just an architect. He created and designed a lifestyle and an aesthetic interpretation of Denmark's welfare state. Most Danes encounter his designs on a daily basis, whether in their own homes, in the doctor's waiting room, in lecture halls or in conference rooms. It is Arne Jacobsen's approach to his profession and the creative process that makes him so relevant. This is why so many of his works are so popular and sold in such vast numbers today.

Series 7. The updated colour palette created by the artist Tal R in 2005

The characteristic shape of the Egg chair has often been used in depictions of models and famous people. Here, Michelle Pfeiffer has been photographed for the cover of *Esquire UK*

Photo: Michelle Pfeiffer photographed by Rankin for the September 2007 issue of *Esquire UK*

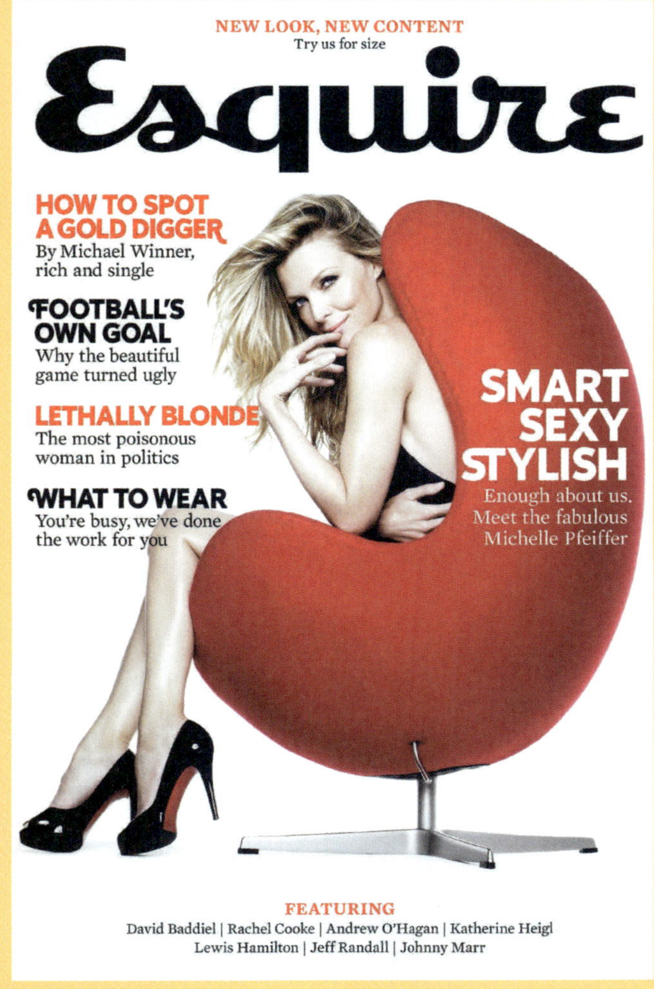

Furniture in the media

In his own lifetime, Arne Jacobsen benefited greatly from media attention. If one takes as a whole the general media coverage, the many advertisements created by the manufacturers and the popularity enjoyed by his furniture among fashion magazines and photographers, Arne Jacobsen's designs are some of the most photographed in the world. With its simple, iconic shape, the Egg chair is a particular media favourite. The Egg and the Series 7 appear in countless contexts across popular culture: in advertisements for everything from cars to heat guns; in movies, magazines and lifestyle features; and on social media. They are often used as props when portraying famous people around the world. Indeed, the Egg chair was also chosen for the cover of this publication.

Over the years, the Fritz Hansen company has successfully reinterpreted and reinvented the ways in which they present Arne Jacobsen's furniture, so we still see them as contemporary and modern today. When the Series 7 was first launched in 1955, it was accompanied by texts telling readers that 'wherever you need to sit comfortably, whether you are many or few, working or a listening audience, the Series 7 chair is the logical solution' (Fritz Hansen's archives). Visually, the Series 7 and Ant chairs were presented as ideal choices for the modern family and as innovative, resilient, affordable chairs for canteens, offices and lecture rooms. Today, the manufacturers' presentation of Arne Jacobsen's design focuses on words such as 'iconic' and 'simple'.

Archives

Danish National Art Library, Søborg: Arne Jacobsen's scrapbooks, The Collection of Architectural Drawings and The Collection of Architectural Photographs

Fritz Hansen's archives, Allerød

Novo Nordisk History Collection, Bagsværd

RIBA – Royal institute of British Architecture, London: Photo Collection and Collection of drawings

The Danish National Archives, Copenhagen: Arne Jacobsen's business archives

Bibliography

Andersson Møller, V. (2009). *Farver i funktionalismen*. Copenhagen: Nationalmuseet og Forlaget Rhodos

Andersson Møller, V. (2013). *Danske kunstnertapeter 1930-1965*. Copenhagen: Nationalmuseet og Ruben Blædel

Bostrup, E. (1954). Man kan godt standardisere uden at gøre Husene ens. In: *Jyllandsposten*, 16 october 1954

Dahlkild, N. (2015). *Huse der har formet os: Arkitekturhistorien bag danskernes institutioner og offentlige rum*. Copenhagen: Museum Tusculanum and Danmarks Kunstbibliotek

Dahlkild, N. (2018). *Sommerlandets arkitektur: drømmen om det gode liv*. Copenhagen: Museum Tusculanum

Dybdahl, L. (2017). *Det danske møbelboom 1945-1975*. Copenhagen: Strandberg Publishing

Faber, T. (1964). *Arne Jacobsen*. Stuttgart: Hatje

Hansen, P.H. (2006). *Da danske møbler blev moderne : Historien om dansk møbeldesigns storhedstid*. Odense: Syddansk Universitetsforlag & Aschehoug

Holm, M.J.; Kjeldsen, K. & Vindfeld, T. (2002). *Arne Jacobsen – Absolut moderne*. Humlebæk: Louisiana

Kaiser, B. (1992). *Den ideologiske funktionalisme*. Copenhagen: Gad

Lidegaard, B. (2013). *En fortælling om Danmark i det 20. århundrede*. Copenhagen: Gyldendal

Møller, E.; Lindhe, J. & Vindum, K. (1991). *Aarhus Rådhus*. Copenhagen: Arkitektens Forlag

Olsen, T.O. (2002). *Arne Jacobsen i Gentofte: 24 udvalgte bygninger: arkitekturguide*. Gentofte: Gentofte Kommune

Pedersen, J: (1954). *Arkitekten Arne Jacobsen*. Copenhagen: Arkitektens Forlag

Sheridan, M. (2006). *Room 606 : the SAS House and the work of Arne Jacobsen*. London: Phaidon Press

Solaguren-Beascoa, F. (2002). *1. Approach to his complete works 1926-1949, 2. Approach to his complete works 1950-1971, 3. Drawings 1958-1965* Copenhagen: Arkitektens Forlag

Staunsager, S. & Stenum, K. (ed.) (2018): *Arne Jacobsens Kubeflex*. Kolding: Trapholt

Thau, C. & Vindum, K. (1998). *Arne Jacobsen*. Copenhagen: Arkitektens Forlag

Tøjner, P.E. (2002). *Atlas: Arne Jacobsens akvareller*. Copenhagen: Aschehoug

Tøjner, P.E. & Vindum, K. (1996). *Arne Jacobsen. Architect & designer*. Copenhagen: Dansk Design Center

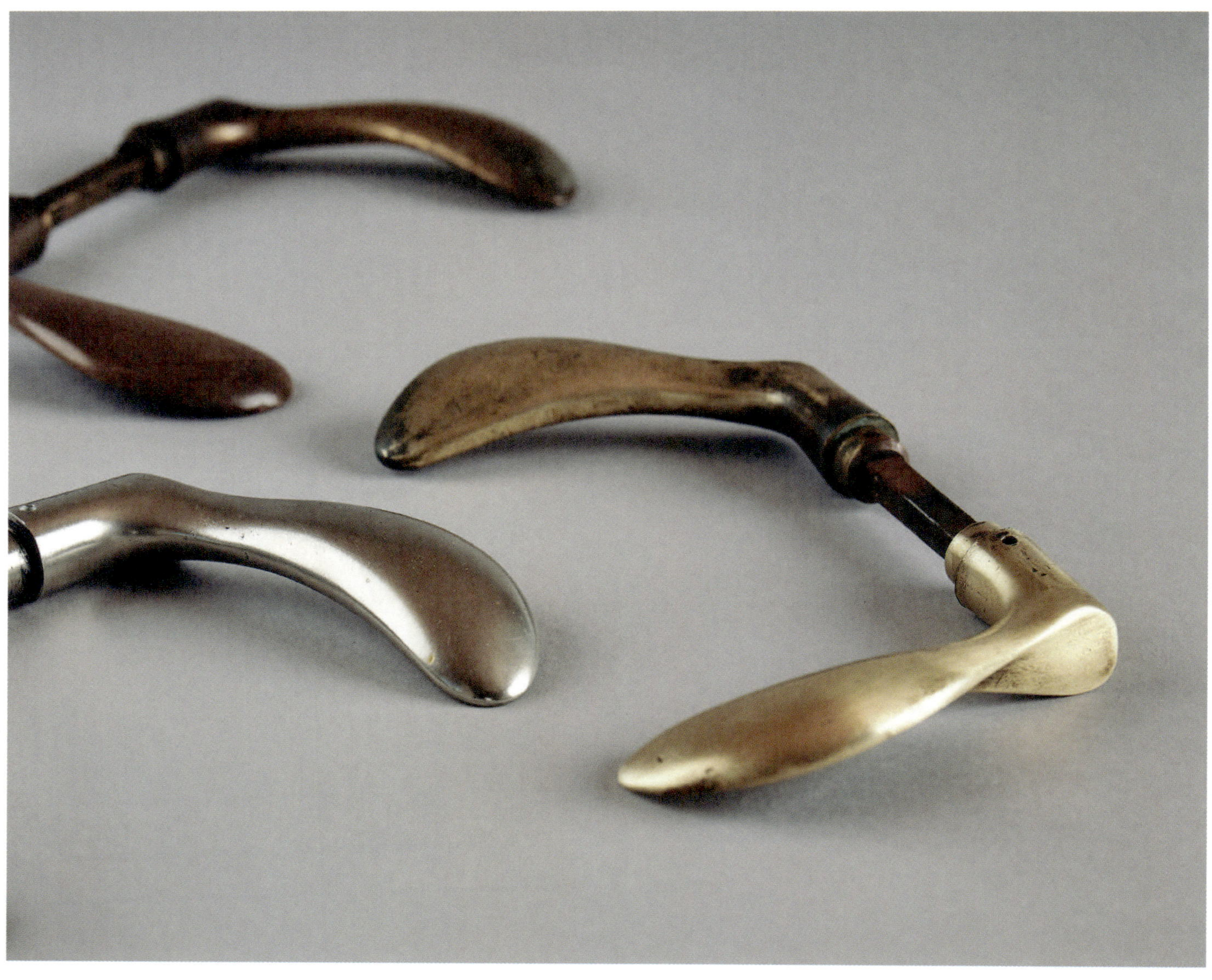

The AJ door handle (1956)

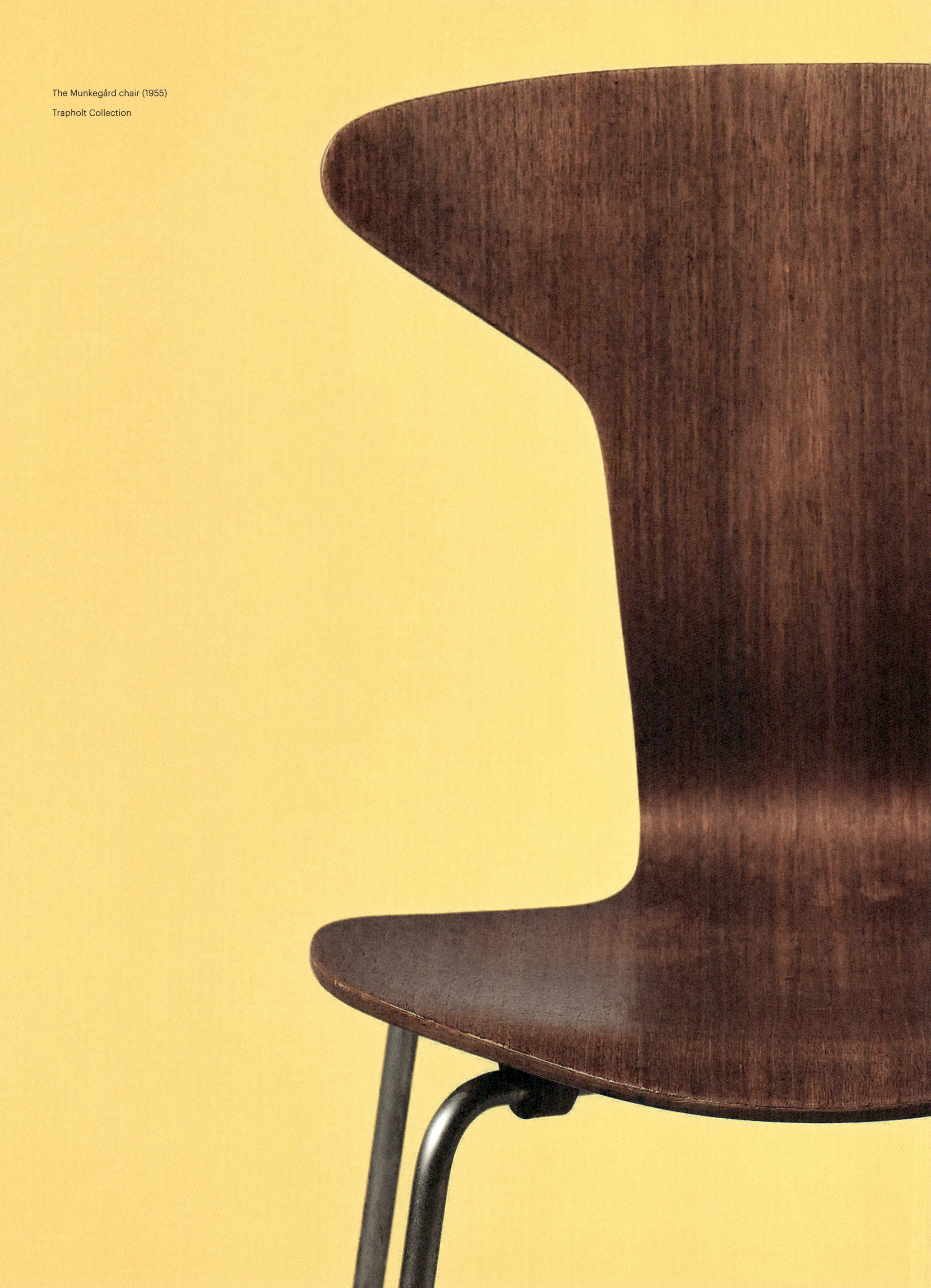

The Munkegård chair (1955)

Trapholt Collection

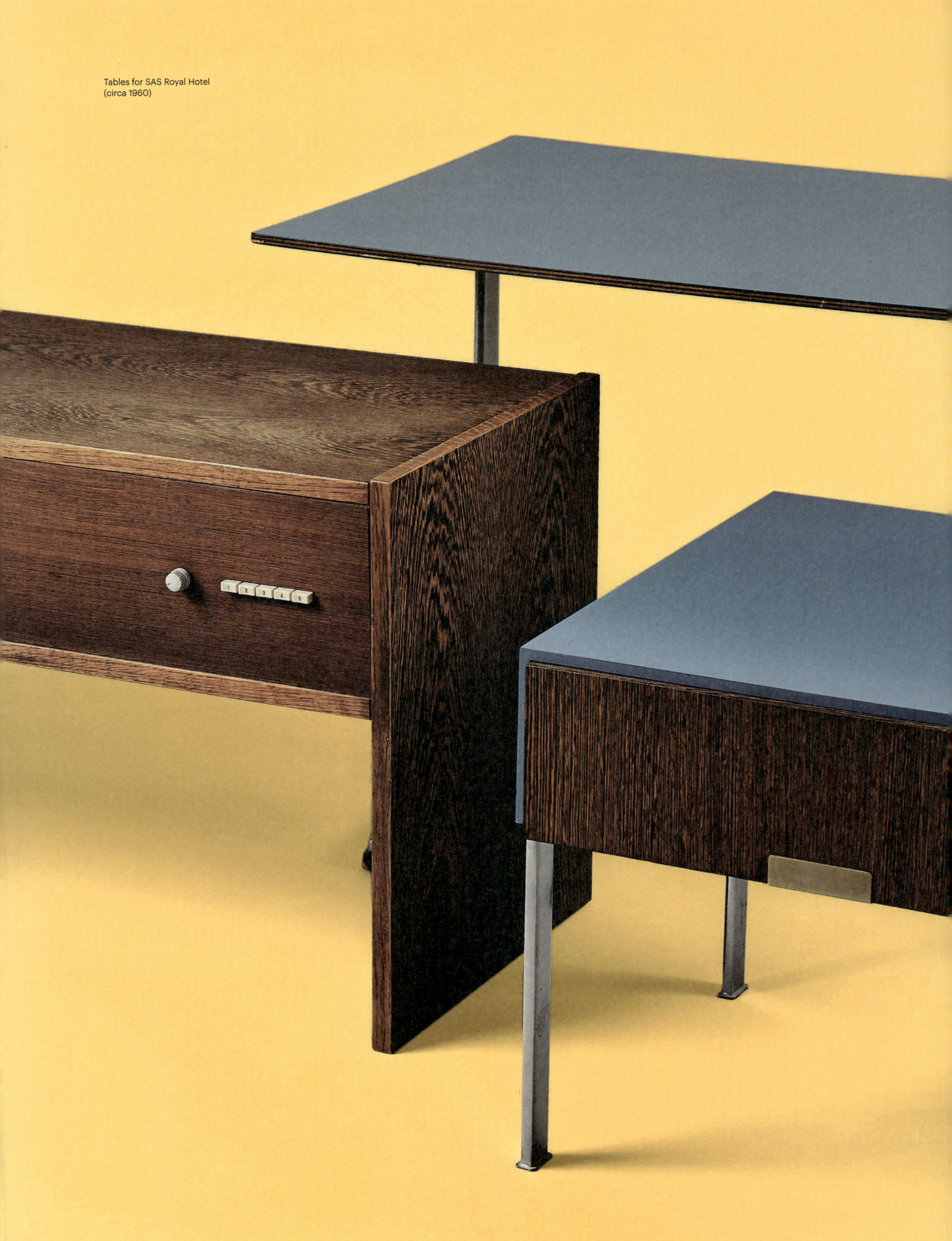

Tables for SAS Royal Hotel
(circa 1960)

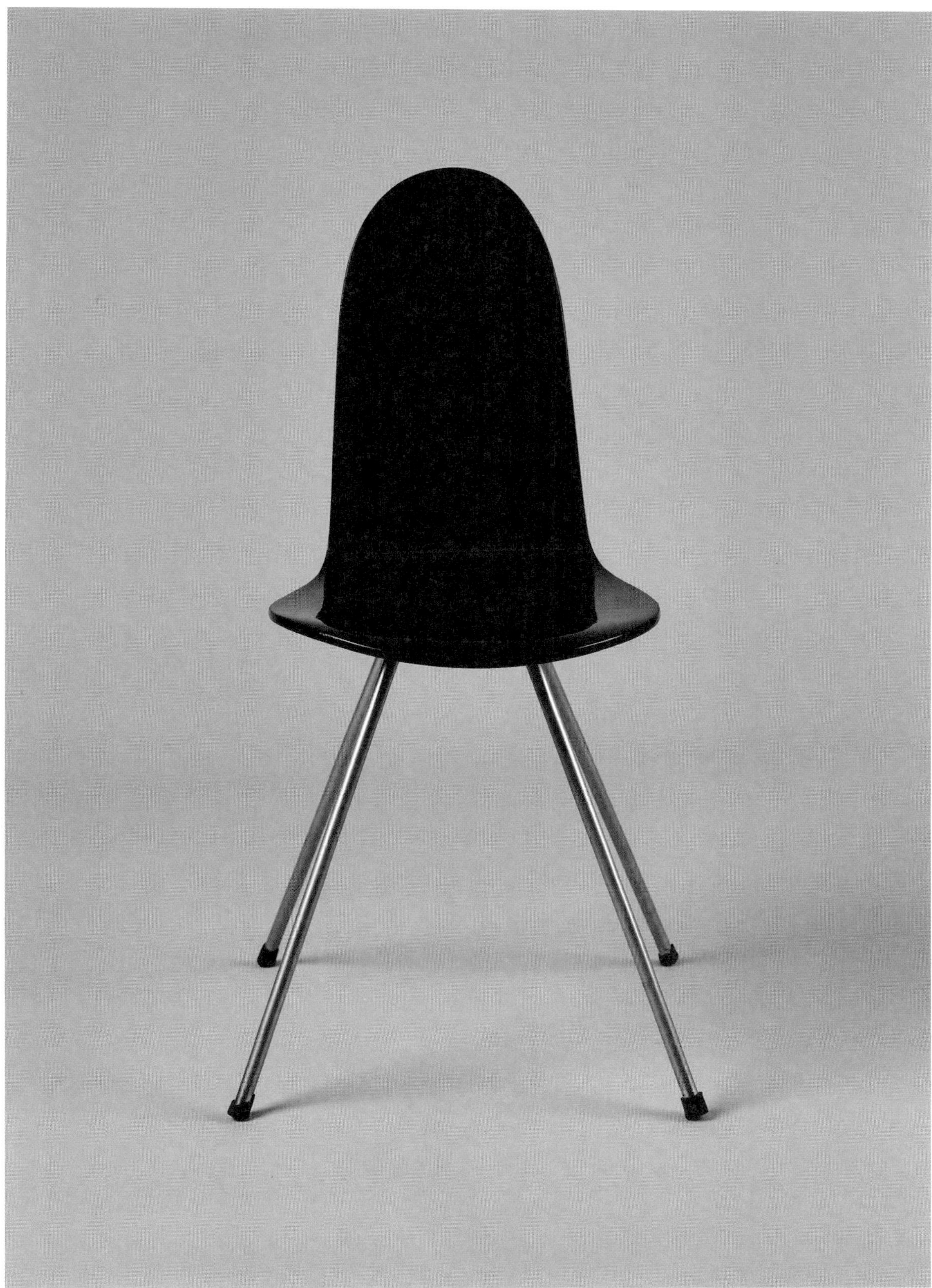

The Tongue chair (1955)

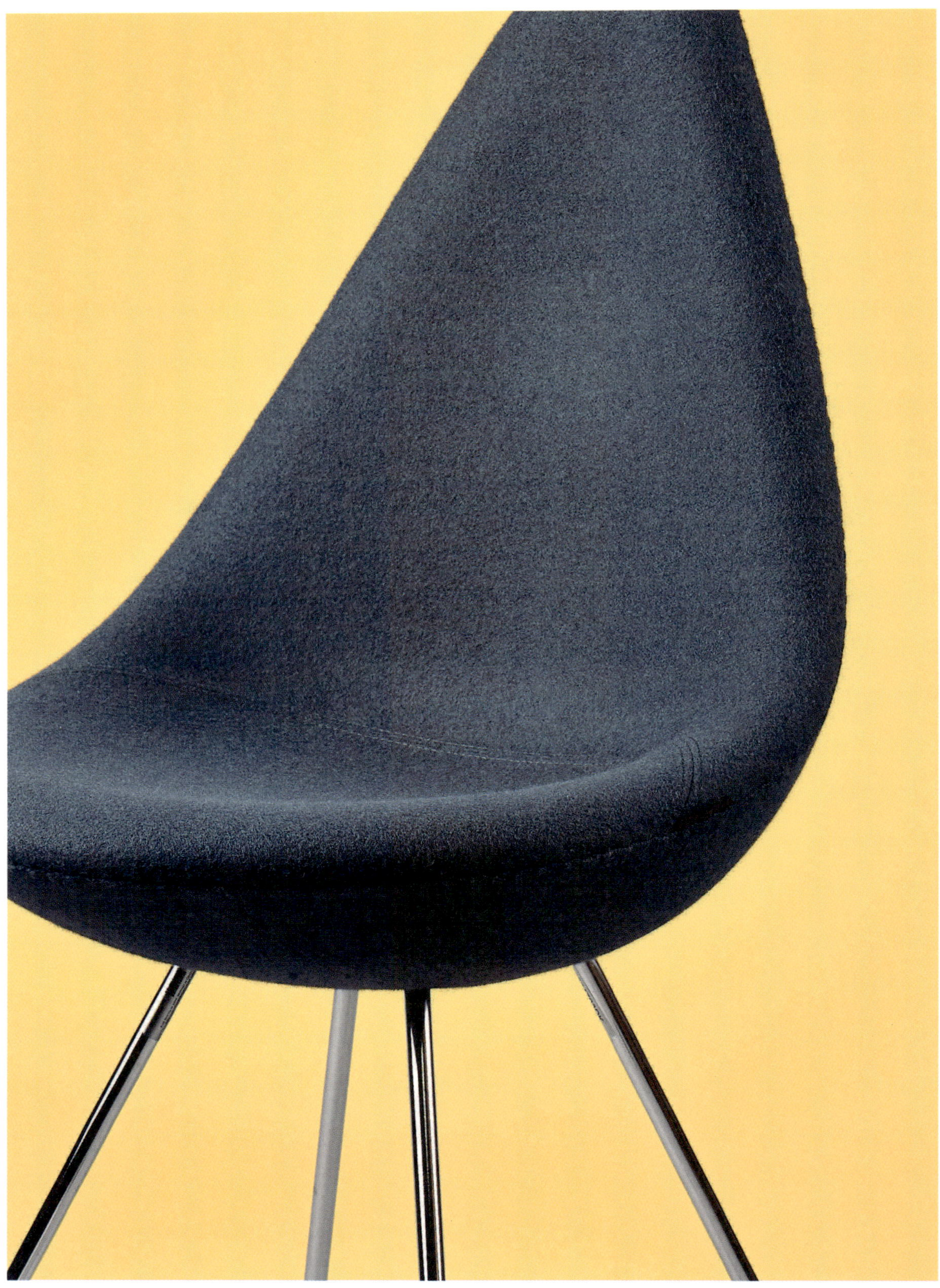

The Drop chair (1959)

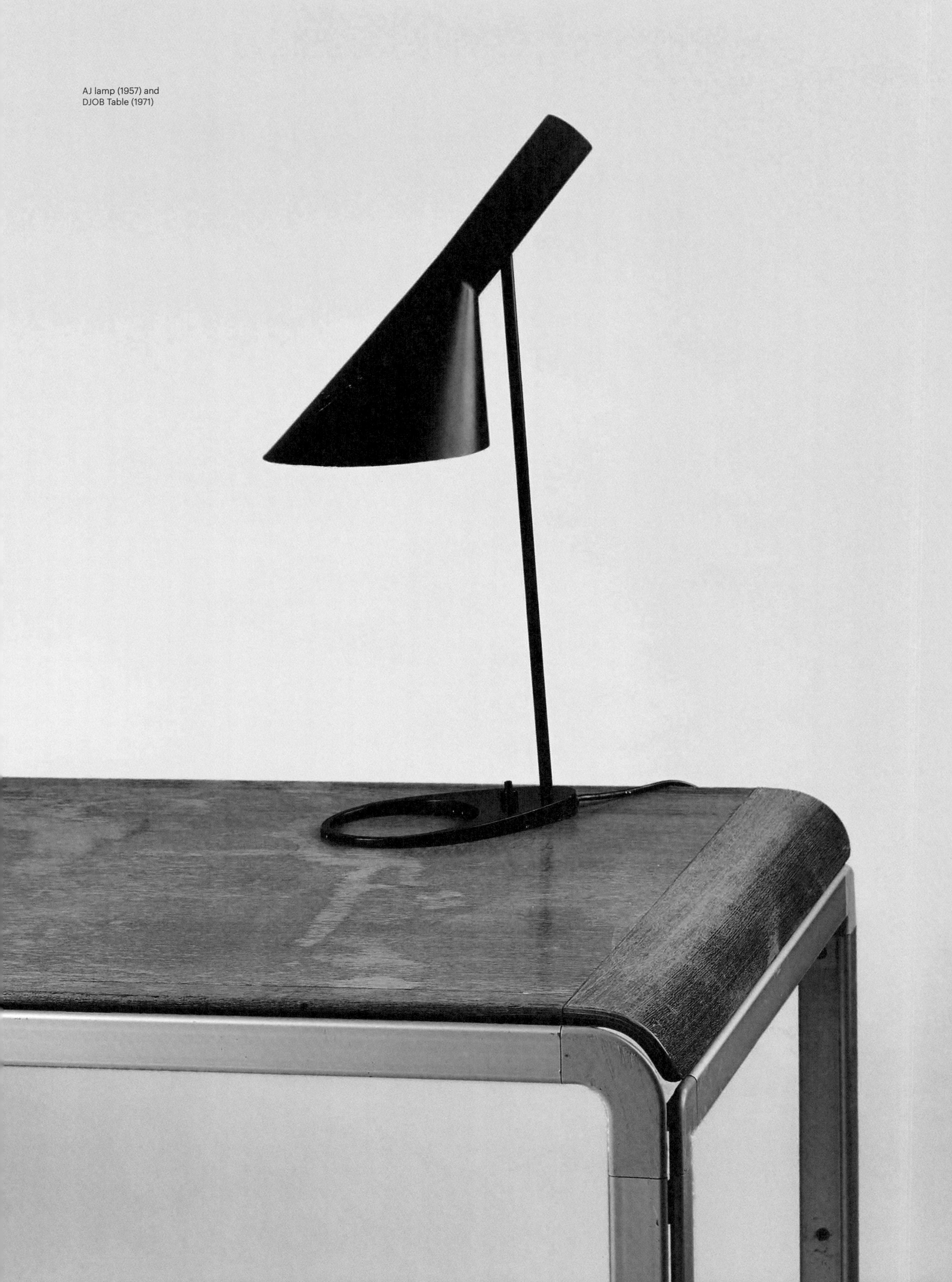

AJ lamp (1957) and
DJOB Table (1971)

Can something like that be made?

Art and creativity at Arne Jacobsen's design studio

Annika Skaarup Larsen

Art Historian, Arne Jacobsen Design I/S

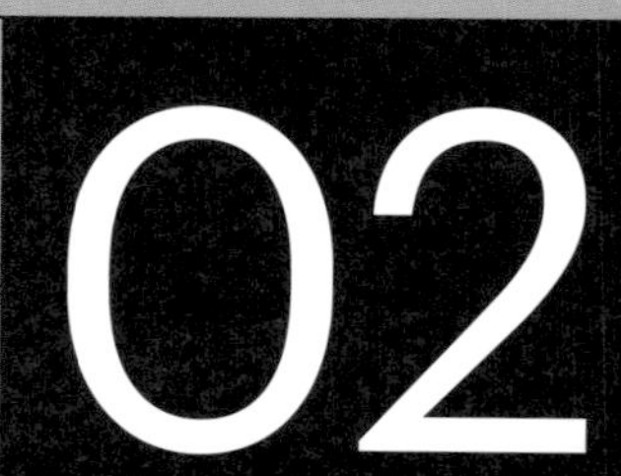

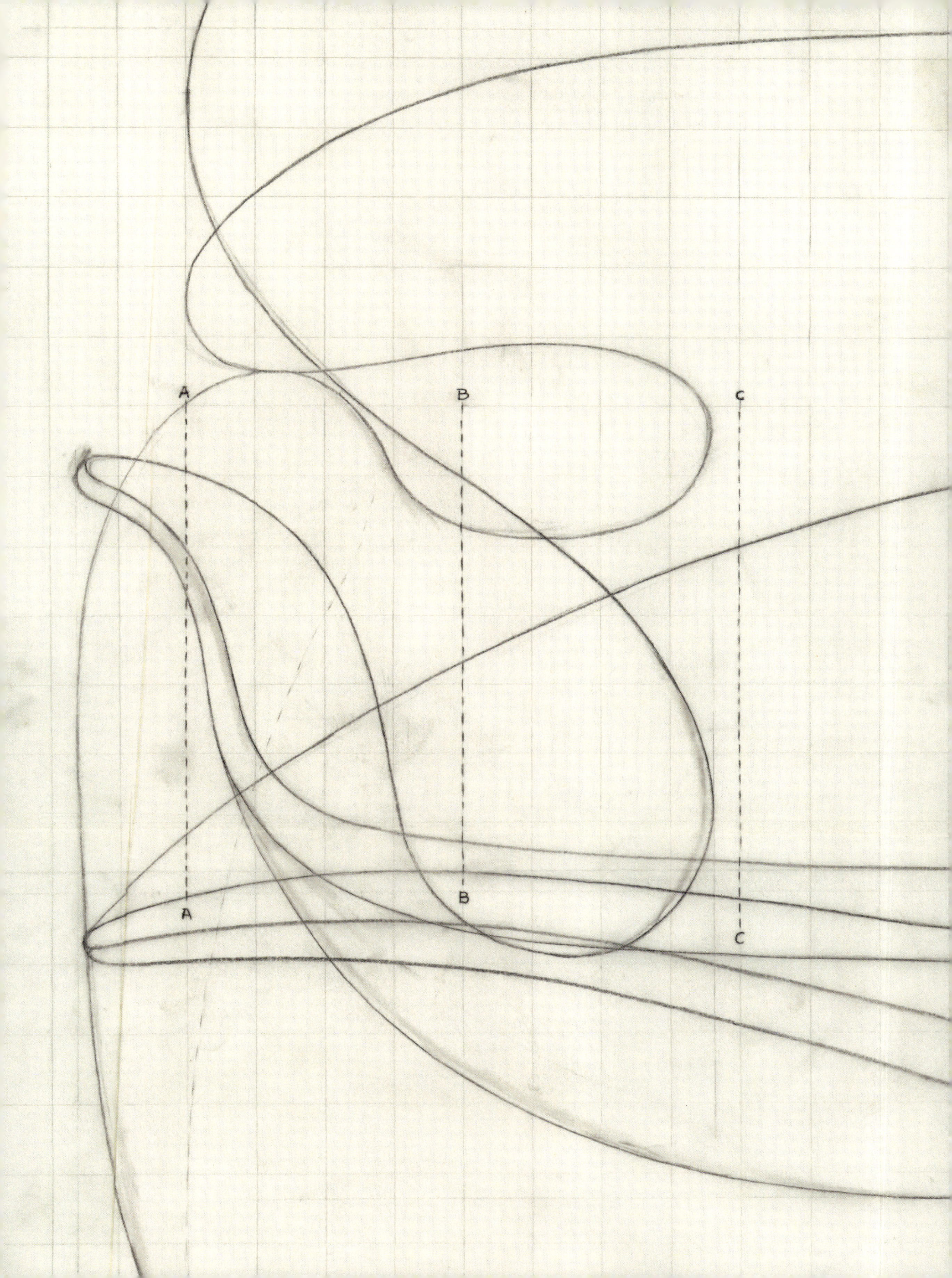
A
B
C
B
A
C

'Inspiration? A new city hall doesn't come to you in dreams.'

– Arne Jacobsen, 1967

Previous page: Drawing of a precursor of the Swan chair

Photo: The Royal Danish Library – Danish National Art Library

Creativity and innovation are much-debated topics in current discussions. How will Denmark make its money in the future? And how can we use design and innovation to solve the challenges currently facing the world? These are some of the questions frequently asked today, often considered in numerous books on the subject of creativity and in research on how we might design our schools to promote the students' desire and ability to be creative (e.g., Tanggaard & Brinkmann, 2012). This article will explore the phenomenon of creativity by looking at how Arne Jacobsen created buildings and design products that helped transform how we live and made Denmark an internationally recognised nation of design in the middle of the last century.

The quote by Arne Jacobsen was printed in the newspaper *B.T.* in 1967. The text goes on to say: 'There is no other way to do it than through work. You are given a task and then you have to think it through and draw and work. There is no other method than simply getting started'. (Jessen, 1967). Arne Jacobsen's description of his working process goes against the grain of how we typically understand creativity, where we tend to think of good ideas appearing in a sudden burst of clarity or a result of an inner, cognitive thought processes (Tanggaard, 2013; Ingold, 2010; Nielsen, 2009). By contrast, Jacobsen describes a working method where creative development takes place and unfolds over time, and which includes a concrete, tangible processing of the physical world. His description forms the starting point of this article, which examines how Arne Jacobsen used his surroundings in his creative process – and what we can learn from his method.

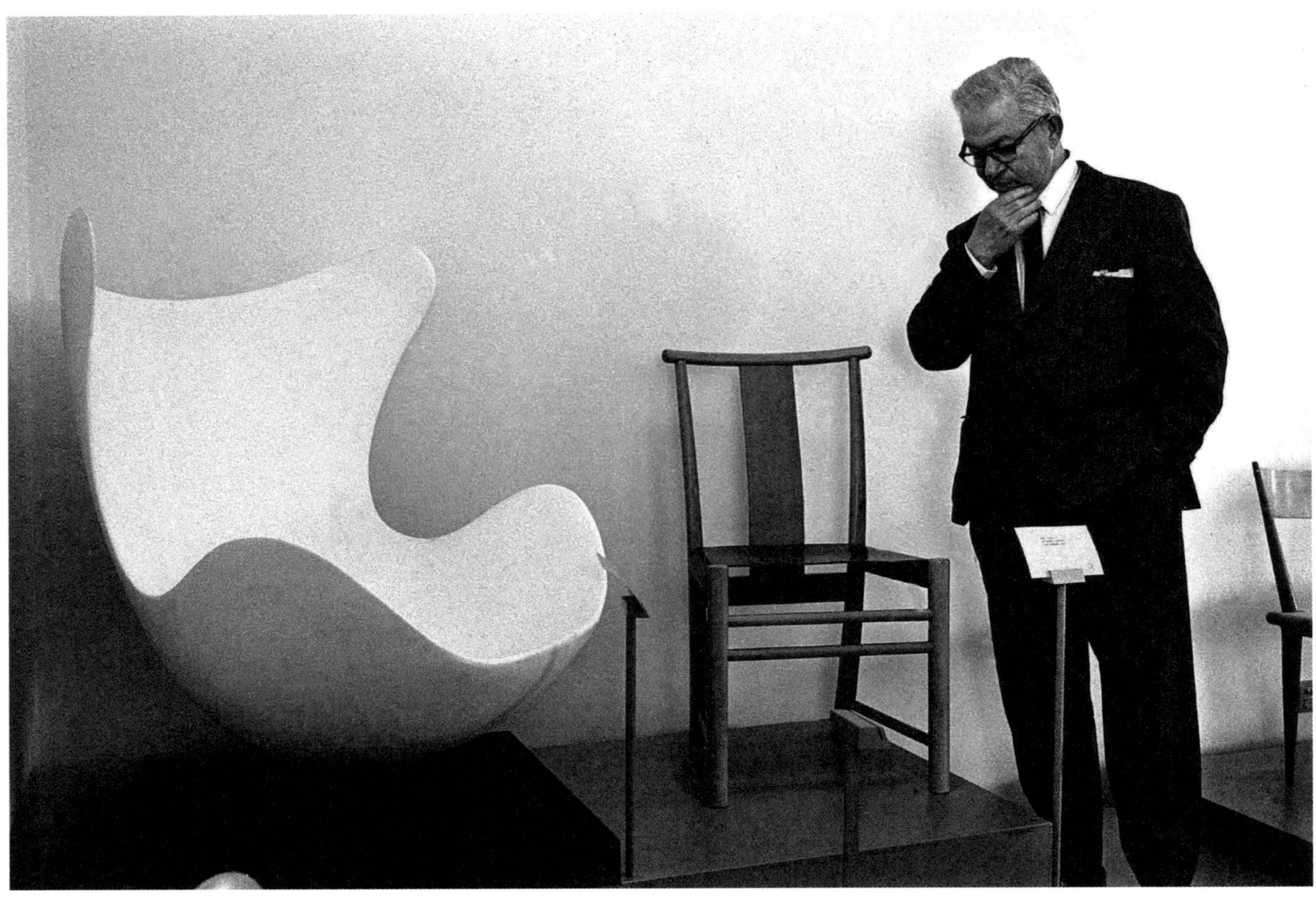

Arne Jacobsen with a plaster model of the Egg chair

Photo: Bjarne Lüthcke/Scanpix

What is creativity?

Taking my point of departure in the ideas put forward by Professor of Educational Psychology Lene Tanggaard, Anthropologist Tim Ingold and Professor of Visual and Museological Anthropology Elisabeth Hallam, I will consider creativity as a relational phenomenon, meaning that creativity always unfolds in relation to something. According to Hallam & Ingold (2007), creativity should not be traced backwards from the finished product, but instead be seen as a forward-looking process, driven by *improvisation*. They use the metaphor of a house whose final design depends on the architect's plans, but also on the materials and craftsmen who make the house a reality. According to Ingold (2010) we tend to erroneously read creativity as a process in which the individual devises a design and then translates it into physical reality by means of passive materials. Ingold believes that creativity should instead be understood as an improvisational journey of discovery that unfolds within a moving, changing world. With Arne Jacobsen's description of 'just getting started', we find *improvisation* coupled with the more tangible idea of the *experiment*.

Tanggaard (2013) also rejects the idea that creativity should be read as an exclusively cognitive process, as ideas cannot be created, developed or realised without materials and tools. She emphasises the relationship between continuity and renewal, as 'materials, tools, things, institutions, normative practices and 'ways of doing' already in the world are taken as starting points for new creations.' (p. 20). Such an approach implicitly rejects the idea that the new emerges only in the individual's struggle against the constraints of society, hitherto something of a cornerstone of the modern conception of creativity. With statements like 'first you bristle a bit, then you get used to it – and find it beautiful', Arne Jacobsen staged himself as part of an avant-garde that challenged his conservative peers (Tiden arbejder altid for den gode kunst, (1952, p. 9).

This narrative endures today; for example, the furniture company Fritz Hansen tells the story of how the young Arne anticipated Modernism's revolt against the widespread penchant for decoration when he covered the Victorian wallpaper of his nursery with white paint. 'Even as a child, Arne Jacobsen was ahead of his time,' they conclude (Fritz Hansen, 2020). In this article, I offer another reading of creativity and innovation, one that does not celebrate Arne Jacobsen's rebellion, but instead his ability to transform existing norms and practices by actively engaging with them.

Working at Arne Jacobsen's studio

The working environment at Arne Jacobsen's studio was characterised by dialogue, collaboration and practical experiments rather than by discussions on architectural theory (for more on working at the studio, see: Tøjner & Vindum, 1996; Thau & Vindum, 2002; DR, 2003). During most of its existence, the studio was essentially an extension of Arne Jacobsen's own home, employing a substantial number of architects and designers over the years; between six to ten would work there at any given time. A hive of activity, the studio's work revolved around the famous architect, and an important part of the process involved the production of models and visual representations: sketches, technical drawings, architectural models made of wood and cardboard, chair models made of plaster and presentations of the project executed in watercolours. Often, the employees would start working on a range of drafts themselves while Arne Jacobsen surveyed the studio, offering comments and making corrections with a bold 6B pencil. He did the charming watercolours himself; these were instrumental in convincing the client and everyone else about the value of the project at hand.

The work itself centred on experiments, tests and practical action. 'His method was quite simply to experiment his way to a solution,' says architect Knud Holscher, who worked at the design studio from 1960 to 1964 (Tøjner & Vindum, 1996, p. 100). The desire to experiment and test things is a trait also found in other great Danish designers of the period, see for example the writings of innovation researcher Rajiv Vaid Basaiawmoit about the Danish Architect Kay Bojesen (2017).

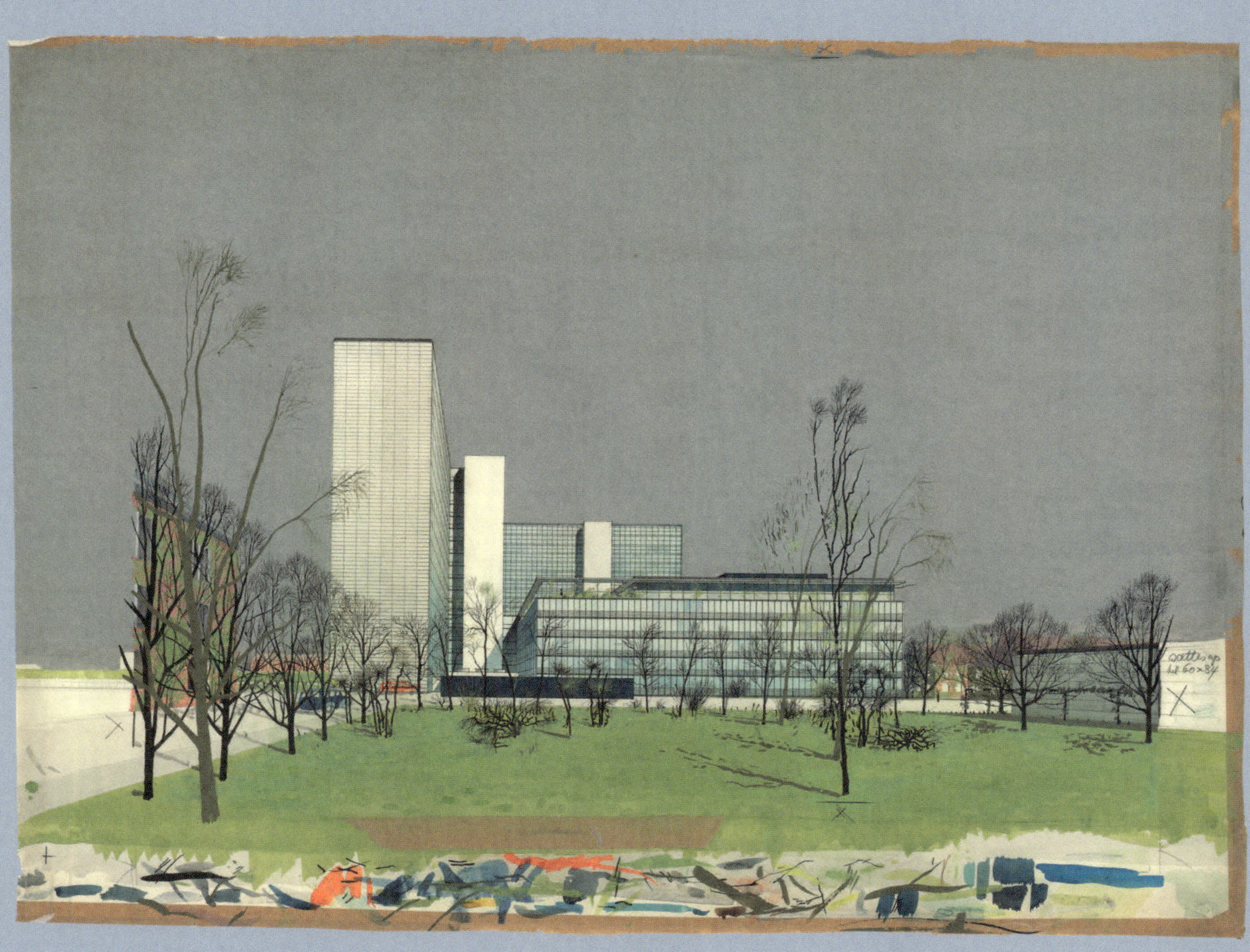

Watercolour by Arne Jacobsen submitted for a design competition for a new National Archive at Frederiksholms Kanal, 1954. The project was never realised

Photo: The Royal Danish Library – Danish National Art Library

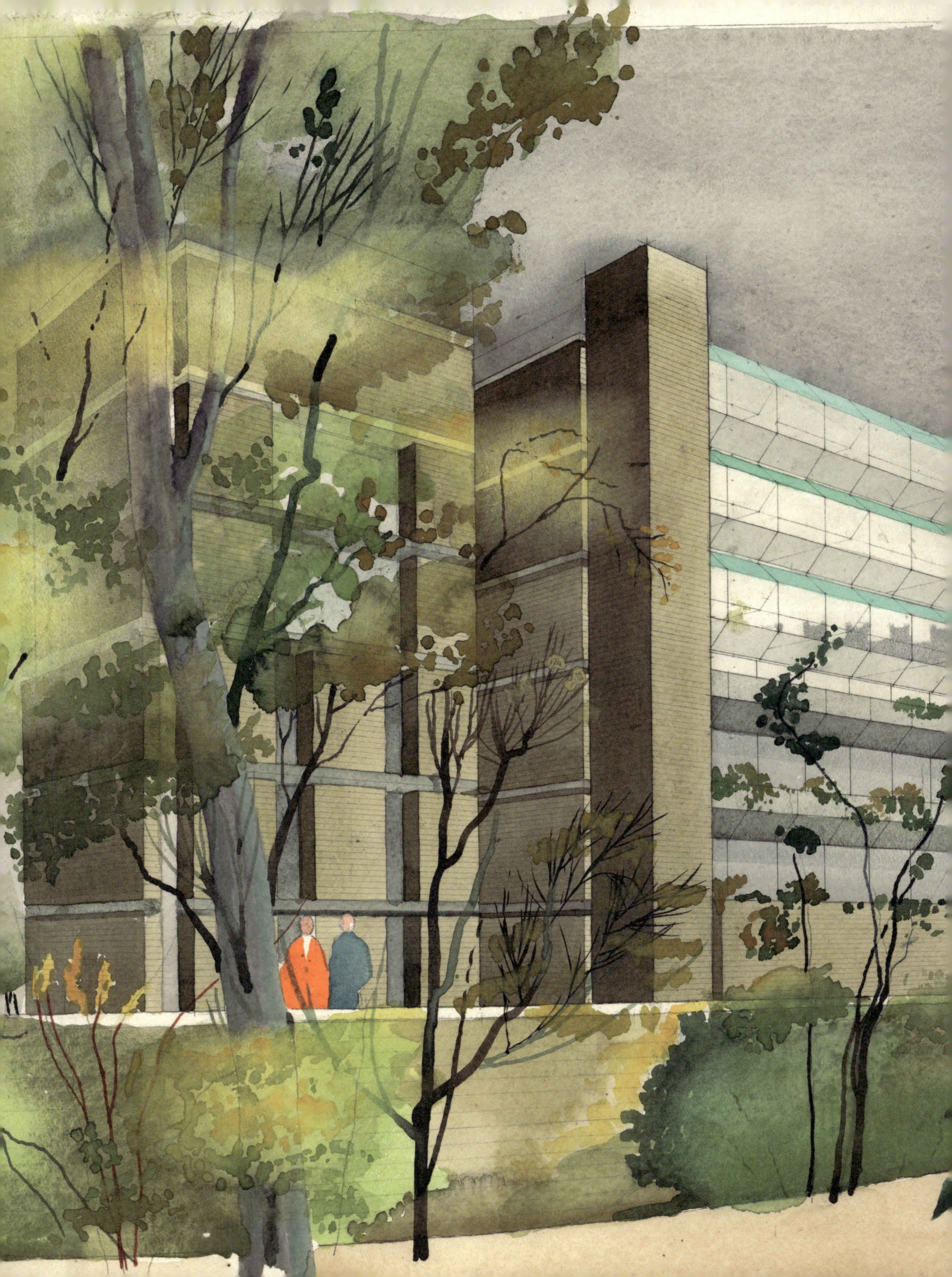

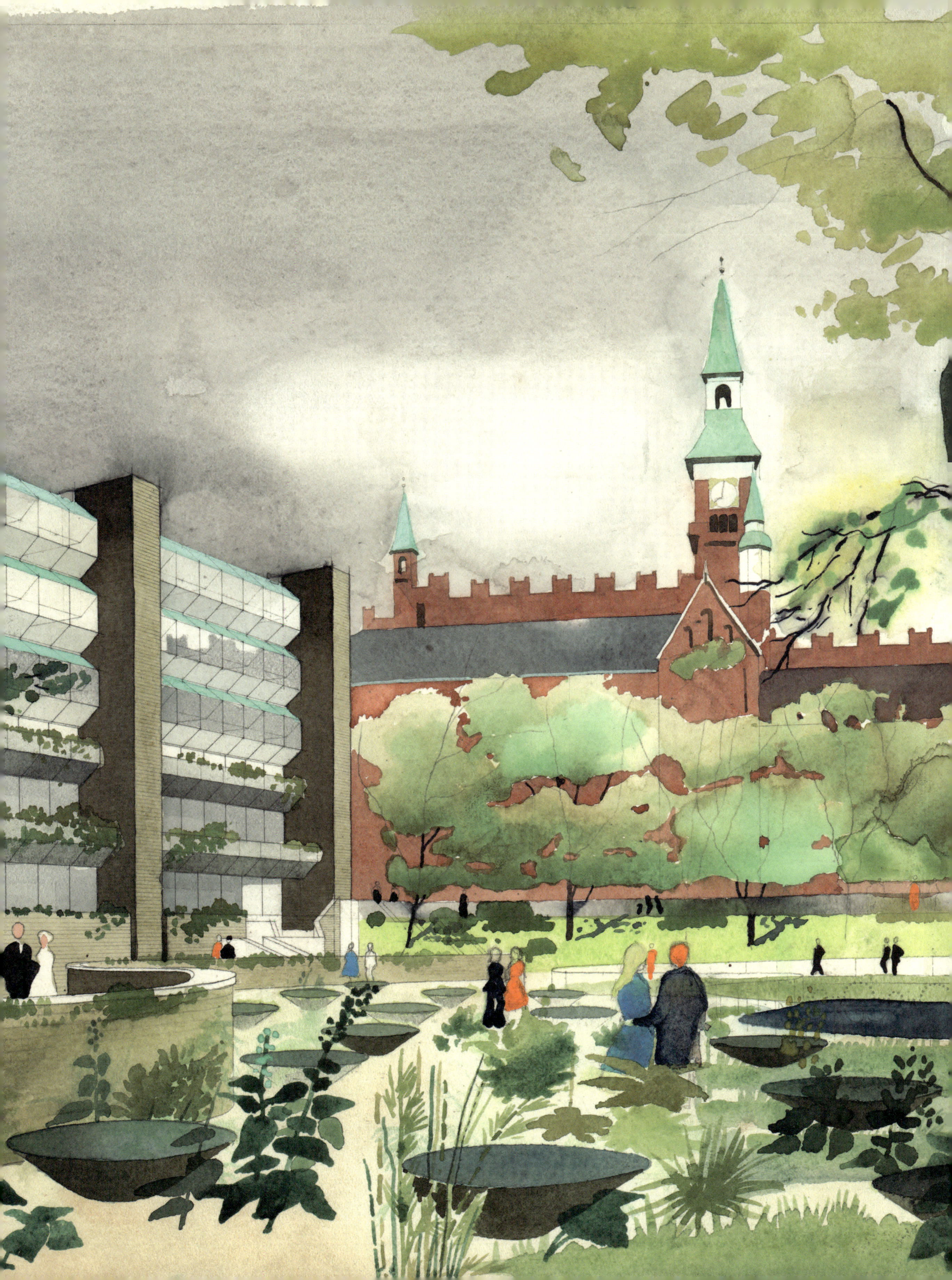

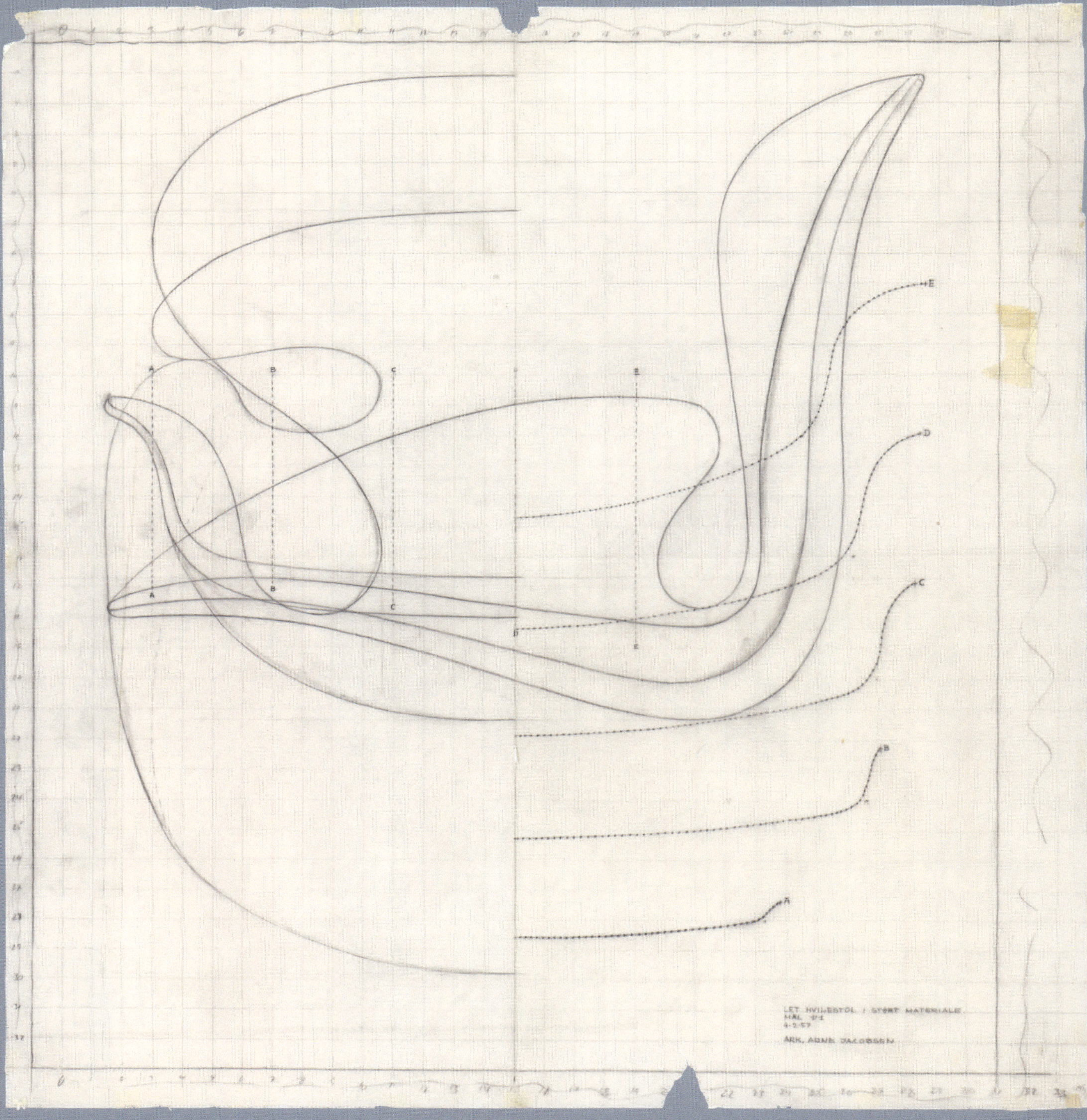

Drawing of a precursor to the Swan chair. The Swan chair was originally envisioned as a shell chair in veneered wood

Photo: The Royal Danish Library – Danish National Art Library

Previous page: This watercolour of Industriens Hus is an example of how Arne Jacobsen used his gift for watercolour painting to win architectural competitions and convince customers. The proposal came first in the competition, but was never realised

Photo: The Royal Danish Library – Danish National Art Library

Dialogue and collective design processes at the studio

The working method may have been based on dialogue, but the actual words exchanged were often terse and to the point. Eschewing verbosity, the discussions were based on drawings and models. 'Can something like that be made, Folmer?', Arne Jacobsen would ask his consulting engineer while presenting his drafts (Tøjner & Vindum, 1996, p. 54), and he would say 'Do you think it looks nice?' to the young architects working on a project (DR, 2003, 00:45:45). Often, chimneysweeps and postmen would be involved in the conversation too when they happened to visit the office. If the ideas did not stand up to such scrutiny, they were discarded and everyone started over again.

The absence of a firmly defined method or theoretical framework meant that the early stages of a task were often infused by uncertainty, lack of confidence and a 'flickering nervousness' (Thau & Vindum, 1998, p. 169). According to professor Carsten Thau and architect Kjeld Vindum (1998), that sense of starting from scratch created a mental space that allowed opportunities to sprout freely, nurturing a 'fruitful sense of unease' which urged the participants to offer up their thoughts and suggestions. The practice of staying within the open-ended start phase for a long time – and doing so collectively – was an important tool in their collaboration. Of course, this did not mean that the process was not characterised by a high degree of expertise and professionalism, but rather that these facets were activated by working with tools and materials.

'He was not much of a theoretician, and the communication was practical rather than verbal in nature. It was all about things. During a later stay in Thailand I learned that it's perfectly possible to collaborate on specific design projects without being able to understand each other's language. Arne Jacobsen was a little like that; when he had to comment on your work, he would either say 'That's ugly' or 'That's not too bad'. The last phrase was high praise indeed.'

– Niels Jørgen Haugesen

Collective experiments carried out in plaster

At the design studio, the various design sketches and models served as means of presentation and persuasion, as vehicles for exchanging knowledge and ideas, and as the basis for joint experimentation. The sculptor Sandor Perjesi, who took part in developing the Egg chair back in the late 1950s, describes how he and Arne Jacobsen would spend days working on a plaster model, 'adding more material here, sanding away some there. Back and forth, like a traditional sculptor' (Tøjner & Vindum, 1996, p. 80). One can form some sense of this long, deliberate exploration by looking at a plaster model now owned by the furniture manufacturer Fritz Hansen. Here, all of the individual elements of the chair are different: the two armrests are differently shaped, and the two sides of the back as well as the four spokes of the stand are all disparate (fig. 1).

In one study, interactive design researcher Giulio Jacucci and professor of multidisciplinary systems design Ina Wagner (2007) have described how materials contribute to the collective design process by expanding the scope for communication and action capabilities through their physical properties. They argue that the tangible, material qualities of the models engage us through multiple senses, encourage participation and mobilise the non-linguistic aspects of knowledge and learning. At Jacobsen's studio, the models facilitated collaboration and dialogue at levels other than the purely linguistic and cognitive. Designer Niels Jørgen Haugesen, who worked at the design studio in the 1960s, describes the experience of collaborating with Arne Jacobsen as follows:

'He was not much of a theoretician, and the communication was practical rather than verbal in nature. It was all about things. During a later stay in Thailand I learned that it's perfectly possible to collaborate on specific design projects without being able to understand each other's language. Arne Jacobsen was a little like that; when he had to comment on your work, he would either say 'That's ugly' or 'That's not too bad'. The last phrase was high praise indeed' (Tøjner & Vindum, 1996, p. 108).

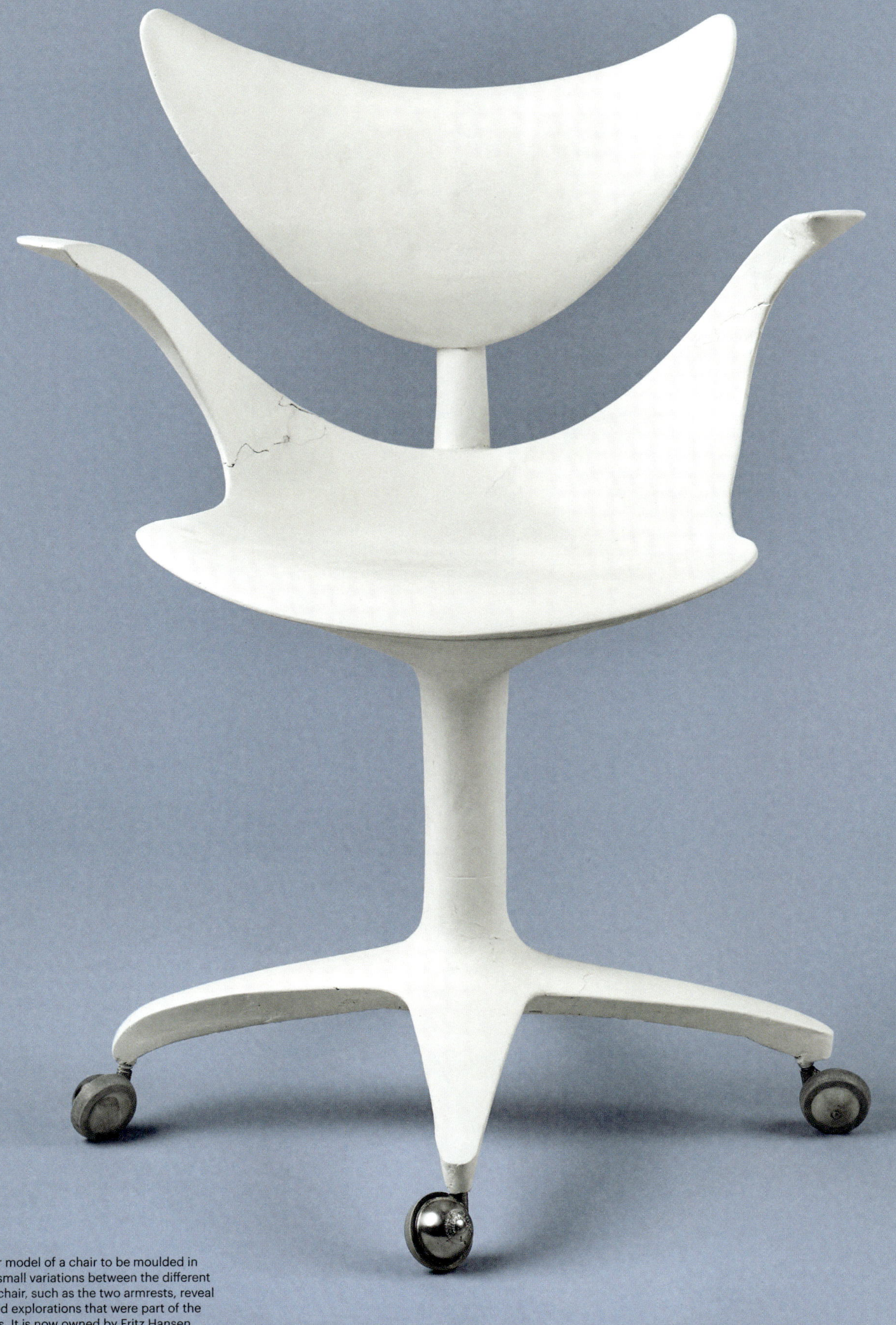

Fig. 1. Plaster model of a chair to be moulded in plastic. The small variations between the different parts of the chair, such as the two armrests, reveal the continued explorations that were part of the work process. It is now owned by Fritz Hansen

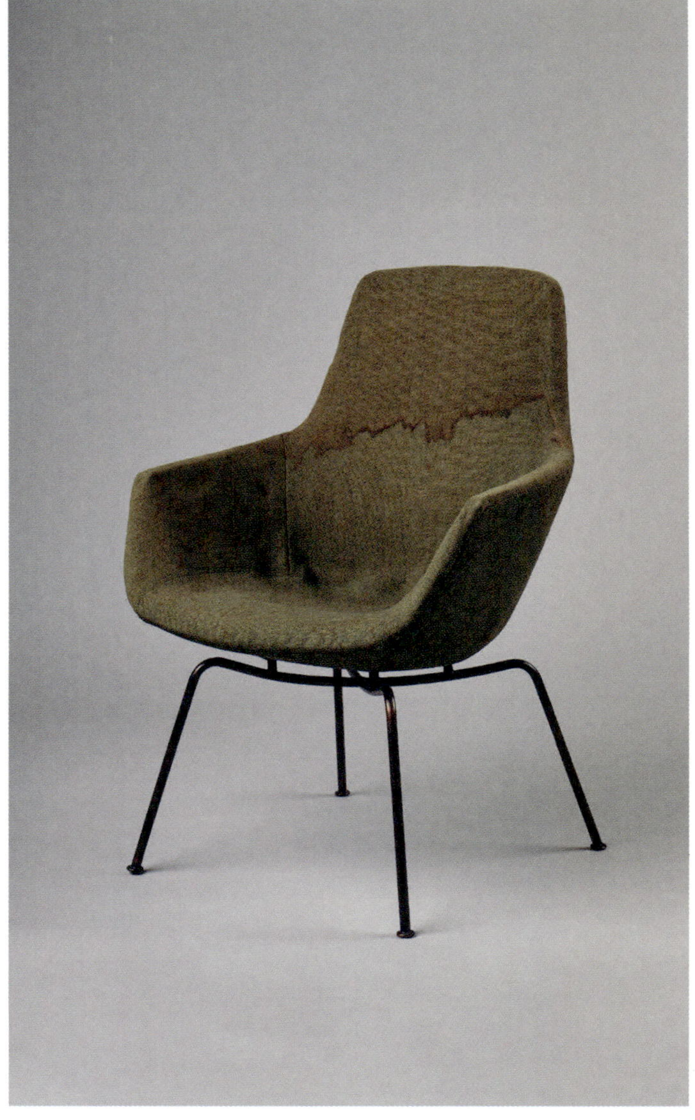

Fig. 2

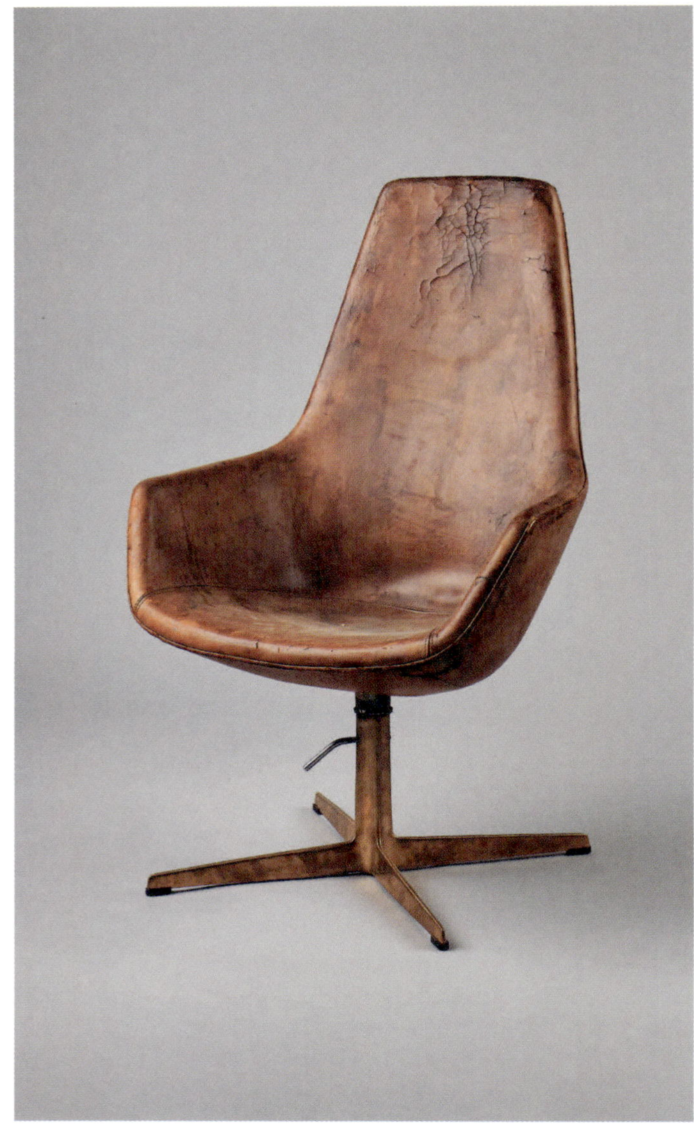

Fig. 3

Fig. 2-5. . Four versions of the Giraffe chair showcasing the iterative processes at the factory. From the left: prototype of the Giraffe chair with a low back (fig. 2), the Giraffe chair as swivel chair, made as a gift for the director of SAS Royal Hotel Alberto Kappenberger (fig. 3), prototype of the Giraffe chair with legs from the plywood Tongue chair (fig. 4) and the Giraffe chair with green fabric, made for the restaurant at the SAS Royal Hotel (fig.5). They are now owned by Fritz Hansen

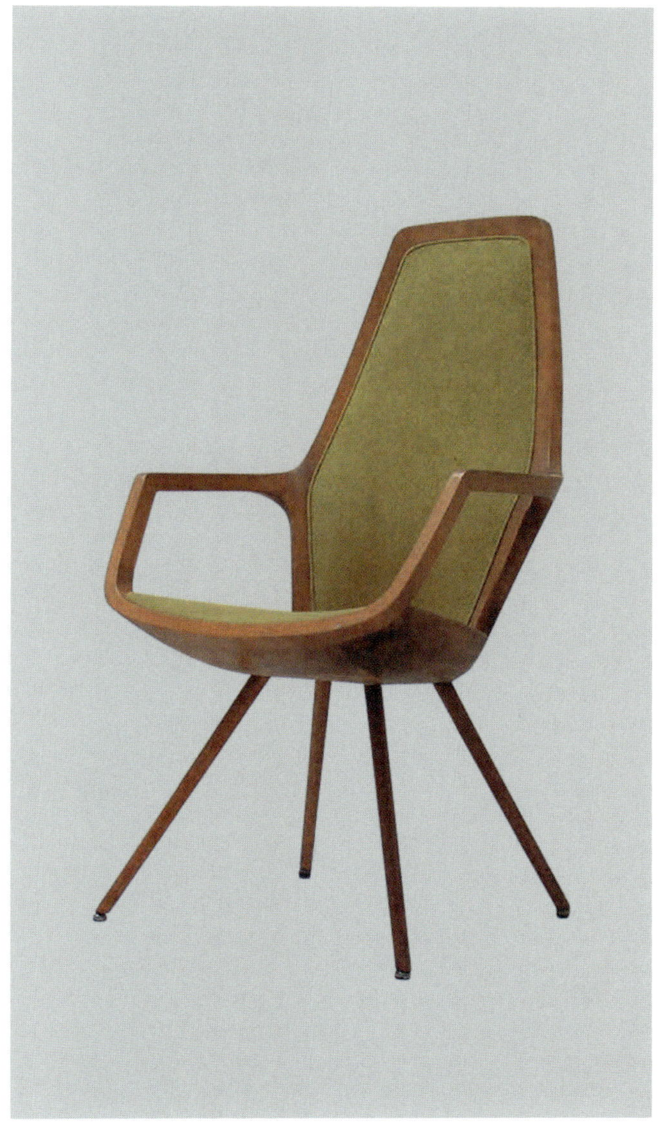

Fig. 4

Photo: Fritz Hansen

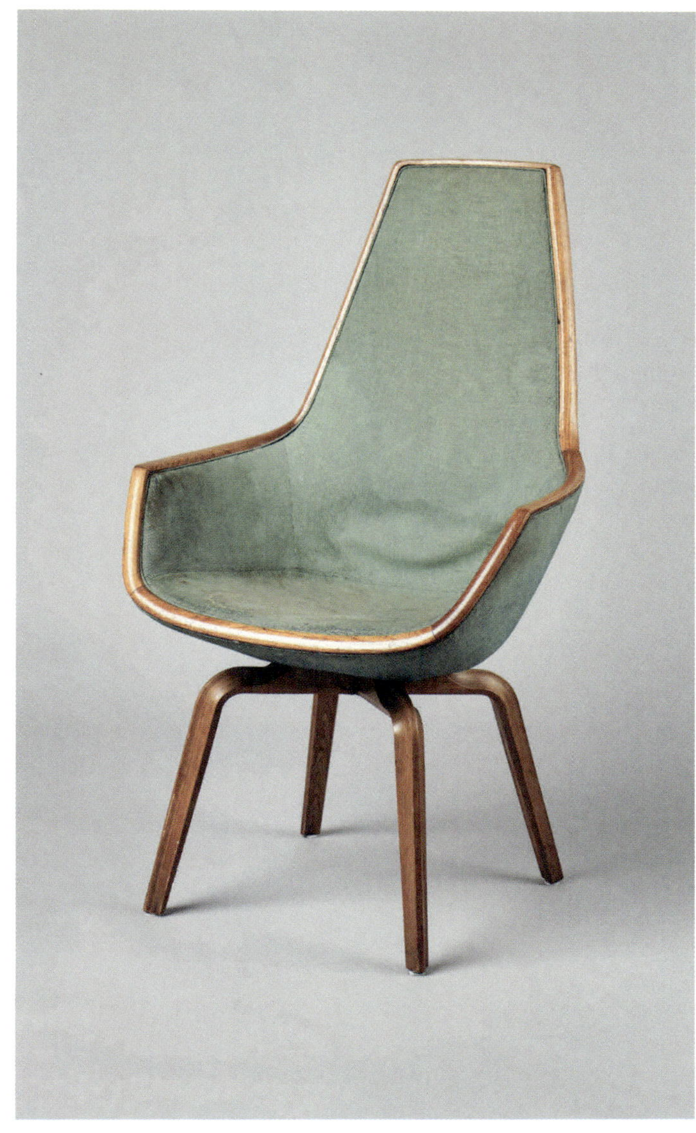

Fig. 5

Multidisciplinary processes at the factory

Four different versions of the Giraffe chair, a design developed in 1958 for the SAS Royal Hotel in Copenhagen, provide some insight into how models and prototypes also formed the basis for the ongoing collaboration between the studio and the furniture manufacturing company Fritz Hansen (figs. 2-5). Two prototypes and two realised chairs represent four different variations on the same seat, each combined with various types of chair legs developed by Arne Jacobsen and Fritz Hansen during that same period. The results reflect processes that are neither linear nor personal, but collective, interdisciplinary, improvisational and iterative.

Arne Jacobsen, whose knowledge of engineering was limited, was deeply dependent on his cooperation with the manufacturers. The process was often initiated by a drawing or model that did not take into account any technical constraints; it was then up to the factory engineers to solve the technical issues involved. A focus on form and considerable pressure on the engineers involved are recurring themes in the manufacturers' descriptions of their collaboration with Arne Jacobsen (Tøjner & Vindum, 1996). The processes were time-consuming, as it was often necessary to develop new machines or even entirely new technologies. For example, the development of the Cylinda Line series took a full three years, while the development of the Ant chair took over a year (Land og Folk, 1957).

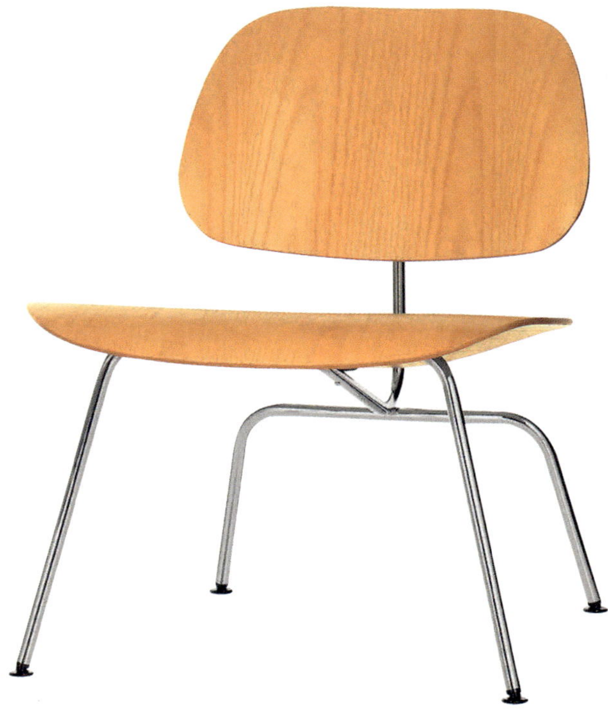

Fig. 7. Charles and Ray Eames's LCM chair from 1946, which Arne Jacobsen kept at his design studio during the development of the Ant chair

Photo: © Vitra

The genesis and life of the Ant chair

Designed in 1952, the Ant chair (fig. 6) arose out of a desire to create a small, stackable chair that would fit into the modern eat-in kitchen and could be manufactured industrially at a low price (Berlingske Tidende, 1953). Here, Arne Jacobsen set himself a task addressed by many of the designers of the period, and during the development stage he drew on lessons learned by others. He bought Charles & Ray Eames's 1946 LCM chair for the design studio, a piece that would set the overall direction for the project (fig. 7). Arne Jacobsen has related how this new type of chair required the designers to work with clay during its creation – because it, unlike previous chairs, was 'three-dimensional' in nature (Berlingske Tidende, 1953). He is presumably referring to the fact that the shell bends in two different directions, an innovation that made it possible to mould the seat and back as a single piece. Verner Panton and Henning Larsen, who worked at the design studio in 1951–52, also took part in the development process, and the final silhouette with the narrow waist was created in collaboration with Fritz Hansen's technicians, partly determined by the technical possibilities available (concerning the development of the Ant chair, see: Thau & Vindum, 2002, p. 169).

The genesis of the Ant is a story of encounters between a wide range of highly diverse actors and factors, including the design experiments conducted at the studio, the new needs and demands of contemporary society, the technical solutions developed at Fritz Hansen and the potentials and limitations inherent in the material. Using the framework of Ingold and Hallam (2007), one may also point out how the Ant became a catalyst for a long-standing relationship between Arne Jacobsen and Fritz Hansen, creating a range of new silhouettes – each one even more popular than the one preceding it – and, later, new materials and new technologies. Today, the Ant and its descendants are still the subject of new interpretations and developments, adapted to present-day tastes and preferences.

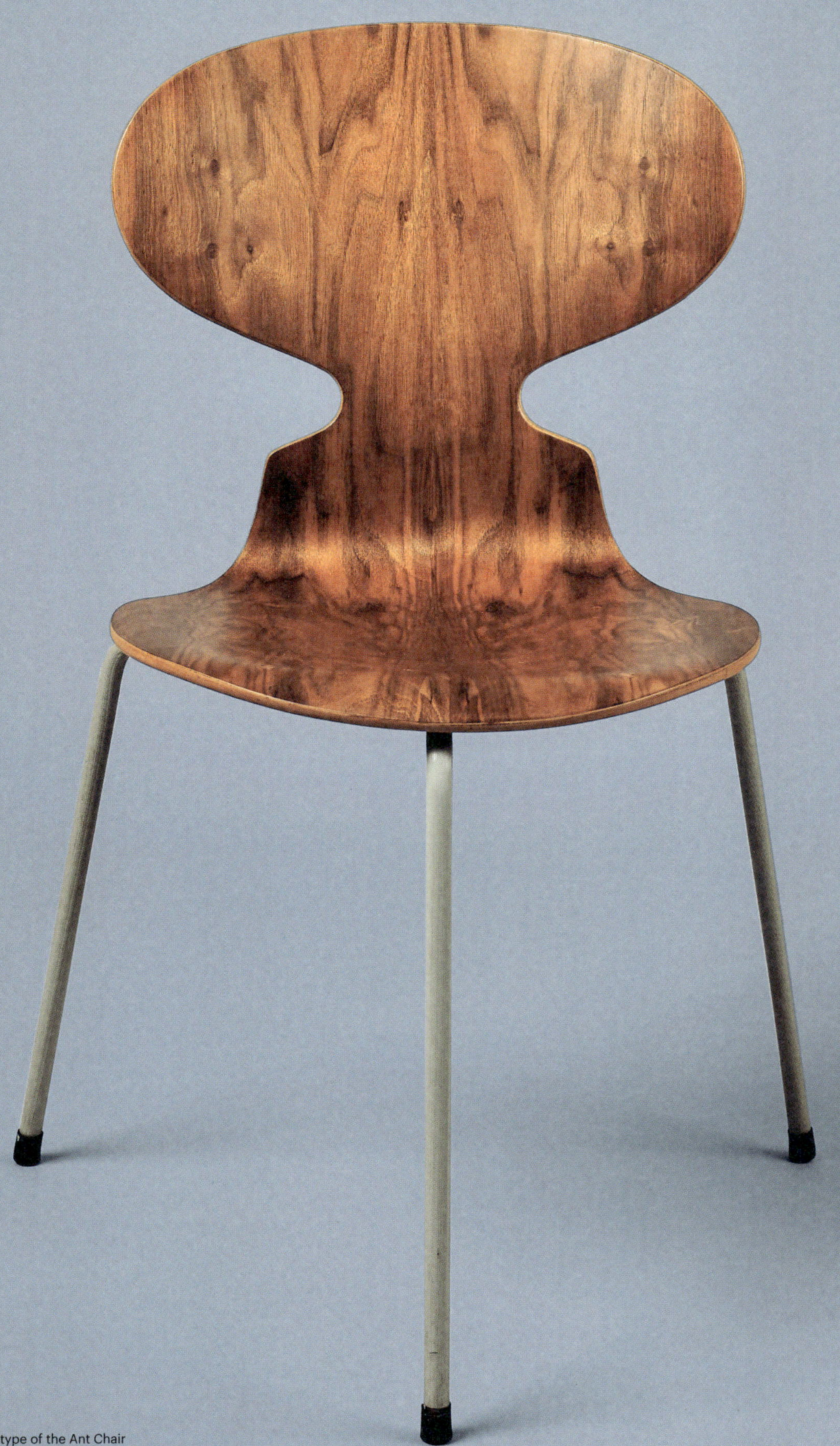

Fig. 6. An early prototype of the Ant Chair in walnut. The first series of chairs had legs covered in grey, fluted plastic

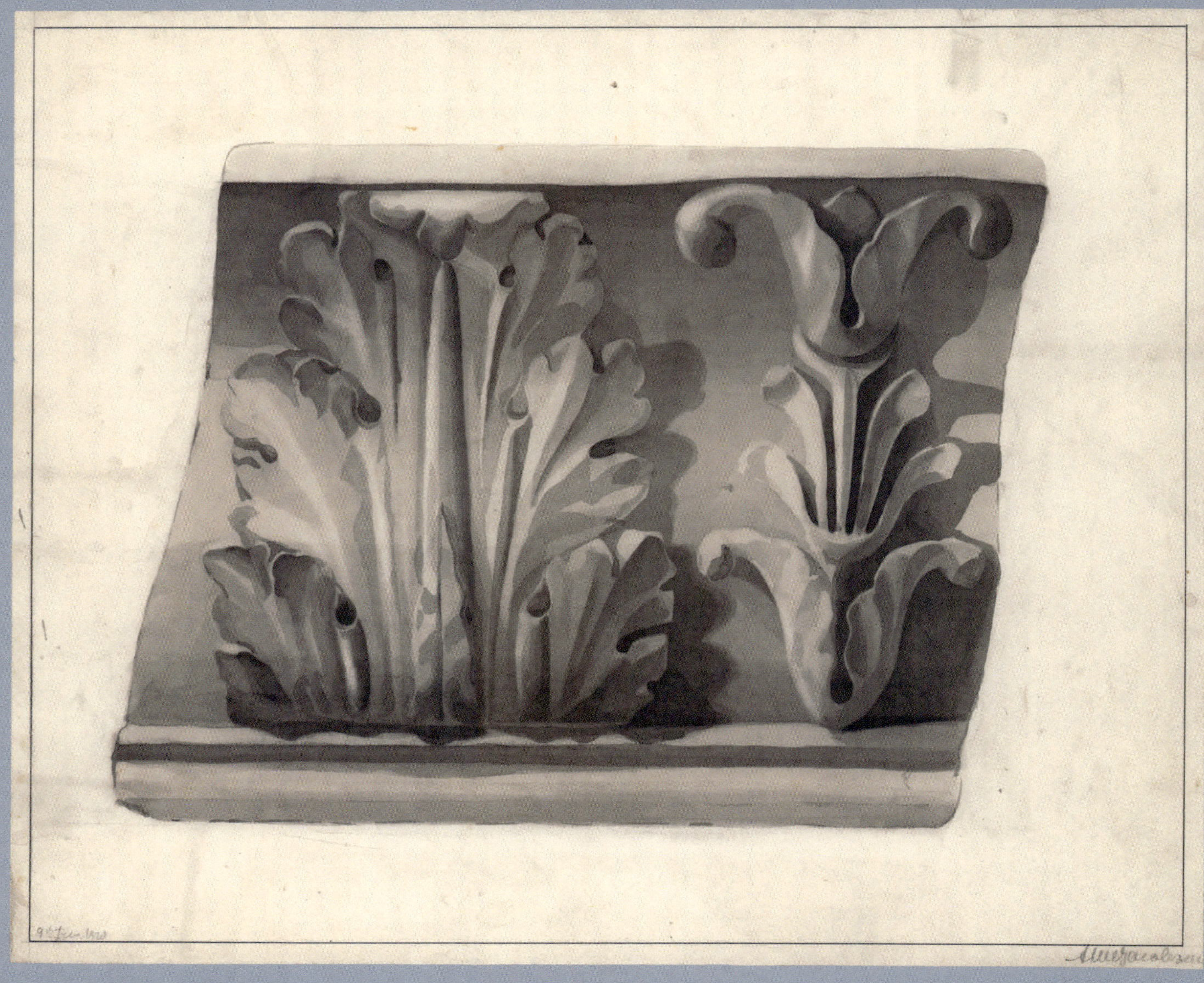

Watercolour after the antique, made during Arne Jacobsen's time as a pupil at the Royal Danish Academy of Fine Arts

Photo: The Royal Danish Library – Danish National Art Library

'... I remember that once, I commented on one of his watercolours, and he just said, in a low, but insistent voice: 'I need to do them'. I can only interpret those words as proof of how important observation was to him, the act of teasing out insight and knowledge from what one sees.'

– Erik Christian Sørensen

Studying the world

Only a faint, almost invisible echo of the Eames chair used as a reference at Jacobsen's design studio can be traced in the Ant chair, but in other Arne Jacobsen designs the inspirations are more clearly evident. The visible world in general remained an important source of inspiration for Arne Jacobsen throughout his life, and he eagerly took in the sights through drawings, watercolours, photographs and films.

At the Royal Danish Academy of Fine Arts' School of Architecture, which he attended from 1924 to 1927, students learned to apply a systematic study of the world and use it as the basis for new works. Classical antiquity was still an important starting point for the teaching provided, and students would absorb antiquity's concept of beauty by drawing and painting after their illustrious role models. Arne Jacobsen, who originally dreamed of becoming a painter, was a tremendously skilled watercolour painter, and the brush remained his favourite means of collecting and translating impressions. Architect Erik Christian Sørensen, who was Arne Jacobsen's assistant lecturer in the 1950s, recollects a conversation he had with the professor: '... I remember that once, I commented on one of his watercolours, and he just said, in a low, but insistent voice: 'I need to do them'. I can only interpret those words as proof of how important observation was to him, the act of teasing out insight and knowledge from what one sees' (Thau & Vindum, 1996, p. 89).

Sørensen's view is mirrored in a 1967 article that describes Arne Jacobsen as someone 'who greedily takes in all of the outside world, as if he notices everything with his vivid, pale blue eyes that look like a young boy's. His attention is total' (Jessen, 1967, p. 32). Private footage from the 1930s allows us to follow Arne Jacobsen's gaze as it pans around the world: cities, buildings or sections of nature. One senses how he scans his surroundings, focusing on selected aspects and maintaining that focus for a long time.

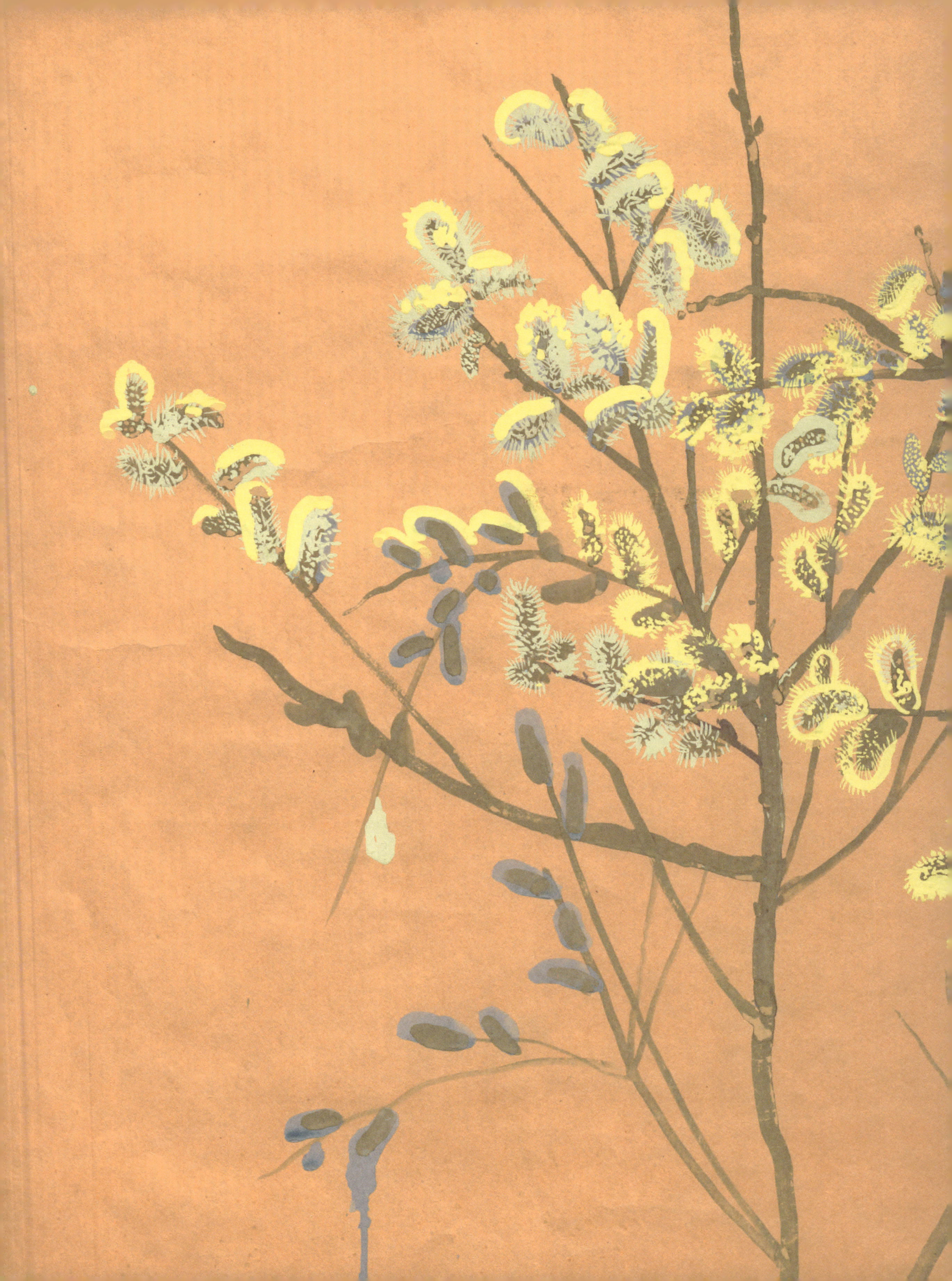

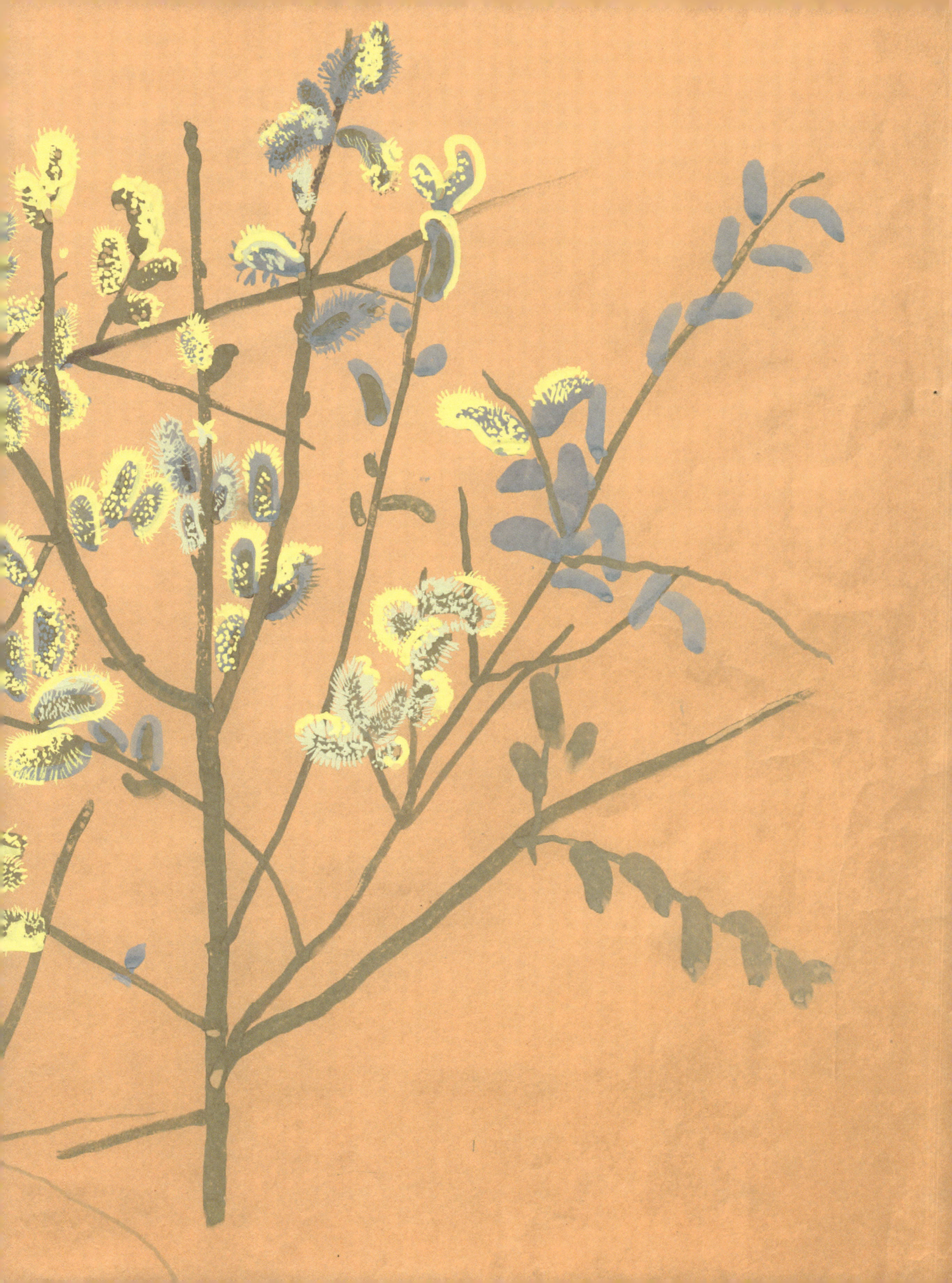

Previous page: Study of willow branches with catkins

Photo: The Royal Danish Library – Danish National Art Library

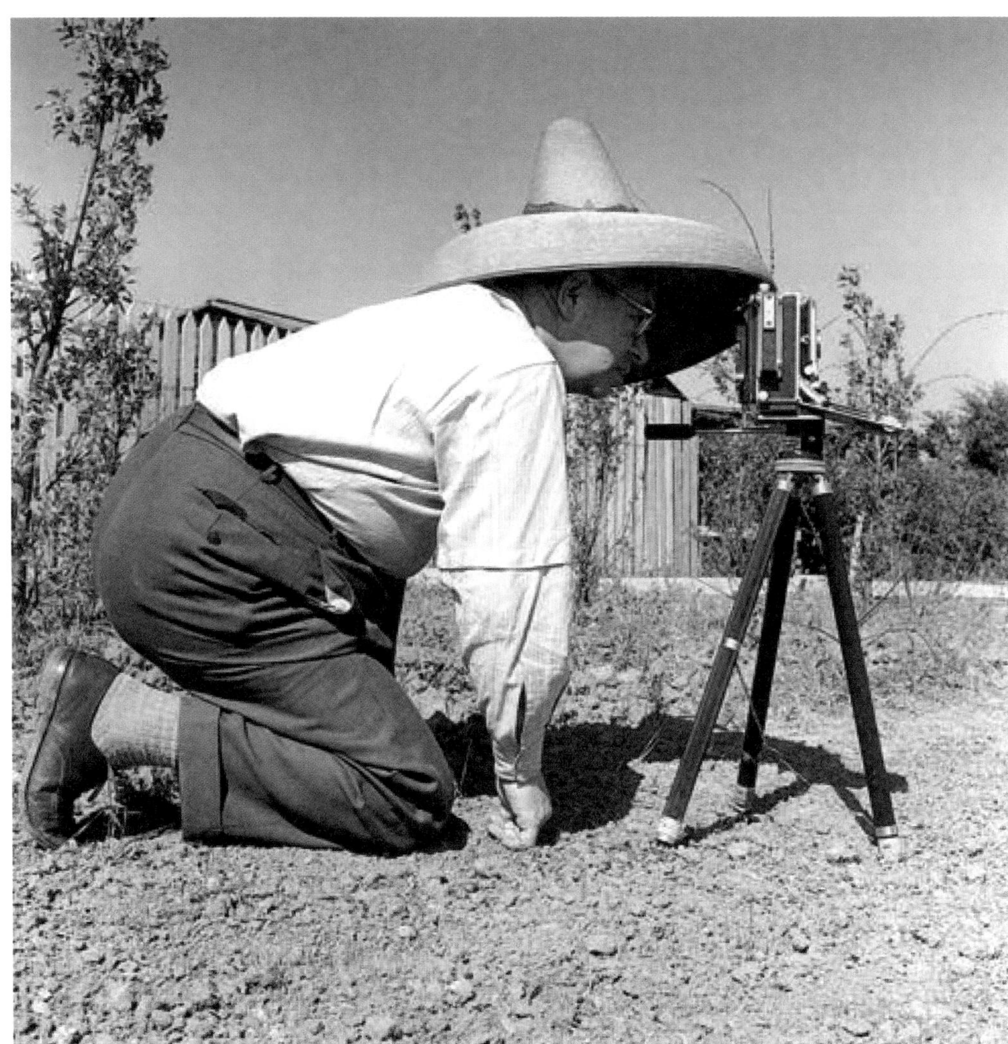

Arne Jacobsen photographing in his garden. Here he found inspiration for design and architecture

Photo: Aage Strüwing © Jørgen Strüwing

Imitation as an artistic pursuit

Some scholars within the study of creativity also consider imitation a creative activity. Tanggaard (2008) argues that being deeply involved in existing practices is a prerequisite for being able to transform them, and Professor of Educational Psychology Klaus Nielsen (2009) states that the ancient concept of mimesis best describes human creation as 'transformations based on what is already present' (p. 210). As described in the above, one of Arne Jacobsen's most important methods focuses on the study of the visible world, something he was taught at the Academy. Even today, one of the central aspects of our notion of artistic creativity is that artists, through their practices, build up a special sensitivity towards what they perceive in the world. For example, innovation researcher Tatiana Chemi (2009) concludes, on the basis of a series of interviews with artists, that artists do one particular thing differently from non-artists: they actively use the impressions that life gives them. 'They choose to be like sponges,' she writes, 'absorbing all the inspirational materials they can get, and then they do something with them' (p. 93).

In his own practices, Arne Jacobsen mirrored the conventionalised methods of artists. Former employee Kaj Blegvad Andersen relates how Arne Jacobsen would often refer to other people's work when developing projects. 'Maybe we can use this?' he would say, pointing to a page in a magazine about architecture. On other occasions he brought potential sources of inspiration in from the garden. 'Just take a look at the colours and the pattern,' he might say while displaying a large toad, 'isn't it beautiful?' (Andersen, 2002). Three preparatory sketches for a textile pattern that Arne Jacobsen designed in the 1960s gives us insight into the process through which Arne Jacobsen transformed what he saw into something new. The sketches very clearly show how his observations of ferns eventually became the abstract pattern Tassel, in Danish 'Kvast' (figs. 8-11).

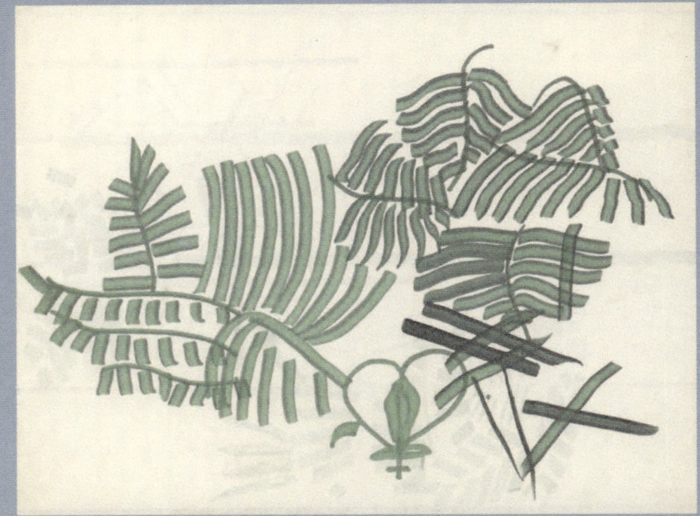

Fig. 8

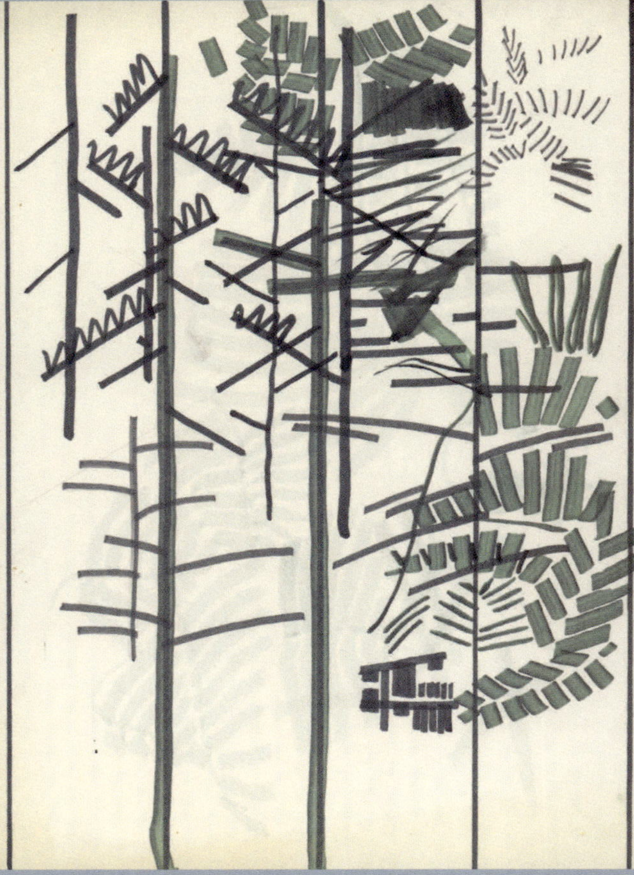

Fig. 9

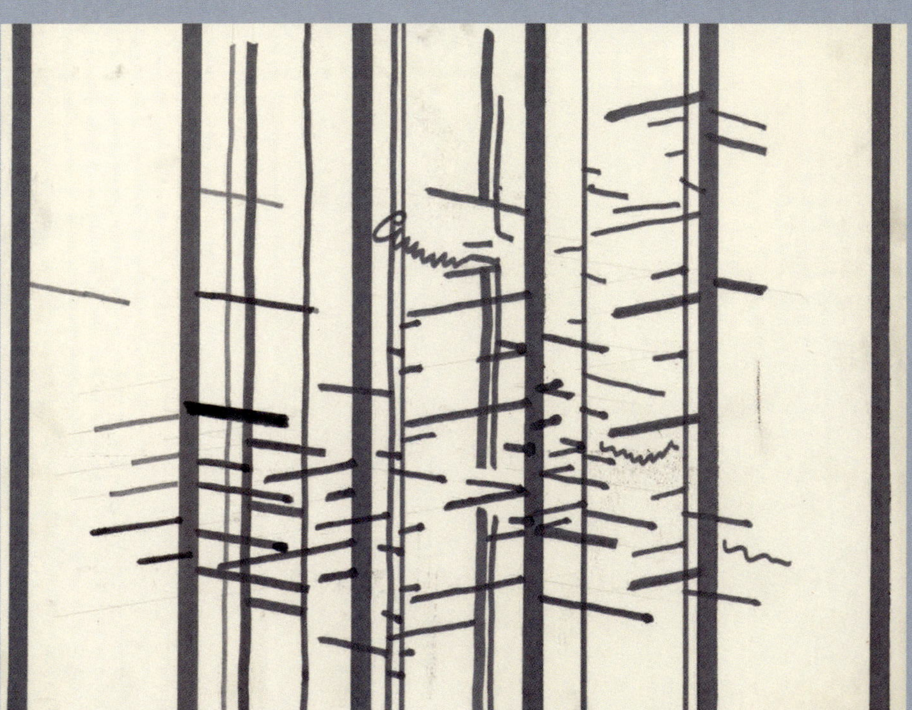

Fig. 10

Figs. 8-10. Three sketches for the pattern Tassel

Photo: The Royal Danish Library – Danish National Art Library

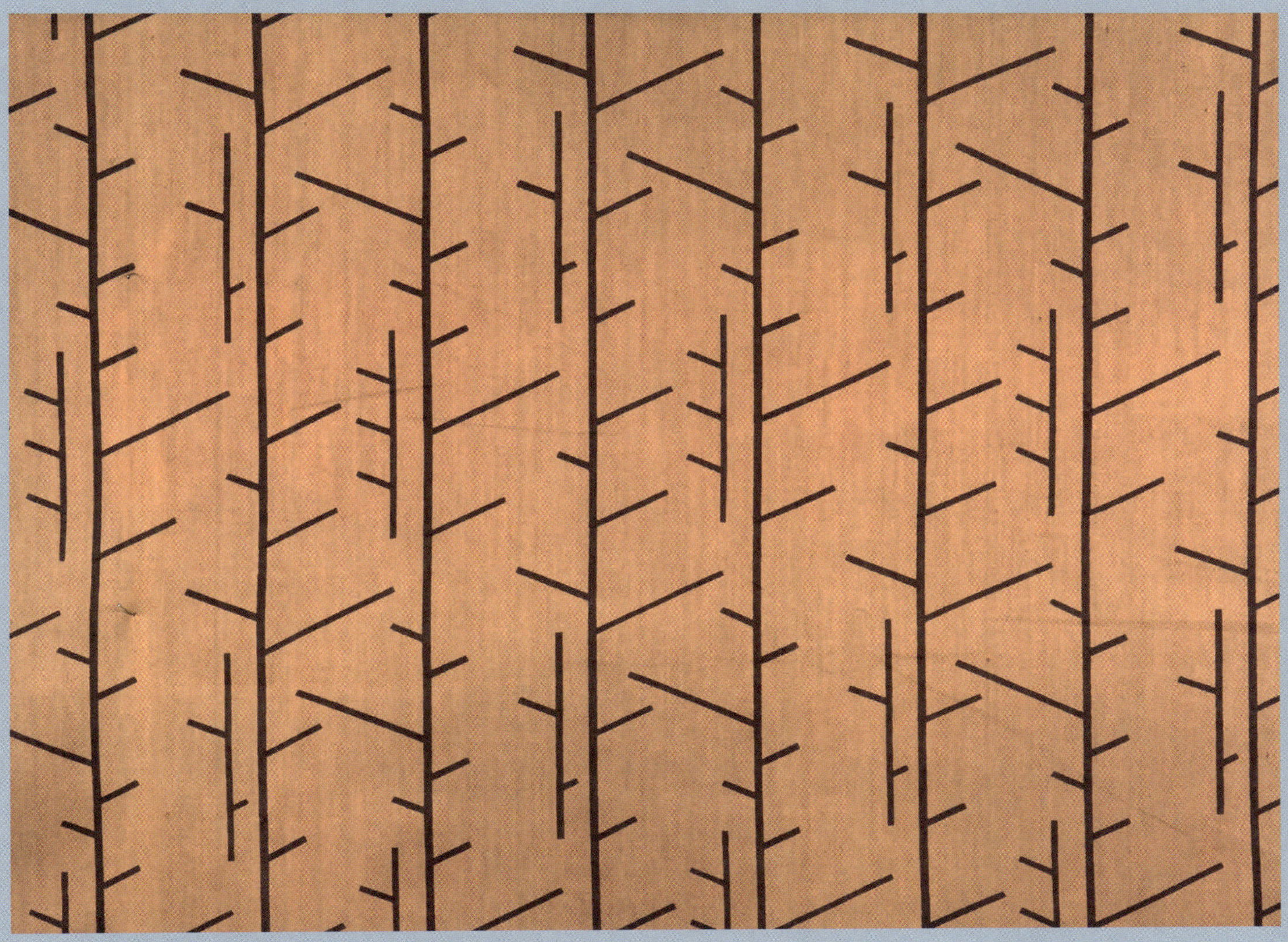

Fig. 11. The pattern Tassel, circa 1963

Photo: Arne Jacobsen Design I/S

'Sadly, I don't have the gift of suddenly having a solution present itself to me in a flash of insight. I don't feel certain until I have compared and contrasted my first solution with other solutions ...'

– Arne Jacobsen, 1971

What can we learn from Arne Jacobsen?

In his 2010 book, Claus Springborg (2010), founder of the Sensing Mind Institute, argues that when we put aside our conceptual brain and allow sensory input to be the basis for sense-making, we keep open a range of options that would otherwise have been cut off by our preconceived ideas and concepts. Here, he says, art can help us perceive and experience the world in new ways. Springborg's point can shed light on the possibilities arising in the environment nurtured in Jacobsen's studio, where a general orientation towards practical action and experimentation with tangible materials formed the basis of a collective process of creation. Plaster, cardboard and paper were the starting point of experiments that continued in the subsequent collaboration with factory technicians and did not stop until the right solution was found. In a 1971 interview. Arne Jacobsen himself said:

'Sadly, I don't have the gift of suddenly having a solution present itself to me in a flash of insight. I don't feel certain until I have compared and contrasted my first solution with other solutions ...' (Tøjner & Vindum, 1996, p. 130).

Alongside the art of experimentation, the ability to study, decode and engage with the outside world was crucial for Arne Jacobsen's opportunities to influence it. In this regard, the most important thing we can learn from Arne Jacobsen may be this total and open-minded outlook on the world as a place you can learn from *and* a place you can shape and influence. He trained and honed this awareness throughout his life by mirroring various artistic practices, including the painter's slow study of the visible world. Tanggaard (2012) states that creativity is that which sets others in motion, and that in order for others to realise the value of the new, it must be possible to understand it within the given worldview. Crucially, Arne Jacobsen created his works in a state of interaction with that of which he was part. It is difficult to quantify the influence of Arne Jacobsen, but for those who worked with him, it was clearly huge. As the Danish Architect Verner Panton put it: 'Arne Jacobsen has taught me more than anyone else about being insecure and never giving up' (Tøjner & Vindum, 1996, p. 40).

Bibliography

Andersen, K.B. (2002). Mig og Arne Jacobsen. *CD NYT* 13. Article ID 64. Accessed 12 March 2020 at: http://www.club-danois.com/news_articles/show_article.php?id=64

Basaiawmoit, R. V. (2017). Kay Bojesen – Eksperimenter, innovation og iværksætteri. In: Staunsager, S. & Stenum Mortensen, K. (eds.), *Kay Bojesen – Humøret i Dansk Design* (pp. 76-97). Kolding: Trapholt

Chemi, T. (2015). Part One: Creativity and Art. In: Chemi, T.; Jensen, J. B. & Hersted, L., *Behind the Scenes of Artistic Creativity. Processes of Learning, Creating and Organising* (pp. 31–146). New York: Lang

DR (2003). *Arne Jacobsen: arkitekt og designer* (TV programme). Producer: Svend Erik Øhlenschlæger; script: Lars Andreas Pedersen, Svend Erik Øhlenschlæger

Fritz Hansen (2020): *REBELLEN*. Accessed 24 April 2020 at https://fritzhansen.com/da-dk/designers/arne-jacobsen

Information (1953). Hvorfor skal en stol have fire ben?. *Information* 9 February 1953 (Arne Jacobsen's scrapbooks)

Ingold, T. & Hallam, E. (2007). Creativity and Cultural Improvisation, An Introduction. In: Ingold, T. & Hallam, E. (eds.), *Creativity and Cultural Improvisation* (pp. 1-24). Oxford, UK: Berg

Ingold, T. (2010). The textility of making. *Cambridge Journal of Economics* 34(1), pp. 91–102

Ingold, T. (2014). The creativity of undergoing. *Pragmatics & Cognition* 22(1), pp. 124–139

Jacucci, G., & Wagner, I. (2007). Performative roles of materiality for collective creativity. Proceedings of the 6th ACM SIGCHI Conference on Creativity & Cognition, pp. 73–82.

Jessen, R. (1967). Inspiration? Et nyt rådhus kommer ikke til én i drømme (Lørdagslæsning). *B.T.*, 24 October 1964, p. 32

Land og Folk (1957). Professoren, der modellerer stole. In: *Land og Folk*. Sunday 6 October 1957, p. 7 (Arne Jacobsen's scrapbooks)

Løhmann Stephensen, J. (2019). Kultur og kreativitet. In: Eriksson, B. & Schiermer, B. (Red.), *Ny Kulturteori* (pp. 253-288). copenhagen: Hans Reitzels Forlag

Nielsen, K. (2009). Kreativitet, kultur og mimesis. Kritiske overvejelser. In: Tanggaard, L & Brinkmann, S. (eds.), *Kreativitetsfremmende læringsmiljøer i skolen* (pp. 193–216). Frederikshavn: Dafolo

Springborg, C. (2010). Leadership as art – leaders coming to their senses. *Leadership* 6(3), pp. 243–258

Tanggaard, L. (2008). *Kreativitet skal læres! Når talent bliver til innovation*. Aalborg: Aalborg Universitetsforlag

Tanggaard, L. (2013). The sociomateriality of creativity in everyday life. *Culture & Psychology* 19(1), pp. 20–32

Tanggaard, L & Brinkmann, S. (2009). *Kreativitetsfremmende læringsmiljøer i skolen*. Frederikshavn: Dafolo

Thau, C. & Vindum, K. (2002). *Arne Jacobsen* (2nd edition, 2nd printing). Copenhagen: Arkitektens Forlag

Tiden arbejder altid for den gode kunst (1952). (Arne Jacobsen's scrapbooks)

Tøjner, P.E. & Vindum, K. (1996). *Arne Jacobsen: Architect & designer*. Copenhagen: Dansk Design Center

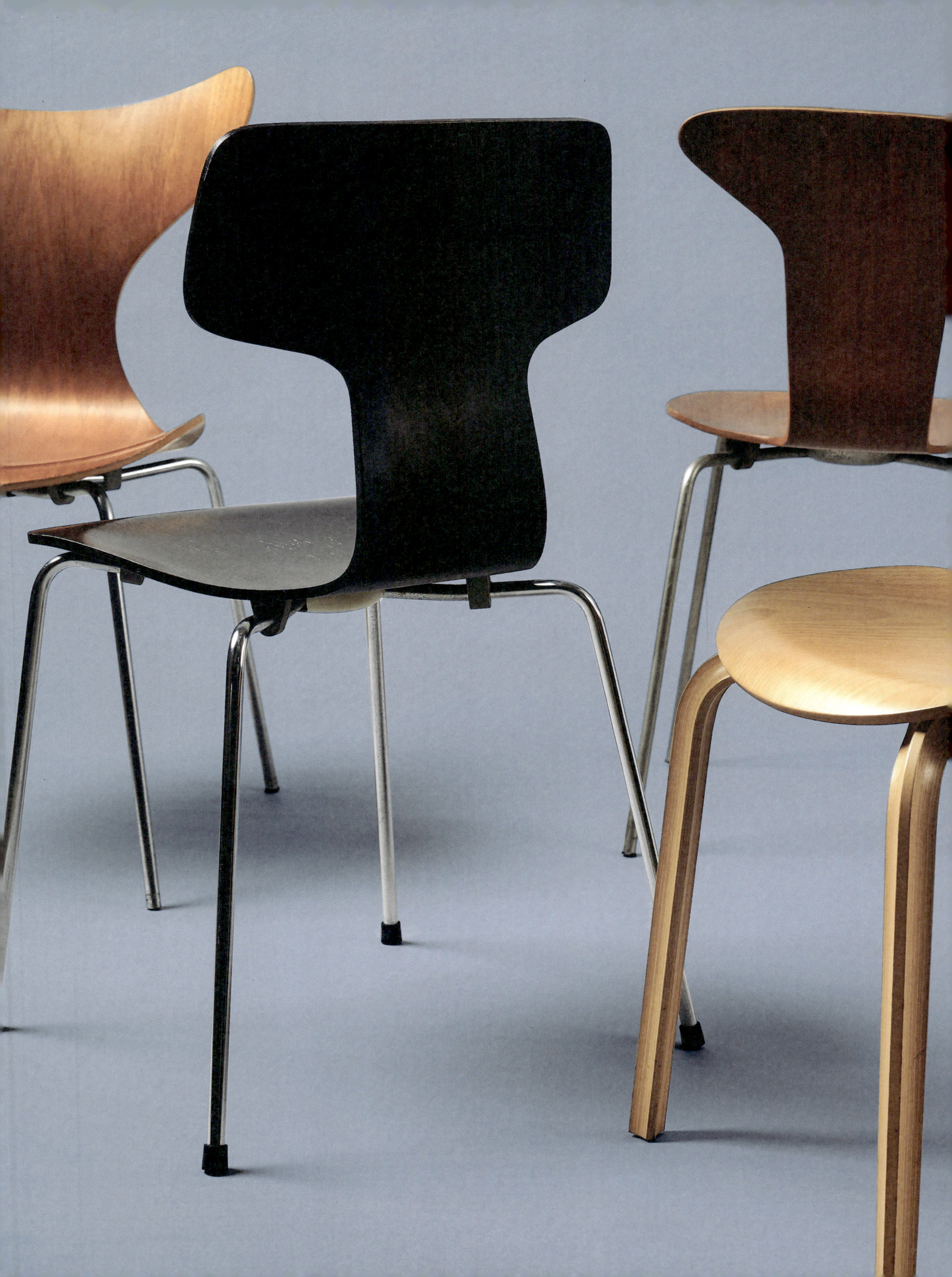

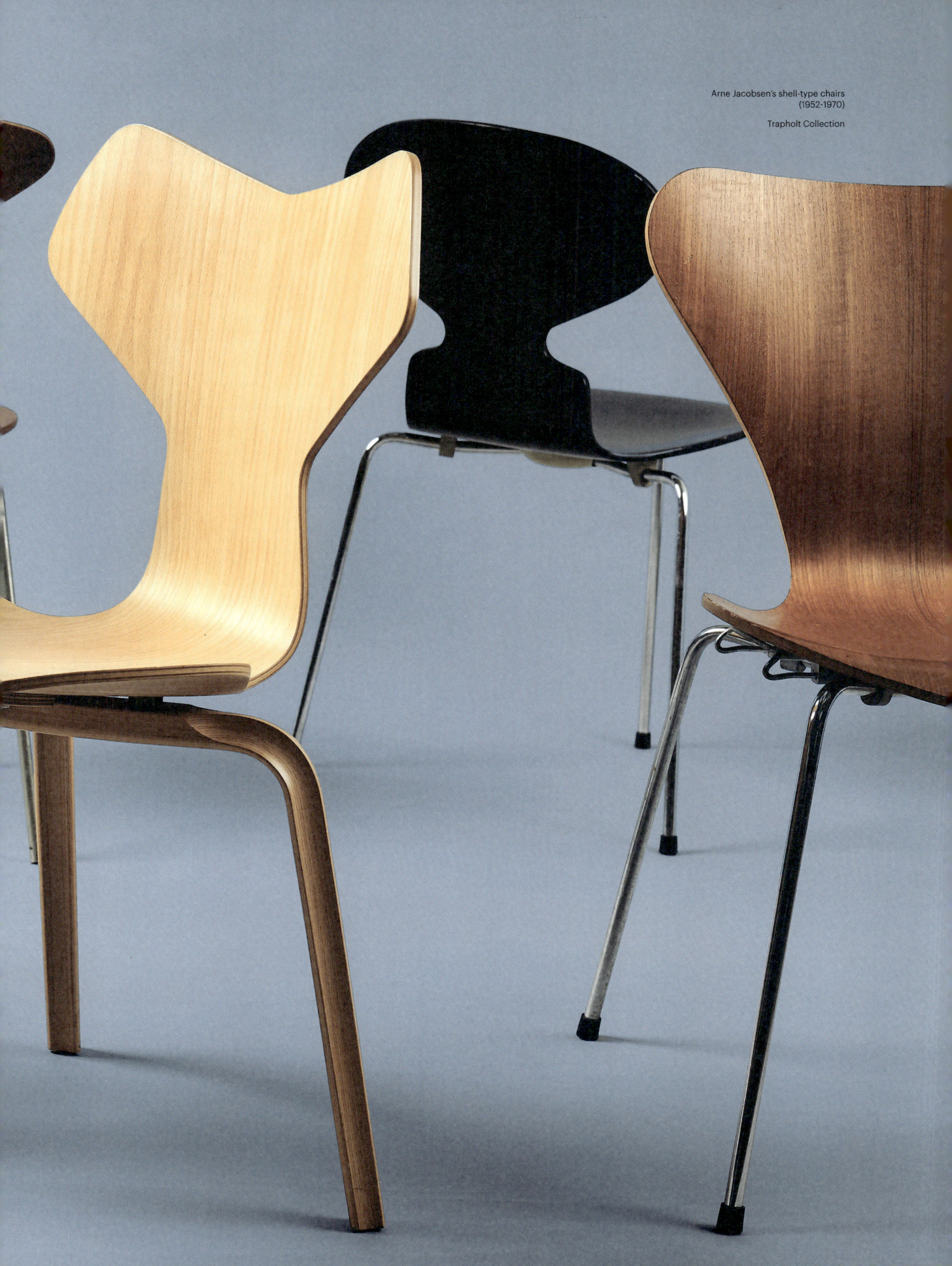

Arne Jacobsen's shell-type chairs
(1952-1970)

Trapholt Collection

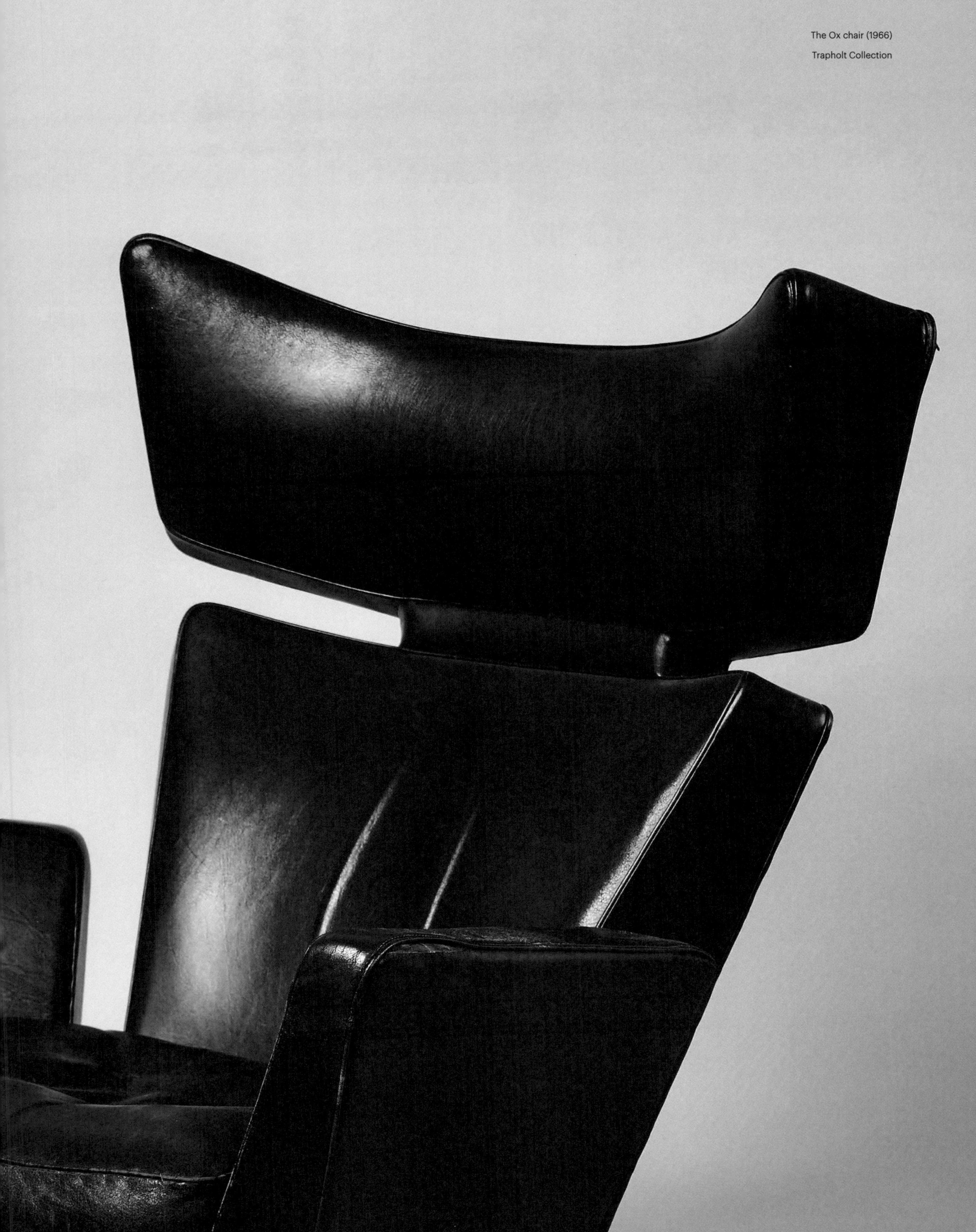

The Ox chair (1966)

Trapholt Collection

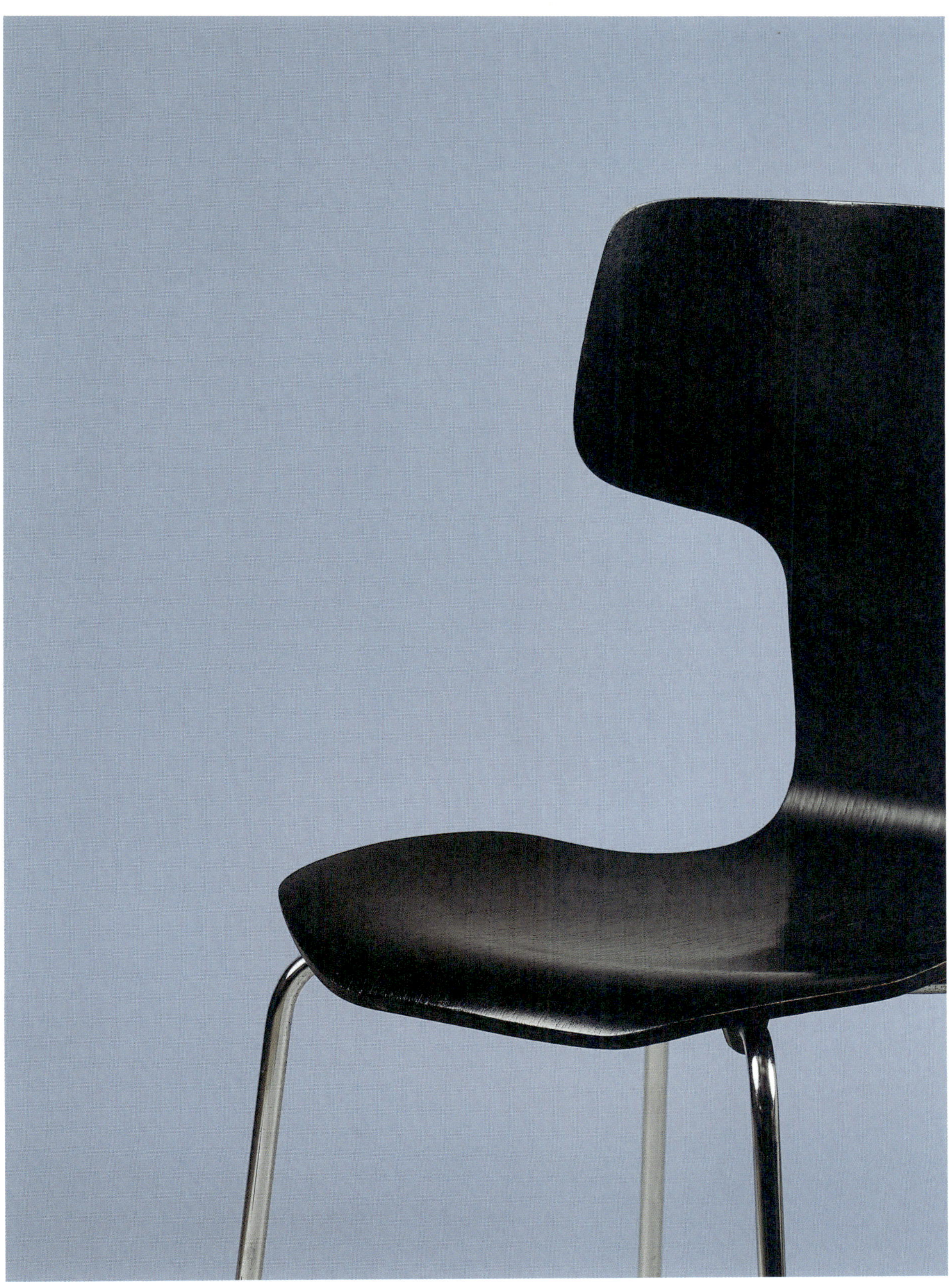

The T chair (1957)

Trapholt Collection

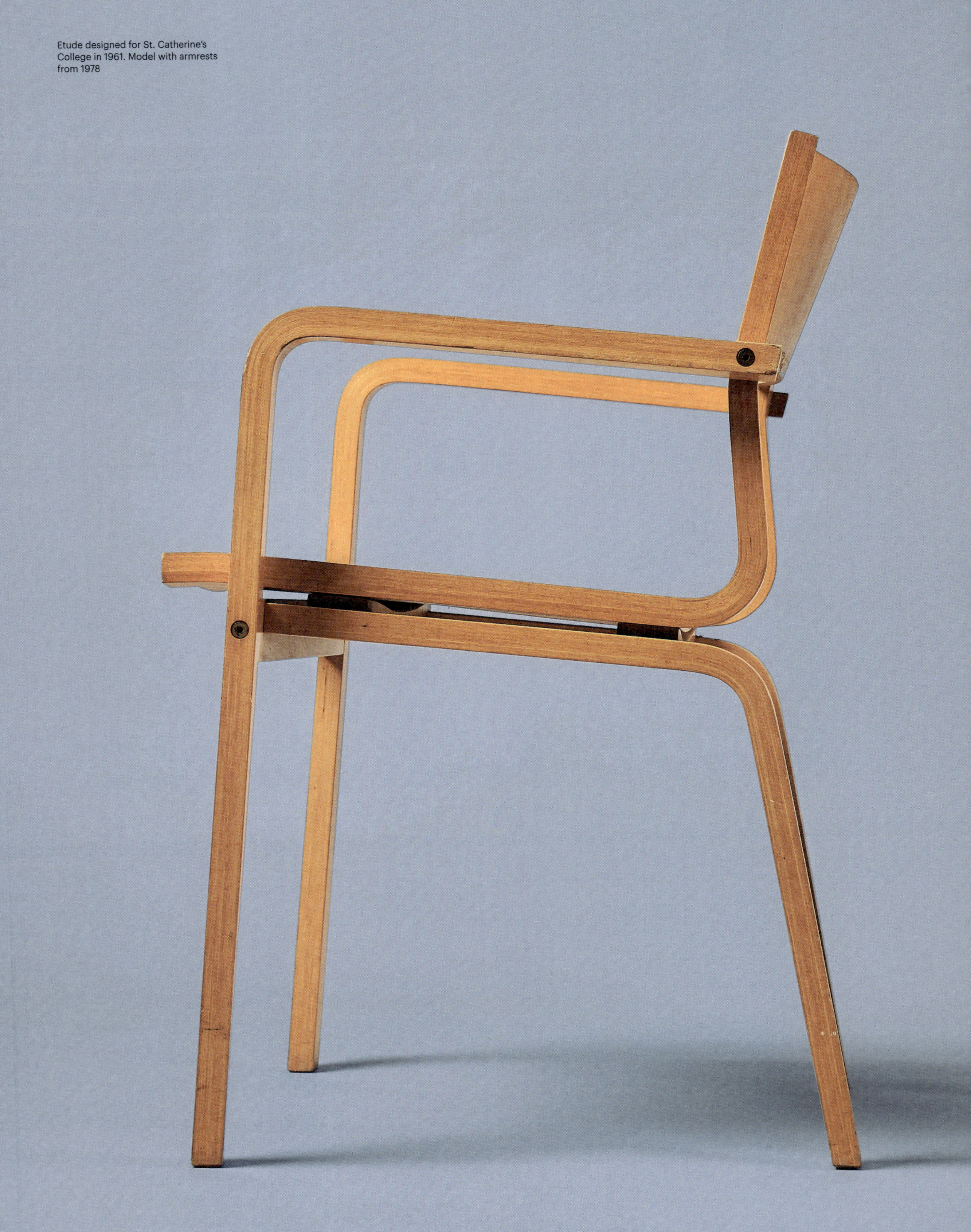

Etude designed for St. Catherine's College in 1961. Model with armrests from 1978

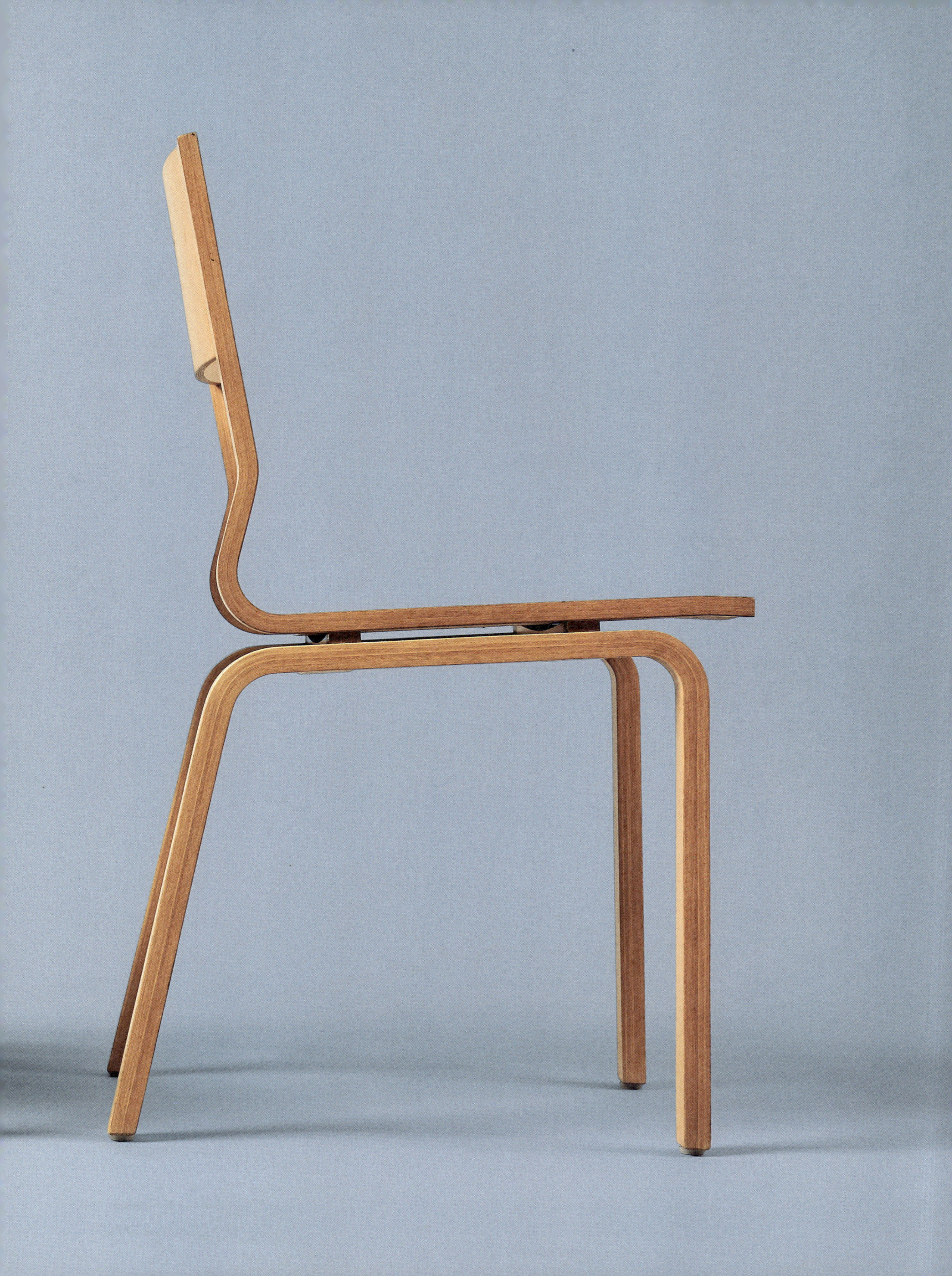

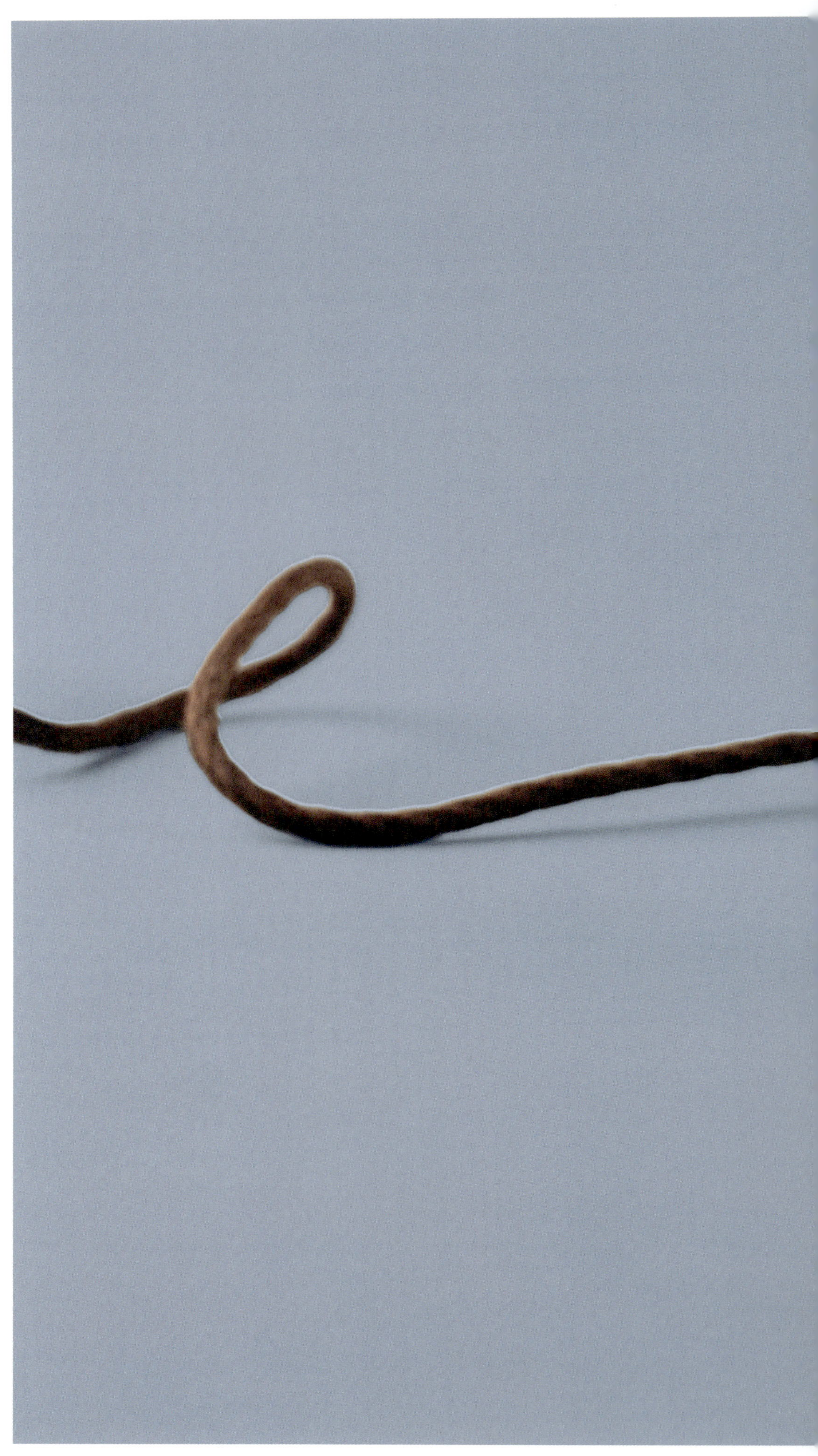

Table clock manufactured by
Lauritz Knudsen (1939)

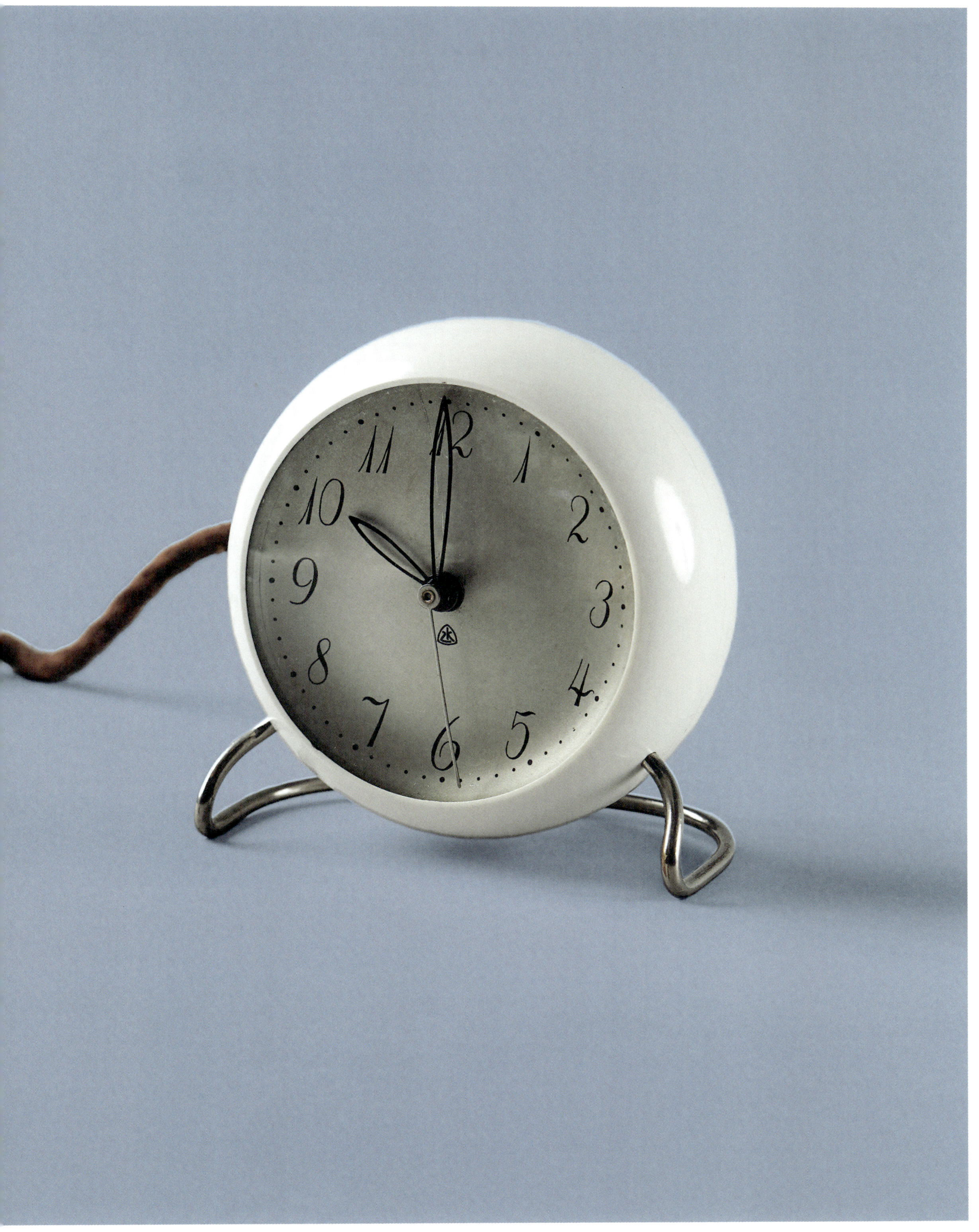

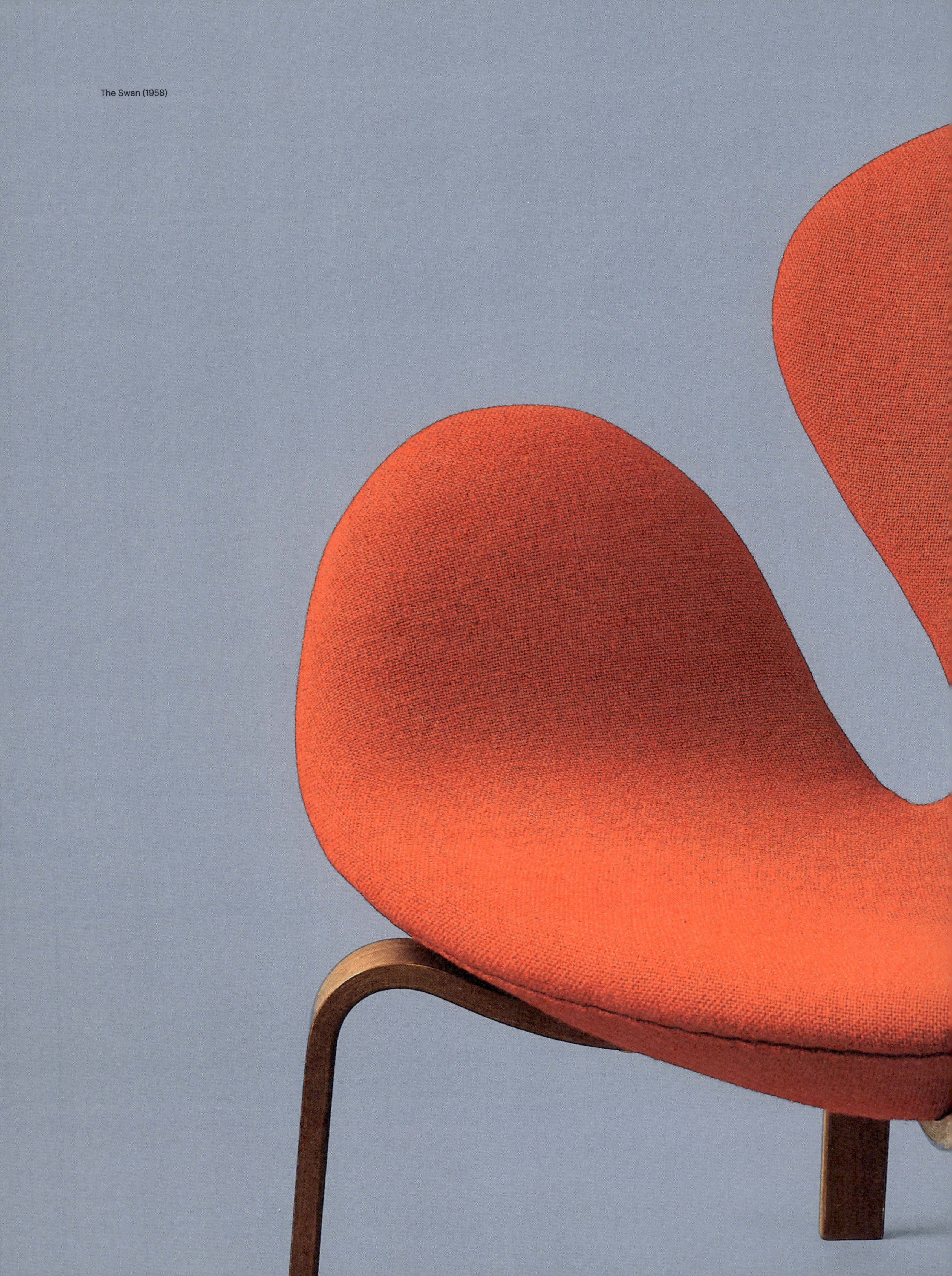

The Swan (1958)

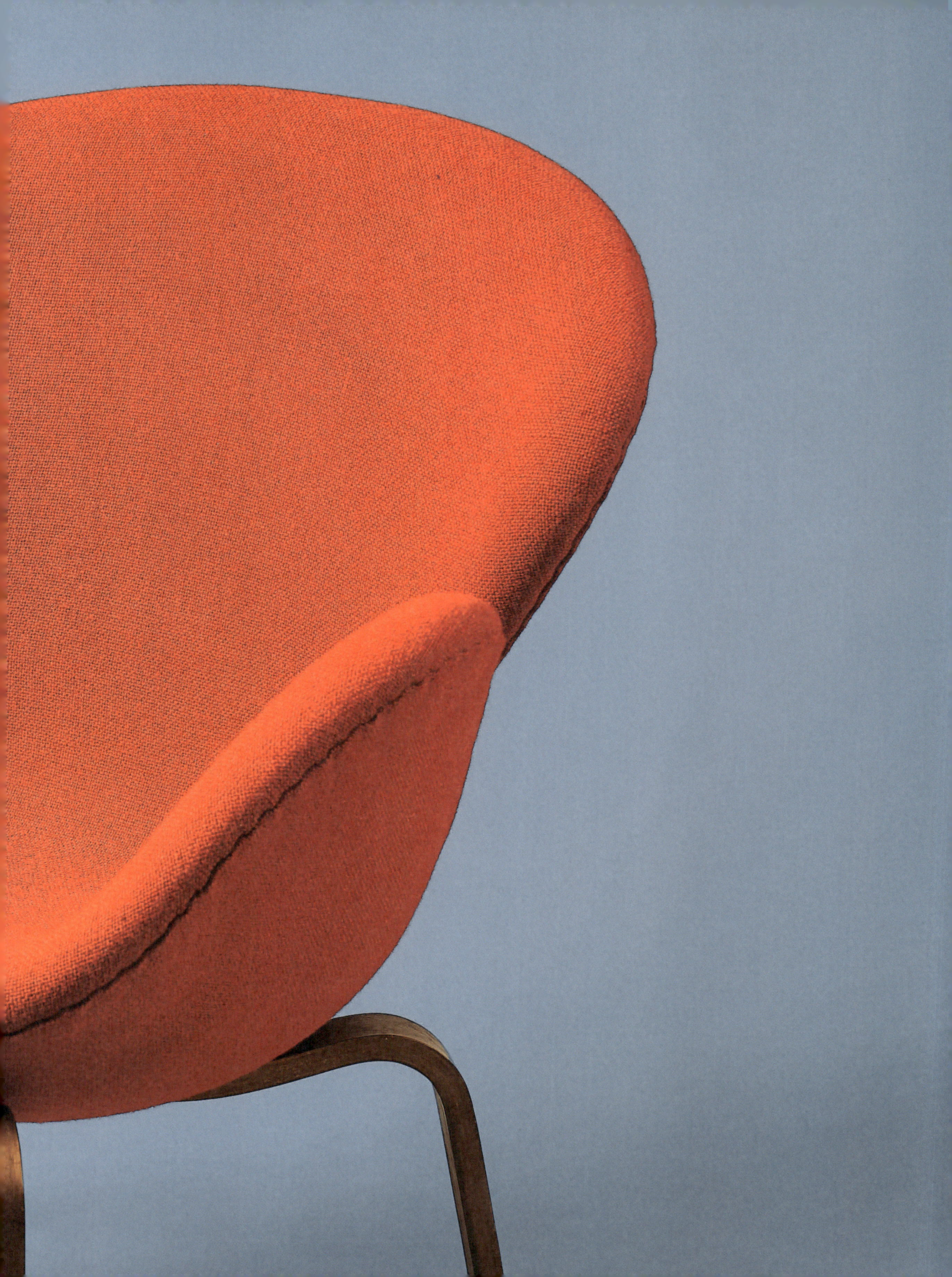

Nature studies and textile patterns 03

Throughout his life, Arne Jacobsen used nature as a source of inspiration. When not working at his office, he would study plants in his garden or in the countryside surrounding his holiday cottage at Gudmindrup Lyng in north-western Zealand. He would capture what he saw with his camera or with a pen and brush.

In 1942, Arne Jacobsen met his future wife and companion, Jonna Møller, who was a trained textile printer. At that point his interest in nature took on a specific purpose. Working with Jonna, he transformed his studies of nature into patterns to be used for textiles and wallpapers. The patterns were often free-form, naturalistic reproductions of meadow flowers and entire plant environments, all conveying the richness of nature. When the couple had to flee to Sweden in 1943, escaping the German occupation forces in Denmark, Arne Jacobsen launched a collaboration with the Swedish department store Nordiska Kompaniet in Stockholm, which means that for some years he devoted himself to working with floral fabrics.

Upon returning to Denmark, he continued to work with patterned textiles concurrently with his architectural projects. He himself stated that working with patterns was a *con amore* project, a space where he could express himself freely. Over time, the designs grew more abstract, and when he launched a collaboration with the textile manufacturer C. Olesen (Cotil) in the 1960s, the designs presented there were rigorous, stringent and characterised by geometric basic shapes. However, Arne Jacobsen's late sketches reveal that he still often found inspiration in nature, for example in designs such as 'Tassel' (see p. 97) and 'Forest' (see p. 242) from circa 1963.

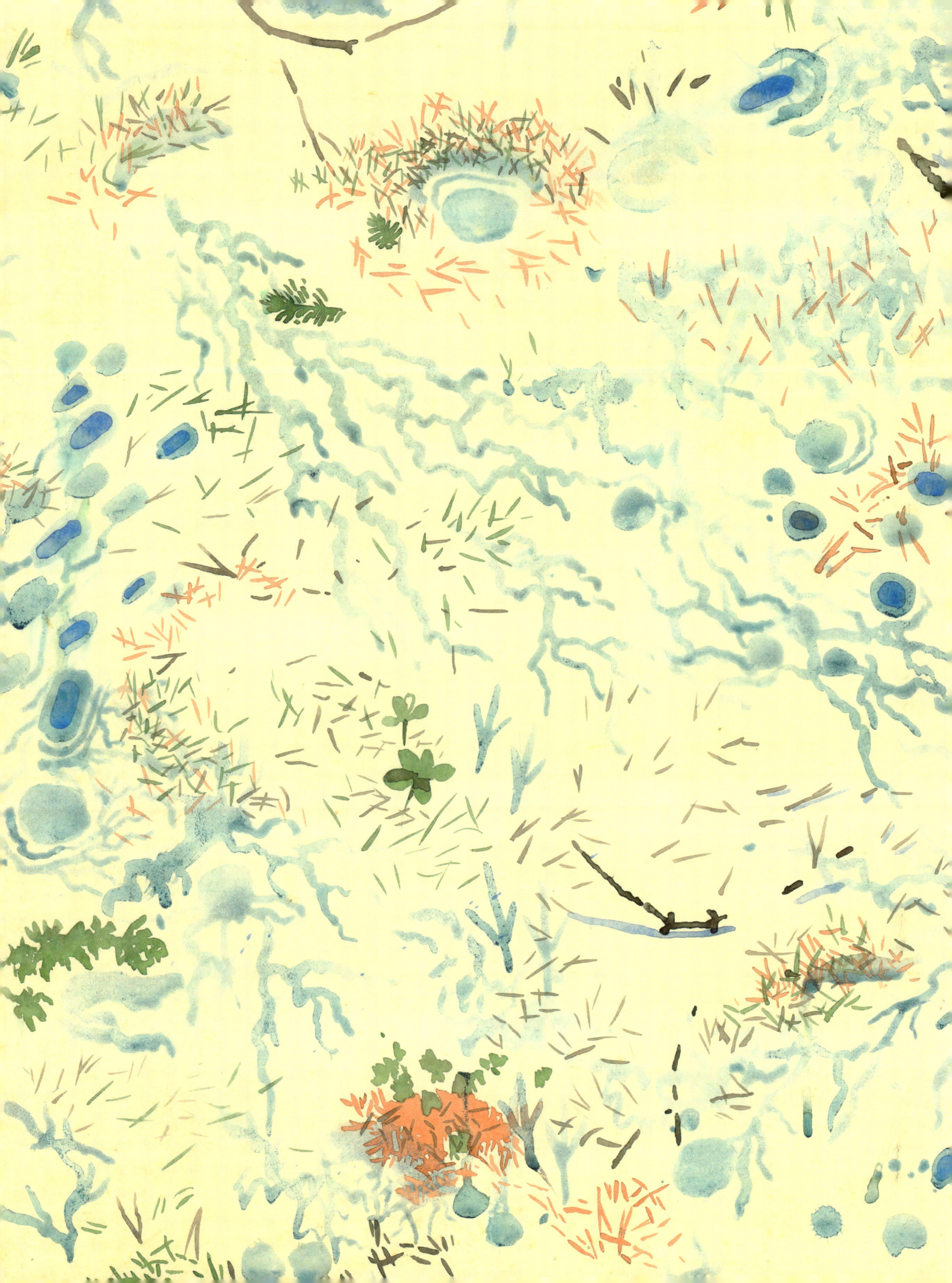

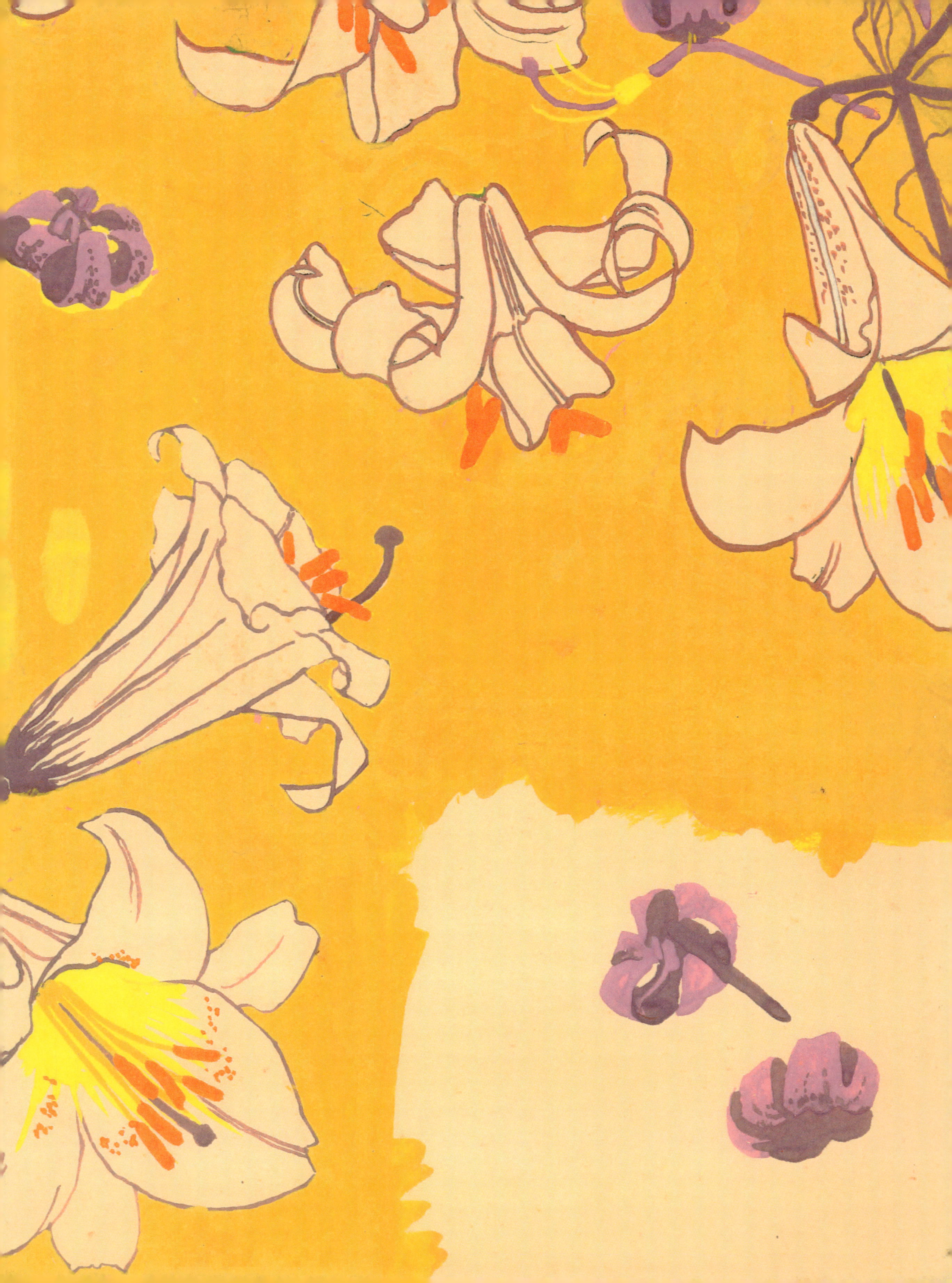

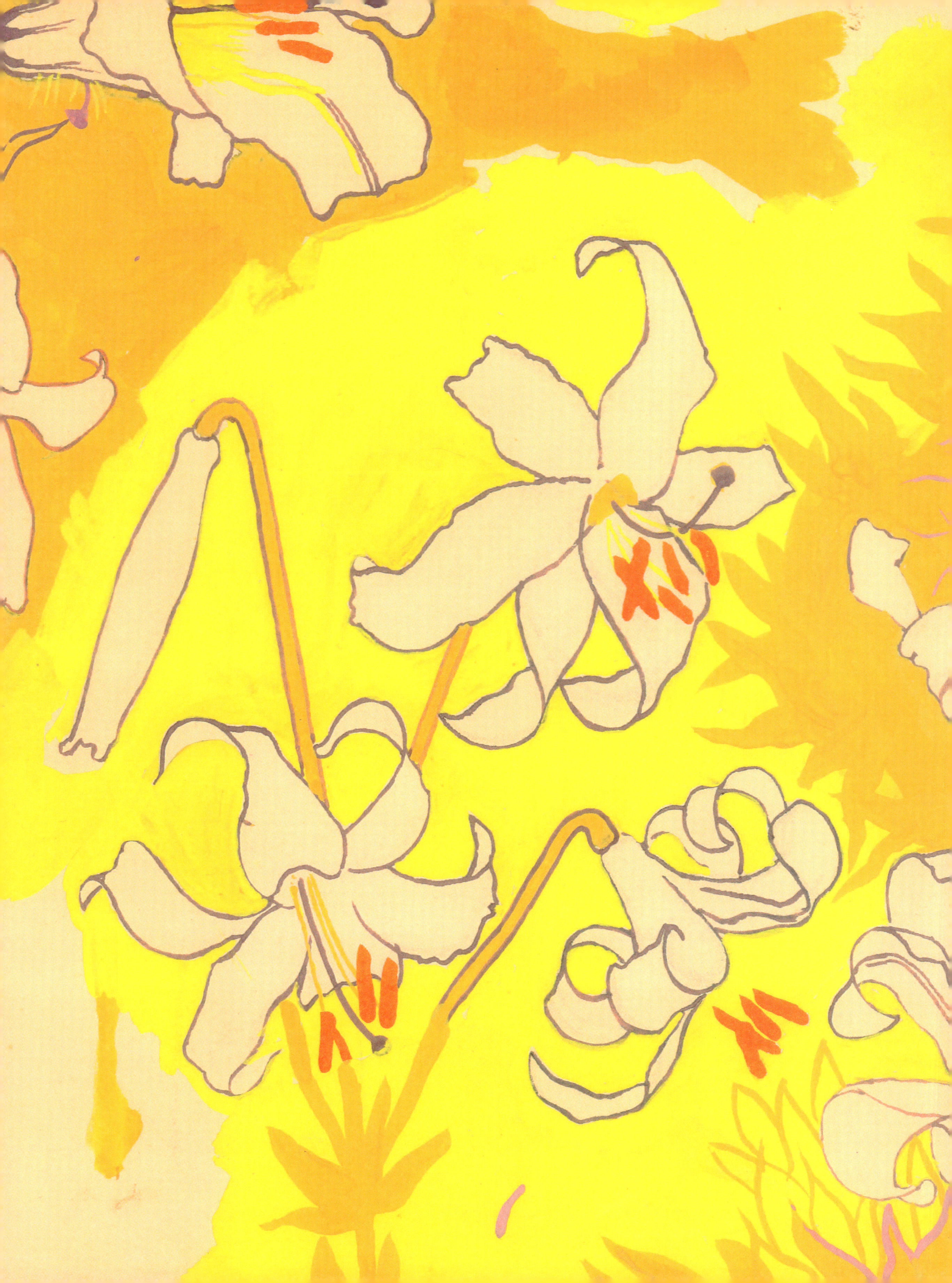

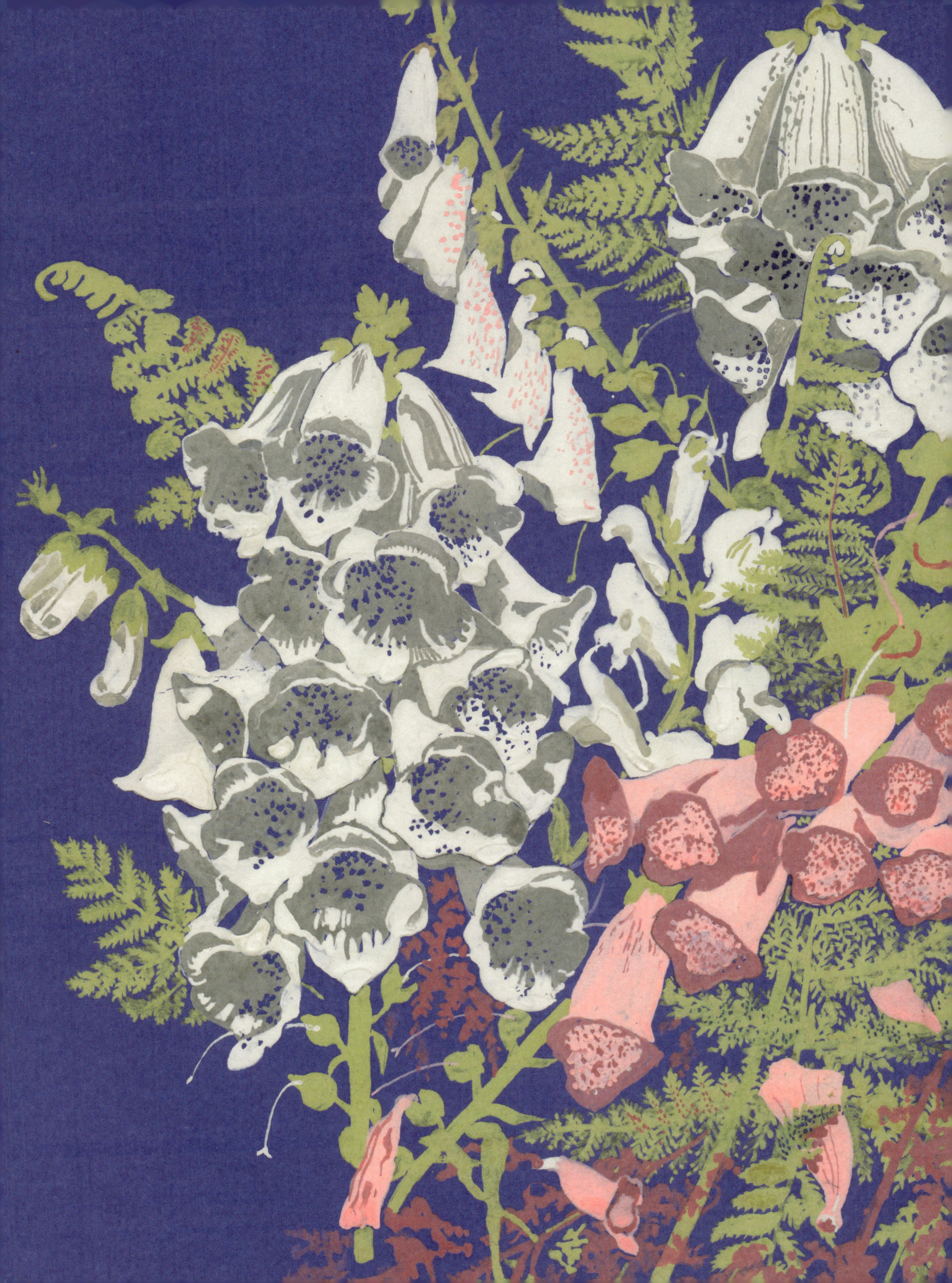

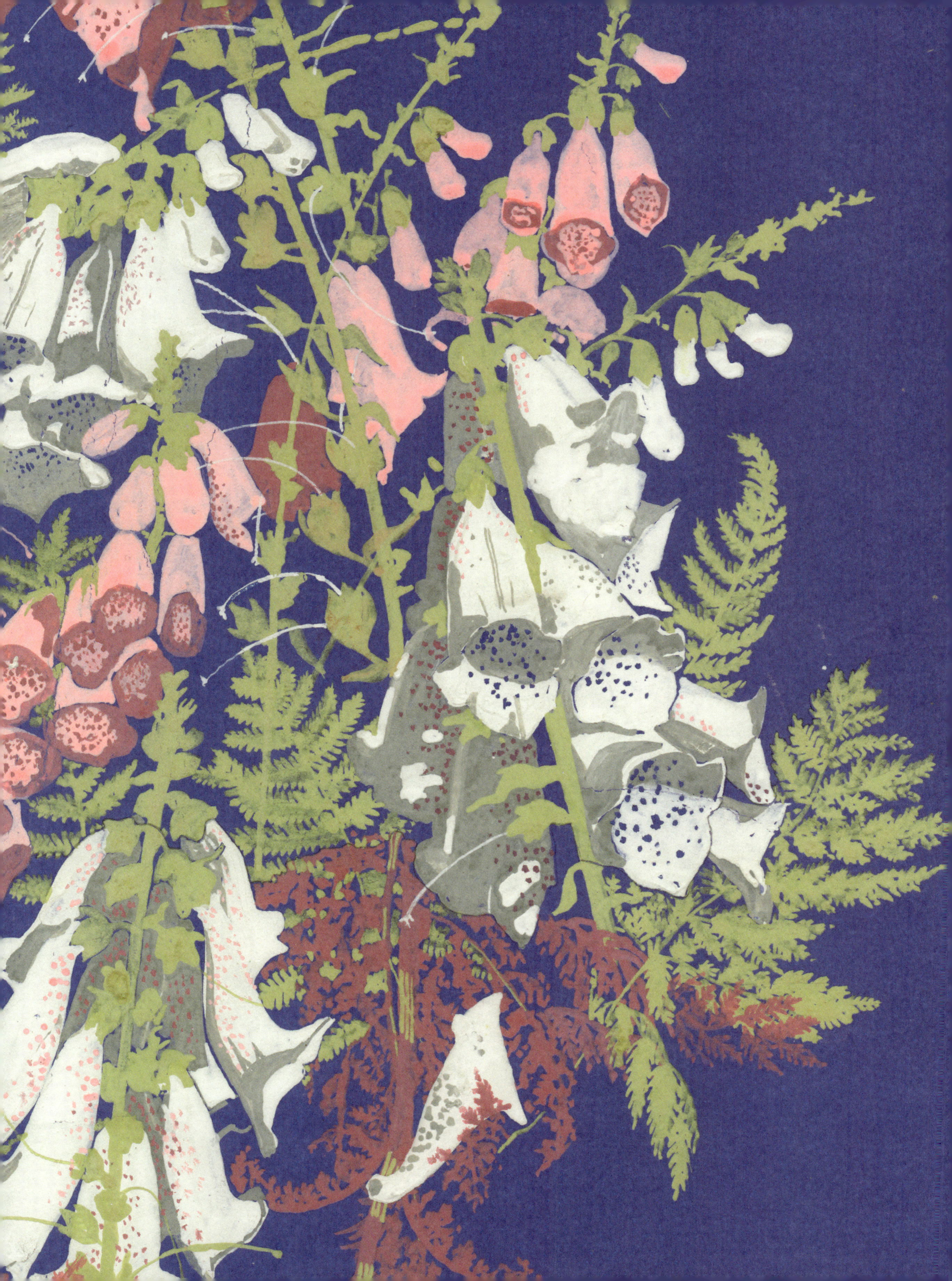

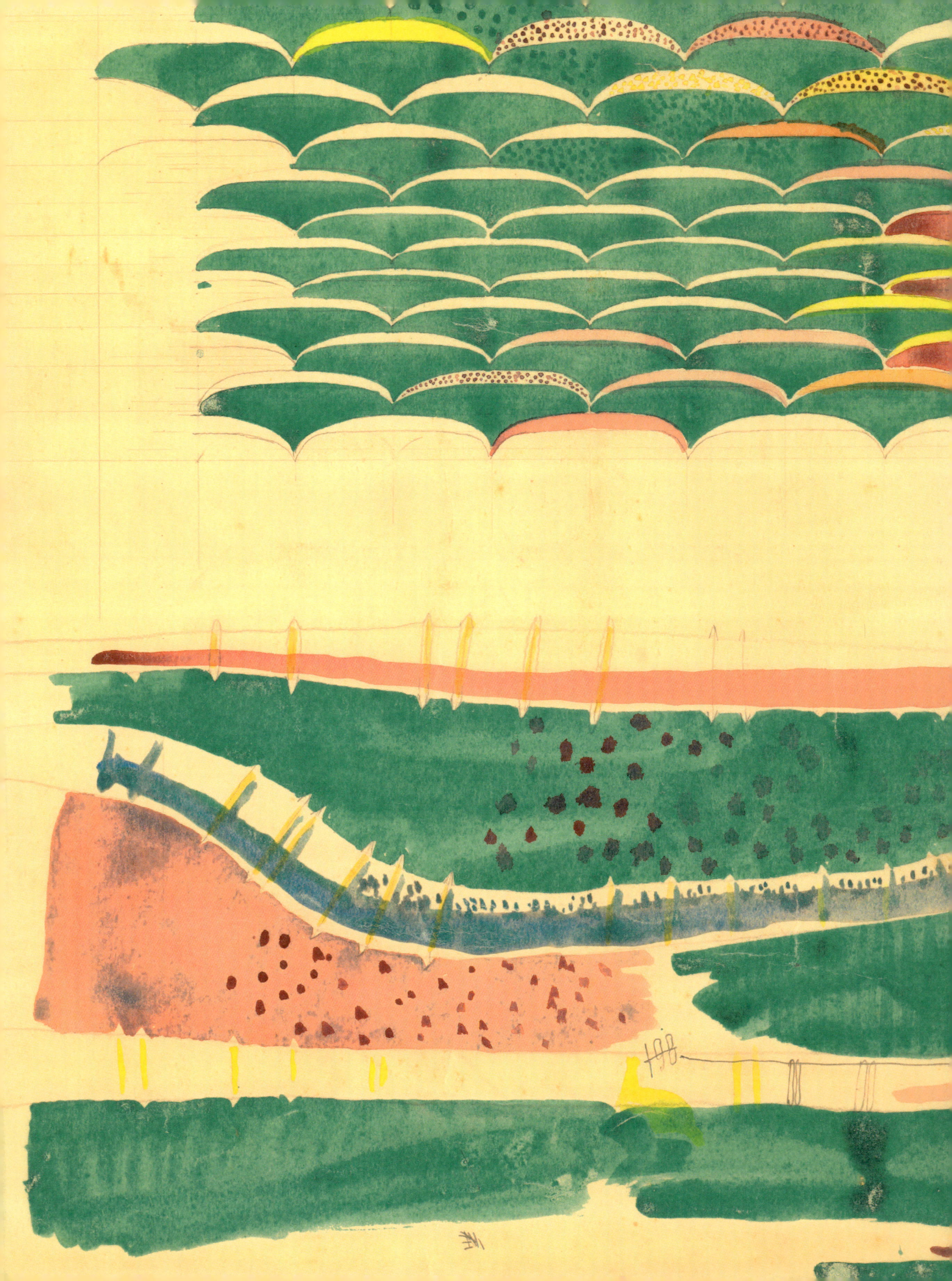

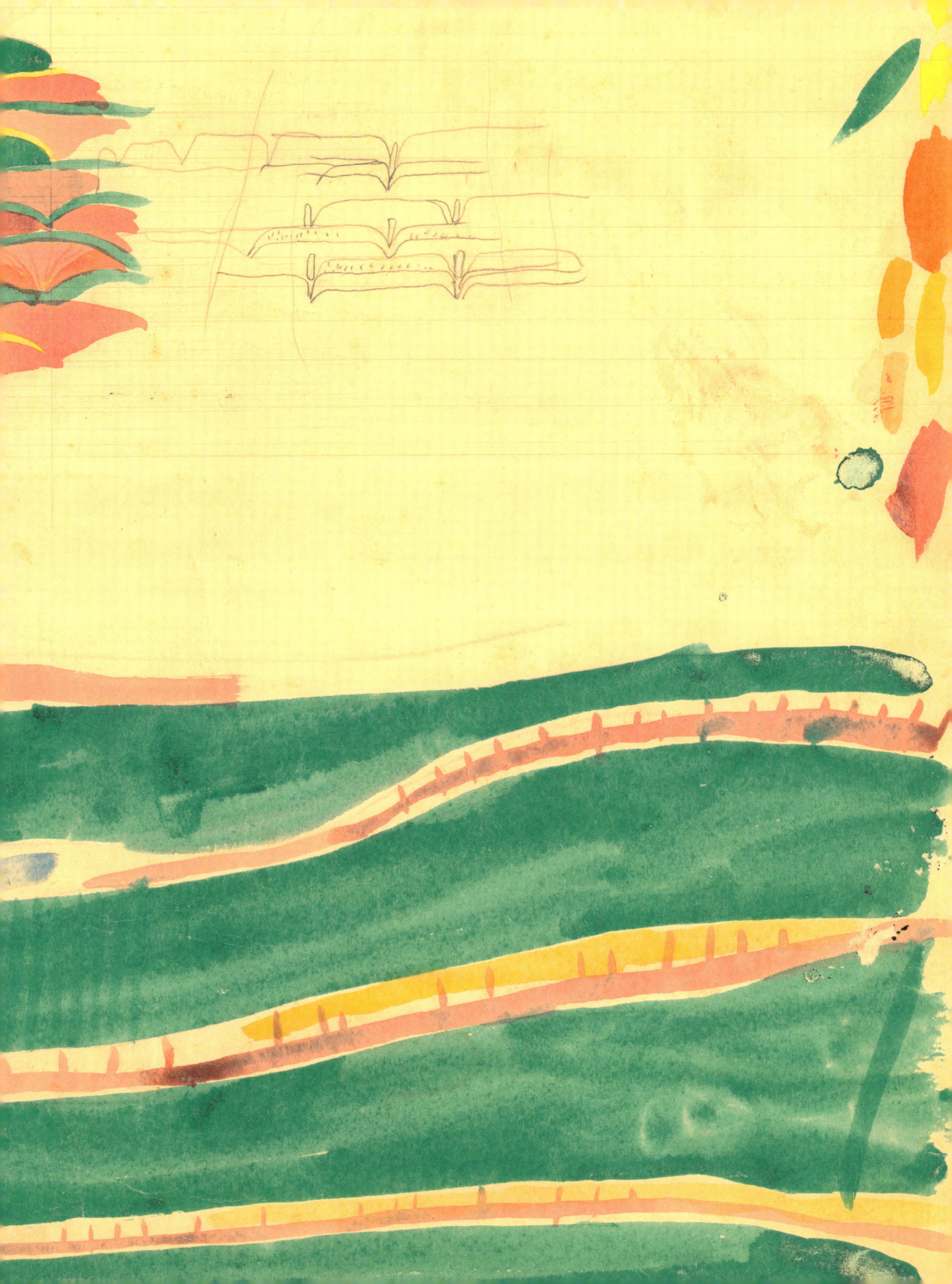

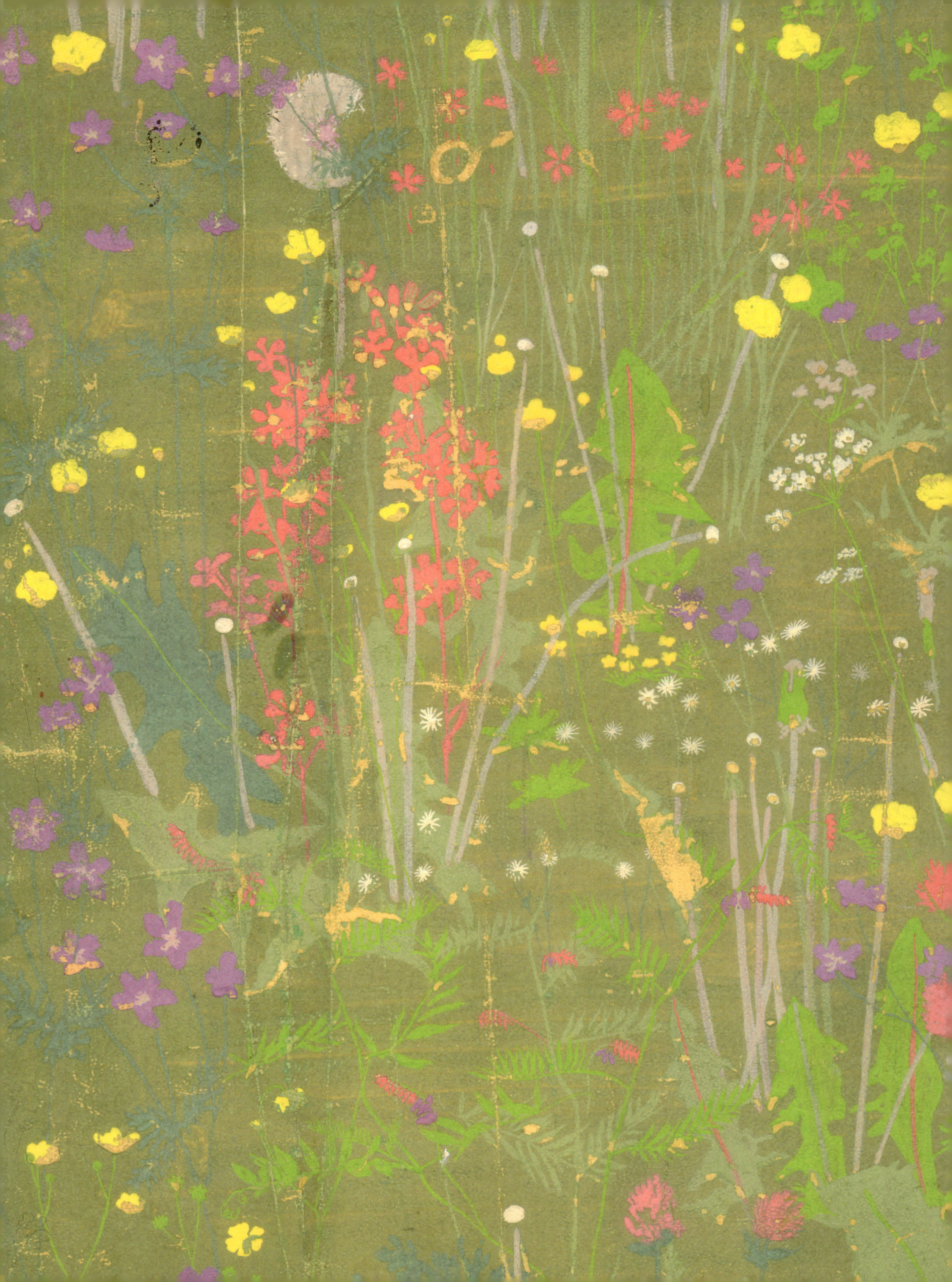

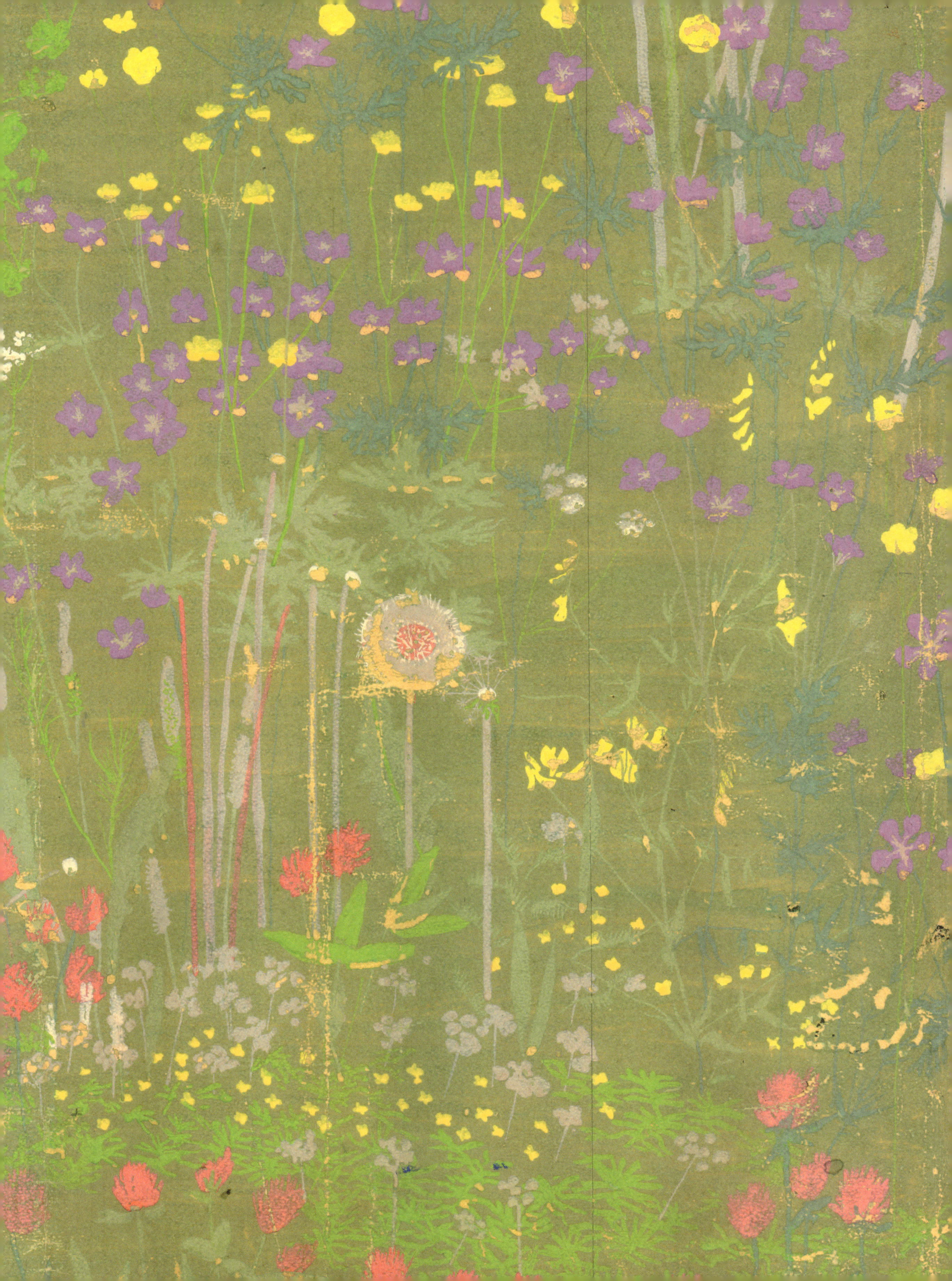

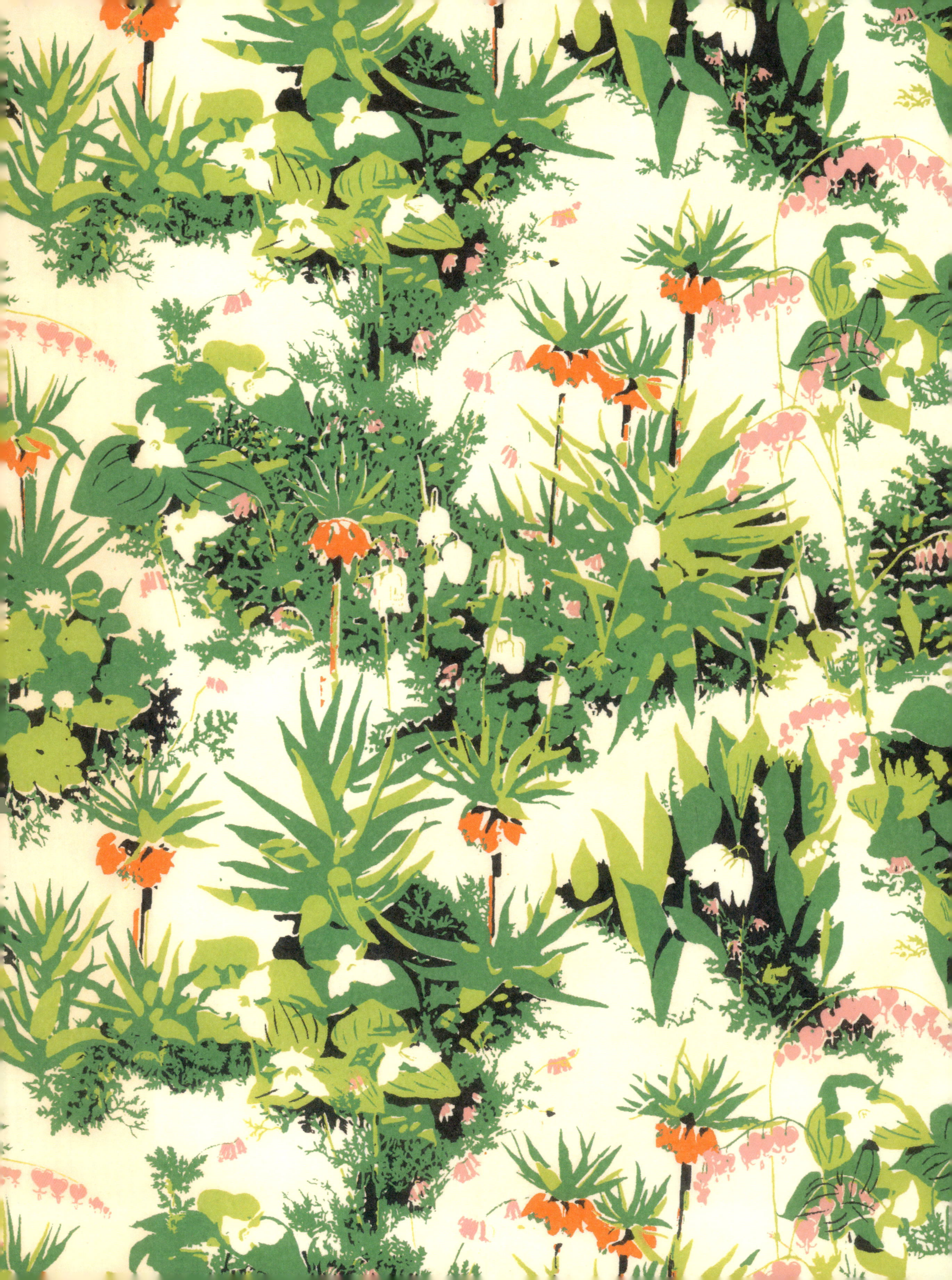

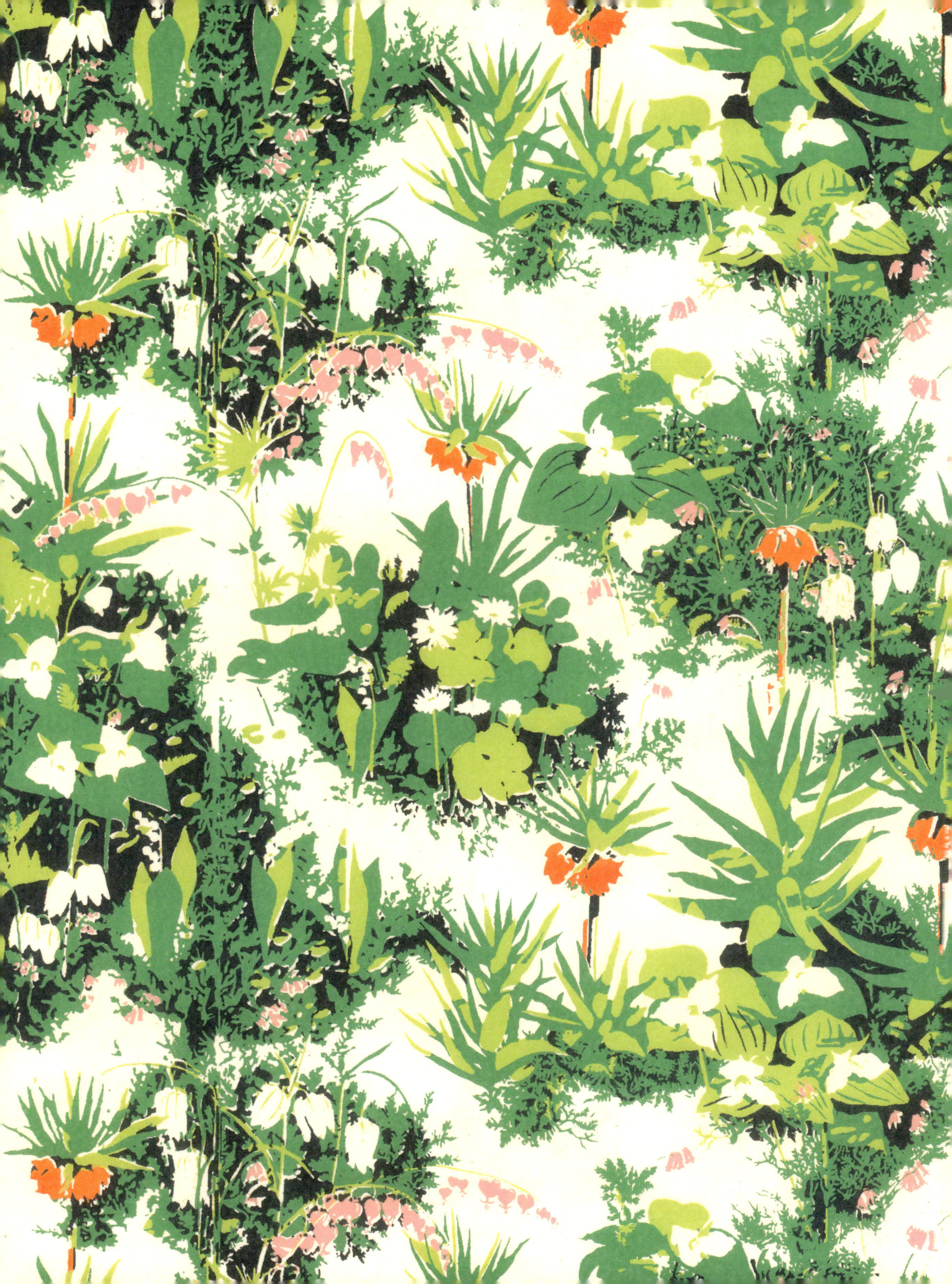

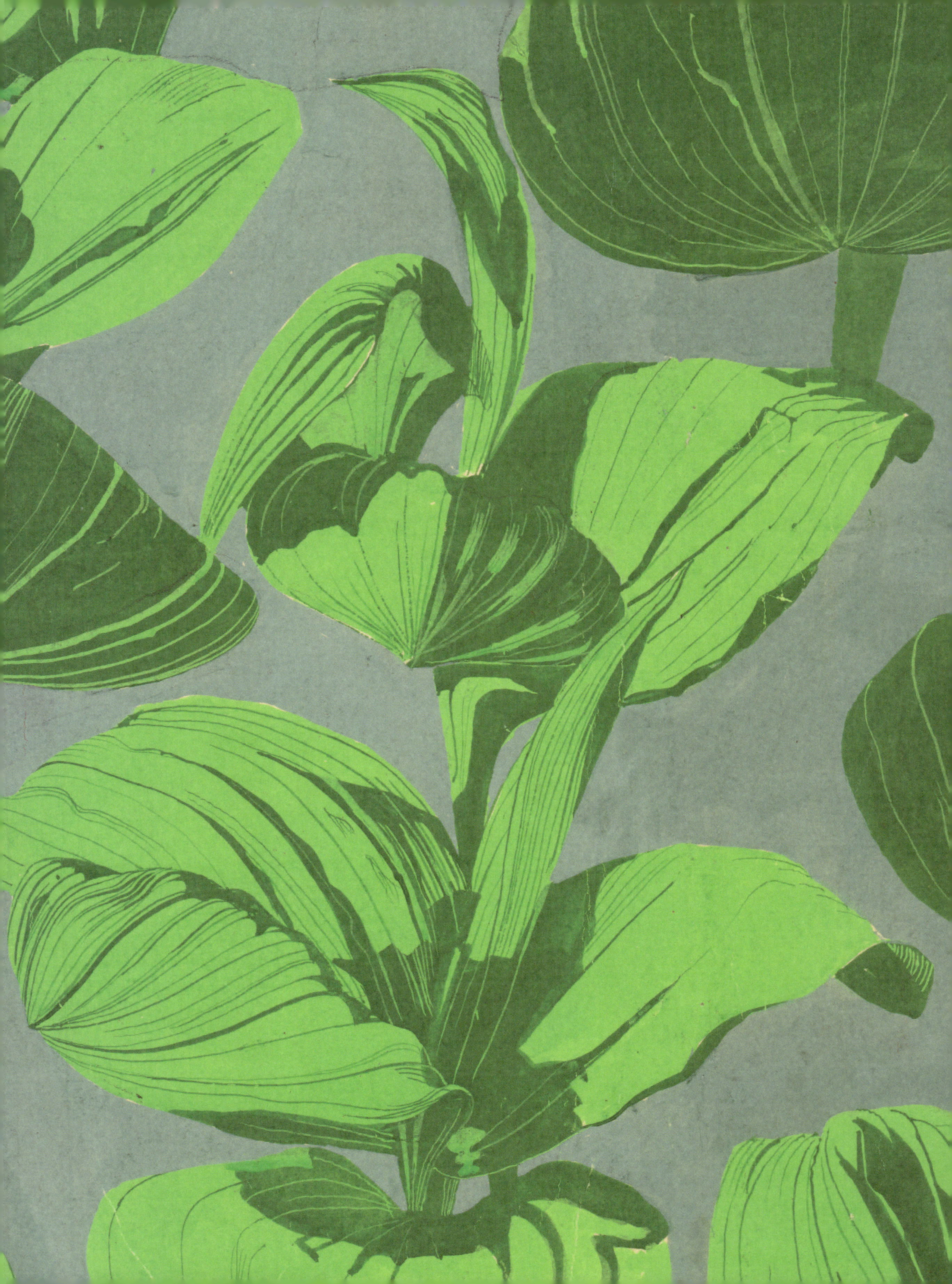

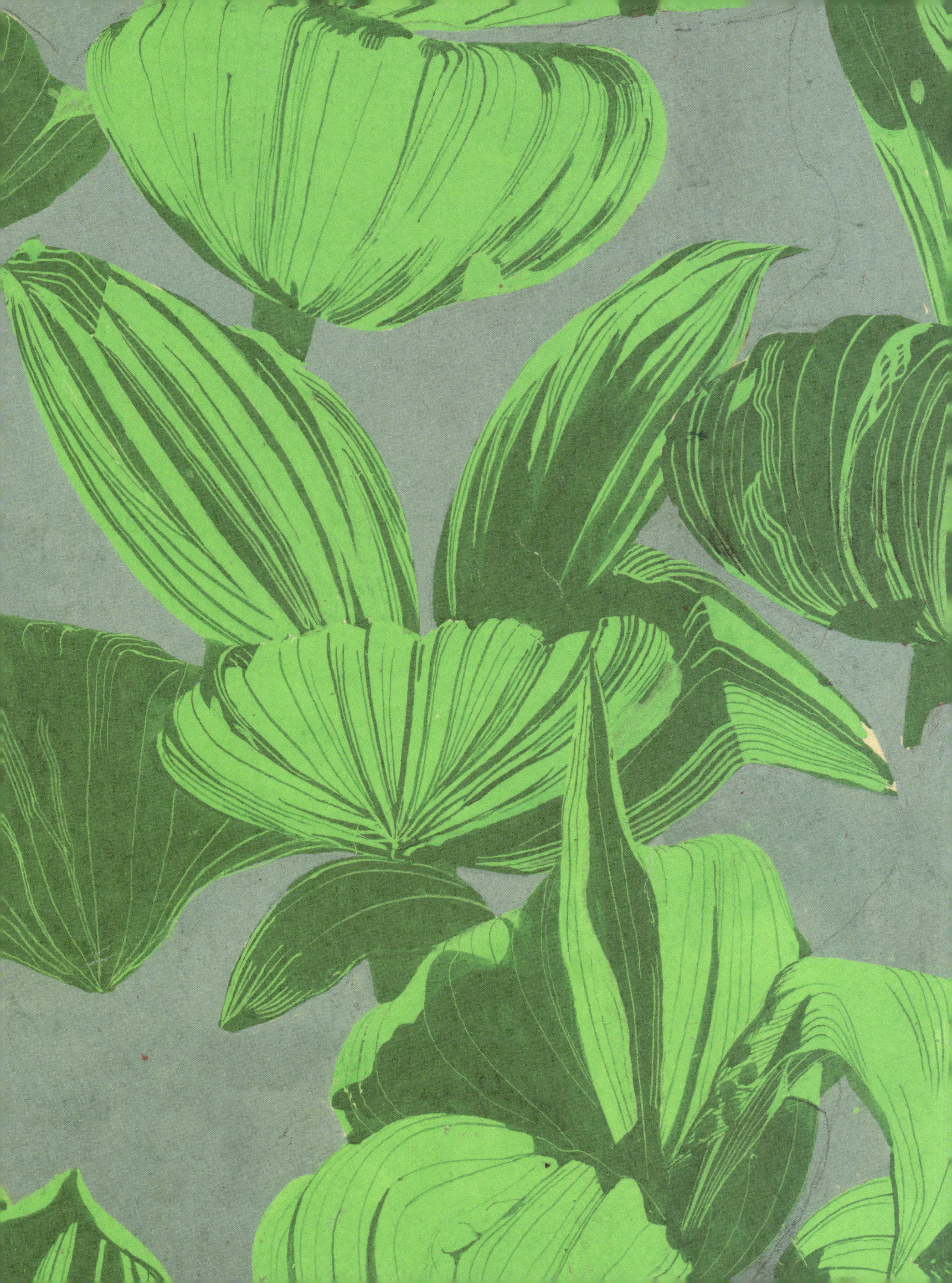

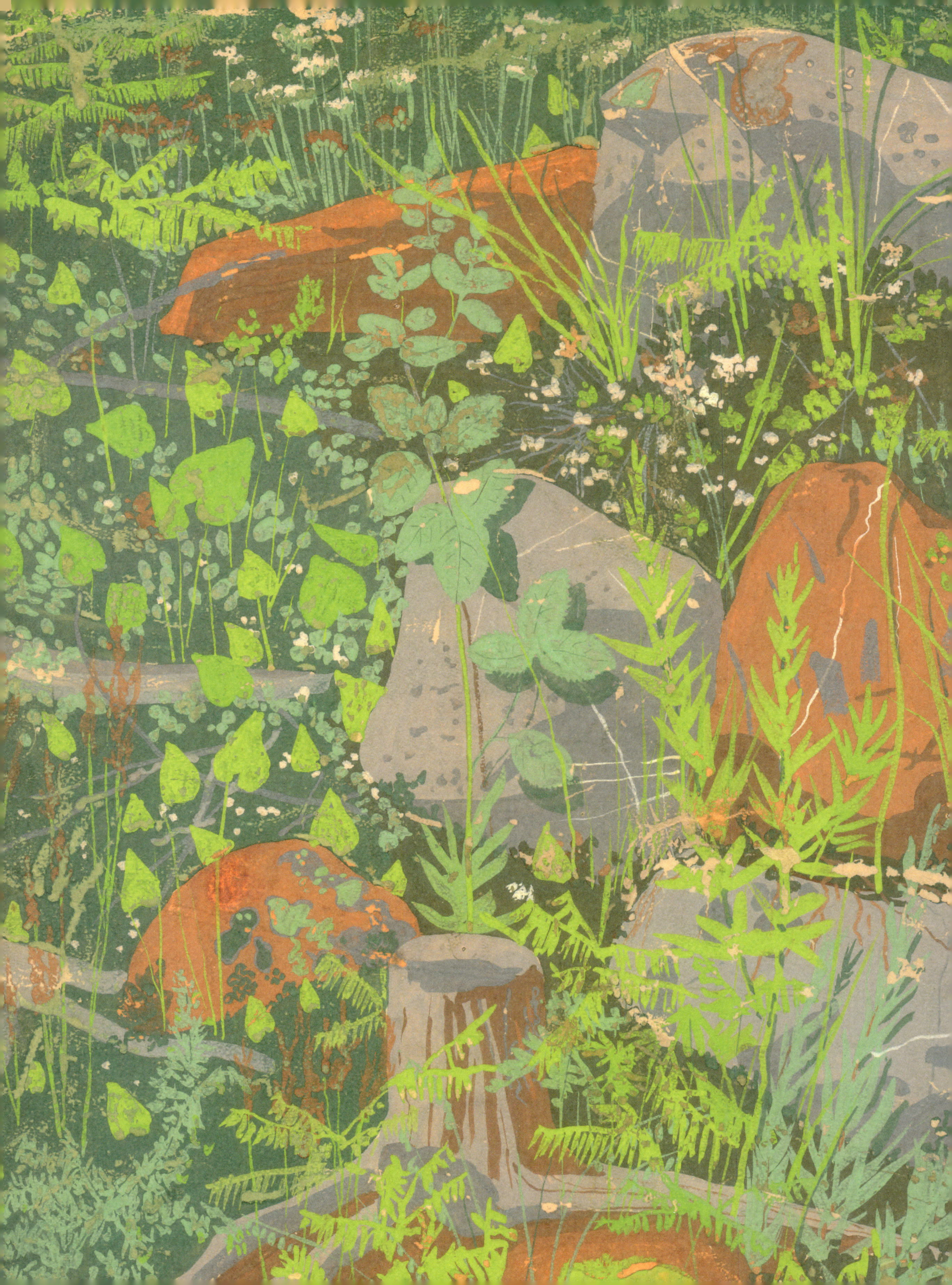

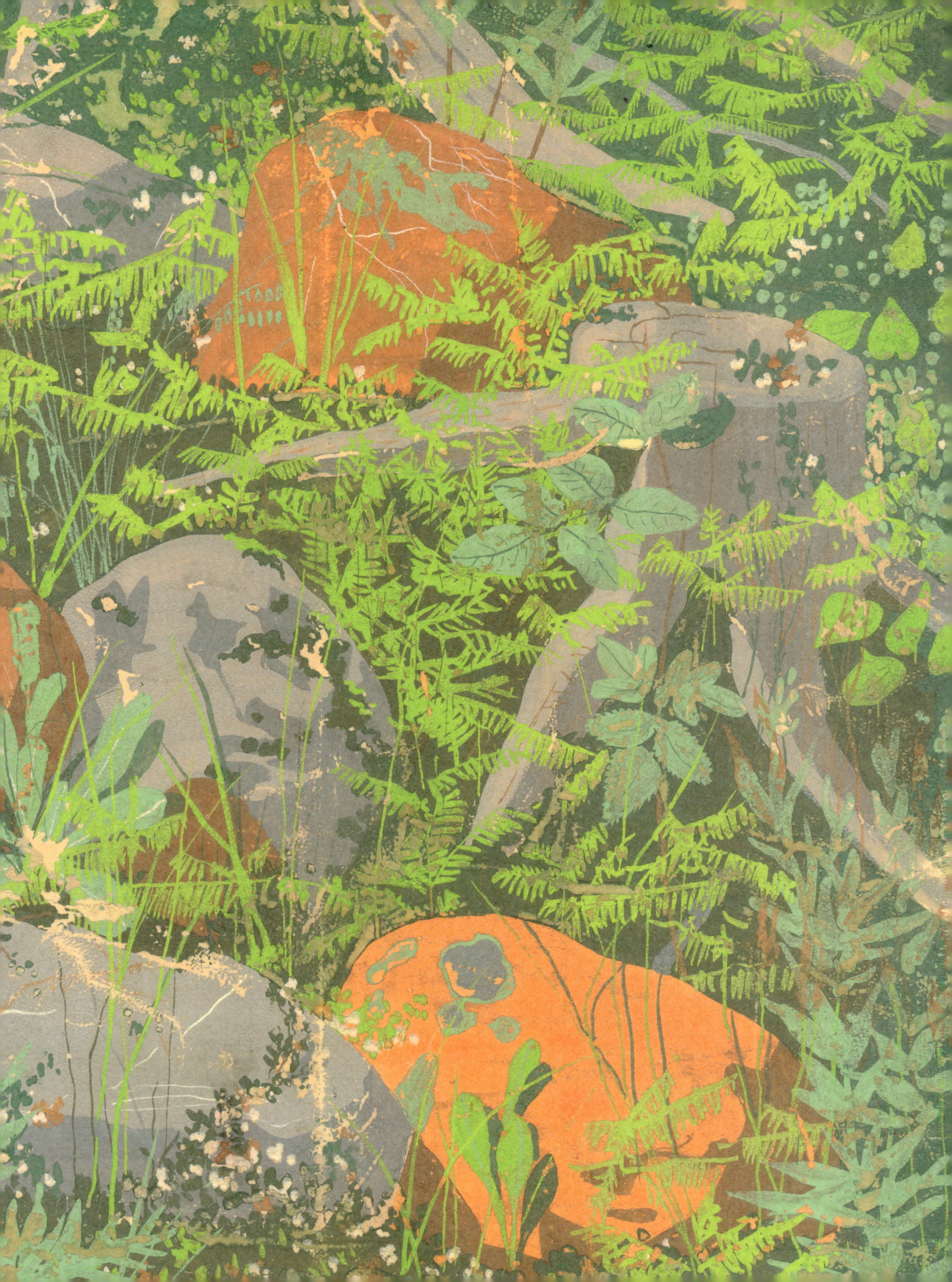

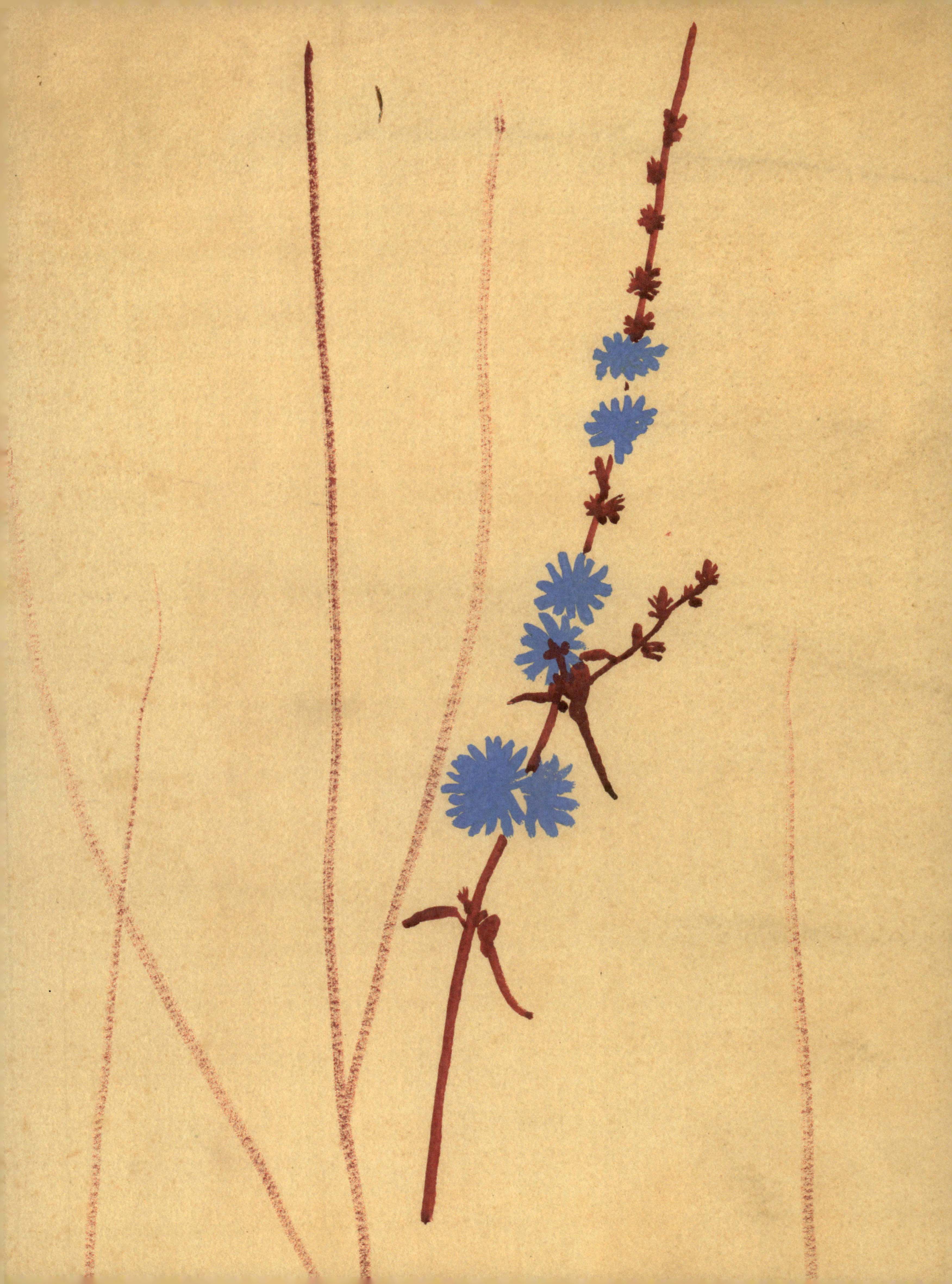

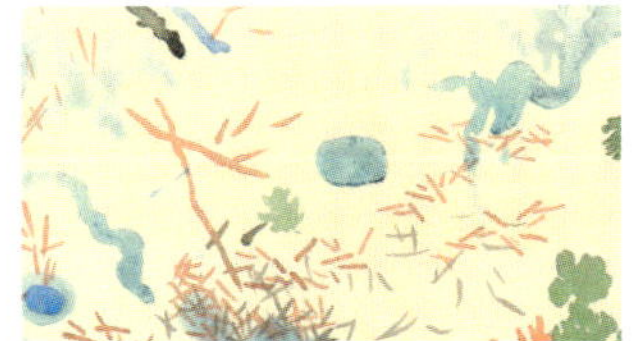

Landscape with Dunes

Preliminary work for an unknown wallpaper or textile design

Photo: The Royal Danish Library – The Danish National Art Library

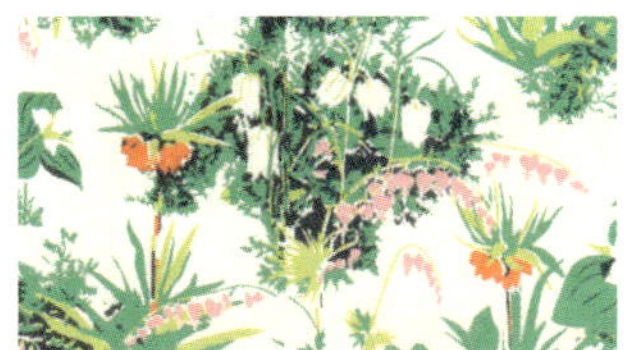

Crown Imperial

Print featuring the textile pattern Crown Imperial (Kejserkrone), which was manufactured by Nordiska Kompaniet in the 1940s

Photo: The Royal Danish Library – The Danish National Art Library

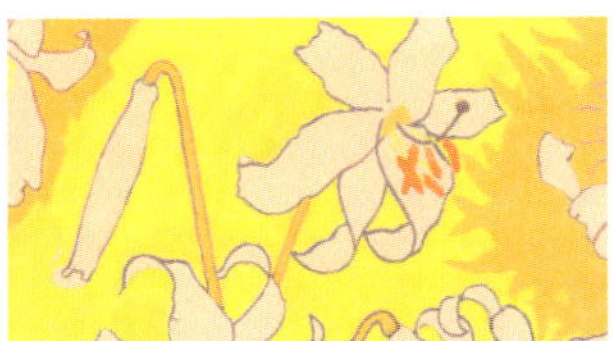

Lilies

Study or preliminary work for an unknown wallpaper or textile design

Photo: The Royal Danish Library – The Danish National Art Library

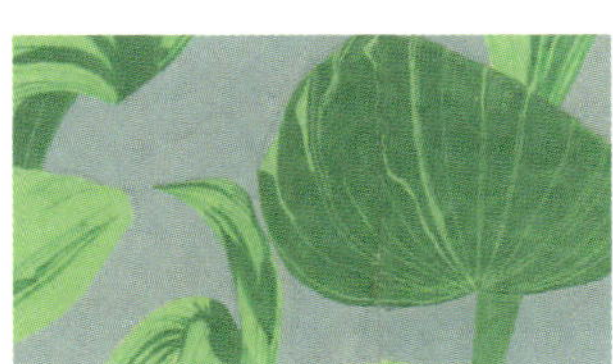

Veratrum

Print featuring the textile pattern Veratrum (Foldblad), which was manufactured by C. Olesen (Cotil) in the 1960s

Photo: The Royal Danish Library – The Danish National Art Library

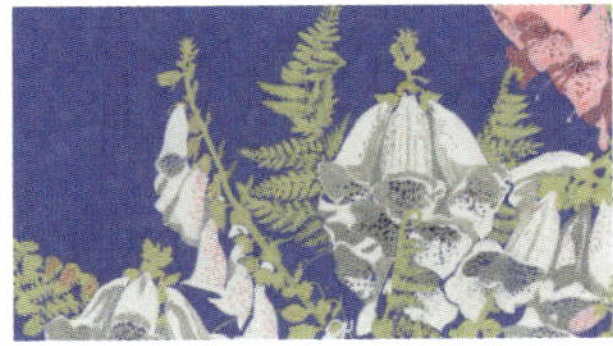

Digitalis

Print featuring the textile pattern Digitalis

Photo: The Royal Danish Library – The Danish National Art Library

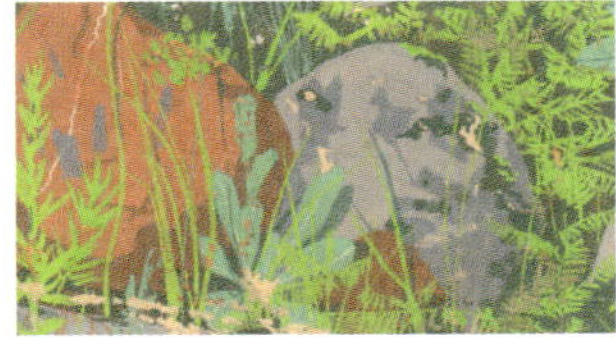

Wood Stumps

Print featuring the textile pattern Wood Stumps (Stubbe) from 1944, which was manufactured by Nordiska Kompaniet in the 1940s

Photo: The Royal Danish Library – The Danish National Art Library

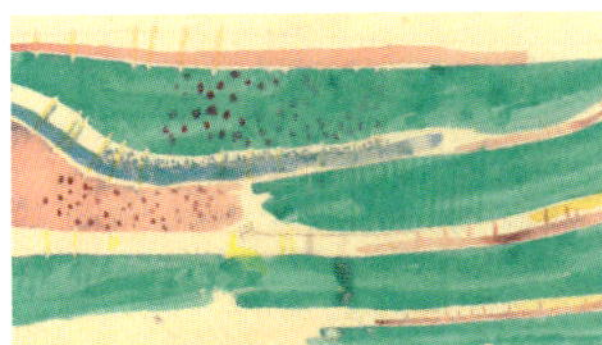

Undulating Lines

Possibly a study or a preliminary work for the wallpaper pattern Bio-Bio, which was manufactured by Grautex and Danske Tapetfabrikker around 1950 (see p. 33)

Photo: The Royal Danish Library – The Danish National Art Library

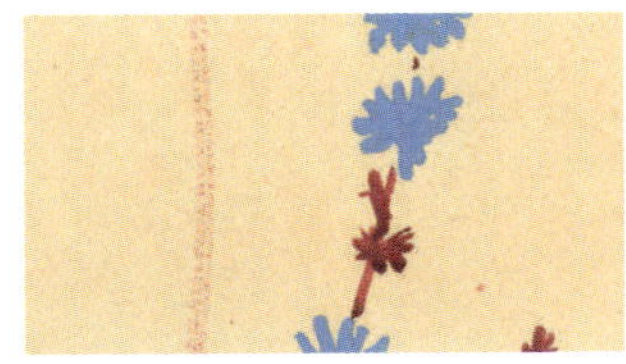

Chicory

Study or preliminary work for an unknown wallpaper or textile design

Photo: The Royal Danish Library – The Danish National Art Library

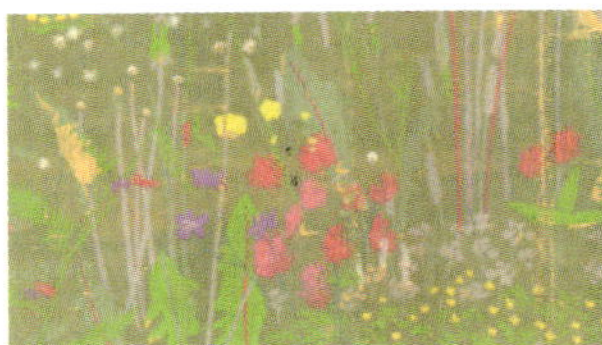

Summer Meadow

Print featuring the textile pattern Summer Meadow (Højsommereng) from 1944, which was manufactured by Nordiska Kompaniet in the 1940s

Photo: The Royal Danish Library – The Danish National Art Library

Art was in his blood

Arne Jacobsen's pursuit of aesthetic cohesiveness

Katrine Stenum Poulsen

Curator, Trapholt

04

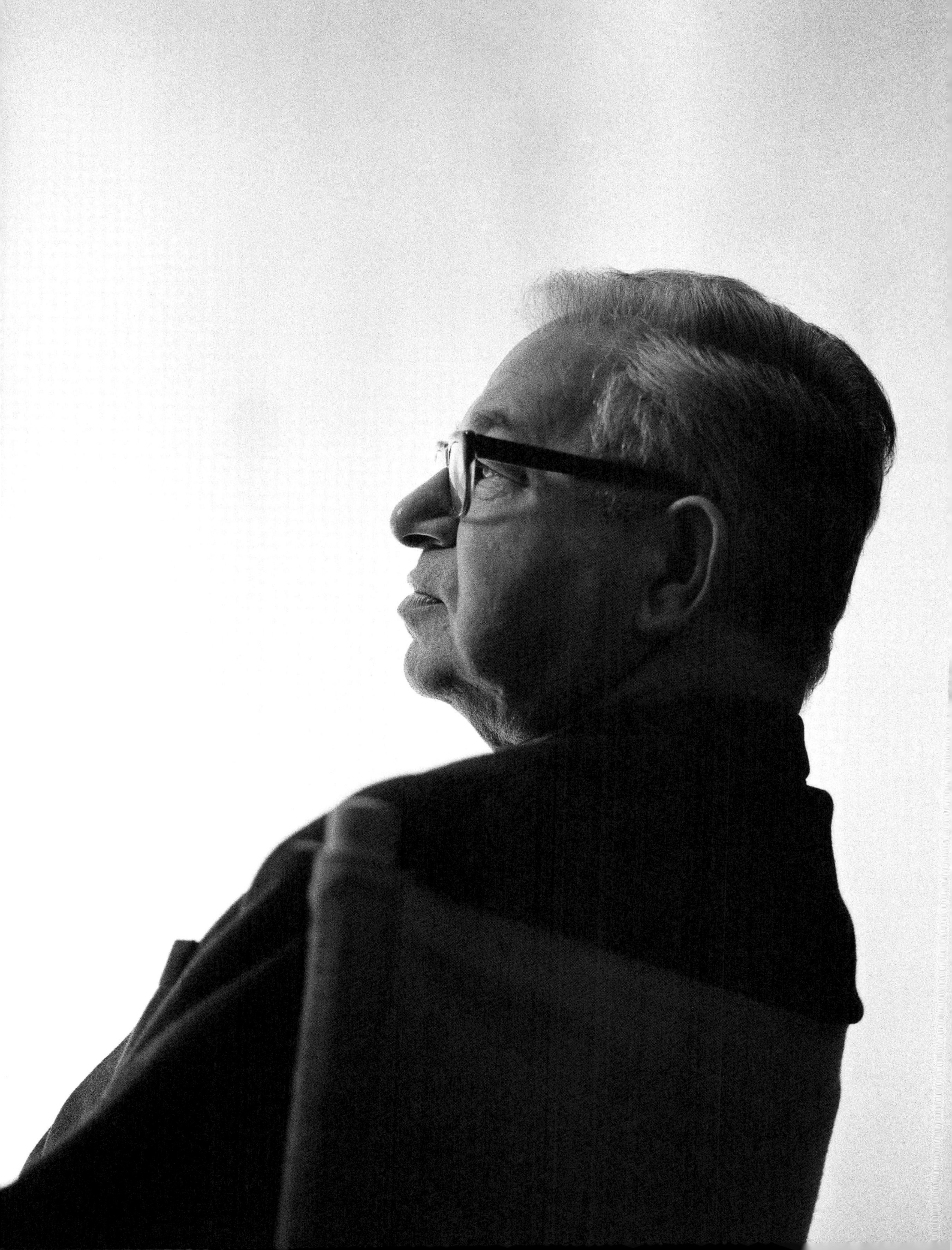

'Architecture and the plastic arts are not just two things that are juxtaposed, they are a solid and coherent whole.'

– Le Corbuisier

Previous page: Arne Jacobsen

Photo: Rigmor Mydtskov

Few Danish designers have had such great and far-reaching success as Arne Jacobsen. His legacy in design, crafts and architecture clearly testify to this, but so too do the many books that have been written about the Danish architect since his death in 1971. There is general consensus that Arne Jacobsen had a particularly keenly honed feel for design. While he originally wanted to be a painter, he was persuaded by his father to choose the more sensible path of training to be an architect. However, his interest in art never went away, and throughout his life Arne Jacobsen distinguished himself as a passionate painter of watercolours and as an art collector.

Arne Jacobsen belonged to a small group of architects who were particularly successful and contributed to the overall development of architecture seen in the early and mid-twentieth century. This was an era infused by the avant-garde's insistence on totally rearranging what had gone before – a simultaneously fantastic and totalitarian project, and one with which Arne Jacobsen's will to renewal was a perfect fit (Thau and Vindum, 2002). With his extensive projects and determination to design even the smallest details, Arne Jacobsen has become an important figure in the narrative of Modernism's total design. Professor at the SDU Department of Design and Communication Anders V. Munch (2012) has studied the *Gesamtkunstwerk* of early Modernism as an artistic project and the later Modernist movement's concept of 'total design' as an overall perspective on issues such as form, function, history, nature and economics. He uses the SAS Royal Hotel in Copenhagen as an example of Arne Jacobsen's total design, where everything from the building itself to its textiles, furniture and lighting was designed by the architect himself. The SAS Royal Hotel is a particularly oft-quoted example of Arne Jacobsen's success and of his ability as a designer. Anders V. Munch has defined *Gesamtkunstwerk* or total design as an attempt to unite the arts (2008/09); Thau and Vindum have defined it as a large-scale joining of many art forms in a single, cohesive work (usually) created by the same author (1998). This makes it all the more startling that neither Anders V. Munch's book *Design as Gesamtkunstwerk* (2012) nor Carsten Thau and Kjeld Vindum's major biographical work *Arne Jacobsen* (1998), nor the various past exhibitions and catalogues about the Danish architect have applied a definite focus on Arne Jacobsen's efforts to integrate art in his work with total design. Rather, he is described in more overall terms as having 'a craving for aesthetic control' (Thau and Vindum, 2002) and as 'uncompromising' (Tøjner and Vindum 1994). As many will know, Jacobsen decorated the SAS Royal Hotel with his own textiles and furniture, but he also saw to the art on the walls in the form of reproductions of Picasso paintings, Bjørn Wiinblad posters and imported tapestries from French Polynesia.[1]

British architect Rod Hackney has described the result of Arne Jacobsen's efforts in these terms: 'Jacobsen perhaps gave a guide during his careerof how the architects and consultants in fine art should work together' (1972). This article examines how Arne Jacobsen worked with art throughout his life. An artist himself, he created watercolours, paintings and textiles, but was also a curator and facilitator of artistic and decorative commissions in his buildings. I also look at how his less successful results shaped his subsequent work with art. Conceptually, I will use the concept 'total design' to describe Arne Jacobsen's projects, as it has wider application than that of a *Gesamtkunstwerk* (see Munch, 2012 for an account of the values and associations embedded in the two concepts).

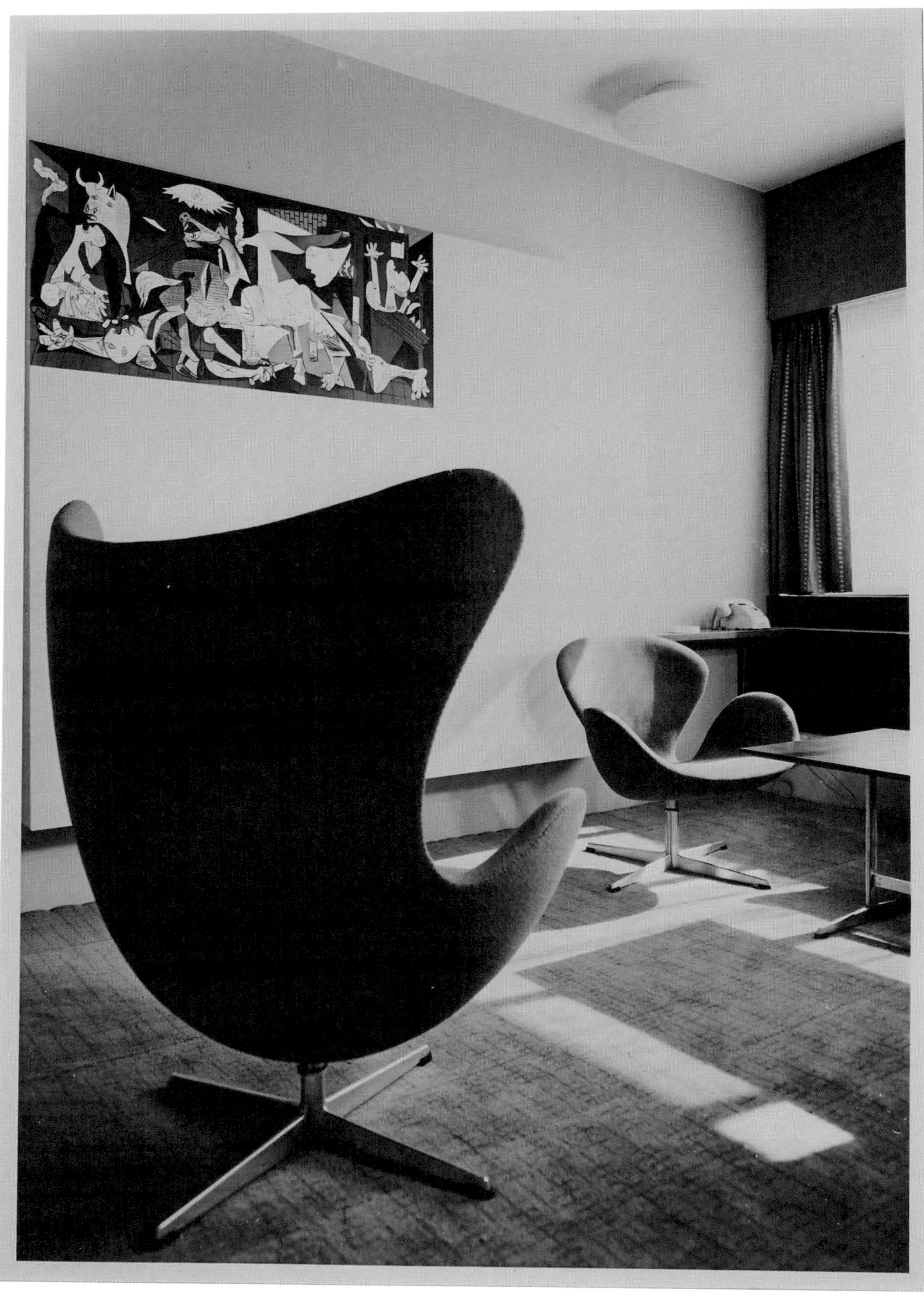

Interior from SAS Royal Hotel with a replica of Picasso's *Guernica* from 1917

Photo: Aage Strüwing © Jørgen Strüwing

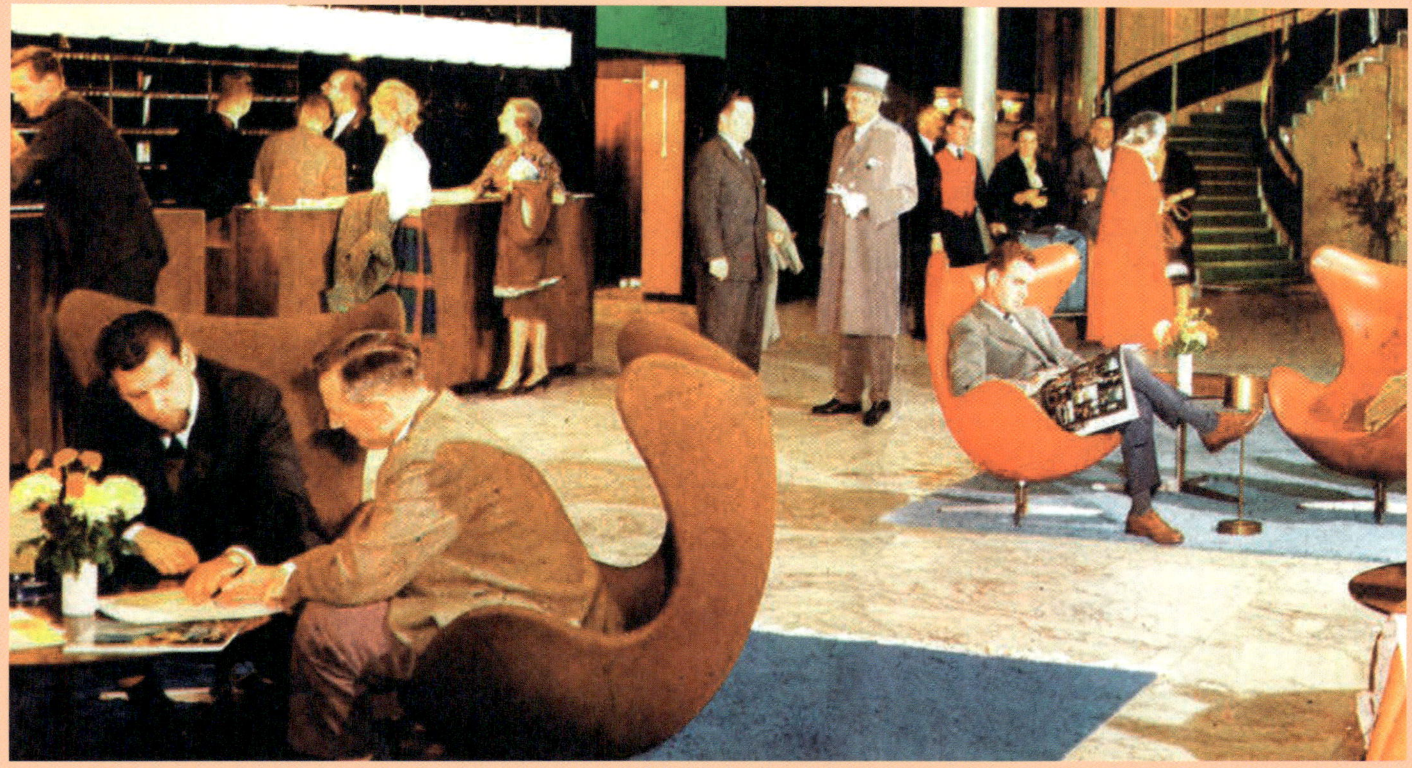

The lobby of the SAS Royal Hotel was impressive with its richness of colours and materials

Photo: Unknown

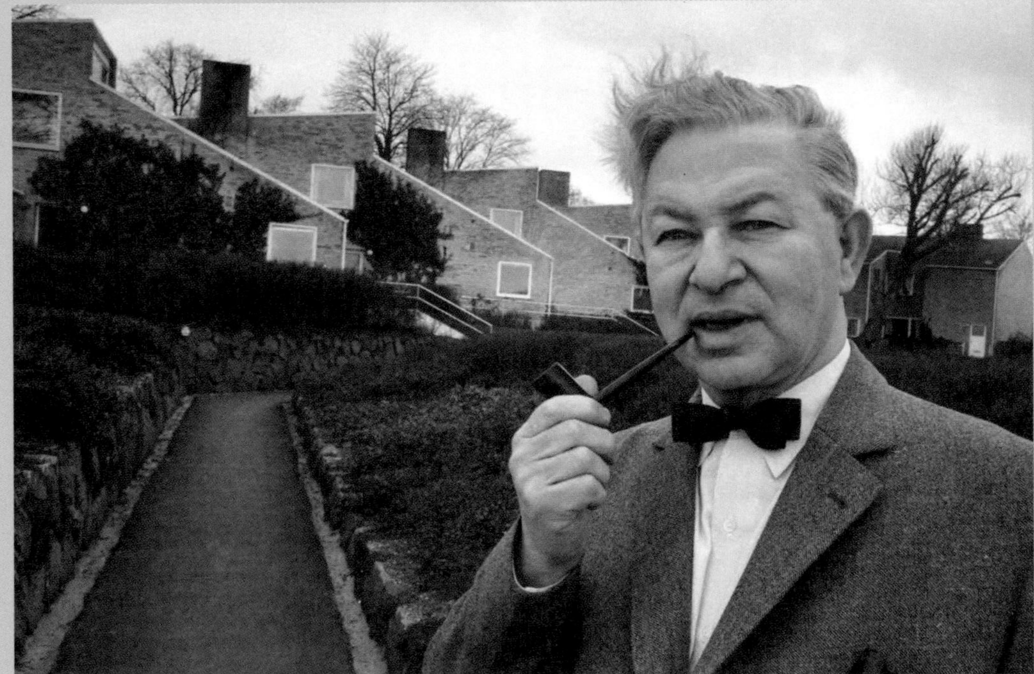

Arne Jacobsen in front of the Søholm I development in 1952

Photo: Willy Henriksen/ Ritzau Scanpix

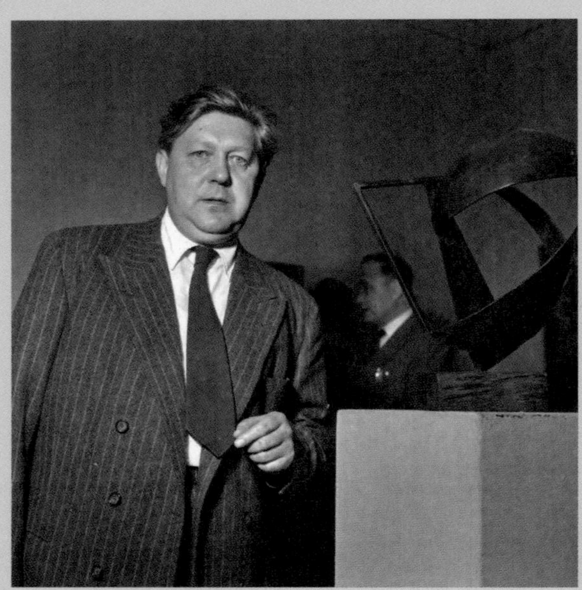

The Danish sculptor Robert Jacobsen in 1953

Photo: Lars Hansen/ Ritzau Scanpix

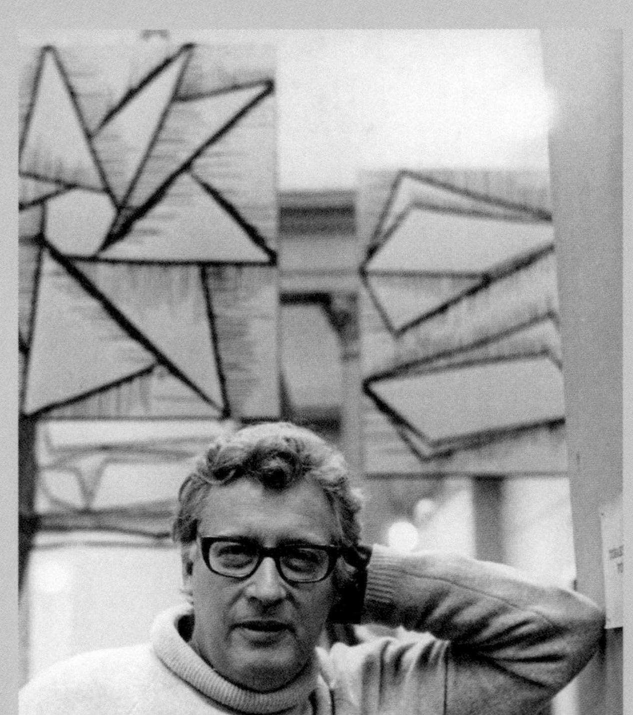

The Danish painter Gunnar Aagaard Andersen

Photo: Asger Sessingø/ Ritzau Scanpix

Arne Jacobsen and the artistic avant-garde

In 1951, the French sculptor André Bloc founded the avant-garde group known as 'Le Groupe Espace' together with a contemporary, the painter Fernand Legér. The objective was to bring together architects, artists and engineers working towards one common goal: achieving a synthesis between the arts of painting, sculpture and architecture. In October of that year, Arne Jacobsen signed the group's manifesto, whose total of thirty-nine signatures also included the two Danish artists Robert Jacobsen and Gunnar Aagaard Andersen.[2]

The road to reaching the group's common goals was to be paved by cutting-edge experiments and collaboration aimed at blowing open the traditional boundaries separating architecture, sculpture and visual arts (Roy, 2013). The Hungarian-born French artist Nicolas Schöffer, who also signed the manifesto, emphasised the group members' sense of the necessity and importance of 'creating an Art that inscribes itself in real space, responding to functional necessities and to all of Man's needs from the simplest one to the highest one ... caring for collective and private living standards' (Dossin, 2019). For some of the group's members, the project represented a new way of thinking and working; for others, its ideas had been a common thread throughout their careers (Roy, 2013). For example, this was not André Bloc's first attempt. In 1935, he partnered with French architect Auguste Perret to found L'union pour l'Art (the Association for Art), and in 1949 he and the world-famous French architect Le Corbusier founded the Association pour un Synthése des Arts Plastiques (The Association for a Synthesis of the Visual Arts) (Dossin, 2019). For Arne Jacobsen, the work on integrating art and architecture took place behind the scenes, but it had been going on for many years. Unlike fellow architects Poul Henningsen or Børge Mogensen, Jacobsen was not known for expressing political views. Carsten Thau and Kjeld Vindum, the authors of the comprehensive book *Arne Jacobsen*, have criticised Arne Jacobsen for lacking the vision and panache that many other of the greatest architects of the twentieth century possessed, but also for his lack of eloquence, his difficulties in articulating his ideas. Perhaps that is why the example of the Groupe Espace appears with particular prominence. It demonstrates a special case where Arne Jacobsen rallied round a clearly formulated programme, but is also something that may be interpreted as the culmination of many years of work on perfecting the interaction between art and architecture. However, the Groupe Espace never achieved any great success and gained little prominence in the history of art or architecture. Even during the group's own lifetime, there was some confusion about how the synthesis of the arts should be achieved in real life (Dossin, 2019), and at the same time the group members struggled to raise the funds necessary for their ambitious exhibition projects (Roy, 2013).

Thau and Vindum regard Arne Jacobsen as a consolidating character – as someone who brought together and fused different trends and professional disciplines. There is also much to indicate that Arne Jacobsen's wide outlook meant that he was often, to a greater or lesser extent, inspired by other architects for his projects (Thau and Vindum, 1998). However, that trait may also be a sign of great innovative intelligence (Basaiawmoit, 2018). For example, Verner Panton highlights how Arne Jacobsen began to design various objects because he was not satisfied with what was already available on the market (Tøjner and Vindum, 1994). Arne Jacobsen improved on that which already existed. He saw the movements of his time clearly and perfected them. Throughout his life, he worked diligently towards achieving greater symbiosis between architecture and art, and he repeatedly demonstrated his ability to put himself in the artist's place as well as the architect's. For these reasons, his commitment to the Groupe Espace is crucial for our understanding of Arne Jacobsen's outlook on art, but also his insight into the artistic and architectural trends found outside Denmark. A passionate art collector, he filled his own home with paintings and sculptures, primarily Concrete, Modern and Expressionist in style.[3] Arne Jacobsen's own collection included works by the Danish painters Asger Jorn and Richard Mortensen as well as the by the sculptor Robert Jacobsen and the painter Victor Vasarely, both of whom were fellow members of the Groupe Espace. He also owned the preliminary works for Preben Hornung's large-scale work at the Rødovre City Hall, to which I shall return below.

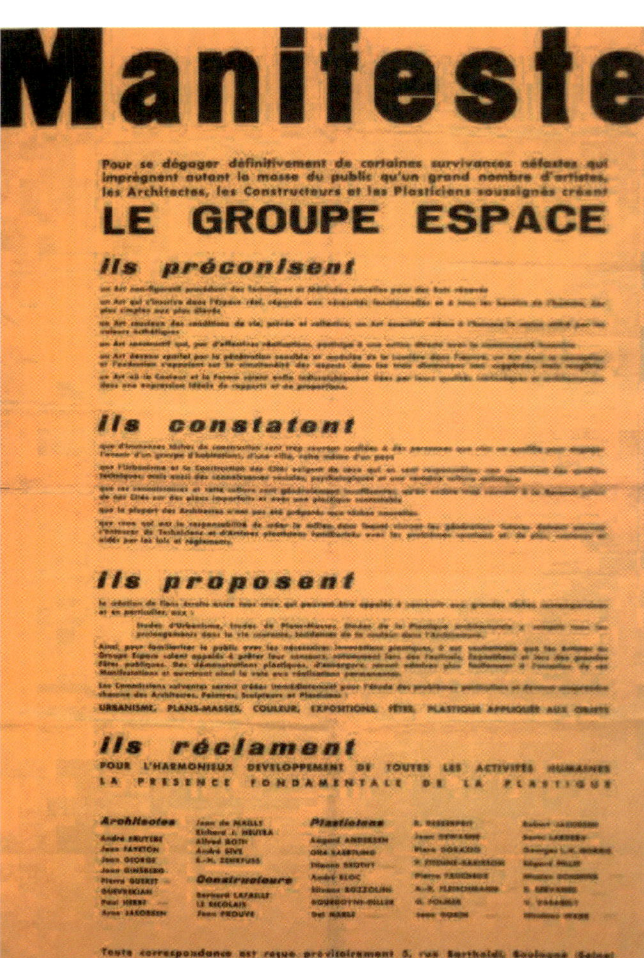

Manifeste

Pour se dégager définitivement de certaines survivances néfastes qui imprègnent autant la masse du public qu'un grand nombre d'artistes, les Architectes, les Constructeurs et les Plasticiens soussignés créent

LE GROUPE ESPACE

Ils préconisent

Ils constatent

Ils proposent

URBANISME, PLANS-MASSES, COULEUR, EXPOSITIONS, FÊTES, PLASTIQUE APPLIQUÉE AUX OBJETS

Ils réclament

POUR L'HARMONIEUX DEVELOPPEMENT DE TOUTES LES ACTIVITÉS HUMAINES LA PRESENCE FONDAMENTALE DE LA PLASTIQUE

Architectes

Constructeurs

Plasticiens

Toute correspondance est reçue provisoirement 5, rue Bartholdi, Boulogne (Seine)

List of the 39 artists and architects who signed Le Groupe Espace's manifesto in October 1951

Architects: André Bruyére, Jean Fayeton, Jean George, Jean Ginsberg, Pierre Guéret, Gévrékian, Paul Herbé, Arne Jacobsen, John De Mailly, Richard J. Neutra, Alfred Roth, André Sive, Bernard-Henri Zehrfuss

Engineers: Lafaille, Le Ricolais, Jean Prouvé

Artists: Aagaard Andersen, Ole Baertling, Etienne Béöthy, André Bloc, Silviano Bozzolini, Burgoine-Diller, Felix Del Marle, Roger Desserprit, Jean Dewasne, Peiro Derazio, P. Etienne-Sarisson, Pierre Faucheux, A-R. Fleischman, Georges Folmer, Jean Grin, Robert Jacobsen, Berton Lardera, George L. Morris, Edgar Pillet, Nicolas Schöffer, Simone Servanes, Victor Vasarely, Nicolas Waarb

'The task of the architect is first and foremost to combine the aesthetic and the practical.'

– Arne Jacobsen (Hansen, 1959)

Architecture as an art form

In the old days, architecture was ranked alongside painting and sculpture as one of the fine arts; like the other two, architecture speaks directly to the eye and our aesthetic sense (Rasmussen, 1995). In ancient Rome and ancient Greece, the architect and artist (sculptor) had a close kinship with each other; often, they were even one and the same person. After the Renaissance in Europe, the two art forms gradually separated, with sculpture being delegated to ornamentation or later additions to architecture. The members of the Group Espace wanted to put an end to such separation.

Like art, architecture speaks to our senses and our physical perception of the world, but architecture also relates specifically and concretely to man's fundamenal need for space and boundaries. Like artists, architects have materials, textures and colours at their disposal. The architect creates a composition with surfaces, lines and colours. In his 1971 article *Concerning Sculpture and Architecture*, American artist and sculptor Art Brenner (1924–2013) argued for a better understanding of the connection between architecture and art and how the two mutually inform and nourish each other. Brenner's mission is similar to that of the Groupe Espace, but whereas the French avant-garde group wanted to break down the boundaries completely, Brenner suggested that the artist should be included as part of the construction process on par with the architects. Arne Jacobsen, who in many ways took an artistic approach to his own work, alternated between working with artists and doing the decorations for his buildings himself.

Brenner believed that by looking at architecture as works of sculpture in their own right, we may learn more about the harmony between architecture and art (Brenner, 1973). In keeping with Munch's description of the concept of total design, it may be helpful to look at the totality, scale and interaction between all the various elements, rather than to insist on distinct genres such as design, architecture and painting.

The programme presented by the Groupe Espace in the manifesto was an affirmation of what Arne Jacobsen had practiced himself – a close synergy between architecture and art, blurring the boundaries between the two. Even as a young man, Arne Jacobsen demonstrated his keen interest in artistic work that extended beyond the architect's usual metier.

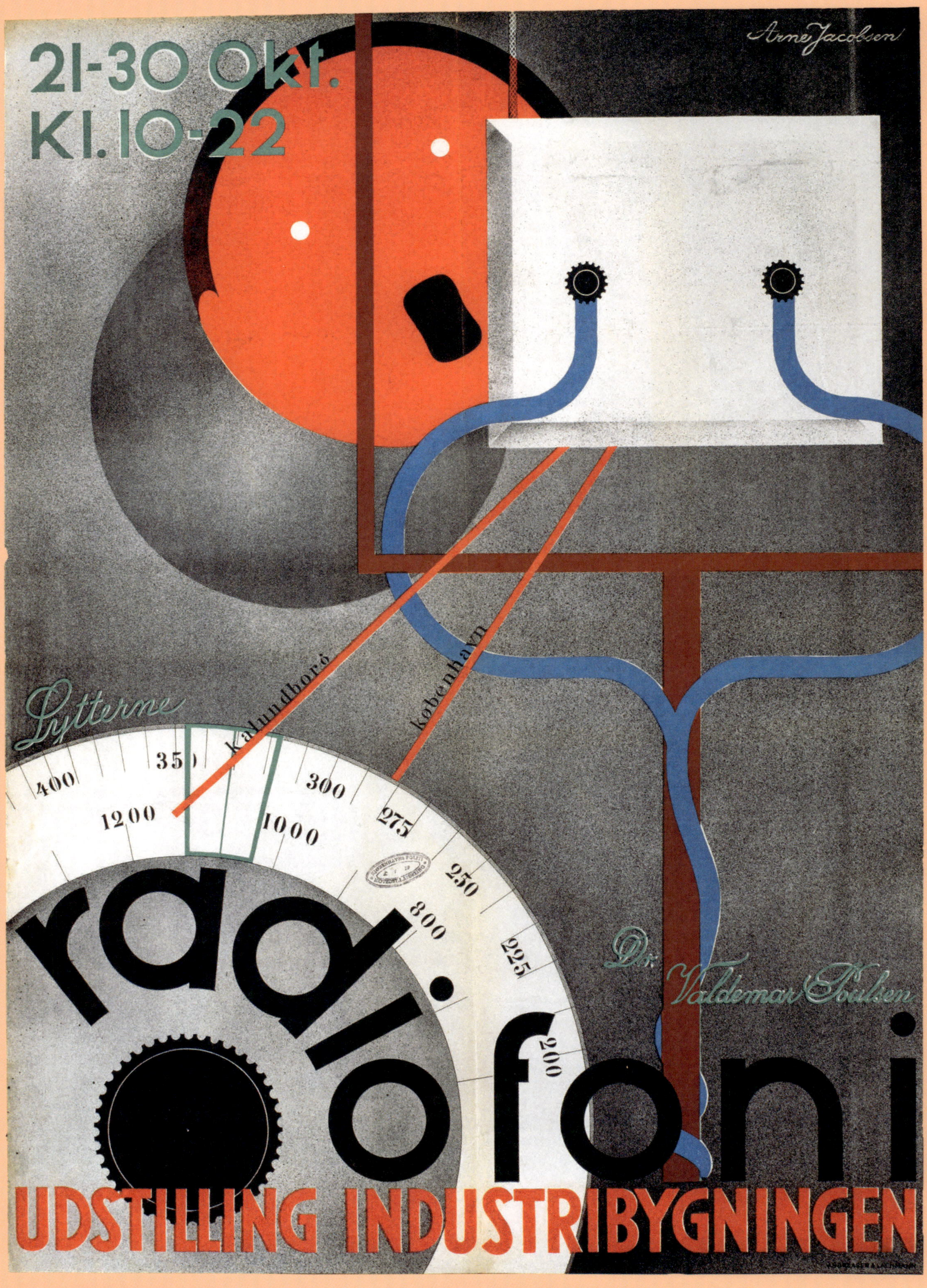
Arne Jacobsen
21-30 Okt.
Kl. 10-22
Lytterne
Kalundborg
København
400
350
300
275
250
225
200
1200
1000
800
Dr. Valdemar Poulsen
radiofoni
UDSTILLING INDUSTRIBYGNINGEN

Poster for the Radiofoni exhibition, 21-30 October 1932, designed by Arne Jacobsen

Photo: Pernille Klemp

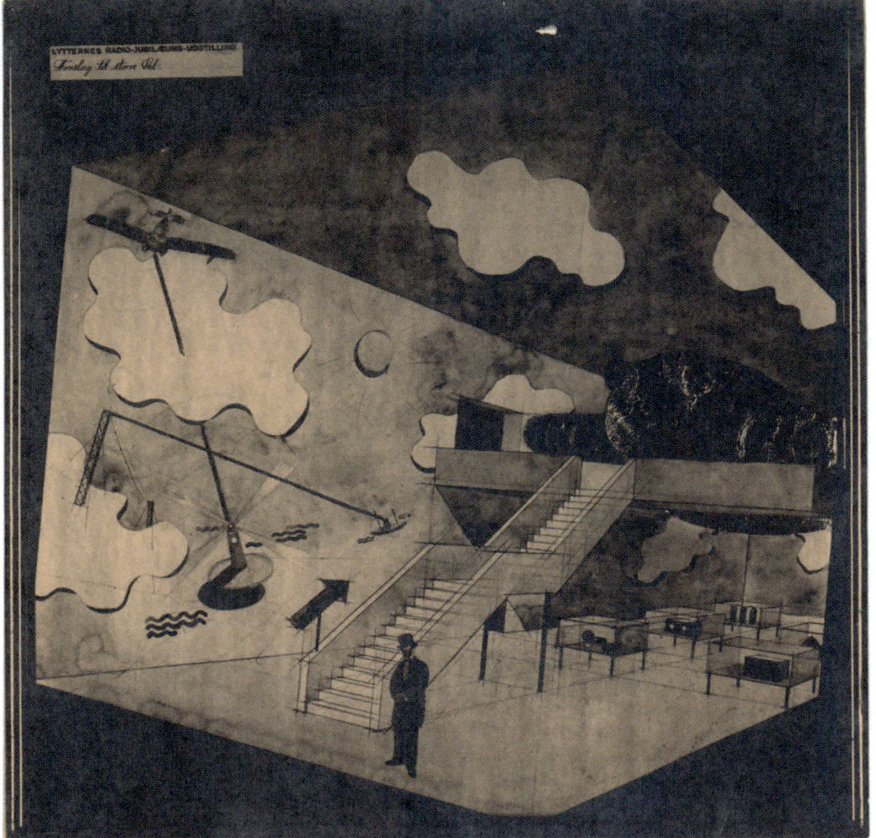

Arne Jacobsen's proposal for the design of the Radiofoni exhibition (1932)

Photo: The Royal Danish Library – Danish National Art Library

Arne Jacobsen at exhibitions

In his work as an exhibition architect and as an exhibiting artist, Arne Jacobsen gradually built a skill set and an authority that extended beyond architecture. On several occasions he presented a different side to his aesthetic, an ability to collaborate with visual artists and a gift for conducting independent work that extended beyond the formal qualities of architecture.

A successful example of such work appeared in 1932, at which point Arne Jacobsen worked as an architect on the Radiofoni exhibition in the Industrial Society of Copenhagen's Building in Vesterbrogade in Copenhagen. In addition to designing the extensive scenography of the exhibition, he also designed the exhibition poster, creating artwork that channelled the futuristic and technological spirit of the time.

A lesser-known collaboration took place in 1941, when Arne Jacobsen joined artist Anker Hoffmann in taking part in a design competition for a monument in memory of Vitus Bering. The partners won a bronze medal for their proposal (Hackney, 1972). Arne Jacobsen also distinguished himself as an exhibiting artist, and in late 1948 he took over the Danish Museum of Decorative Art (now Designmuseum Denmark) alongside sculptor Hugo Liisberg. Arne Jacobsen showed a large selection of textiles, and Hugo Liisberg exhibited new sculptures. Several reviews and articles praised the two artists for the quality of the exhibition, and Arne Jacobsen's already world-famous textiles were hailed as examples of successful, skilful craftsmanship, prompting predictions for a bright future ahead in Danish homes.[4] A review published on 27 November 1948 ends by stating that: 'This is art that could hold its own in any art museum in the world'.

These examples illustrate how Arne Jacobsen worked outside the traditional framework of architecture at an early stage of his career. The Radiofoni exhibition was in itself a total design in which scenography, colours and architecture formed the framework of a sensory experience for the more than 35,000 visitors. In the next section I will look more closely at Jacobsen's 'House of the Future' as an architectural sculpture or total design relating to the overall artistic aesthetic of the time.

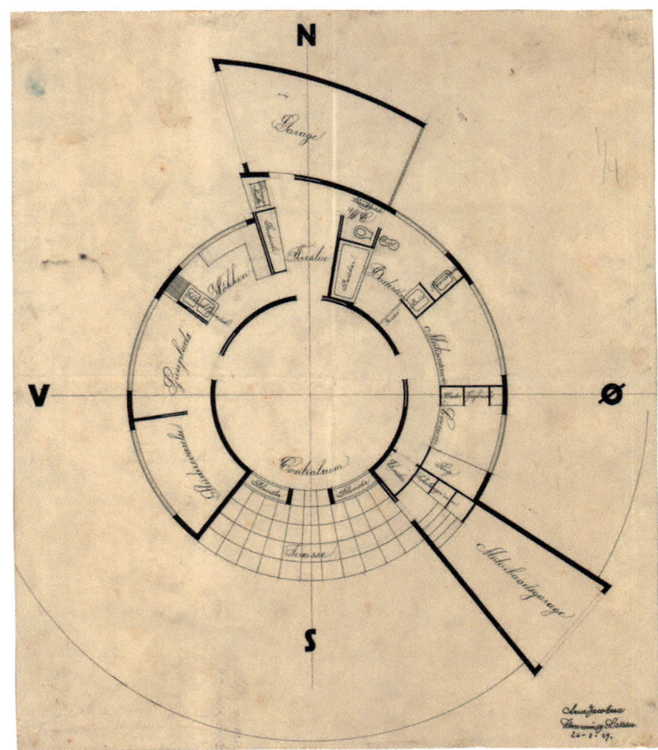

The sculptural architect of the future

Arne Jacobsen and Flemming Lassen's take on a house for the future, presented at the Danish Association of Architects' exhibition in 1929, ushered in a technical emancipation in Danish design (Thau and Vindum, 2002). The house won first prize in the competition for 'the ideal house'. It pointed to the role of the architect as more than just the creator of a blank canvas. As an architectural sculpture, the House of the Future distinguished itself by its unique interpretation of the circle as a basic form. The floor plan clearly shows how the house is constructed around a central circle surrounded by two concentric semicircles of different width and height. Ever since antiquity, the circle has held a special status among the basic forms. Throughout history, the circle has been a key figure in times of turmoil and revolution. For example, the circle was central to artists and architects in the years around and after World War I. These years saw the advent of the artistic movement known as 'Orphism', named by the French poet Guillaume Apollinaire. Orphism was an offshoot of Cubism, drawing inspiration from Fauvism in its search for pure abstraction executed in light, clear colours. Some of the most prominent artists of the Orphism movement were Fernand Léger (who later co-founded the Groupe Espace, which Arne Jacobsen joined) as well as Sonia and Robert Delaunay. The movement's artistic studies of geometric shifts had reverberations in the realm of architecture. The House of the Future was decorated with furniture of steel and glass, and the walls and ceilings were painted in bright primary colours. The dining room walls and ceiling were yellow, while the floor was red. With its vivid colours and staggered circles, the House of the Future looked almost like a three-dimensional Orphist painting. See for example Sonia Delaunay's *Prismes électriques* (1914) in The Centre Pompidou, Paris.

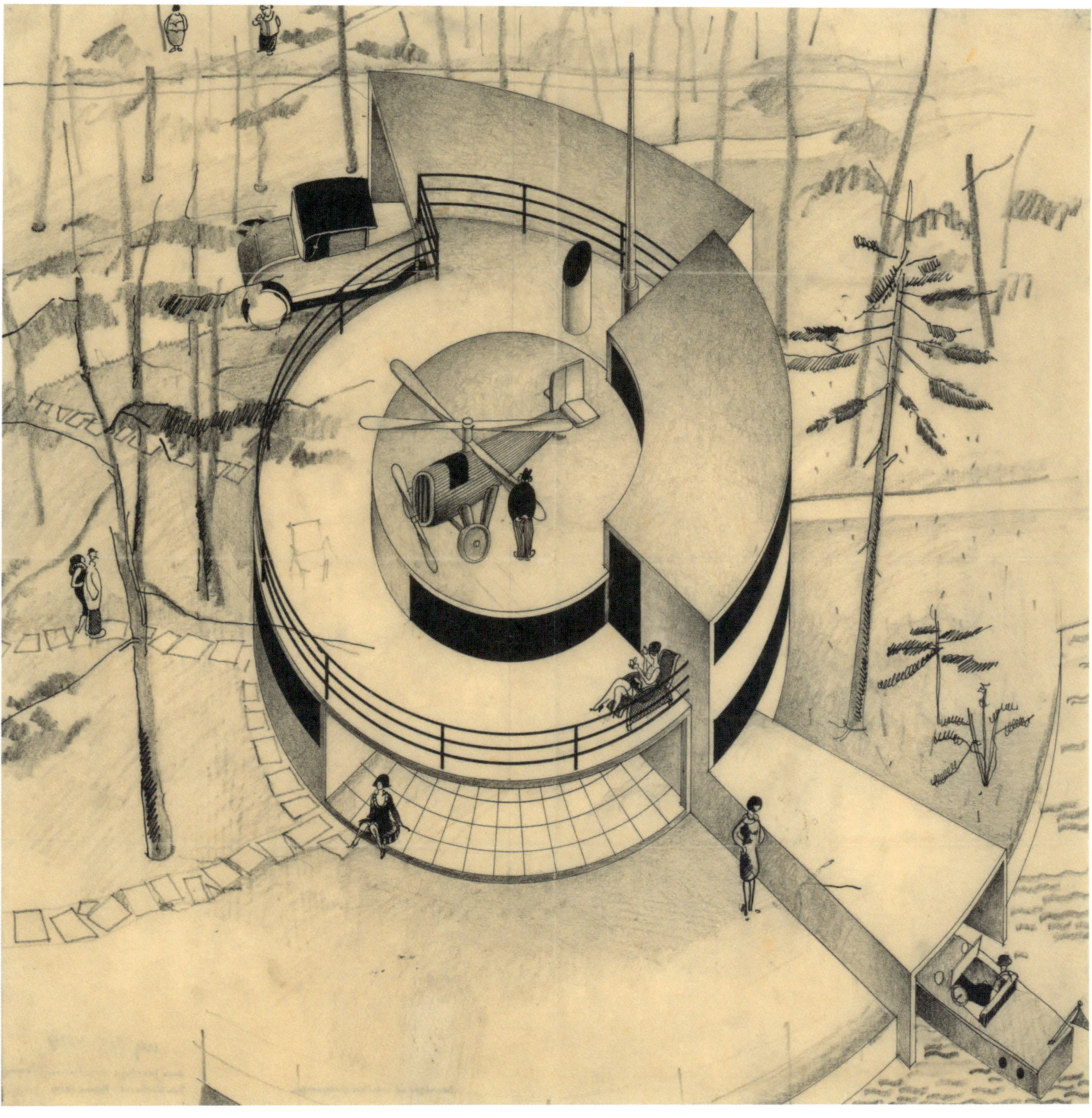

Arne Jacobsen and Flemming Lassen: two drawings of the House of the Future

Photo: The Royal Danish Library – The Danish National Art Library

Thorvald Hagedorn-Olsen mural
Human Society at Aarhus City Hall

Photo: Carsten Andreasen/
Ritzau Scanpix

The Aarhus City Hall and the trouble with the blue painting

One of Arne Jacobsen's most hotly debated buildings through the years was the Aarhus City Hall, designed in collaboration with fellow architect Erik Møller in 1939–42. All the more appropriate, then, that the Aarhus City Hall was also the subject of a much-discussed mural. The New Carlsberg Foundation pledged to fund the project and had appointed the artist Thorvald Hagedorn-Olsen before construction was even completed. In the 1930s, protests initially directed towards the building itself soon turned against Hagedorn-Olsen's monumental blue painting *Human Society* instead (Kayser, 2016). The citizen of Aarhus and the various reviewers did not consider the painting successful or in keeping with the times. Arne Jacobsen, who commented on the issue later, described the painting as 'unsuitable for its position' (Mentze, 1945). Instead, Jacobsen had wanted a light fresco painting that he believed would be a better fit for the architecture (Mentze, 1945).

Aarhus City Hall in itself became an example of Jacobsen's total design, but having no control over the artistic decoration he failed to achieve a complete symbiosis between its various elements. The disappointment at the art installed at the city hall became an important lesson for Arne Jacobsen, one which he did not wish to see repeated. In future projects, such as Rødovre City Hall, we see how he insisted on having the last word – including on the art commissioned to adorn the buildings.

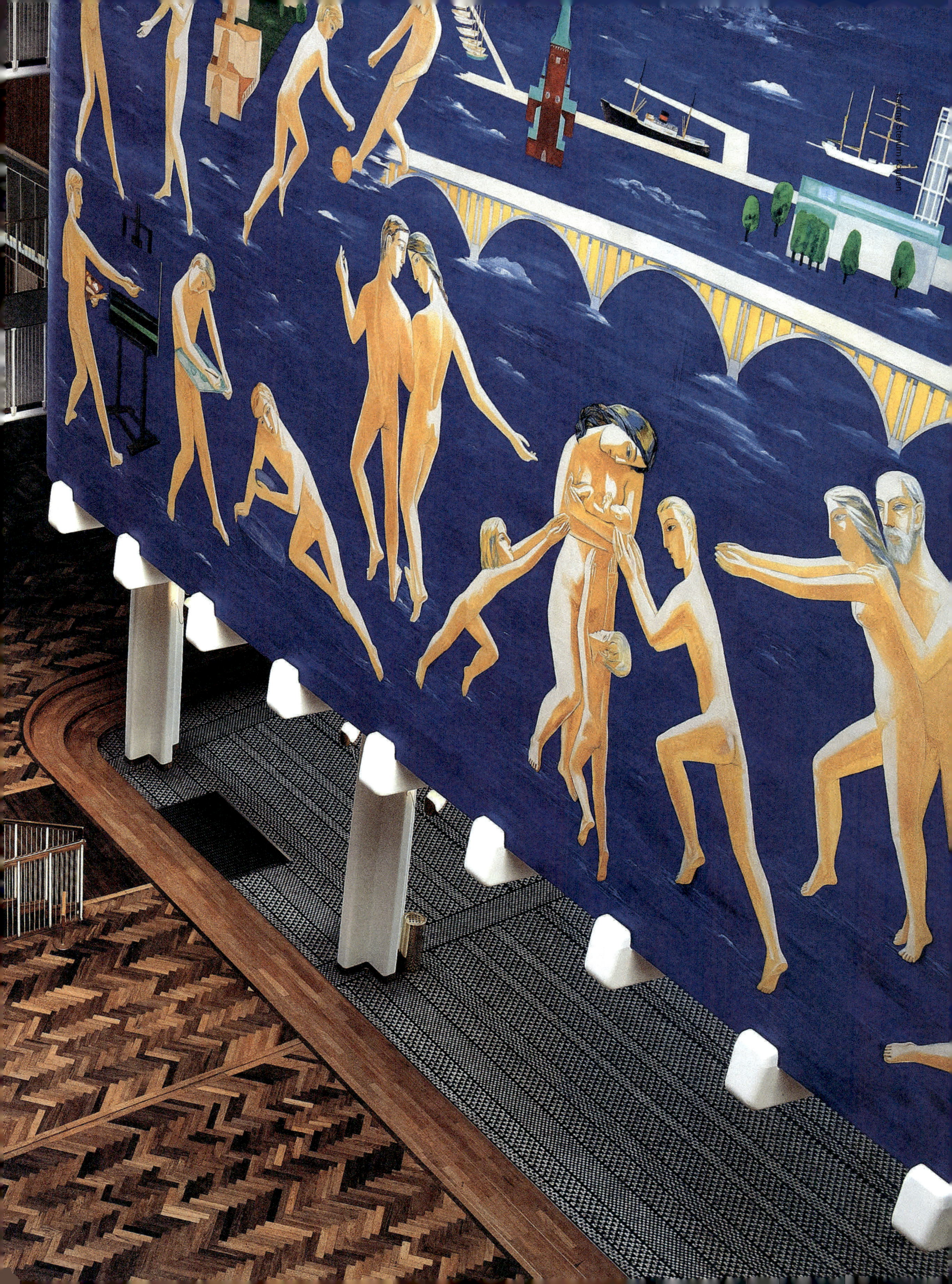

Katrine Stenum Poulsen

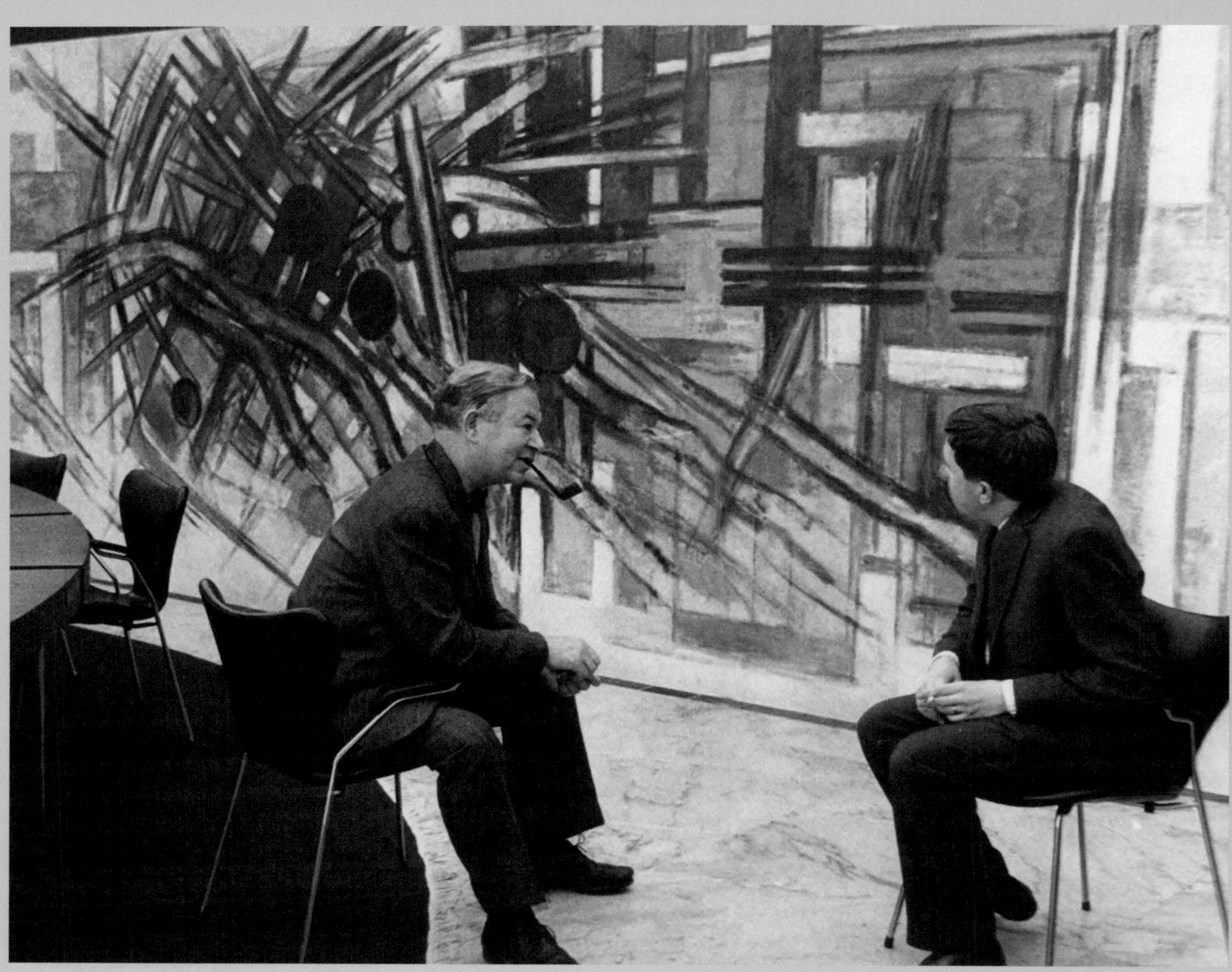

Arne Jacobsen in conversation with artist Preben Hornung in front of the painting at Rødovre City Hall

Photo: Lars Hansen/Scanpix Denmark

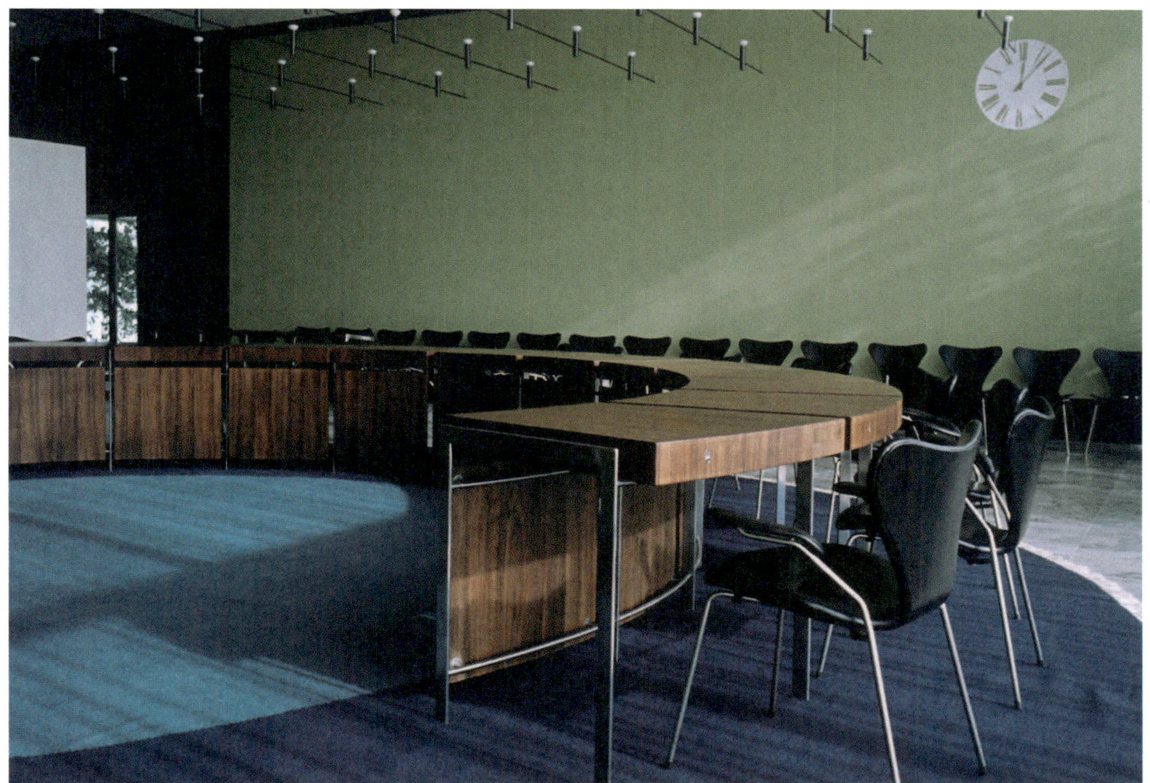

The Rødovre Town Hall council chamber at Rødovre town hall before Hornung's monumental painting was installed

Photo: Arne Jacobsen. The original can be found in: The Royal Danish Library - The Danish National Art Library

Rødovre City Hall and the picture in the middle of the room

On the subject of art integrated in buildings, Arne Jacobsen himself said: 'Yes, it can be an excellent thing if the art is good, but in order to yield natural results, it requires collaboration between the architect and artist from an early stage' (Jerrild, 1952).

When Arne Jacobsen was commissioned to design the new city hall for Rødovre (1954–56), he immediately began to plan the art to be featured in the city council's assembly room - and he had the Danish artist Preben Hornung in mind (Zibrandtsen, 1959; Hornung, 2018). The plan was to incorporate a monumental painting measuring 6 x 2.35 metres, a work that was intended as more than an appendix to the room. The painting was to form part of the architectural totality and serve to screen off the lavatories and wardrobes. Equally, it was to act as a contrast and backdrop to the arch-shaped arrangements of tables and chairs (Hornung, 2018). However, once a sketch for the painting had been drawn up, it was subjected to a good deal of municipal humming and hawing (Zibrandtsen, 1959). The proposal submitted by Preben Hornung went against the prevailing conservative approach to decorating city halls, which often involved a traditional tableau depicting the city's history and creation. Hornung's painting continued in the vein of his railway images of the mid-1950s, featuring an exploded motif that merges the aesthetics of nature and the human world. Arne Jacobsen ended up being an important voice advocating this modern and abstract art. One of the weighty arguments was that Hornung's painting actually symbolised the development of the Greater Copenhagen area (Hornung, 2018). The work was finally greenlighted on 27 May 1958 and ended up being paid for by Arne Jacobsen himself alongside Dansk Almennyttigt Boligselskab (the Danish Nonprofit Housing Association) and the Danish Arts Foundation. Hornung's distinctive painting contributed to the total design, extending the structure's overall affinity with the American curtain wall façade technique, the most advanced construction technique available at the time. The building and its art both embraced and celebrated the technological advances of the time.

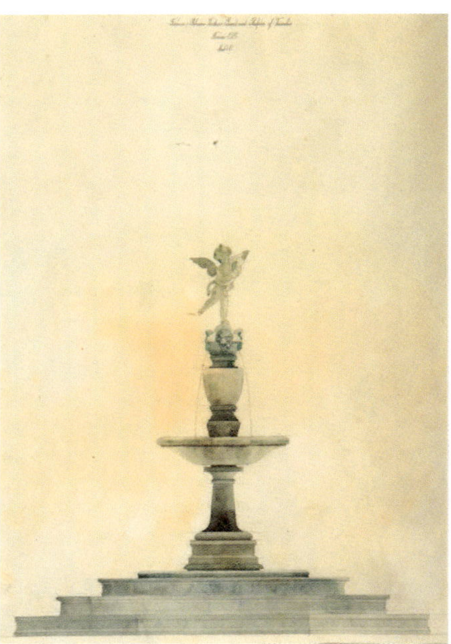

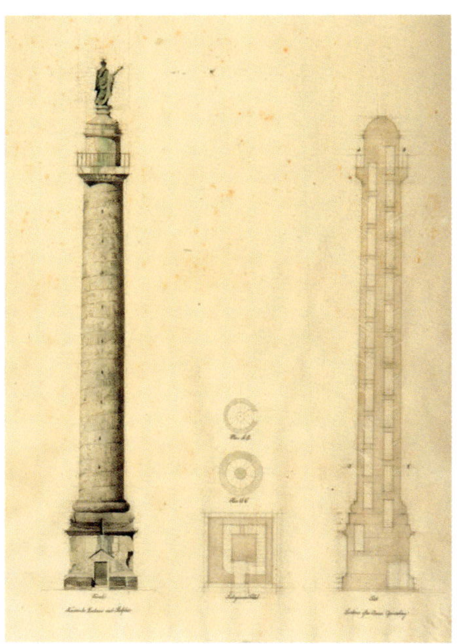

Studies from Italy. The fountain in the courtyard of the Palazzo Vecchio in 1925 and measurement of column

Photo: Private photo

The Munkegård School – sculptural edification

Beginning during his academy days, Arne Jacobsen continued to study the history of art and architecture. His lifelong interest in the subject is clearly evident in his many sketches and watercolours from journeys, where his fascination with ancient buildings and monuments is particularly noticeable. In an interview with the Danish newspaper *Politiken* in 1971, he himself said: 'The main thing is proportion. The proportioning is what gives ancient Greek temples their classic beauty'.

Arne Jacobsen's classical education within the realms of architecture and art was shored up by Kaj Gottlob's 'temple class' at the academy and by study trips to Italy, where he drew and studied ancient architecture and art. This would be the cornerstone of Arne Jacobsen's historic education, and in the late 1940s he was given the opportunity to pass on the legacy. In 1949, the Municipality of Gentofte was planning a new primary school intended to accommodate 850 pupils. The core idea was to create a large school with the intimate atmosphere of a small school (Gentofte, 2013). The Munkegård School comprised 24 classrooms arranged in pairs sharing a common courtyard. Joined by the school's two-storey main building and a series of rooms devoted to specialist subjects, the various spaces were arranged in a grid system. Large windows and south-facing courtyards ensured an even distribution of light in the classrooms, and sixteen courtyards were established between them. Each courtyard had its own distinctive feel with individual paving and planting. In addition, Arne Jacobsen had been allocated a set amount for artistic decoration of the school, and he was free to spend that money as he wished (*Politiken*, 1955). He used the funds to commission artificial stone casts of some of the important sculptures of art history. Each courtyard was given one or two sculptures, which included copies of a Head of Apollo from approx. 450 BC, a bust of Caesar, and a relief of a ship from the Borobudur Temple, Java, Indonesia, circa 750-800 CE.

The choice of classical and ancient examples of sculpture was in line with what Arne Jacobsen himself had studied over the years. This was how he himself got started, making such sculptures an excellent fit for a school – a place where the seeds of art appreciation are sown. Arne Jacobsen strove for full authority and control, not only as regarded his architecture and interiors, but also in terms of artistic decoration. Arne Jacobsen was the architect, artist and curator of this project. As such, he had the final word, not only on what was aesthetically appropriate, but also on what would be most relevant and educational to the students.

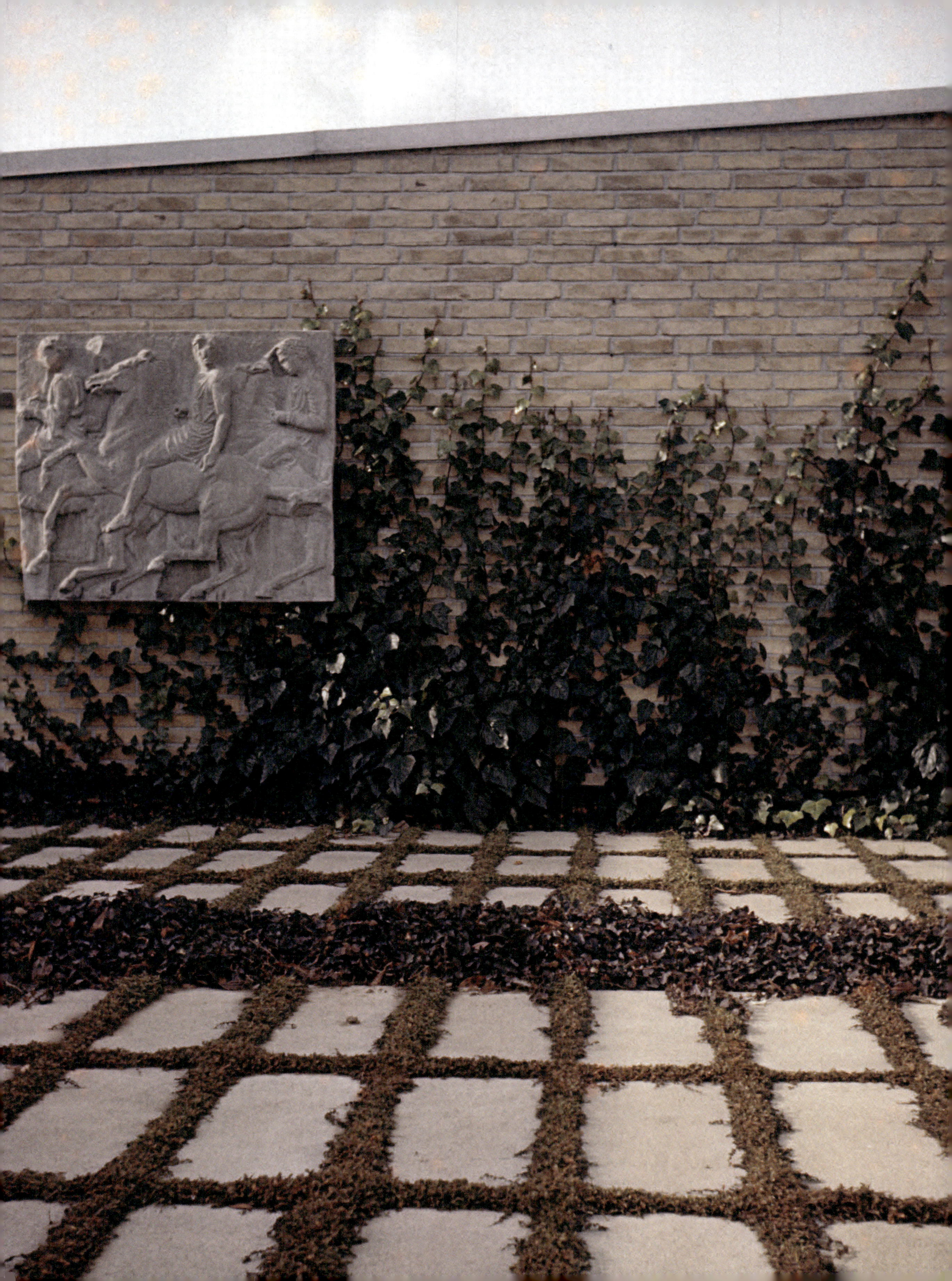

Previous page: One of the courtyards at The Munkegård School

Photo: Arne Jacobsen. The original can be found in: The Royal Danish Library – The Danish National Art Library

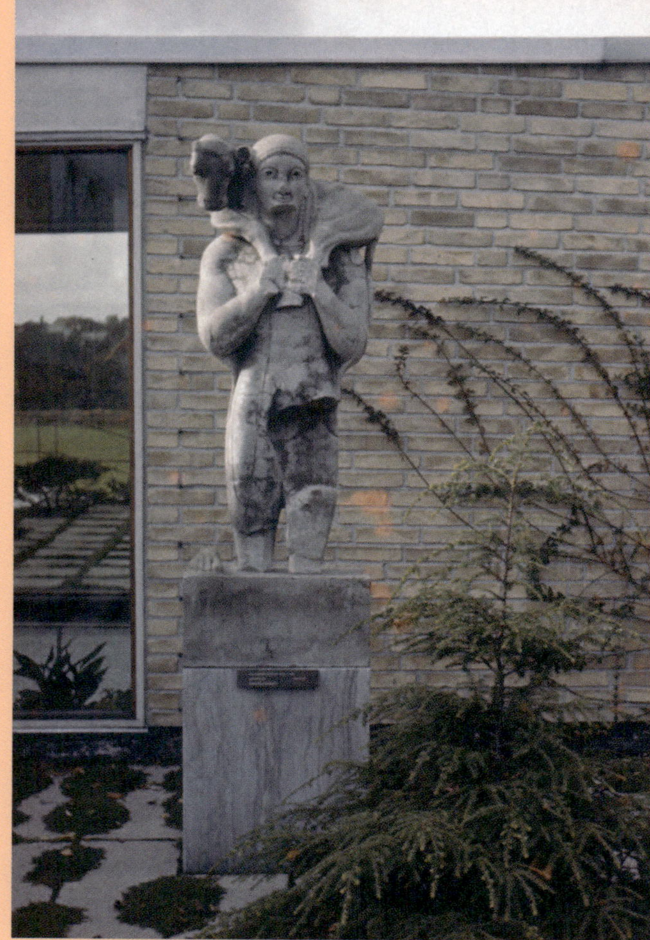

One of the courtyards at The Munkegård School

Photo: Arne Jacobsen. The original can be found in: The Royal Danish Library – The Danish National Art Library

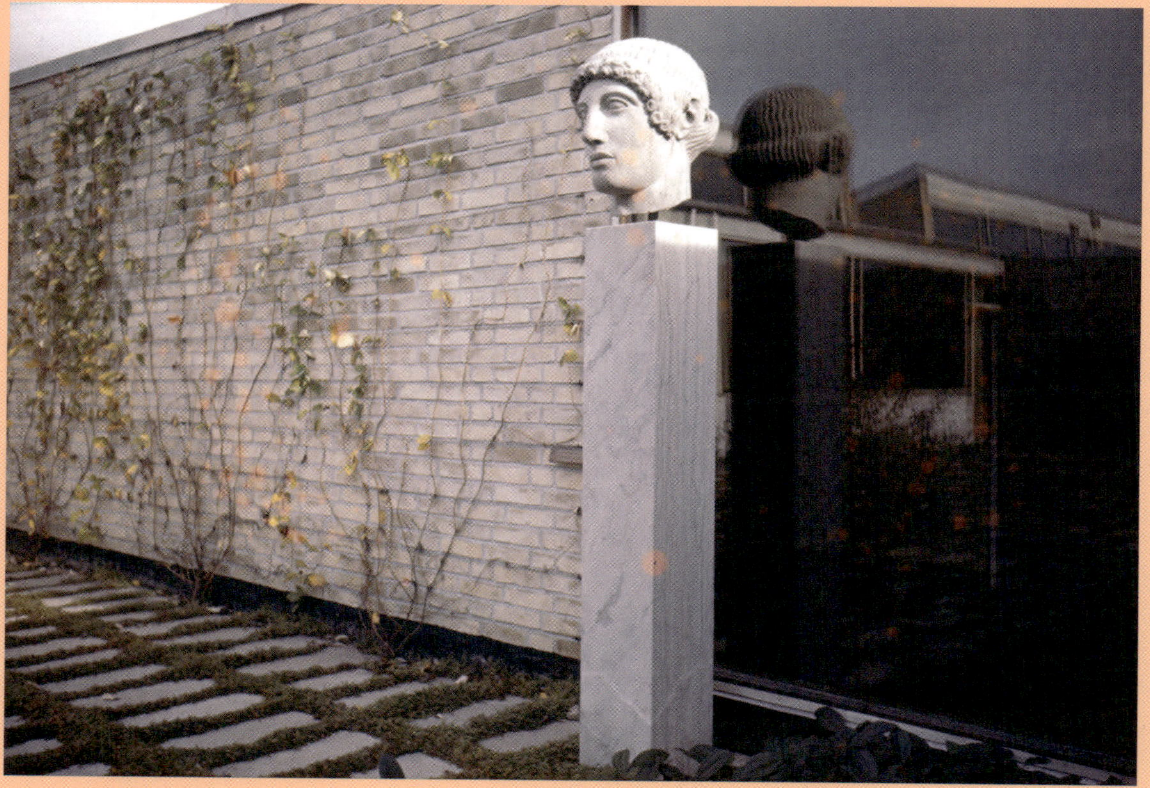

One of the courtyards at The Munkegård School

Photo: Arne Jacobsen. The original can be found in: The Royal Danish Library – The Danish National Art Library

A life-long engagement with art

This article opened with a quote by Le Corbusier: 'Architecture and the plastic arts are not just two things that are juxtaposed, they are a solid and coherent whole'. Arne Jacobsen, who regarded Le Corbusier as a great source of inspiration, leaned towards similar sentiments when he stated that architecture was largely 'bound by the material, function and environment' (Hansen, 1959) or that 'if architecture had nothing to do with art, then it would be astonishingly easy to build houses' (Ninka, 1971). In this article I have presented examples of Arne Jacobsen's involvement in the world of art, his collaboration with artists and his work on achieving synergy between architecture and art. When the results were not satisfactory, as in the case of the Aarhus City Hall, he lamented this fact. If his vision met opposition, as was the case with Preben Hornung and the Rødovre City Hall, he got involved in the political decision and even went so far as to finance part of the project himself. The way Arne Jacobsen saw it, art was not simply an addition to architecture; it was an important part of the overall work – a crucial piece in the puzzle of his total design. By signing Le Corbusier's manifesto in 1951, he underlined his convictions most emphatically. Despite his lack of ability or willingness to speak publicly about the role of art in architecture, the work speaks for itself. Today we once again debate the role of art in public spaces and in new public buildings such as schools, universities, courts and hospitals. In this context, Arne Jacobsen's sense of the interaction between architecture and art offers very relevant input in a debate that is often tinged by arguments about economics and quantity.

Endnotes

1. A list of the 39 signatures of the Groupe Espace manifesto, October 1951.

2. Architects: André Bruyére, Jean Fayeton, Jean George, Jean Ginsberg, Pierre Guéret, Gévrékian, Paul Herbé, Arne Jacobsen, John De Mailly, Richard J. Neutra, Alfred Roth, André Sive, Bernard-Henri Zehrfuss.

   Engineers Lafaille, Le Ricolais, Jean Prouvé

   Artists: Aagaard Andersen, Ole Baertling, Etienne Béöthy, André Bloc, Silviano Bozzolini, Burgoine-Diller, Felix Del Marle, Roger Desserprit, Jean Dewasne, Peiro Derazio, P. Etienne-Sarisson, Pierre Faucheux, A-R. Fleischman, Georges Folmer, Jean Grin, Robert Jacobsen, Berton Lardera, George L. Morris, Edgar Pillet, Nicolas Schöffer, Simone Servanes, Victor Vasarely, Nicolas Waarb.

3. Upon Arne Jacobsen's death his art collection was passed down to his family, who have graciously allowed me to view and register the collection in connection with this article.

4. A review found in an unidentified newspaper clipping from the archives of the furniture manufacturer Fritz Hansen, which collected material about Arne Jacobsen for many years, forming extensive scrap books.

Bibliography

Brenner, A. (1971). Concerning Sculpture and Architecture. *Leonardo* 4(2)

Corbusier, L. (1923). *Towards a New Architecture*. New York: Dover Publications

Kayser. J. (2016). Det store ikon, der blev en del af Aarhus' DNA. *Jyllands Posten*, 27. juni 2016. Lokaliseret på www.jyllands-posten.dk/aarhus/ECE8801035/det-store-ikon-for-byen/

Dijkema, J. (2018). How Art Enhances Architecture. *Chapman Taylor Retail Insights*. Chapman Taylor, pp. 1-12

Dossin, C. (2019). *France and the Visual Arts since 1945: Remapping European Postwar and Contemporary Art*. New York: Bloomsbury Visual Arts, Bloomsbury Publishing Inc.

Gentofte Kommune (2013). *Munkegårdskolen – Arkitekt prof. Arne Jacobsen et al. Vangedevej 178 – Municipal school restored and revitalized*. Gentofte Kommune

Groupe Espace (1951). Manifeste du Groupe Espace. *L'Architecture d'Aujourd'hui* (37)

Hackney, R. (1972). Arne Jacobsen: Architecture and Fine Art. *Leonardo* 5(4)

Hansen, V. (1959). Tænk paa en lagkage og skær saa et stykke ud - Samtale med Professor Arne Jacobsen, hvis navn der fornylig stod blæst om i England i anledning af, at han skal bygge et nyt kollegium i Oxford. *Dagens Nyheder*, 19. april 1959

Hornung, P.M. (2018). *Preben Hornung*. København: Lindhardt og Ringhof

Jerrild, H. (1952). Vilde først være Maler - men blev Arkitekt - !. *Børsen*, 10. februar 1952

Mentze, E. (1945). I: *Berlingske Tidende*. 5. december 1945. (Arne Jacobsens Scrapbøger)

Munch, A. V. (2009). Architecture as Multimedia. Jean Nouvel, the DR Concert Hall, and the Gesamtkunstwerk. I: *The Nordic Journal of Aesthetics* 20(36-37.), 81–101

Munch, A. V. (2012). *Design as Gesamtkunstwerk*. København: Rhodos

Munch, A. V. (2006). Historien bag historierne om moderne arkitektur. I: *Nordic Journal of Architectural Research* 19(1)

Ninka (1971). Det nye kritiseres altid – Interview med Arne Jacobsen. *Politiken* 28. februar 1971.Genoptrykt i Tøjner, P.E. & Vindum, K. (1996). *Arne Jacobsen: Architect & designer*. København: Dansk Design Center

Politiken (1955). 16 haver midt i skolebygning. *Politiken*, 23. november 1955 (Arne Jacobsens Scrapbøger)

Rasmussen, S.E. (1995). *Om at Opleve Arkitektur*. Aarhus: Fonden Til Udgivelse Af Arkitekturværker, Arkitektskolen i Aarhus

Roy, E. (2013). *La présence fondamentale de la plastique - L'exposition du Groupe Espace à Biot en 1954: un essai de synthèse des arts*. Biot: Le Museé Fernand Léger

Thau, C. & Vindum, K. (1998). *Arne Jacobsen*. København: Arkitektens Forlag

Thau, C. & Vindum, K. (2002). Af en helt anden verden. Jacobsen og idéen om gesamtkunstværket. In: Holm, M.J., Kjeldsen, K. & Vinfeld, T. (Red.). *Arne Jacobsen. Absolut Moderne*. Louisiana Revy 43, p. 20-43

Tøjner, P.E. & Vindum, K. (1994). *Arne Jacobsen: Architect & designer*. København: Dansk Design Center

Zibrandtsen, J. (1959). Billedet midt i rummet. *Berlingske Tidende*, 30. april 1959

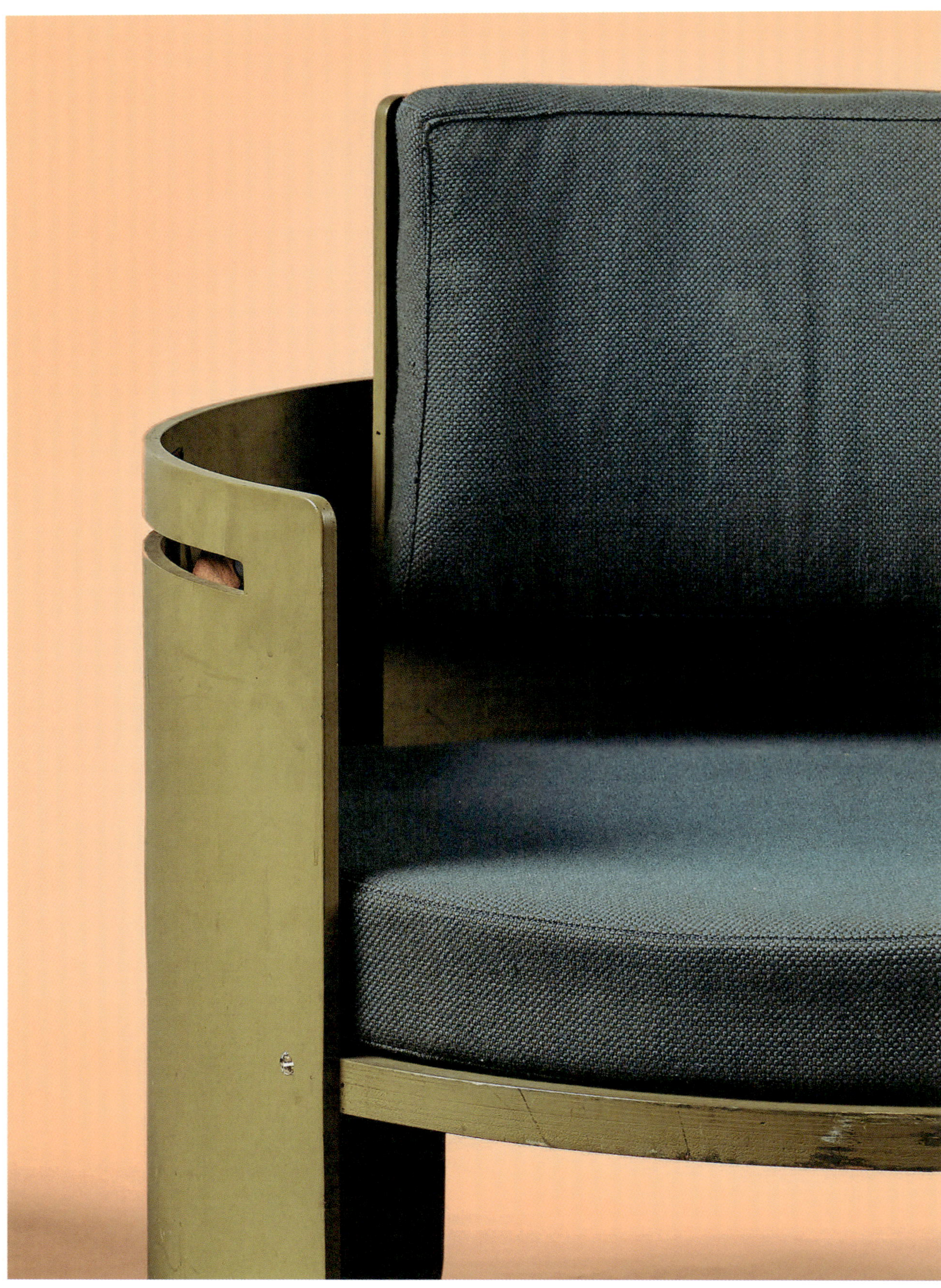

Prototype (1960s)

Trapholt Collection

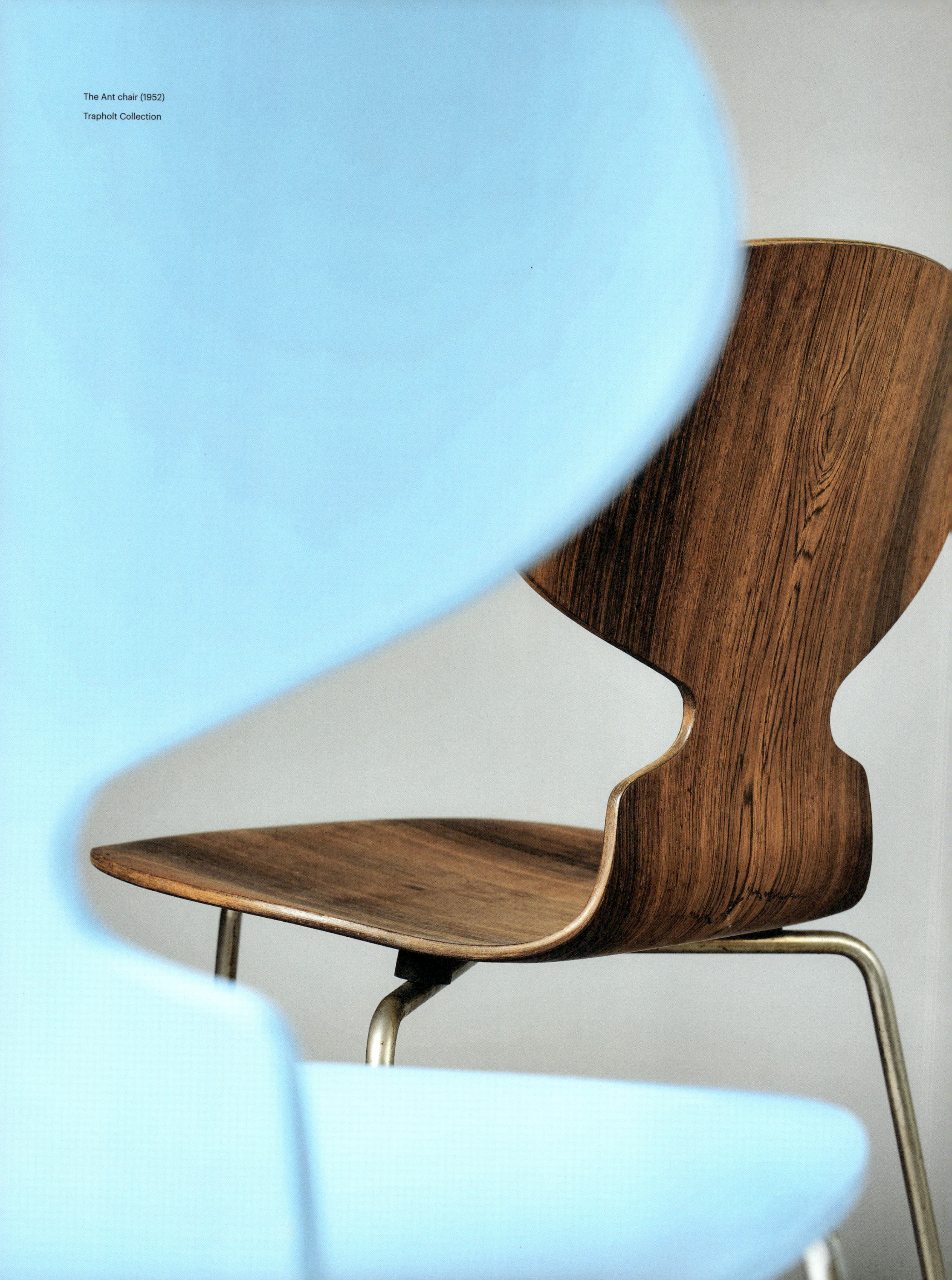

The Ant chair (1952)

Trapholt Collection

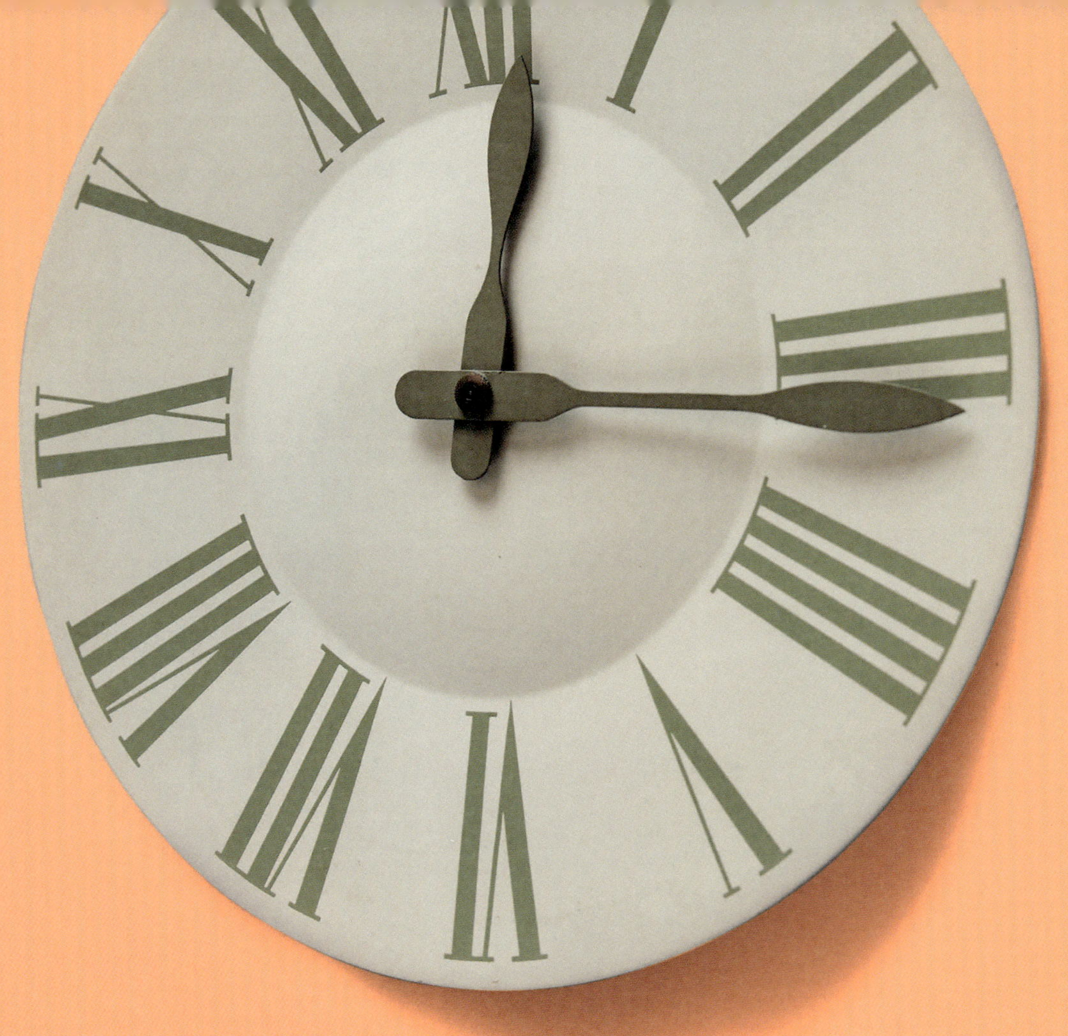

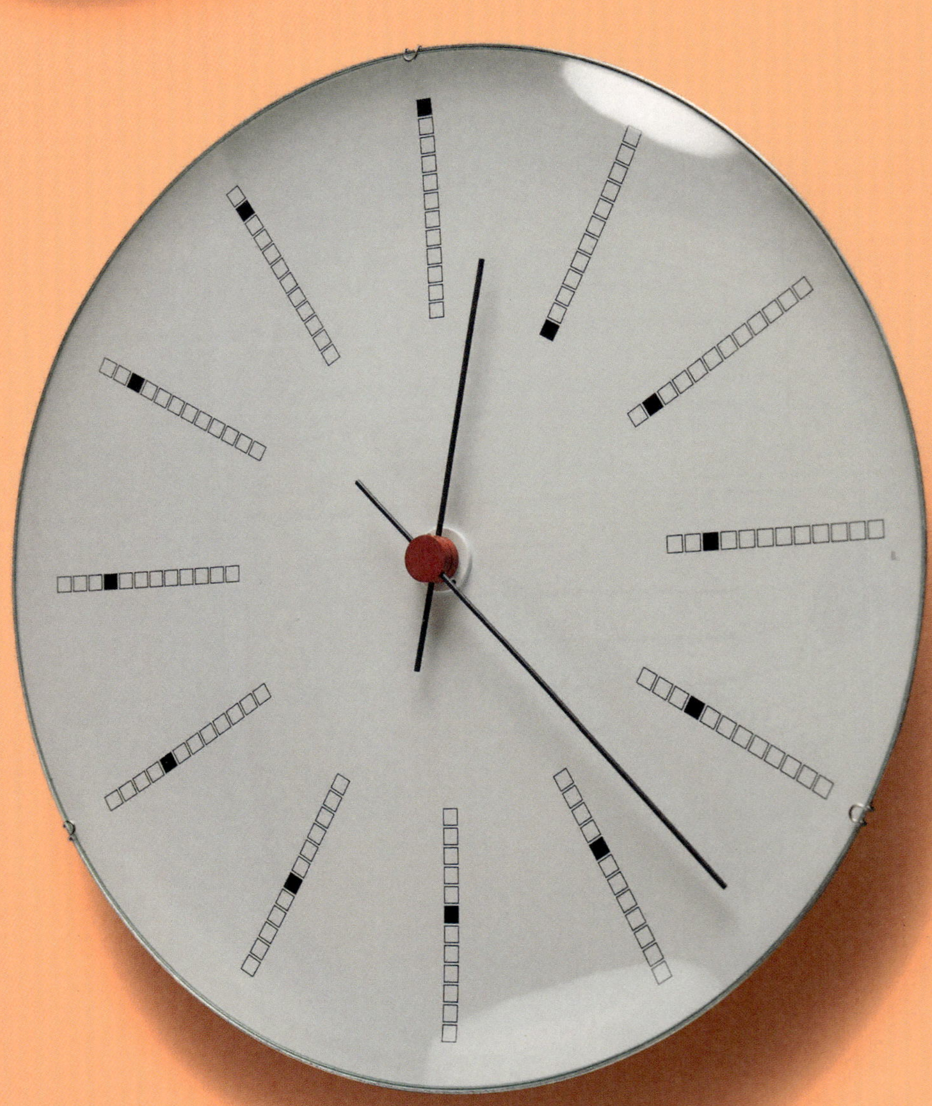

Clocks by Arne Jacobsen: Roman (1946), City Hall (1955), Bankers (1970) and Station (1939)

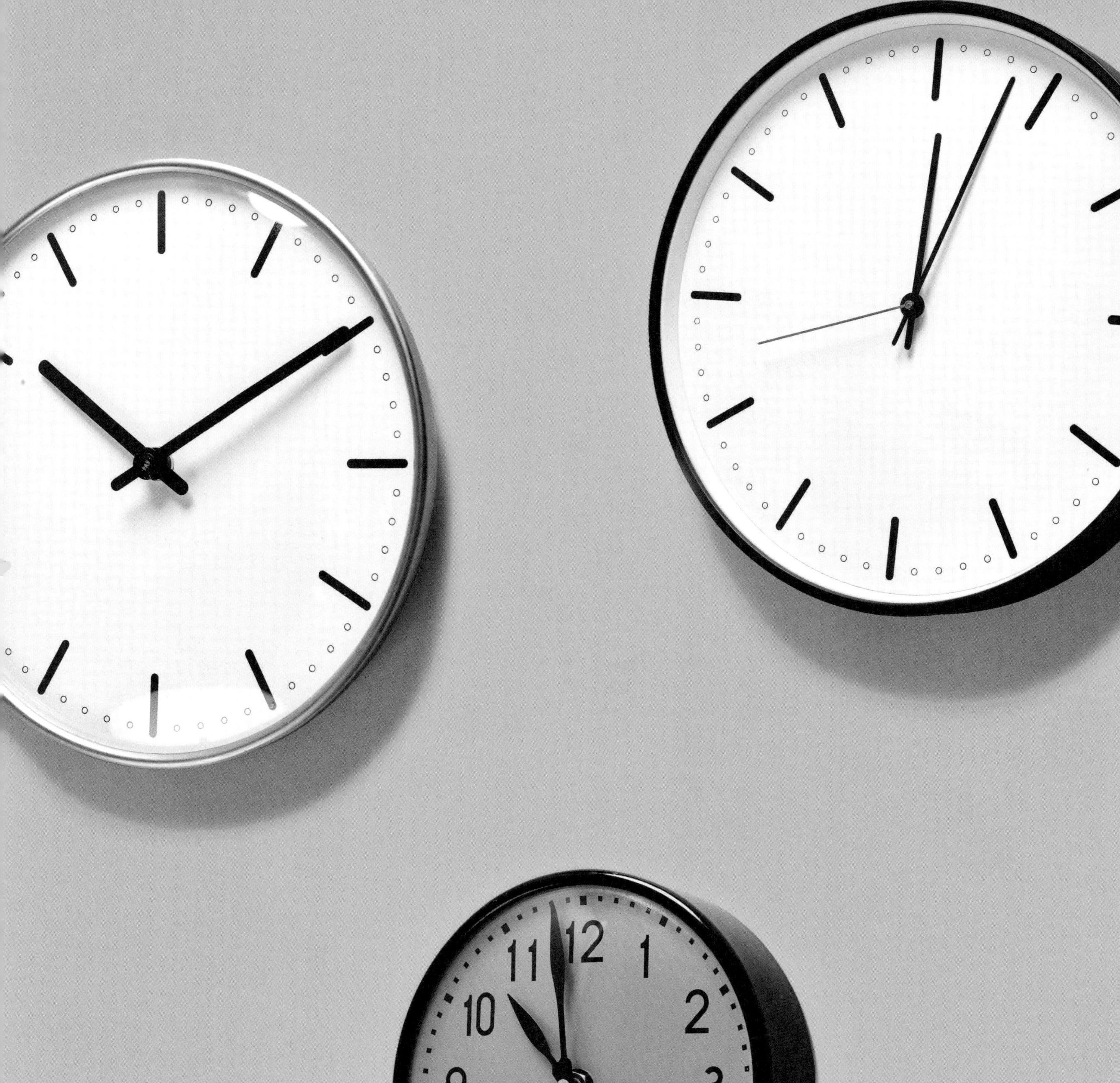
12 1 2 3 4 5 6 7 8 9 10 11

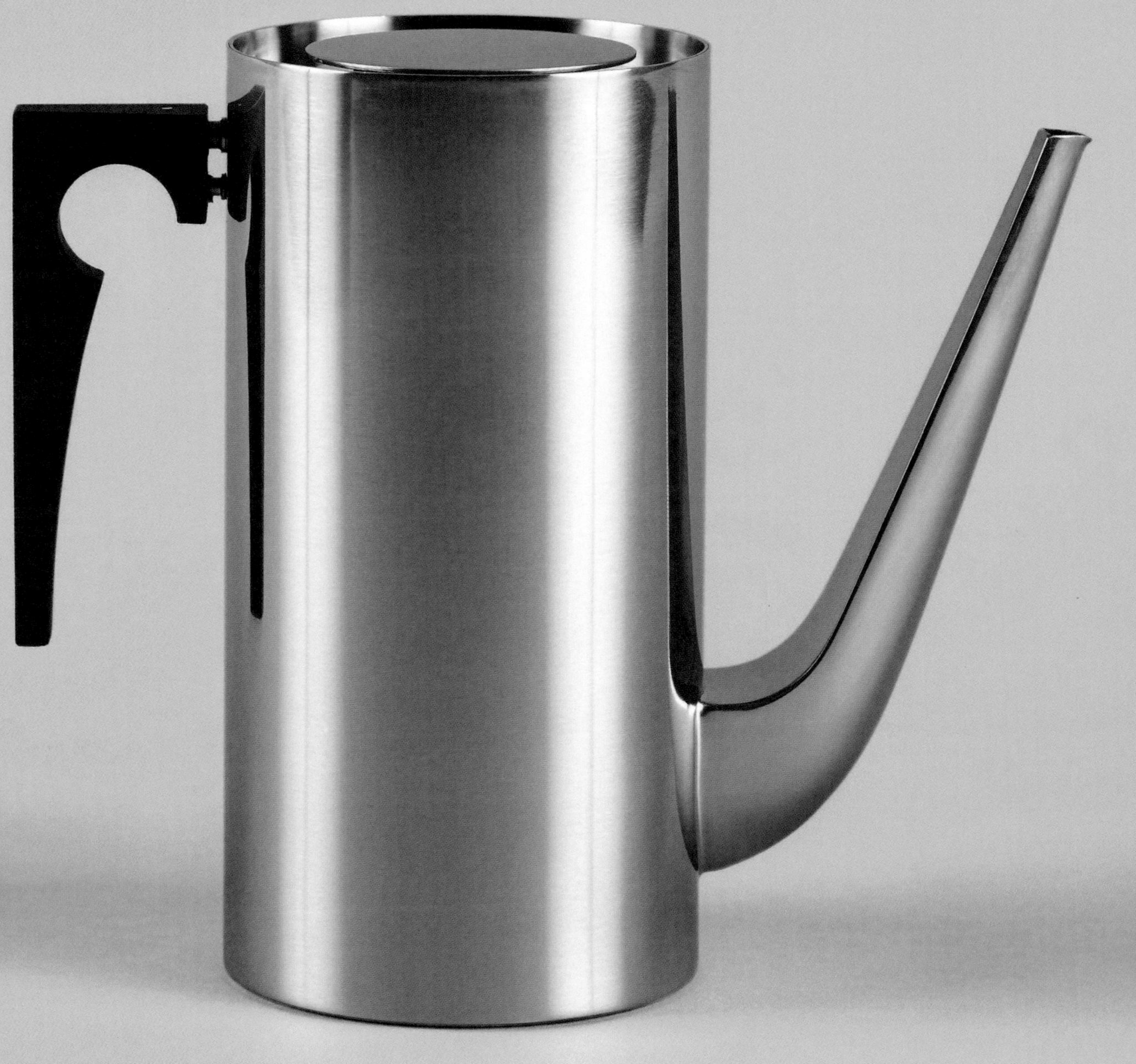

Cylinda Line coffee pot (1967)

Trapholt Collection

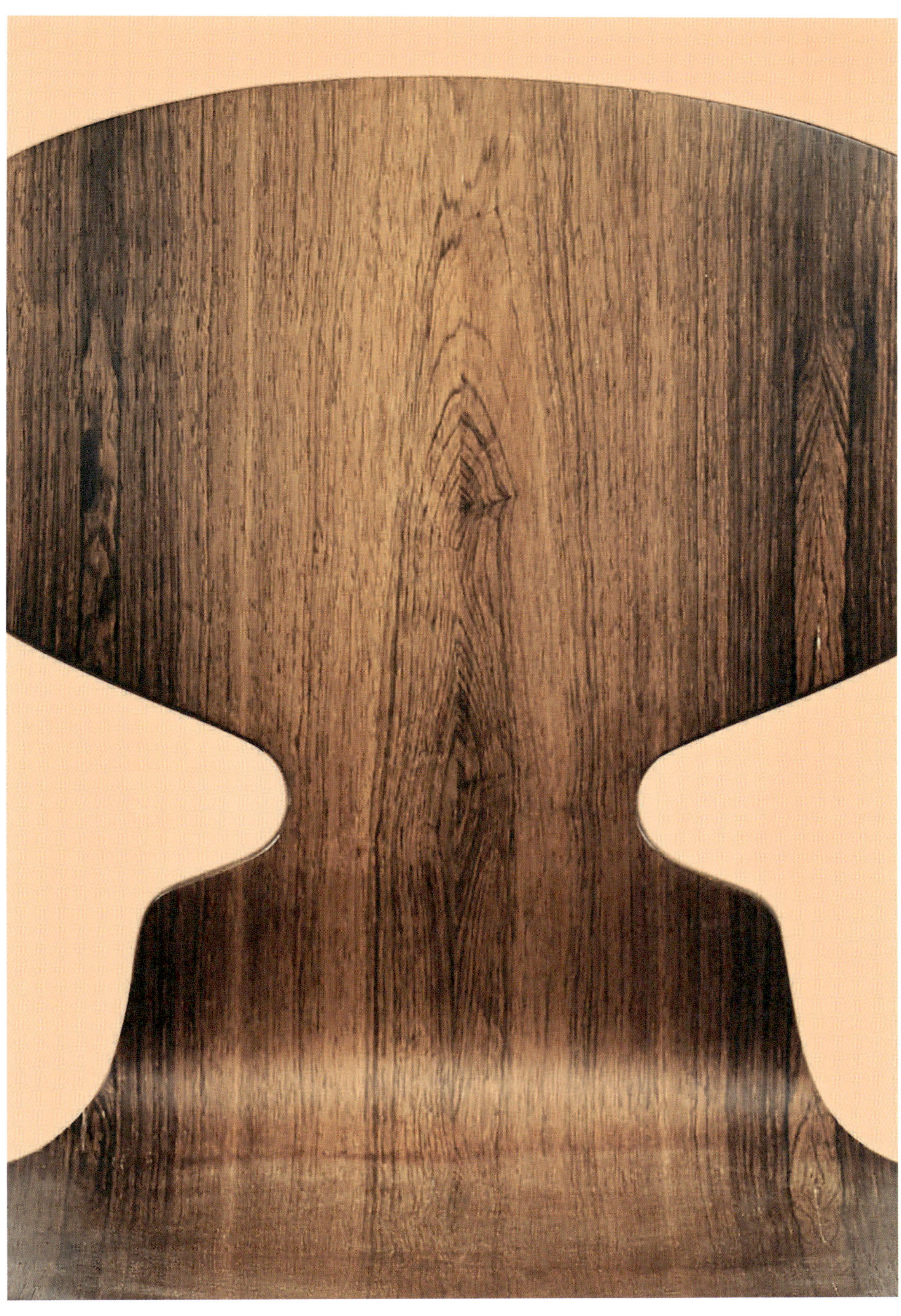

The Ant chair (1952)

Trapholt Collection

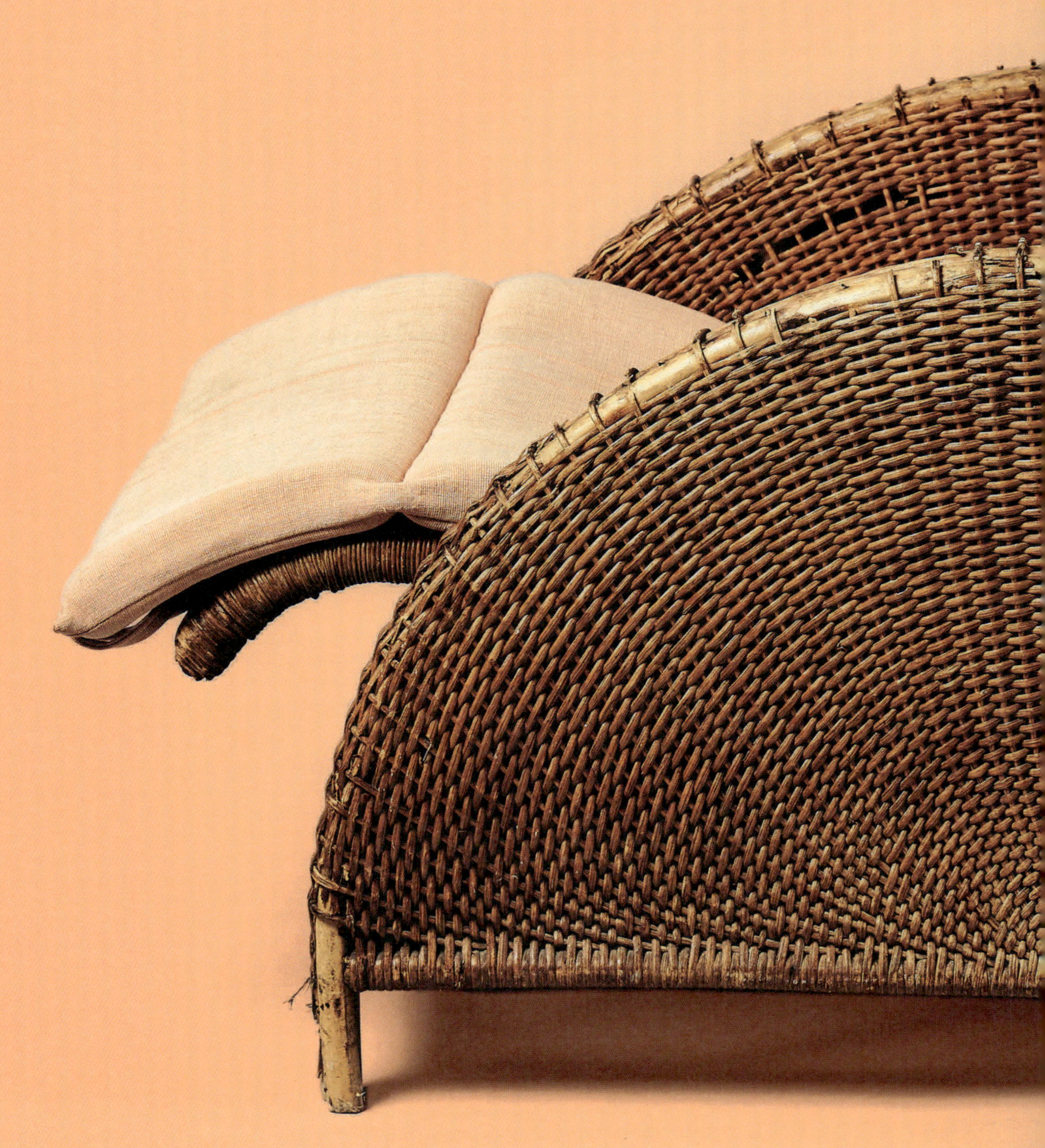

Forest Snail chair

Trapholt Collection

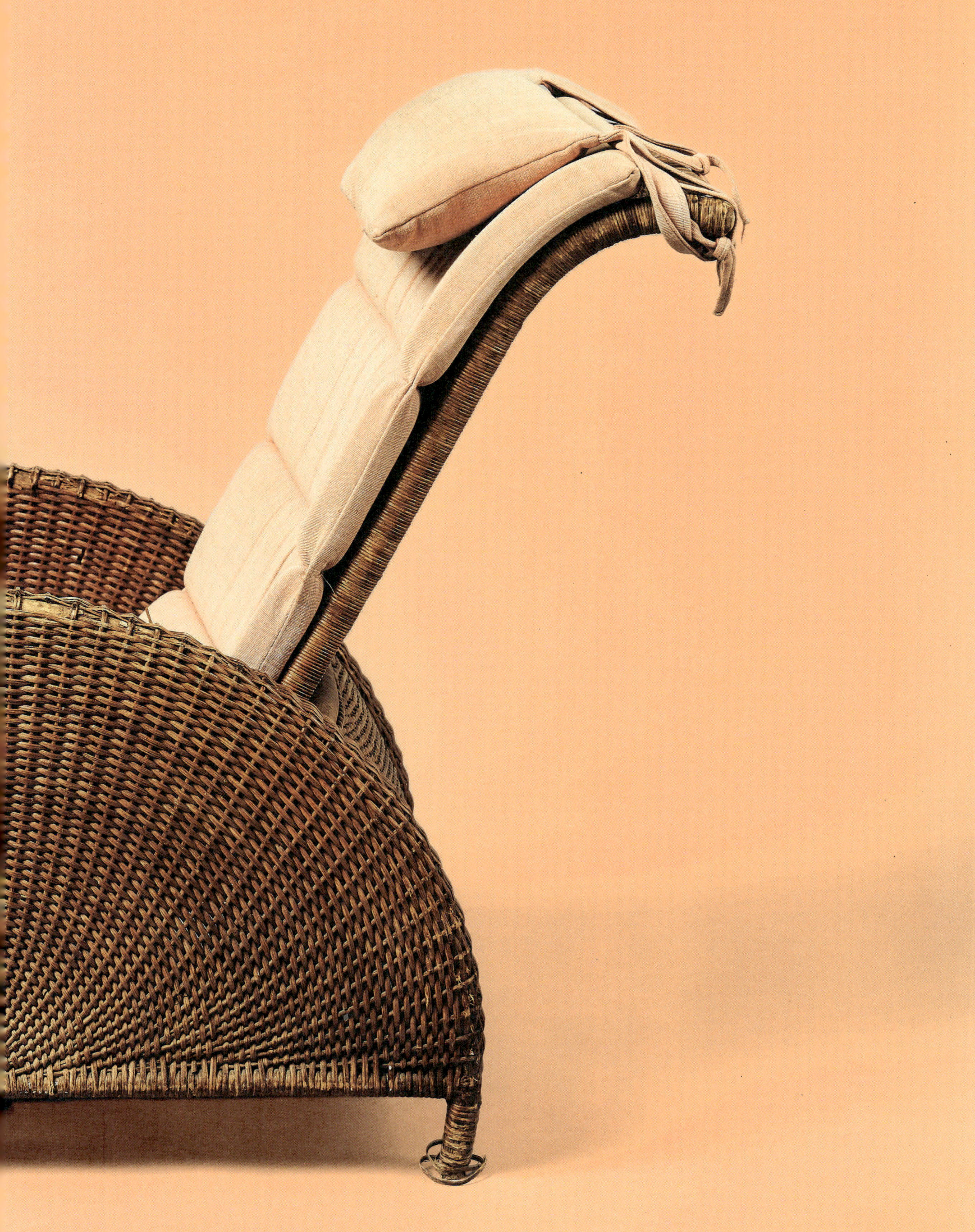

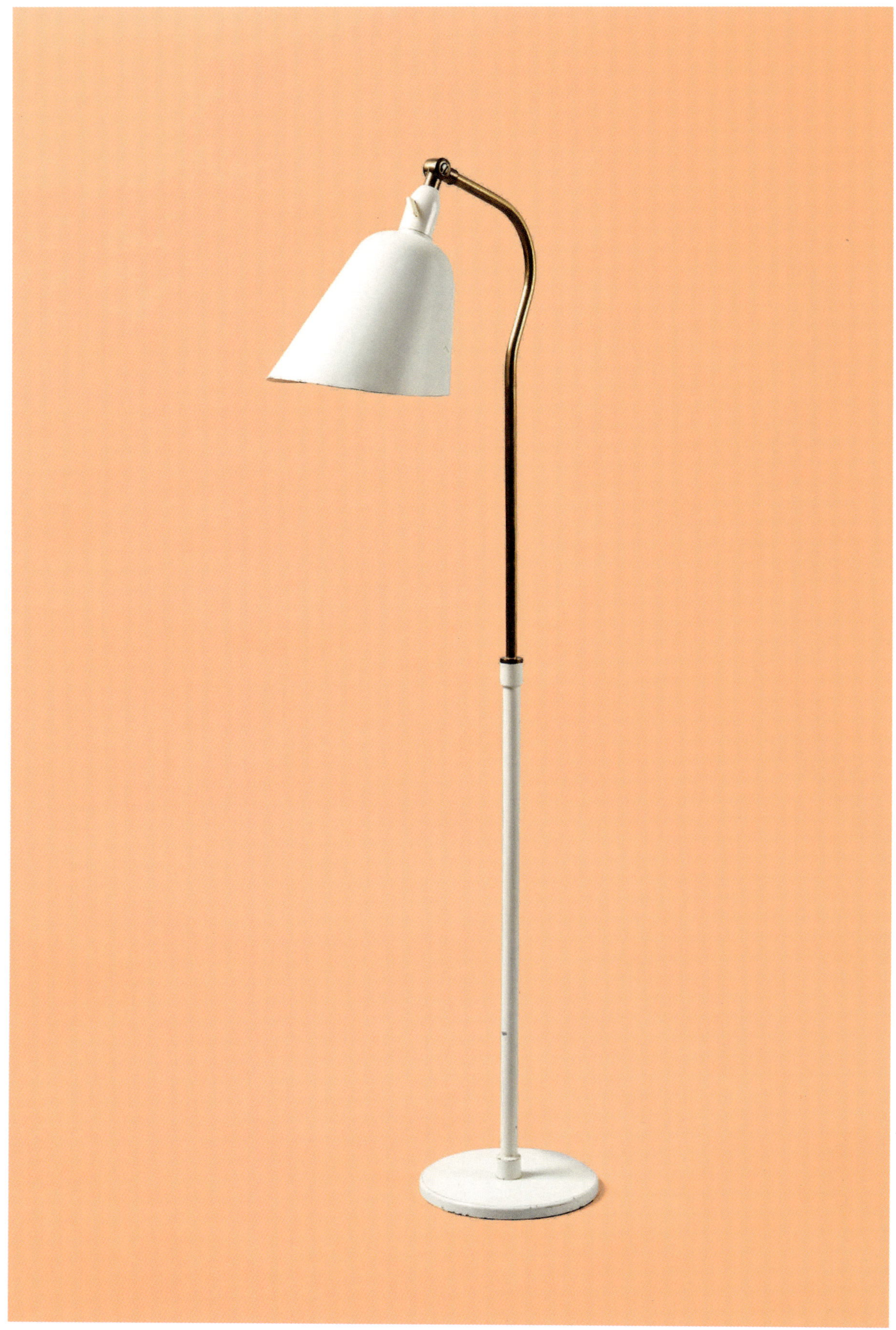

The AJ reading lamp

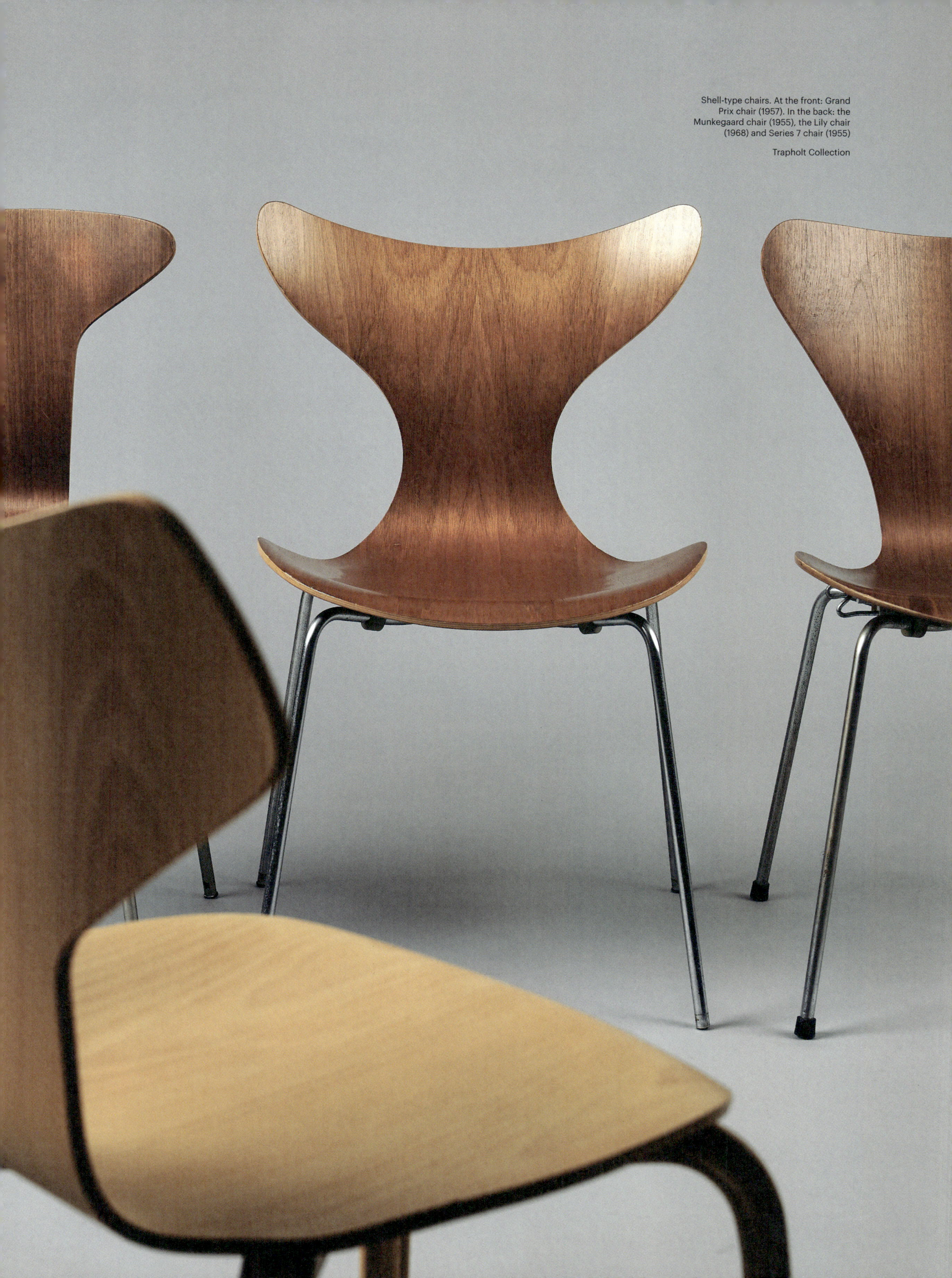

Shell-type chairs. At the front: Grand Prix chair (1957). In the back: the Munkegaard chair (1955), the Lily chair (1968) and Series 7 chair (1955)

Trapholt Collection

Furnishing Welfare Society

Why have Danish design icons become so widespread?

Nan Dahlkild

Associate professor, PhD at the Department of Communication, University of Copenhagen

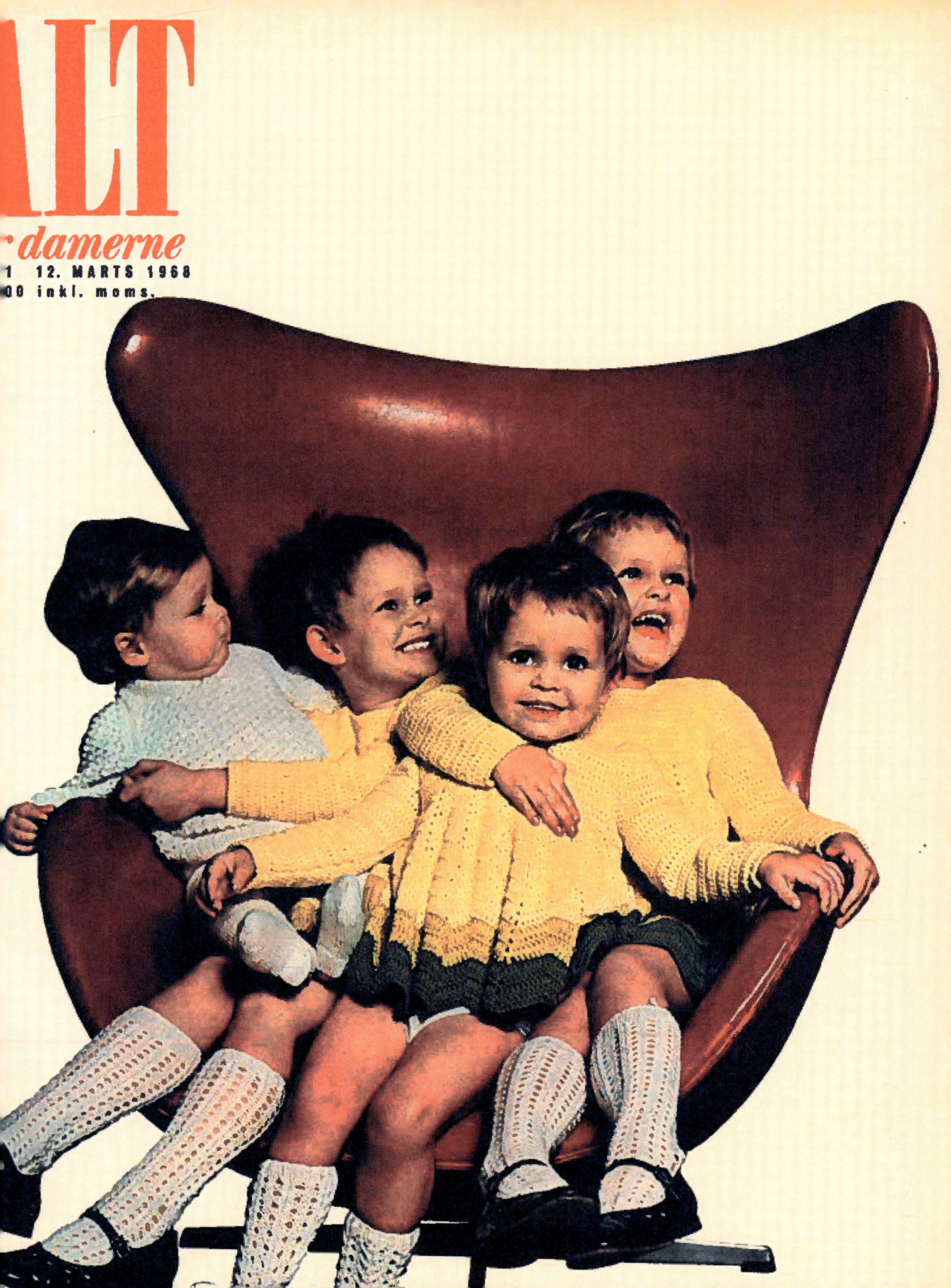

ALT
damerne
1 12. MARTS 1968
00 inkl. moms.

The front cover of the Danish Magazine *Alt for Damerne* combines the elegance of the Egg chair with its function as a family chair

Photo: Alt for damerne, 12 March 1968

Whenever one visits public institutions and large companies in Denmark, one cannot help but notice the prevalence of Danish design icons such as the PH Lamp, Børge Mogensen's Folk Chair and Arne Jacobsen's extensive range of furniture, lamps and utensils. A similar observation can be made in countless private homes.

While it can be difficult to quantify the extent of this trend and document it accurately, the prevalence of such furniture is nevertheless sufficiently conspicuous to incite a sense of curiosity; a desire to know more and to better understand the background for their popularity.[1] The spontaneous, immediate answers would be that these icons achieved widespread popularity due to their originality, quality, elegant design, well-chosen materials, ease of use, durability – and, undoubtedly, even more of these excellent features all rolled into one. Such answers are not necessarily inaccurate, but others may apply, too. The issue can be further unpacked by considering aspects of design with a sociological approach.

Is there a connection between the spread of Danish design and the evolution of the Danish welfare society? Is there a correlation between welfare philosophy and Modernism in architecture and design? How have icons of Danish Design been presented, advertised and disseminated? Are they widespread not only in Denmark, but also internationally? Why did some icons become popular, while other aspects of Modernism failed to make an impact, such as Arne Jacobsen's Kubeflex series of modular holiday homes?

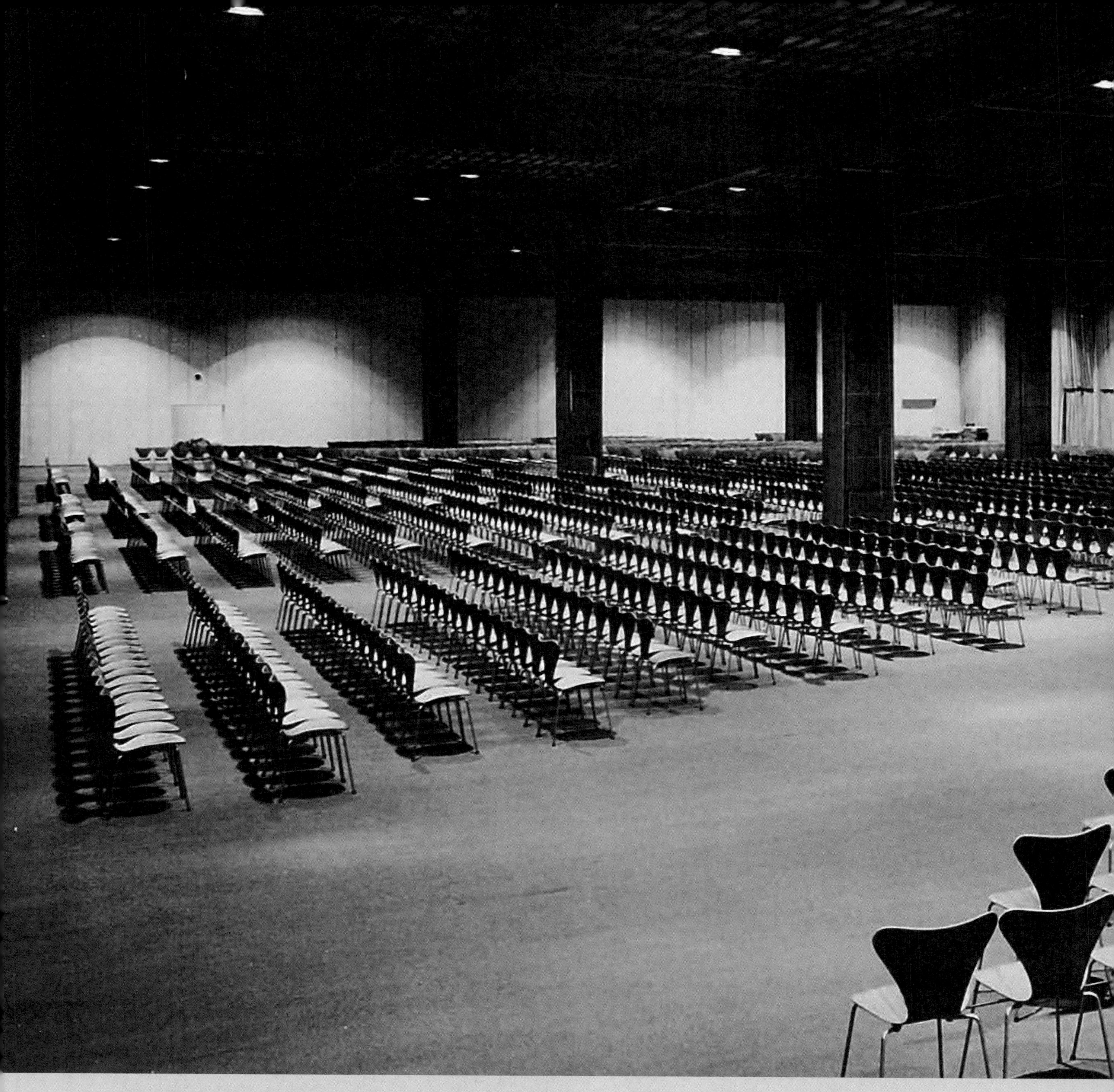

det store auditorium
dagen før lægekongressen
stilhed før stormen
2350 roligt afventende FH-stole

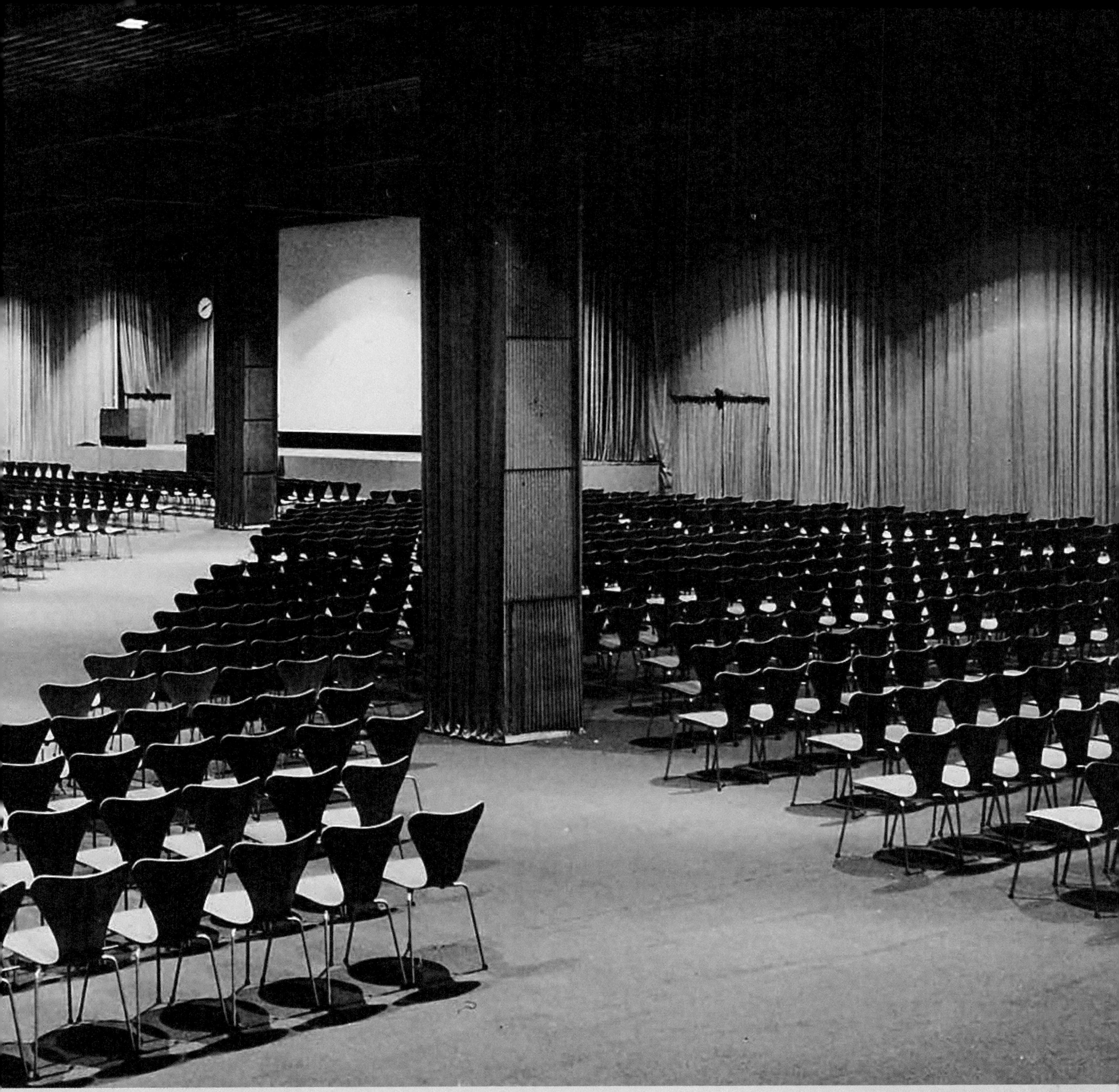

stålstole i rytmisk formation
stabelstole med 5 års garanti
2350 stk. = 3 dages produktion
stole man stoler på . . . . . FH-stole

Arne Jacobsen's designs were an important part of the furnishing of the public institutions for welfare society as well as private homes. Their prevalence in many institutions presumably gave added momentum to their emergence in popular culture

Previous page: 2,350 Series 7 have been set up for a medical conference

Photo: Aage Strüwing © Jørgen Strüwing

This page: The same chair was also presented in a more traditional, homely context, combined with antiques

Photo: Fritz Hansen's archives

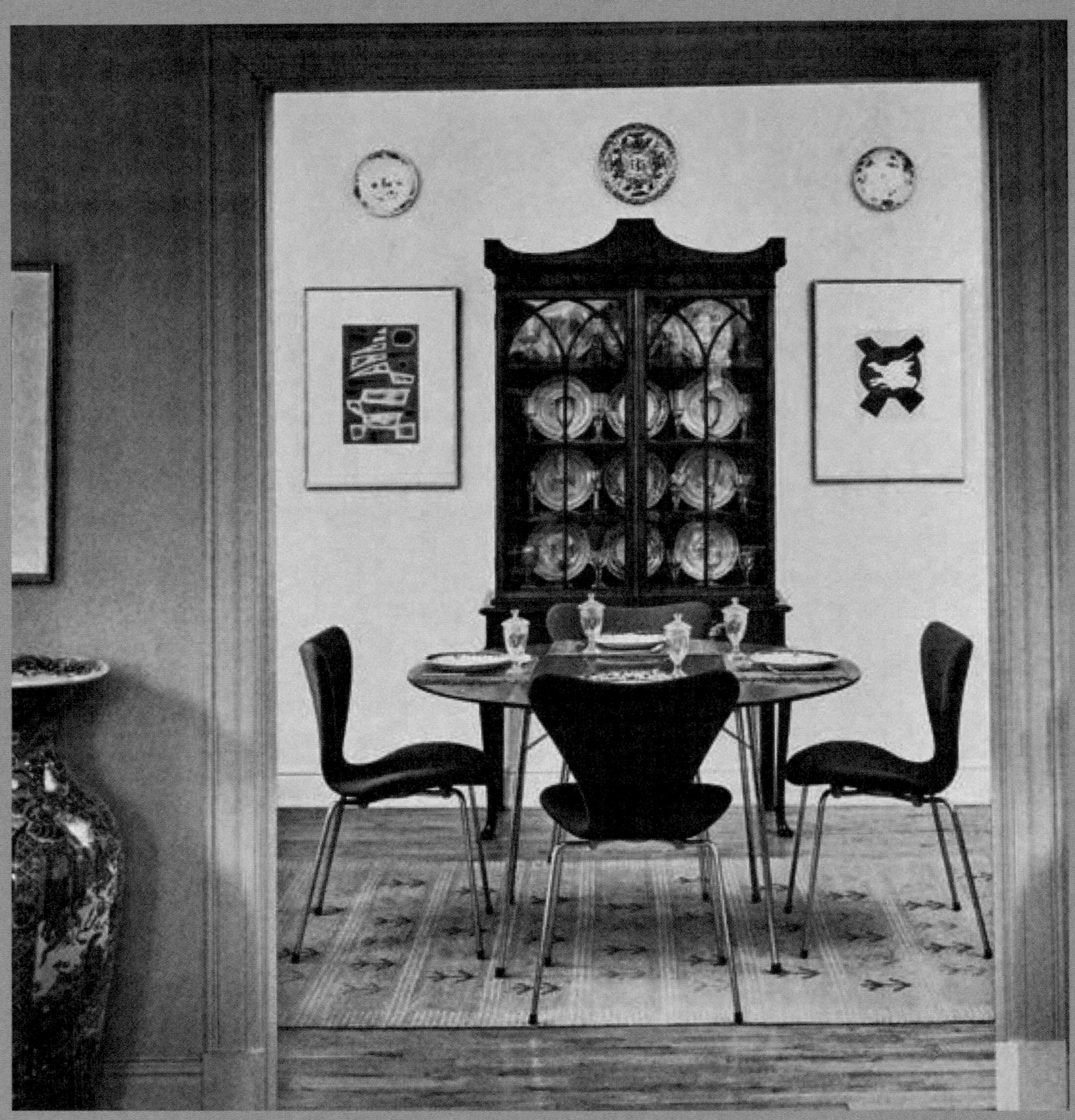

Correlations between the welfare philosophy and Modernism

When Modernism arrived in Denmark during the interwar period, social Functionalism was already a strong movement in the field of architecture and design (Dahlkild, 2019).

A manifesto like Edvard Heiberg's book *To Vær. straks* (Two rooms urgently required) (Heiberg, 1935) emphasised the social dimensions of the issue. As the title makes clear, the book was an attack on the housing shortages seen at the time and against poor housing – problems which the incipient welfare state sought to alleviate through initiatives such as a State Housing Fund that helped support large social housing projects. Heiberg was part of the circle associated with the journal *Kritisk Revy*, which wrote about 'Modern urban construction, social architecture, financially viable technology and real-life engineering and industry' (*Kritisk Revy*, 1926a).

Several historians of architecture and design have seen a connection linking twentieth-century Modernism and the 'Scandinavian Style' with the continued development of the Nordic welfare societies, a process that gained momentum in the decades after World War II. Among them we find Nils-Ole Lund, for whom social responsibility and thinking is an expression of the 'genius loci' of the Nordic countries: 'History has placed the Nordic peoples under very specific geographical conditions. The challenges faced by these people, and the influences to which they have been exposed, have tinted their outlook and attitudes' (Lund, 1991, pp. 9-10). These values would prove to greatly affect how the international movements were adapted to northern settings. In the Nordic countries, Modernism prevailed in a different way compared to anywhere else in the world. It was 'softened' and fused with local materials and traditional motifs, creating a vernacular 'Folkhem' variation that reflected the budding welfare state. The social dimension became an important part of the Nordic tradition, where ordinary buildings and homes are also regarded as architecture: 'The marriage between social commitment and a professional insistence on quality may be the most important part of the Nordic tradition. Our political and cultural history makes it quite natural for us to see connections between form and content, between ideology and society' (Lund, 1991, p. 17).

This development applied to architecture and design alike. Just as the 'functional tradition' in architecture combined international modernism with Danish building materials and traditions, the 'golden years' from the post-war years until the end of the 1960s saw the emergence of a new vein of furniture design and applied art created through collaborative efforts that involved architects, furniture makers and private companies.

In the minds of the creators of the welfare state, ethical, cultural and social values played a major role, one that reached beyond purely material progress. Society should be rich not only in material terms, but culturally too. In his book *Velfærdsteori og velfærdsstat* (Welfare Theory and Welfare State, 1962), Ivar Nørgaard, who was Minister of Economic Affairs in the 1960s, wrote: 'When material concerns are no longer the one main necessity, there are excellent opportunities for cultural and ethical matters to play a greater role in life. Politics will then increasingly transition from being a discussion about finances and economics to become a cultural debate, and the financial issues will be pushed into the background in favour of educational, psychological and general cultural affairs' (Hoffmeyer, 1962, pp. 83-84).

In the cultural debate of the 1960s, which very much revolved around the development of the welfare society, one of the pervasive themes was that material growth should be followed by cultural growth. This was especially true of the founder of the Louisiana Museum of Modern Art, Knud W. Jensen, who articulated this position in countless lectures, essays and newspaper chronicles, all compiled in a book tellingly entitled *Slaraffenland eller Utopia. Artikler om Velfærdsstatens Kulturpolitik* (Land of Plenty or Utopia. Articles on the Cultural Policy of the Welfare State) (Jensen, 1966).

The founding of the Louisiana Museum of Modern Art north of Copenhagen in 1958 was in itself a manifestation of these ideas, and its interiors reflected this view. With its relaxed, informal lounge-like space complete with a fireplace, it not only became a template for a new, more home-like approach to museum presentations; it also became a role model of interior design emulated by the many one-story detached houses being built around the time. Louisiana Modernism was not just about the dissemination of contemporary art, but also of contemporary design (Breunig, 2013, pp. 53–78).

To Knud W. Jensen's mind, the growing wealth and welfare in Danish society ought to pave the way for entirely new opportunities for enlightenment and quality as counterpoints to pop and mass culture: 'Precisely because the widespread rubbish found among entertainment and consumer goods contributes to creating a pattern of life that does not promote well-being, it must be considered legitimate to fight such things through enlightenment. A sense of quality is conducive to independence and broadens your choice. The more you know, the less likely you are to have the wool pulled over your eyes' (Jensen, 1966, p. 101).

The cultural-political charge of the 1960s reached a conclusion with *Betænkning 517. En Kulturpolitisk redegørelse* (Report 517. A Report on Danish Cultural Policy), which offered a vision of the future of Danish cultural policy in the broadest sense, including the framework offered by everyday life (Danish Ministry of Cultural Affairs, 1969, pp. 268–271).

Flagships of cultural life such as Louisiana not only set the new standard for the presentation and dissemination of contemporary art, but also for interior design and furnishings. Thinkers, architects and designers reached out to each other.

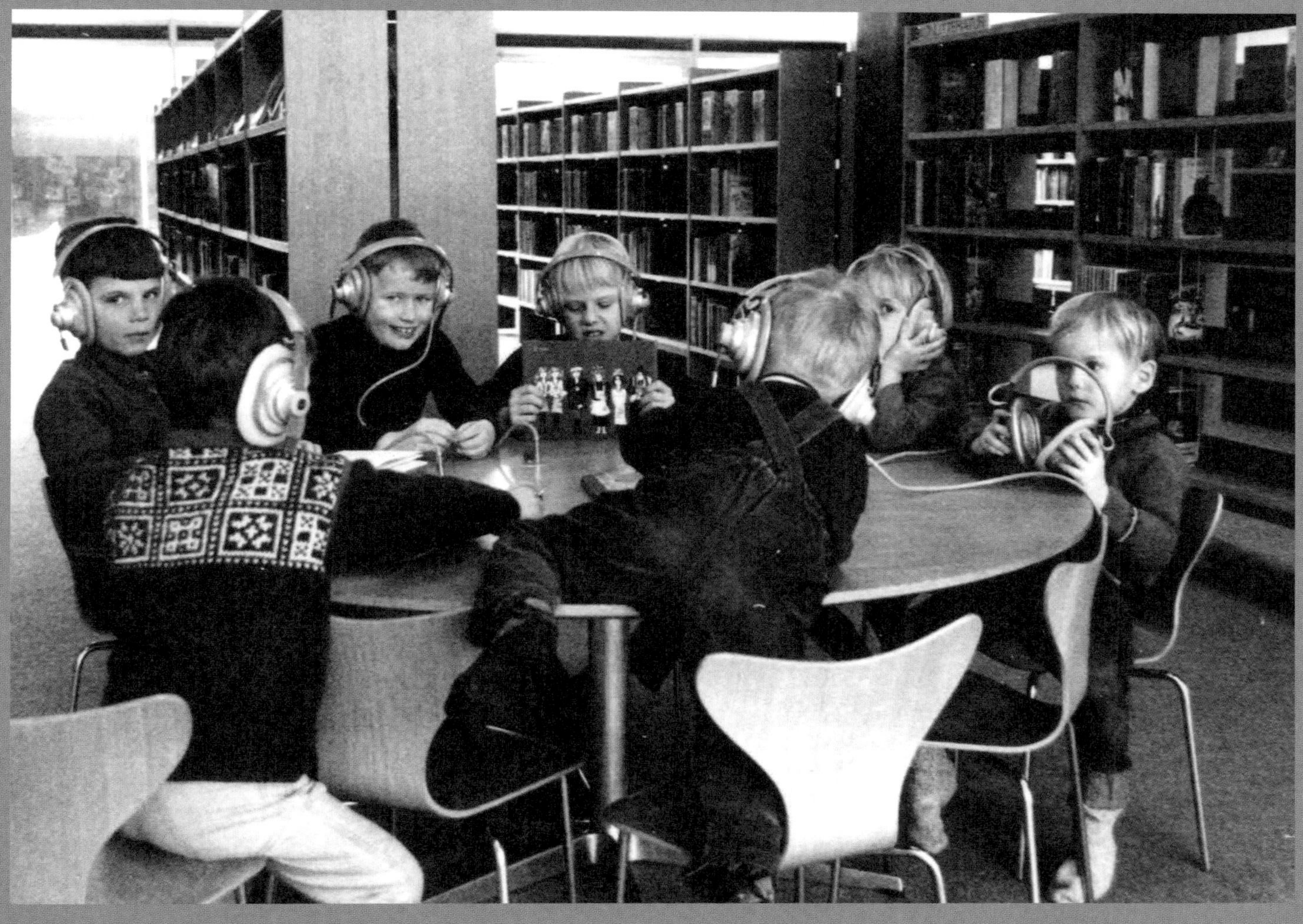

The cultural institutions and community centres of the 1960s and 1970s were 'spearheads of welfare society', and as such were furnished with Danish design. Here we see the children's section of the Rødovre library in 1970, furnished with child-sized chairs by Arne Jacobsen

Photo: Eigil Malmer

The journal *Kritisk Revy* presented the practicality and ideology of the PH lamp through texts, pictures and advertisements alike, thereby laying down the foundations that helped Danish Design take on an identity that extended beyond its purely practical function. Ideology and advertising converged in a synthesis

Photo: Kritisk Revy 3, 1926

The creation and dissemination of Danish Design icons

There can be doubt, then, that those who created and discussed welfare society looked beyond purely material growth and put great store by cultural values. The cultural institutions were the 'spearhead of welfare', but there was a belief that everyday life should also be infused by quality in art, architecture and interior design. The development of 'Danish Design' and 'Danish Modern' reflected similar concerns.

A reference work on Danish history, *Politikens Danmarks-historie* from 1972, illustrates the culmination of the 'golden years' of modern Danish furniture by showing, in the last section of the last volume, a furnished 'welfare state home' with a distinctive caption. In its concluding section on Modernism, the editors chose to show images from the 1965 spring exhibition of Danish Design at the venue Den Permanente and a full-page colour photo from the Louisiana Museum of Modern Art, describing it as 'an entirely new kind of museum'. The good times had reached their peak, and welfare and modernity had merged to harmonious effect. The text emphasised that Danish applied art experienced international success due to its high quality. 'Yet even more important than these victories on the world market is the fact that Danish applied art in its many forms has, over the last decades, contributed so much to beautify the settings in which Danish families live their lives. The boost in housing culture that the Danish people have achieved since the war is due not only to the efforts of the architects and the applied arts, but also to the growing general prosperity during this period. Far more people than ever are now able to afford partaking in the joy of living among beautiful things every day' (Wendt, 1972, pp. 524–526).

A number of social agents, media and forms of public life contributed to the creation and dissemination of this concept and to its tangible expression in the form of furniture, textiles and utensils. The creative inner circle included architects, furniture makers and textile artists who, among other things, presented their creations at the annual exhibitions arranged by Københavns Snedkerlaug (the Copenhagen Cabinet-makers' Guild), a series of shows first launched in 1927 that ran until 1969. The cabinet-makers' exhibitions facilitated direct contact between craftsman and customer, and, importantly, gave rise to publicity and critique in newspapers and magazines. Landsforeningen Dansk Kunsthåndværk (The National Association of Danish Crafts) arranged exhibitions and lectures on housing, living and furnishings in Copenhagen and major cities in Denmark. In 1939, the touring exhibition *Bo Godt* (Live Well) showed examples of interior design of modern homes, complete with a dining area, workplace and rest area. The venue Den Permanente (The Permanent Exhibition) was launched as an exhibition venue for artisans and companies, but soon progressed from being a commercial exhibition venue to becoming an actual shop on Vesterbrogade in Copenhagen. The Copenhagen department stores also had large furniture departments. In particular, the company Fritz Hansen mass-produced architect-designed furniture from the late 1930s onwards. The leading journals of the time included *Arkitekten, Nyt Tidsskrift for Kunstindustri* and *Snedkermestrenes Medlemsblad*. In the 1920s, *Kritisk Revy* played a particularly important role.

LAMPEREKLAME

NAAR vi staar med Ansvaret for Sammenhængen mellem det, vi skriver og det, vi skaber, maa vi ogsaa hente Eksemplerne, hvor det passer os. Hvad er Realisme? Det er ikke som Billedet tilvenstre et forlorent Digt om Teknik. „Lysekronen" er tegnet af Walter Gropius. Den er tilsyneladende meget teknisk, minder om Radioapparater, Højspændingsledninger osv. gennem to af de ti Aluminiumsrør, har de elektriske Ledninger den Ære at blive ført hen til fire Rørlamper, som lyser, ganske som da de kom fra Butiken. Resten er, for at der kan være noget at støve af. Om Belysning, om Teknik, om Dygtiggørelse og Indleven i Emnet er der aldeles ikke Tale. Dette „Beleuchtungskörper" er een stor Løgnehistorie og ingenlunde saa hæderlig som den forgyldte Trælysekrone nedenunder, som dog er Mindelser om Kultur, der har eksisteret, medens Gropius fabler om en, der aldrig skal komme. — Mon ikke Opgaven skulde være at arbejde med Belysningen med Realiteterne, og ikke slippe dem for noget som helst smagsmæssigt.

P. H.

Billedet er fra „Bauhausbücher" (Arn. Busks Bogh)

FRA STUDENTERSAMFUNDETS DECEMBER NUMMER

TIL EN

P.H.

LAMPE

Det Lys, der skaber
alt, vi ser —
find mig saa fint
et Skaberler!

Hvad er den grove
Ordmusik
mod Lampens lysende
Logik?

Se paa en graa
Decemberdag
i en P. H.

den gamle Pagt
af Aand og Lys
fornyes!

Otto Gelsted.

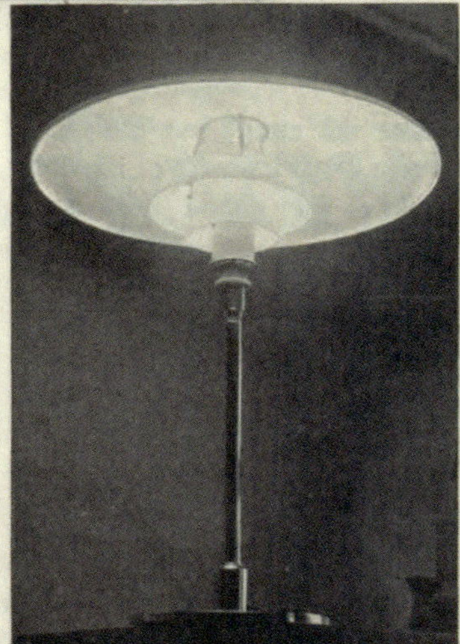

FDB MØBLER

Sikker Hansen 49

ANDREASEN & LACHMANN KØBENHAVN

F.D.B. REKLAME

Aage Sikker Hansen's 1949 poster shows a housewife seated at her sewing machine on Børge Mogensen's Windsor chair, sewing or repairing clothes for her family, a familiar sight in the austere post-war years. The FDB furniture series ushered in 'a bright and happy future' and became very widespread in the welfare society that was soon to come

Photo: Pernille Klemp

The creation of the individual design icons can, like the early beginnings of the welfare philosophy, be traced back to these first formative decades. For example, the PH lamp was a recurring theme in *Kritisk Revy*. In its first year, 1926, several issues of the magazine contained editorial material as well as advertisements about the lamp. Several articles delved into the refraction of light and how this affected its appearance. The lamp had its praises sung in poetic prose and in actual advertisements. The PH lamp was not just a regular lamp, but a progressive invention that combined technical studies of illumination with the poetry of light as in Otto Gelsted's poem: 'The Light that makes up all we see – find me a finer clay, prithee! How could word-music ever hope to match the lamp's bright, logic scope? Behold, on a grey December day, the P.H. shall renew the ancient covenant of spirit and light' (*Kritisk Revy*, 1926b, p. 29). The Danish Design icons took on an aura and identity that extended beyond their actual function.

The company Louis Poulsen followed up on their Danish advertising campaigns by launching international marketing and exhibition efforts. Louis Poulsen collaborated with the German company Siemens, and the lamp became so well-known internationally that it was installed at the Bauhaus movement's new buildings in Dessau and in Haus Tugendhat in Brno, designed by Mies van der Rohe. Louis Poulsen built a network of 372 dealers worldwide. The many international contacts gave rise to a large and colourful range of material about the lamp in a wide variety of languages (Jørstian & Nielsen, 1994, pp. 207–228).

Initially, the lamp was mainly used in institutions and public spaces, but with the introduction of the PH5 in 1958, a pendant lamp that could be hung over a dining table without causing any glare for diners, it began to break through into private homes too. Small red and blue diffusers were introduced to add colour to the spectrum of light emitted. It is estimated that the PH lamp can be found in approximately 20 per cent of all Danish homes (Littrup, 2004, p. 80).

The FDB furniture series have a somewhat different back story. Beginning in the autumn of 1942, Børge Mogensen, acting in his capacity as head of the newly established Møbelarkitektkontor (Furniture Design Office), began developing a furniture programme for FDB, Denmark's co-operative supermarket chain which at the time numbered 2,000 shops and 400,000 members. The objective was to create good, useful and affordable furniture with universal appeal. A particularly important target group were young couples, who would require furniture that would last throughout a long and happy life together. The furniture types and their production were simplified through favourable contracts with manufacturers and, from 1947, by operating their own factory at Tarm.

The designs were inspired by classic furniture types, by Shaker furniture and by Børge Mogensen's mentor, Kaare Klint. The philosophy of the range was that young couples should be able to buy the furniture for their home gradually, acquiring new pieces when they could afford to do so, which meant that they did not have to borrow or buy on an instalment plan. However, Andelsbanken began offering loans for such purchases from 1948. Reflecting on the overall idea of creating furniture for young couples, Børge Mogensen wrote: 'And finally we find our young couple installed in a cosy home where one can be sure of a bright and happy future, one in which the furniture is there to serve them – not the other way around' (Dybdahl, 2007, p. 78). One of the simplified types was the 'Folk Chair', which is made out of four round poles, a braided seat and a curved back. Hans J. Wegner was also attached to the design office, where he created children's furniture that could be easily dismantled.

Boasting its own factory and a strong sales organisation, FDB's furniture had a competitive edge over the rest of the furniture industry. What is more, the co-operative movement carried out a great deal of information work through initiatives such as its own magazine *Samvirke*, exhibitions, consultants, catalogues, evening events for people looking to set up home, lectures and two films: *En lys og lykkelig fremtid* (A Bright and Happy Future) from 1945, the year in which the war ended and Denmark was liberated, and *Næste Generation* (The Next Generation) from 1955. Both were aimed at young people who were about to set up home together. FDB also ran a large export business.

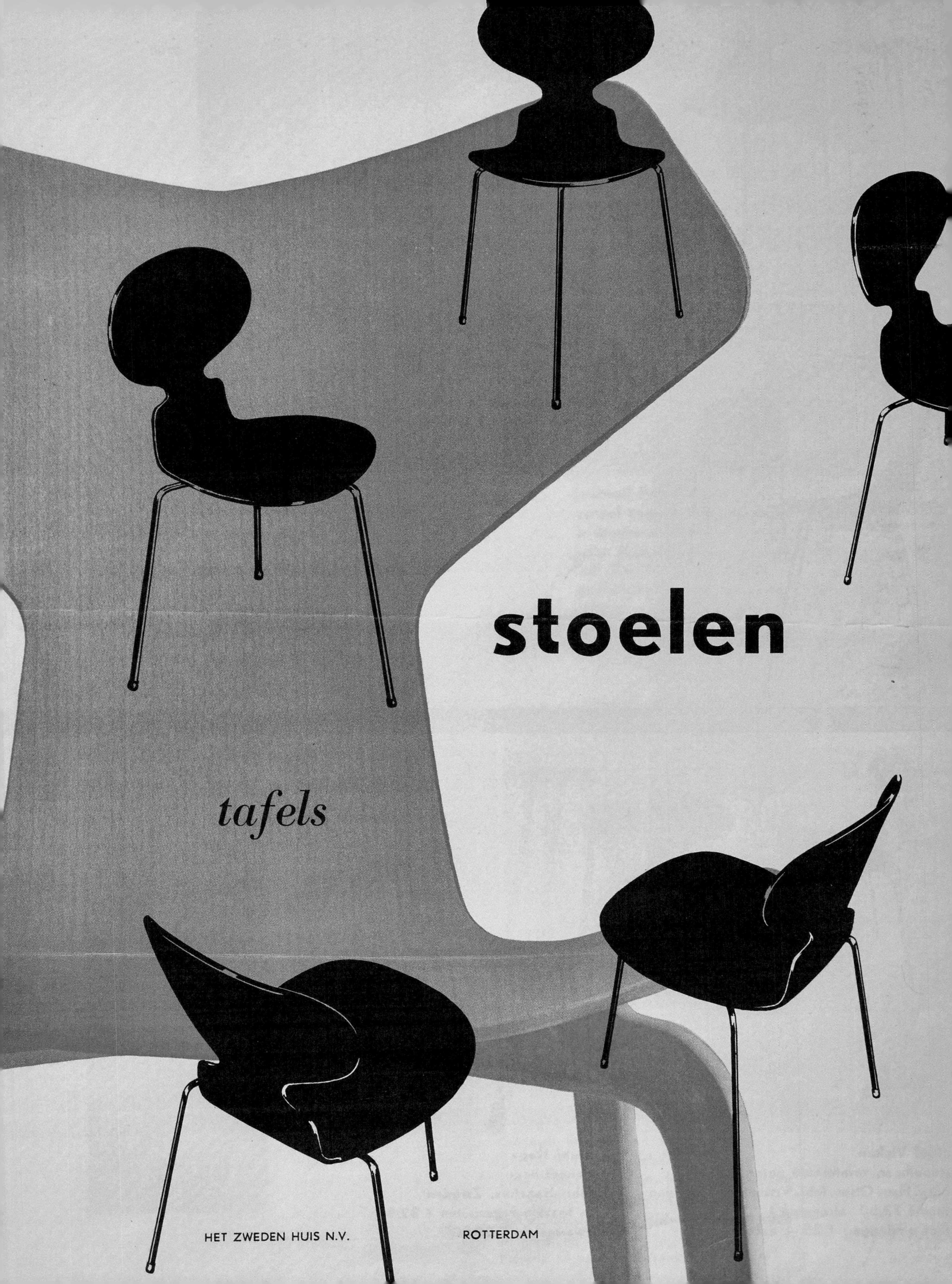
stoelen
tafels
HET ZWEDEN HUIS N.V.
ROTTERDAM

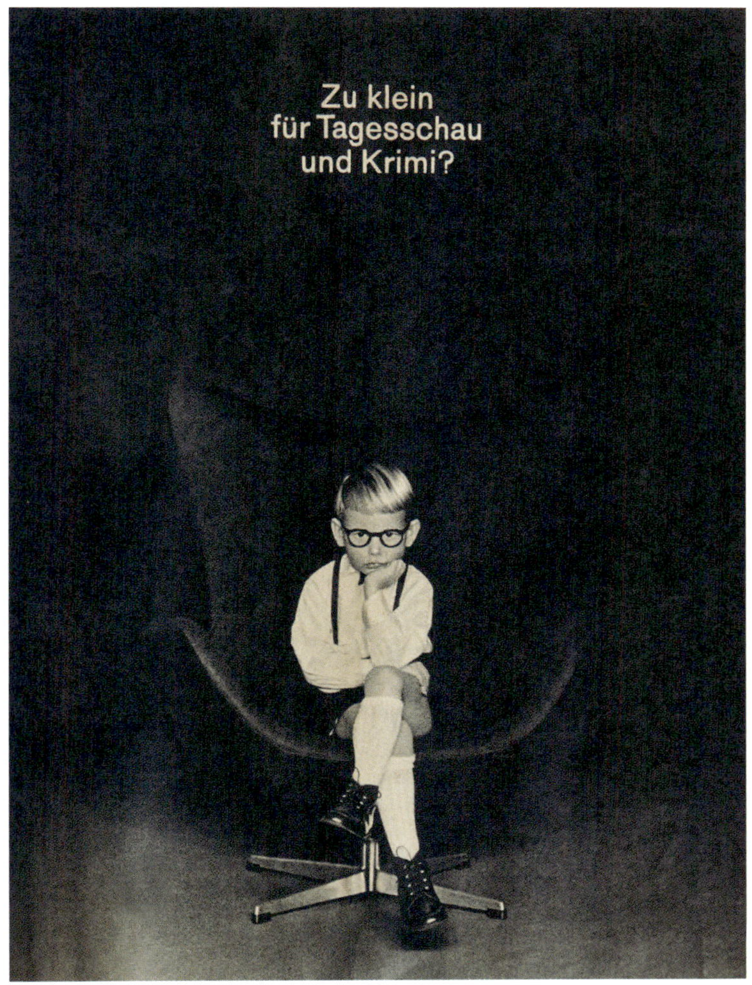

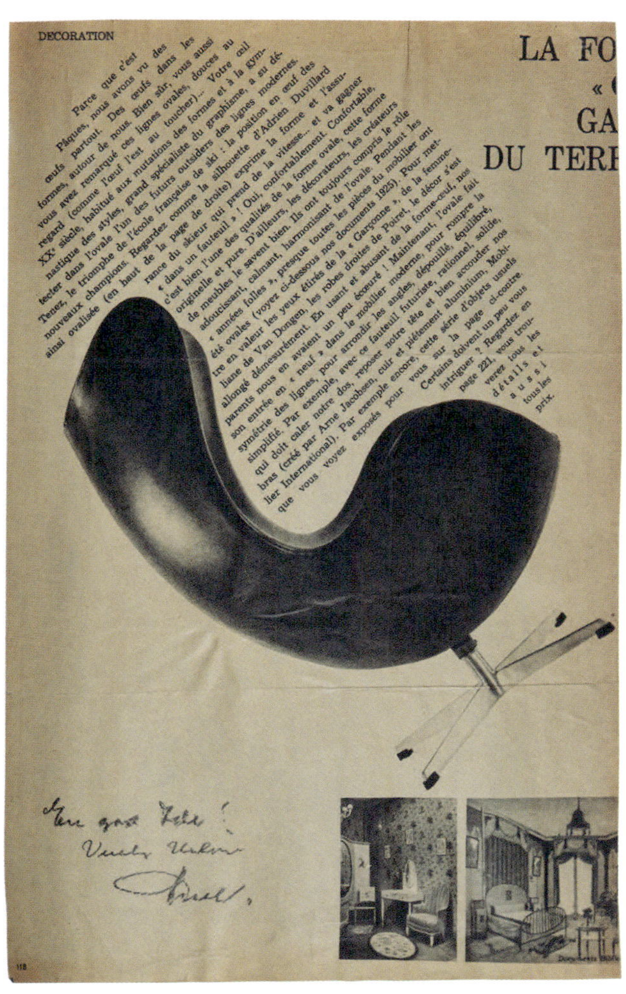
DECORATION

LA FO
« (
GA
DU TERI

The furniture company Fritz Hansen promoted Arne Jacobsen's furniture in Denmark and abroad. Shown here are Dutch, German and French advertisements

Photo: Fritz Hansen's archives

Advertisement for Brugs møbler, bringing together a number of Danish Design icons: Arne Jacobsen's chair, Børge Mogensen's sofa and the PH lamp above Piet Hein's table

Photo: Samvirke

Arne Jacobsen's furniture was widely marketed by the manufacturer Fritz Hansen: at fairs and exhibitions, by means of leaflets and photo series intended for advertisements in all types of newspapers and magazines. There were no ideological intentions here, no specific allegiance to the Cultural Radical or cooperative movements; the objective was simply to sell quality furniture to Danish and international audiences with disposable income.

The Ant chair was created in 1952 as the first of a series of chairs with moulded wooden seats and lightweight metal legs. The Series 7 followed in 1955. Both chairs were inspired by designs created by the American couple Charles and Ray Eames, but had a more organic and varied appearance. The foam-padded and more comfortable variants known as the Swan and Egg chairs arrived in 1958 as part of the seamless integration of architecture and design found in the creation of the SAS Royal Hotel in Copenhagen. Here, the shell shape was adapted to allow for leather upholstery. Several of Arne Jacobsen's furniture designs were created in connection with projects for corporations like Novo, the SAS Royal Hotel, the Nationalbanken or projects associated with the City Hall and library of Rødovre. The minimalism of the City Hall signalled a less lofty and more democratic approach to administration and politics. The library was an example of the new cultural venues and community centres emerging in the suburbs, bringing along many activities and new facilties such as a record bar, a new invention aimed specifically at the young. Like the Louisiana museum, the library served as a nexus for the realisation of the welfare state's cultural policies.

Overall, the advertisements praised the modern feel and materials of the furniture, but the Fritz Hansen company also highlighted concepts such as the Scandinavian way of life and 'hygge'. The Series 7 was described in the following terms: 'Series 7 is like a fanfare proclaiming what ingenious design can create out of moulded plywood and chromium-placed steel pipes. These chairs have won worldwide acclaim by being in daily use all over the Earth... the materials selected have facilitated the creation of a chair that is both easy to handle and robust in use. Wherever you need to sit well, whether many or few, for work or for spectators, Series 7 is the logical solution' (Fritz Hansen's archives). Another advertisement accentuated the close links to Scandinavian traditions and ways of life, pointing to qualities beyond the purely functional: '... with an emphasis on displaying Professor Arne Jacobsen's furniture in a setting infused by the Scandinavian tradition where the distinctively Danish concept of hygge arose. Hygge has to do with the sympathetic balance and silent interaction between people and in relation to the environment they enjoy and thrive in' (Fritz Hansen's archives).

Fritz Hansen also presented Arne Jacobsen's furniture series in international contexts, for example in campaigns in the United States, where the company succeeded in getting Jacobsen's pieces on the covers of interior design and lifestyle magazines.

What is more, other companies also used Arne Jacobsen's furniture in their advertisements. The use of striking, evocative names such as the Ant, the Swan, the Egg, Series 7, the Drop, the Pot and the Tongue was presumably also helpful in promoting general awareness of this furniture among the public. Social relationships and word of mouth added yet another layer of influence.

Nan Dahlkild

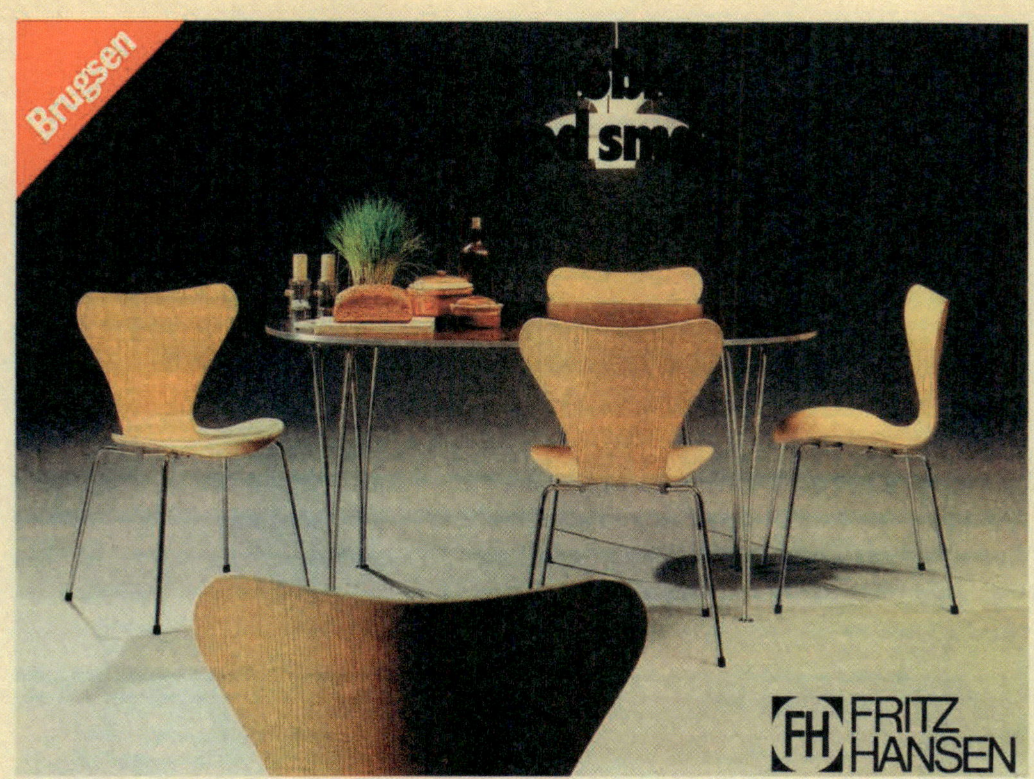

Arne Jacobsen stol

I ægte, tidløs design. Den berømte stol fremhæver det moderne miljø og kan samtidig fremtræde neutral i mere klassiske omgivelser. Her vist sammen med Piet Heins superellptiske bord med praktisk perstorpplade. Stolene fås i naturtræ eller farvelakeret. Bordet fås med brun eller hvid perstorp.

Børge Mogensen sofa

i bøg natur med løse hynder er tegnet i 1945, men stadig lige aktuel. Den højre gavl kan indstilles i 5 positioner ved hjælp af læderstropper.

Reolsystem 60/60

er et reol-modul, hvis mål er 60×60×30 cm. Af 60×60 modulerne kan du bygge lige netop den reol, der dækker dit behov - og samtidig få en reolvæg, der er præget af

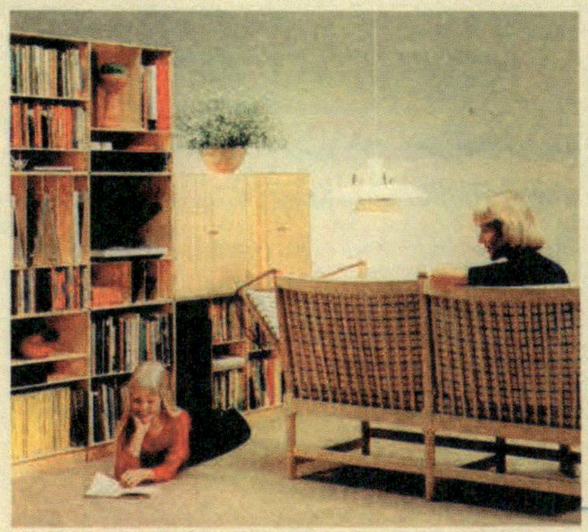

tidløs smag og kvalitet. Modulerne er udført i stavlimet fyr og fås både natur og gråbejdset. Beslagene er af gedigent messing og hyldernes bøjler af kobber.
Design Peter Lassen.

DB Brugsen Møbler, Roskildevej 45, Albertslund, Tlf. (02) 64 19 30 - Nygårds Plads, Rødovre, tlf. (01) 75 46 11 - Nørrebrogade 124, København N, tlf. (01) 37 00 73 - Marienbergvej 90, Vordingborg, tlf. (03) 77 16 55 - Østerbro 41, Odense, tlf. (09) 11 81 11 - Arnfredsvej, Vejen, tlf. (05) 36 09 44 - Hobrovej 461, Skalborg, tlf. (08) 18 06 44 - Vesterbro Torv, Århus C, tlf. (06) 12 90 00 - Hostrupvej 9, Holstebro, tlf. (07) 42 26 77 - Brugsen Møbler, Jernbanegade 47, Sønderborg, tlf. (04) 42 97 27 - Anva, Vesterbrogade 2 E, København V, tlf. (01) 15 12 15 - Nytorv 24, Ålborg, tlf. (08) 13 30 00 - Kongensgade 25-27, Esbjerg, tlf. (05) 12 01 33.

Brugs møbler

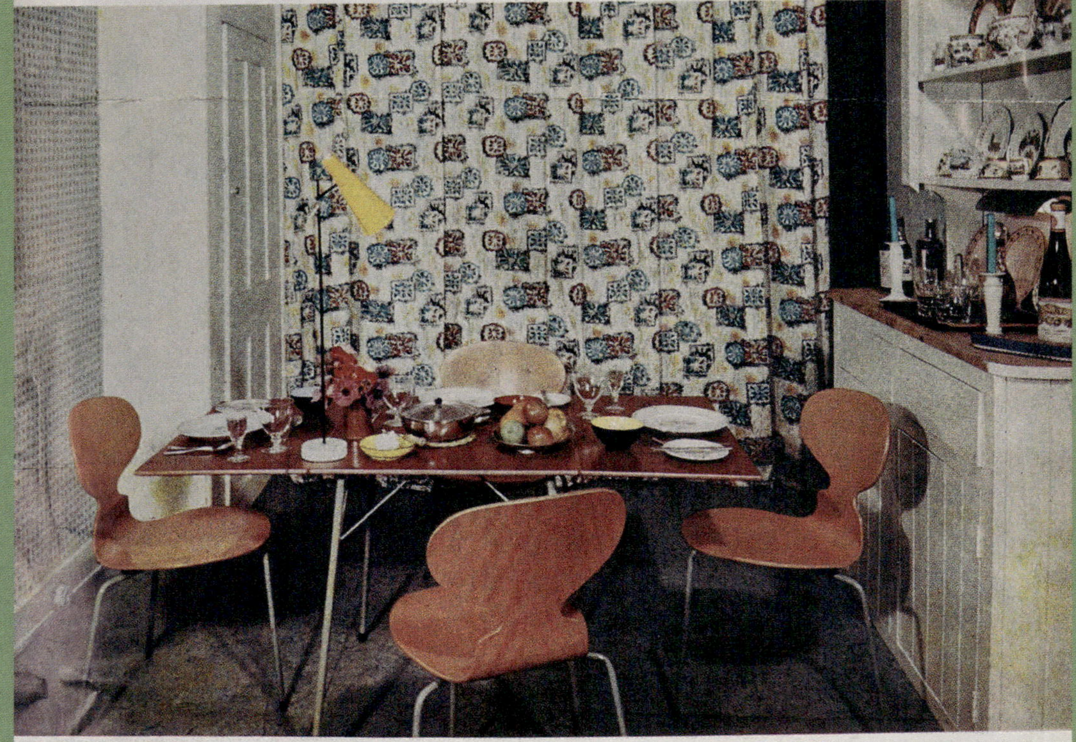

Covers and spreads from American lifestyle magazines. Over the course of several decades, they would present Arne Jacobsen's design in domestic and exclusive settings alike

Photo: Fritz Hansen's archives

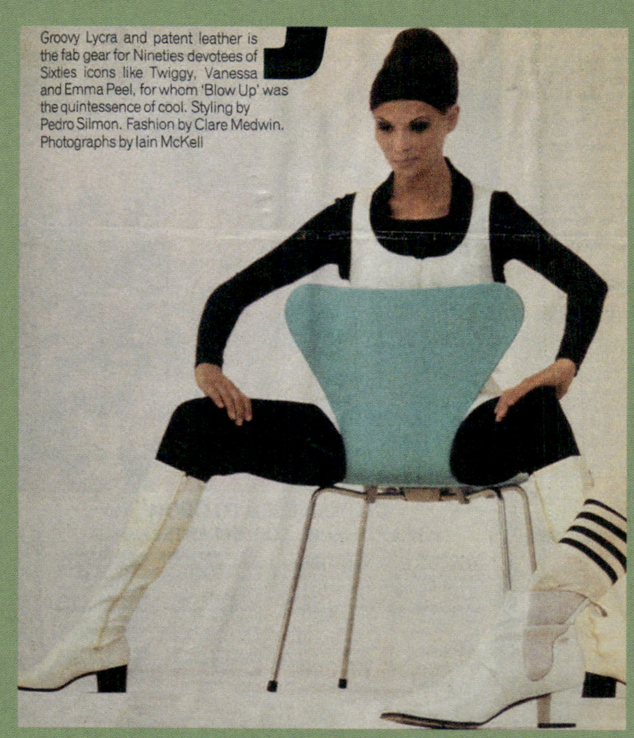

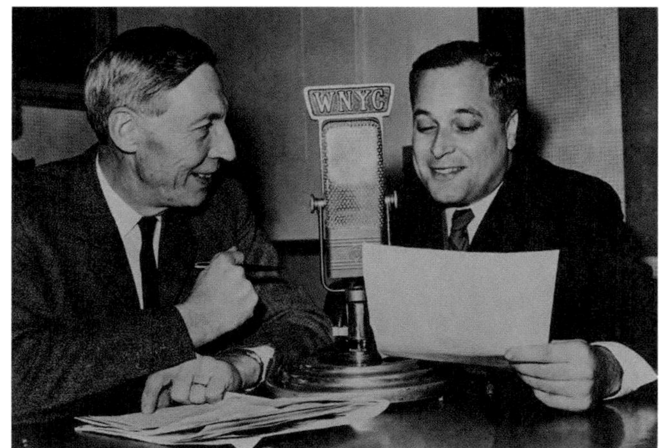

In the 1950s and 1960s, the company Fritz Hansen launched several campaigns to promote Danish furniture in the USA. Here, Mr Søren Hansen is interviewed by the architect Aronin for a WNYC broadcast, New York

Photo: Fritz Hansen's archives

This influence was not restricted to the networks of an inner circle: Danish furniture was also presented through books and magazines on interior design. Prominent books included Esbjørn Hjort's *Bo rigtigt* (Living Right) from 1947 and Finn Juhl's *Hjemmets indretning* (Furnishing the Home) from 1954 which featured Arne Jacobsen's own home, furnished with white Ant chairs, on its cover. Both books combined practical points about interior design with presentations of the new furniture and applied art of the time, accompanied by illustrations. Finn Juhl's book contained three chapters on new Danish and international trends.

First launched in March 1961, the lifestyle and interior design magazine *Bo Bedre* (literally 'Live Better') repeatedly featured Arne Jacobsen's designs on its cover and presented them in interiors in its various features. Still published today, the magazine was initiated by the publisher Palle Fogtdal, while the editor was architect Anker Tiedemann.

The magazine was available from newsagents all over the country, and with the price set at a very affordable DKK 2.50, no less than 100,000 copies were sold within a few months. The actual readership was presumably several times greater than that. The launch was announced with plenty of pathos: 'Coming soon: the big magazine about the home – in colour! The monthly magazine for modern people who are interested in their homes' (Tiedemann, 2013, p. 88). The contents of the magazine were varied, ranging from different house types, interior design, do-it-yourself projects, tests of various types of equipment, recipes for fashionable dishes, articles about Swedish holiday homes or travels to southern Europe – even how to handle teen problems. The advertising profile, which was even more diverse, was out of the editors' hands.

The aim of the magazine was to teach the Danes to live better. It wanted to get rid of the typical features on 'The gracious home of the Rt. Hon. Jane Double-Barrel-Name' with descriptions of expensive antiques, chandeliers and heavy armchairs. 'We wanted to revolt against that way of living, and we definitely felt as missionaries for a particular lifestyle, one which gradually came to be known as the *Bo Bedre style*'. There was a desire to promote the best of Danish design, which was warm, human, child-friendly and affordable. The magazine was itself a way of life: 'We didn't edit *Bo Bedre*. We lived *Bo Bedre*' (Tiedemann, 2013, p. 90).

The *Bo Bedre* approach included many articles that took the form of discussions, and the widespread use of the word 'we' helped to directly include the readers, mediating between experts and ordinary consumers. In the first issue, journalist Inger Lauridsen acted as the reader's representative in a discussion with Louisiana architects Jørgen Bo and Vilhelm Wohlert on the new fashion for glass houses: 'Do we want to live in fish tanks?' (Bo, Lauridsen & Wohlert, 1961). The magazine had its own universe, its own style and a direct, mutual relationship with its own target audience.

'But we had one problem. We couldn't simply go out into people's homes to take pictures. People didn't live the way we thought they ought to live' (Tiedemann, 2013, p. 90). Instead, the magazine set up its own photo studio. Even though the happy family on the cover of the very first issue may seem quite authentic, the image is in fact a staged photo with models placed in Knud Peter Harboe's house, much to the surprise of its actual residents.

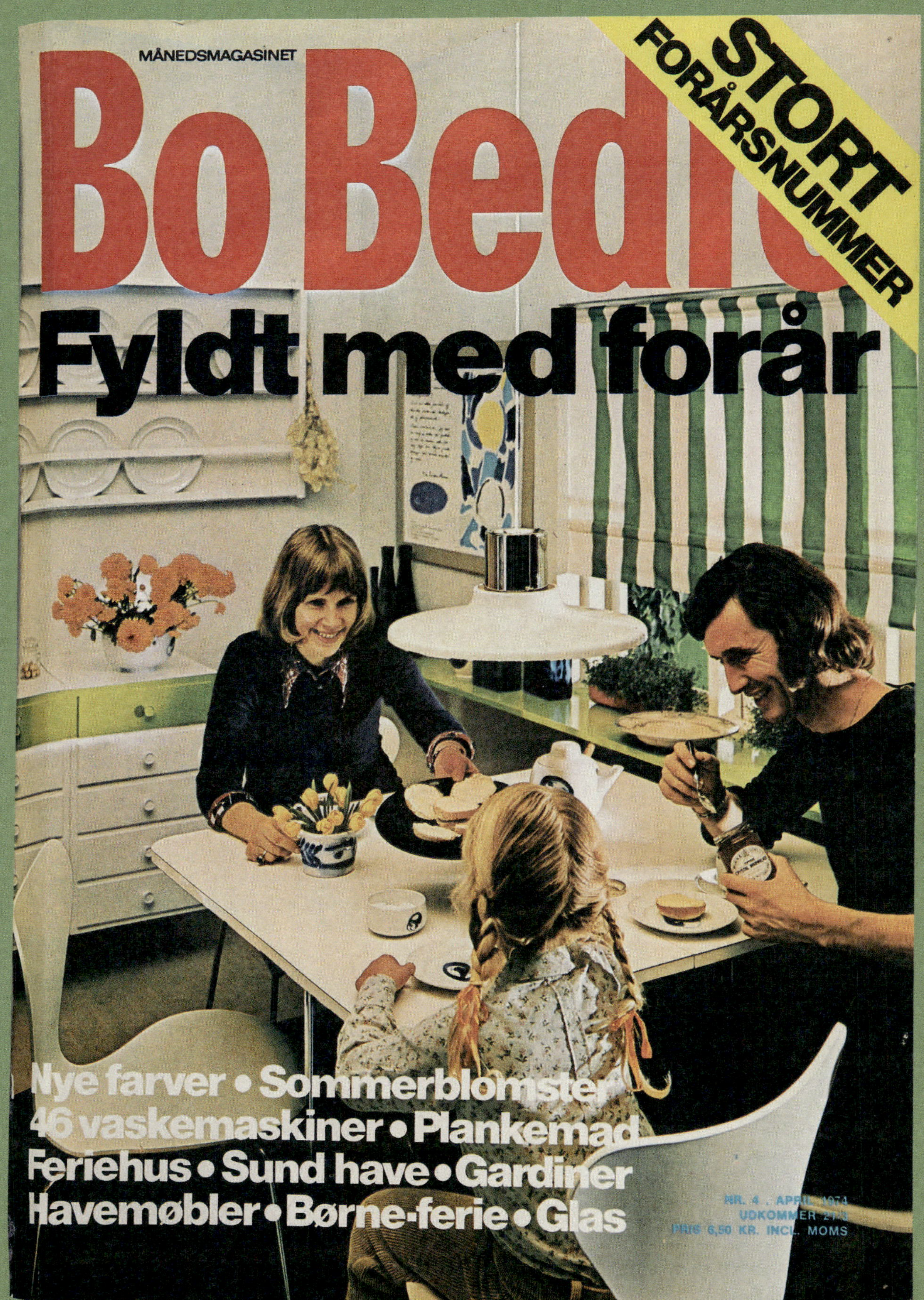

Covers and articles in Danish magazines *Bo Bedre* and *Alt for damerne* made the furniture famous as part of the modern lifestyle of welfare society

Photo: Bo Bedre, April 1974 (left) and Bo Bedre, March 2011

DET NYE
NR. 3 MARTS 2011 · PRIS 56,95 DKR. NORGE 68,90 NOK. SVERIGE 59,90 SEK.

BO BEDRE

FRA DRØM TIL VIRKELIGHED

De vandt konkurrencen:
DANMARKS SKØNNESTE HJEM

VERDENS BEDSTE KOK RASMUS KOFOED:
Forårsmenu, du selv kan lave

BO BEDRE 50 år

NYT **MÅNEDENS OMBYGNING:**
Fra parcelhus til moderne villa

NYT **GRØNNE IDEER** til dit hjem

NYT **MÅNEDENS MIKS:**
Brugbare ideer til dine rum

DE 50 BEDSTE INDRETNINGSIDEER (NOGENSINDE!)

SÅDAN VAR 1960'ERNE:
Klassisk design, vi stadig elsker

STORT
JUBILÆUMSNUMMER

FÅ INSPIRATION TIL ET GODT BOLIGLIV

KR. 56,95
BK 03.03.11-30.03.11
5 701862 000010 00003

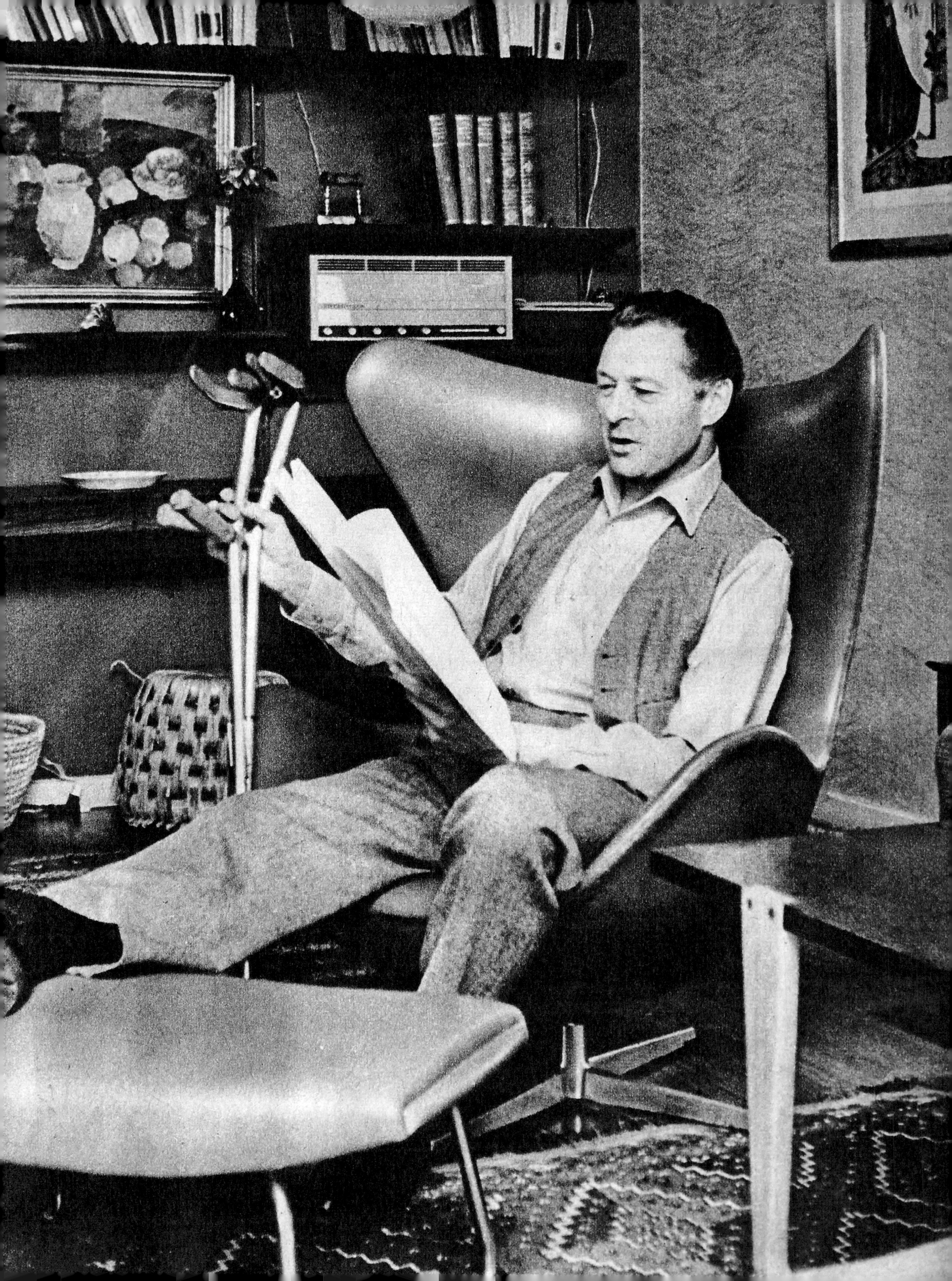

An example of hygge at home: Danish actor Poul Reichhardt reading a script in his Hellerup home

Photo: Fritz Hansen's archives

After books and magazines, the final link in the retail chain was the department stores' furniture departments and high-street furniture stores where the newly affluent consumers of the 1960s could purchase the furniture they had read about and seen pictures of. Many would use them to furnish the new detached houses springing up at the time, complete with an L-shaped living room and fireplace.

In the 1990s, it was estimated that Arne Jacobsen's Series 7 could be found in approximately 15 per cent of all Danish homes (Kaiser, 1992, p. 105). The figure is unlikely to have decreased since. The Danish Design icons were not just tremendously popular in public institutions and private companies, but in private homes too. Arne Jacobsen's furniture designs found widespread use, especially his series of moulded wooden chairs like the Ant and the Series 7, often seen accompanied by a PH lamp. This look was seen in schools and universities, libraries, museums, town halls and administrative buildings ministries, and also extended to banks, insurance companies, administrative headquarters, courtrooms, canteens, hospitals and doctors' offices.

Having a visible presence in so many public spaces undoubtedly aided the dissemination of these design icons. Modern, informal furnishings helped bridge the gap between public and private spaces. Just as Louisiana was made less museum-like by its fireplace, many offices and institutions have been made more home-like by the addition of designer furniture and potted plants.

Bo Bedre was a perfect fit for the welfare society of the 1960s, which the magazine not only reflected, but also helped to furnish.

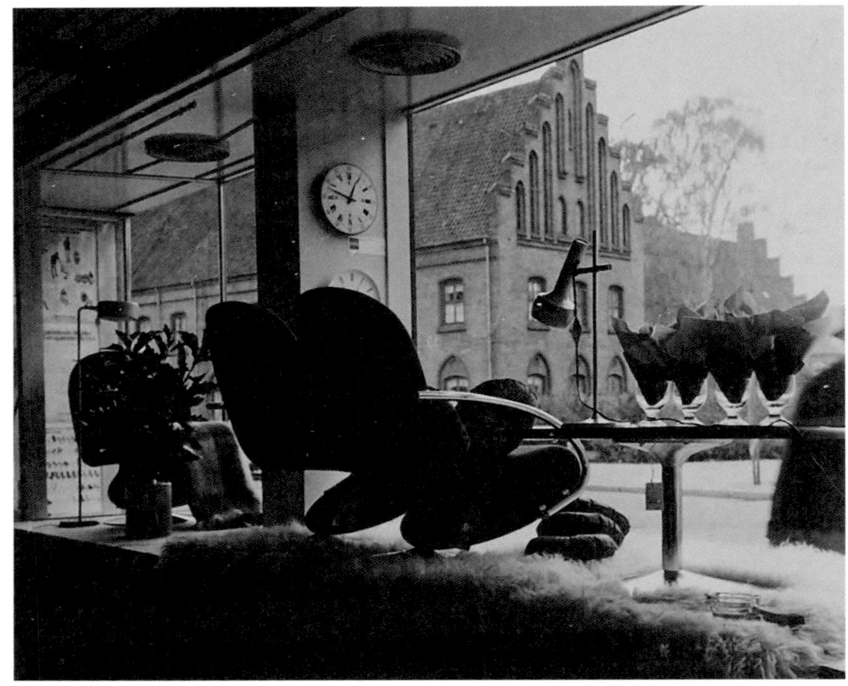

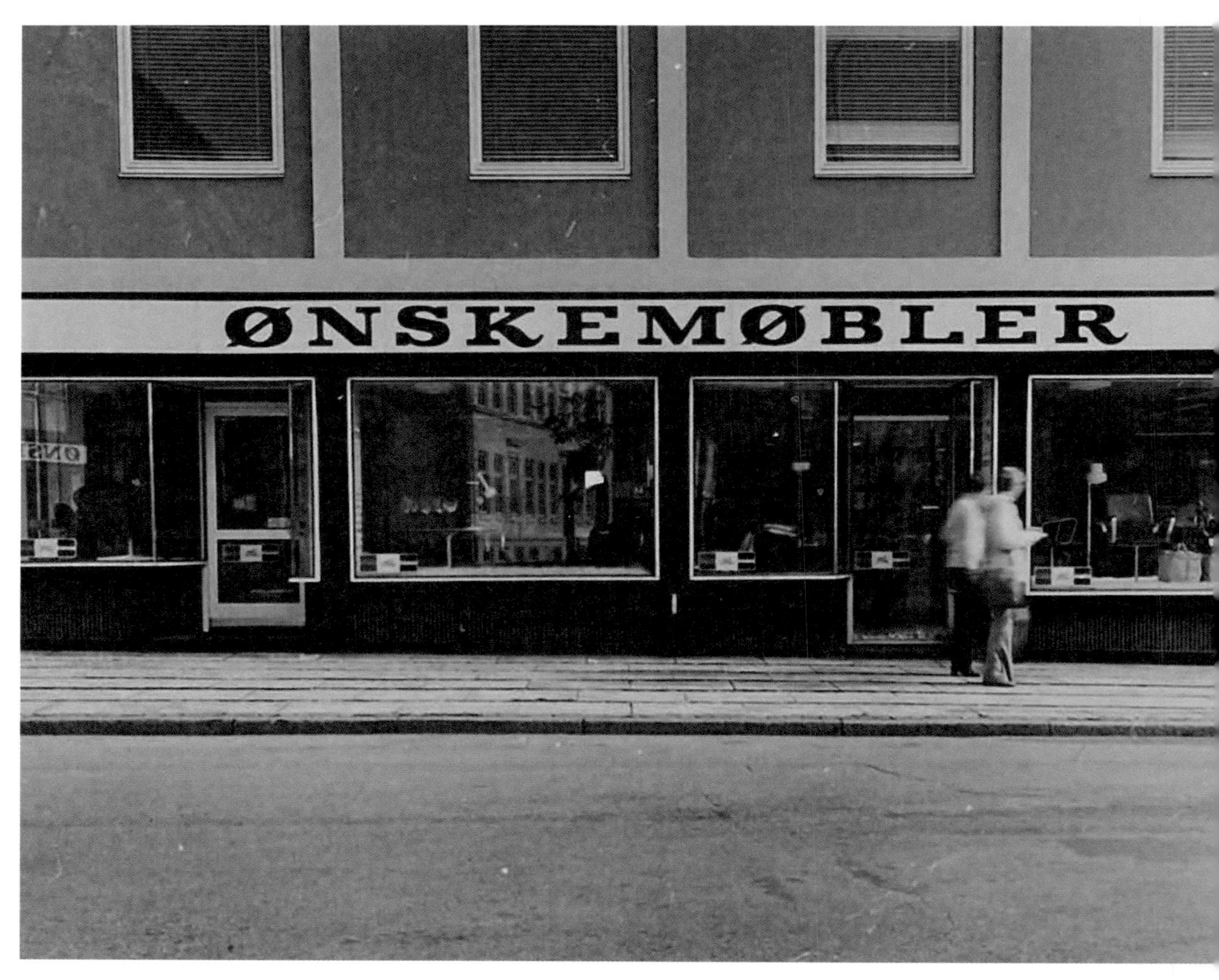
ØNSKEMØBLER

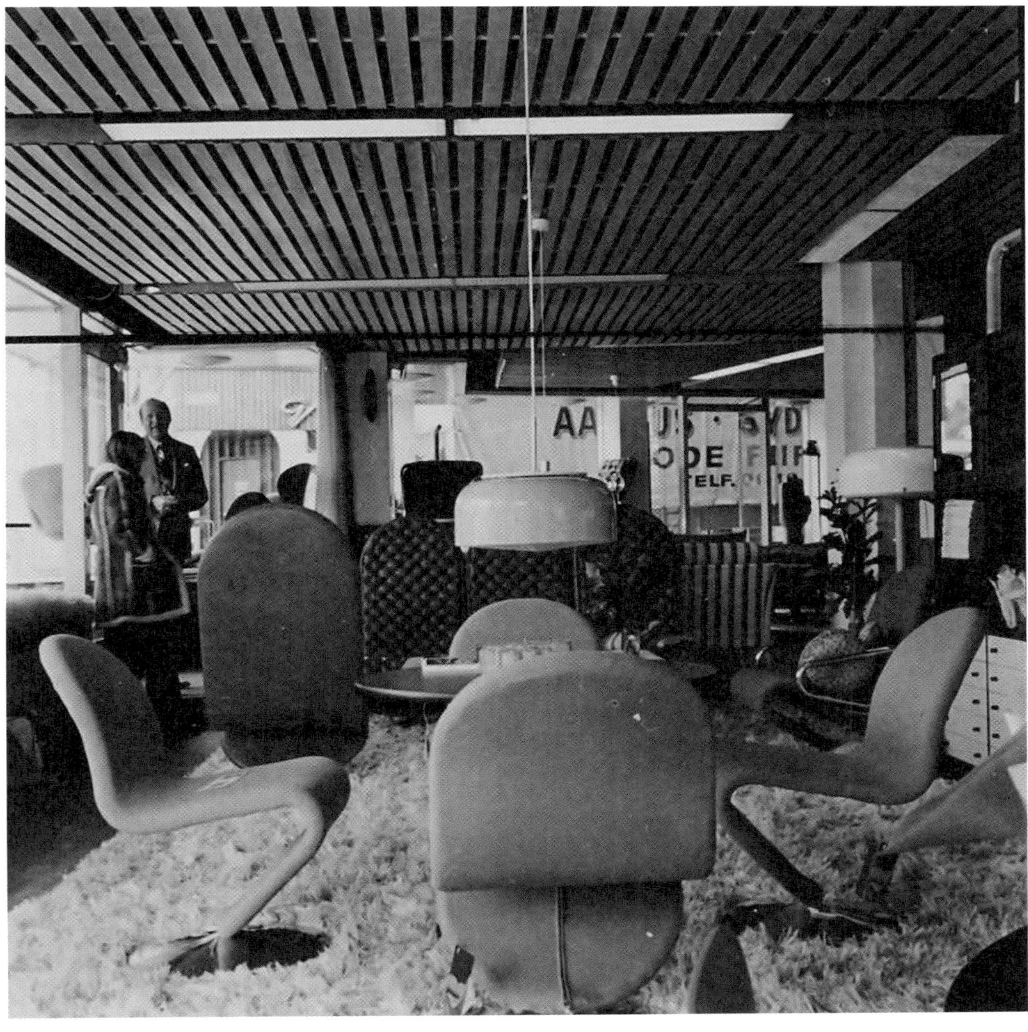

Photographs from the shop Ønskemøbler in Aarhus. After the books and magazines on interior design, the final link in the chain was the displays in the department stores and in the furniture shops of high streets where audiences could try out the furniture, possibly prompting them to buy them

Photo: Fritz Hansen's Archives

Today, a prototype of Arne Jacobsen's modular house Kubeflex is exhibited at Trapholt. It has been restored and features the interior, which Arne Jacobsen created for the prefabricated standard-house exhibition in 1970

Modernism falls out of favour

Modernism fell out of favour in the 1970s and 1980s, both internationally and in Denmark. Post-modernism's new slogan 'Less is a bore' replaced Modernism's minimalist dictum, 'Less is more'. With this, the 'golden years' of Danish furniture came to a close. Since then, the 'retro' movement emerging after the dawn of the new millennium has seen a resurgence of interest in the mid-century design classics. They are now highly sought after, much appreciated and fetch high prices.

Despite the seemingly lasting success of the Danish Design icons, one might still reasonably ask if certain limitations nevertheless apply to their spread, both in the past and present. There can be little doubt that they are most commonly found in homes that possess both cultural and economic capital – to use terms inspired by the French sociologist Pierre Bourdieu's theories of distinctions between the tastes of different social groups, tastes which govern their patterns of consumption (Bourdieu, 1997, pp. 57–78). Looking at the Modernist segment, savvy lifestyle experts will probably be able to further differentiate between environments where Arne Jacobsen's furniture is widely used, where Børge Mogensen's 'Folk Chair' is particularly popular, where Poul Kjærholm's minimalism holds sway, or where Finn Juhl's Chieftain chair is bought for the home.

Ethnologists have investigated the relationship between lifestyle and interior design styles, documenting different environments and their distinctive delimitations and values. In this respect, furniture can also be seen as signs, clues and symbols (Hvidberg, 1989). Their studies identified differences between the interior design found in the homes of workers, of the self-employed and of professionals. The specific examples considered included a rural farmhouse, the home of a metal worker, the home of a pastry chef, the home of a smallholder and the home of a forest labourer, none of which contained designer furniture. These studies are from the late 1980s; social structures and approaches to interior design may have changed since then.

One of these homes was decorated in the 'popular' style commonly seen in many Danish homes. The interior is governed by purchases made in furniture stores, but also by heirlooms and gifts from the family. Shades of brown are a recurring feature, often found on the leather or woollen upholstery of sofas, armchairs and chairs. The living room is decorated with ornaments from Den Kongelige Porcelænsfabrik (now Royal Copenhagen). The owners of this interior did not associate architect-designed furniture with high status or domestic comforts: 'Vagn and Jytte both think it seems "sterile" and "like something from a public building". This is because Danish functionalism has become the style used to decorate public spaces such as libraries, town halls and so on' (Hvidberg, 1989, p. 212).

Modernism was also subjected to criticism within the cultural and philosophical debates of the 1960s. In his 1966 book *Homo Manipulatus. Essays omkring Radikalismen* (Homo Manipulatus. Essays on Radicalism), Johan Fjord Jensen addressed the dilemmas of Modernism, exploring the perfect architecture and planning based on incisive X-ray analyses of pure function and how this might contrast up against the actual use of the settings. In Albertslund, playgrounds were adapted to meet architectural considerations, 'so that the swings are arranged like the lines in a picture by Mondrian' (Jensen, 1966, p. 188).

As a contrast to the victorious Modernism, which Fjord Jensen also associates with a welfare state frame of mind and a firm faith in the future, he points to the Hasmark area north of Odense: 'It is old; created well before the urban planners were out of their diapers. The houses are smack-bang up against each other and do not *match* neatly. Only a few of them are beautiful in a strictly architectural sense. The colours do not mesh, they clash ... the remarkable thing is that in this town you see life unfold itself like in no other seaside resort... You will find that Denmark also has picturesque environments full of human warmth. People will yearn for them. Perhaps they will eventually become fashionable; indeed, maybe the conservation authorities will step in and *protect* them' (Jensen, 1966, pp. 142–143).

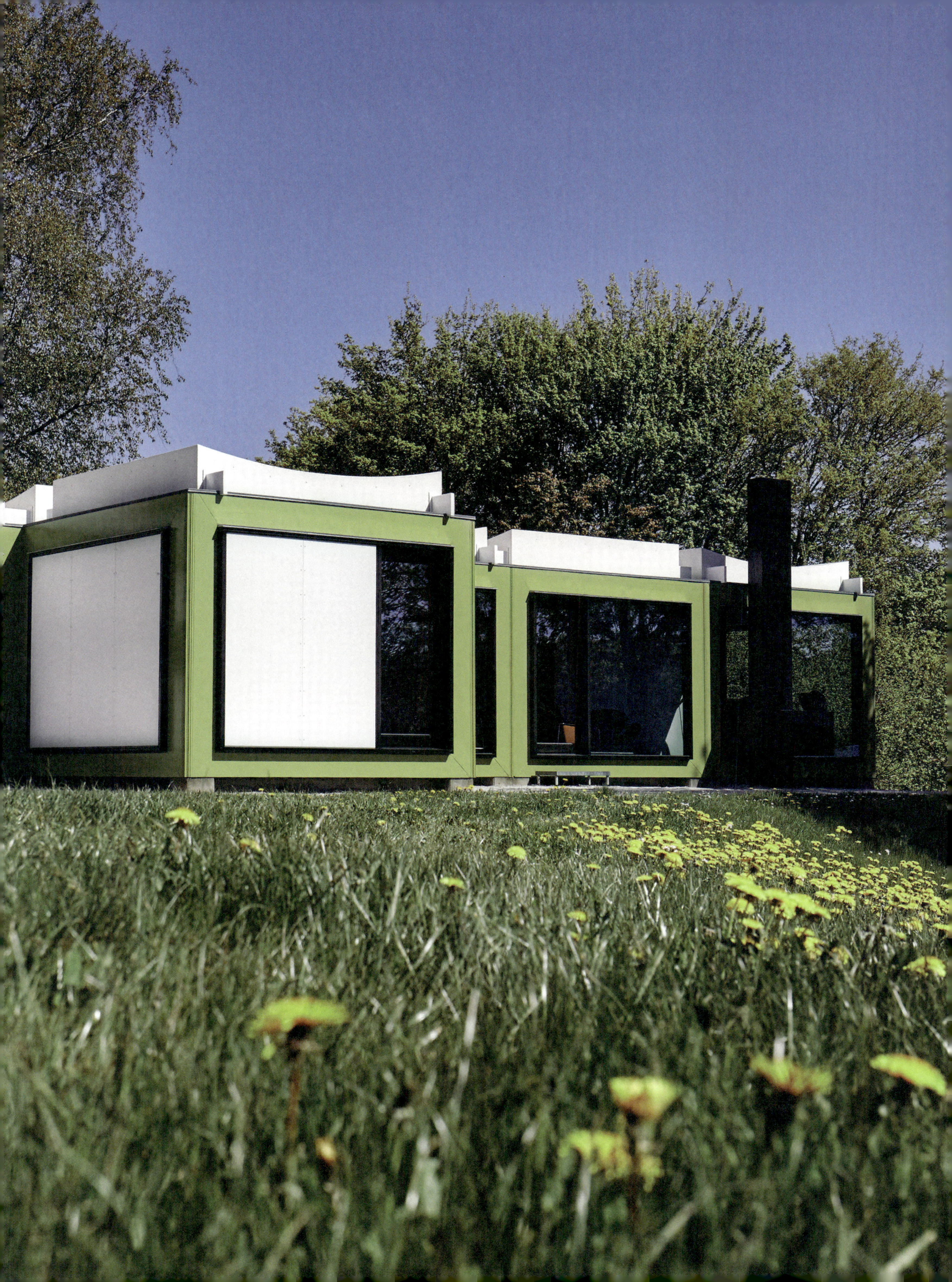

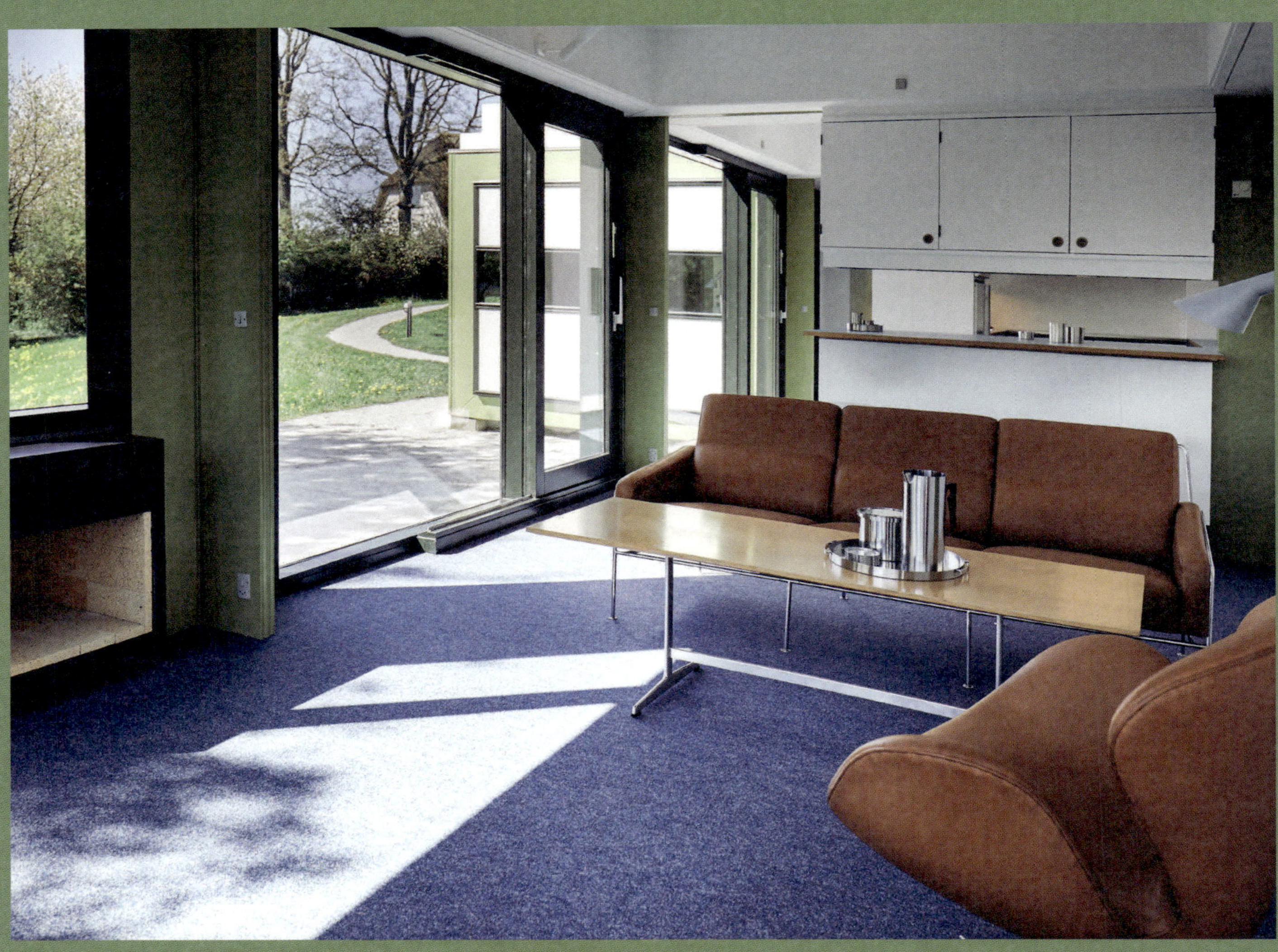

Trapholt's Kubeflex, in which Arne Jacobsen's interior from 1970 has been reinstated

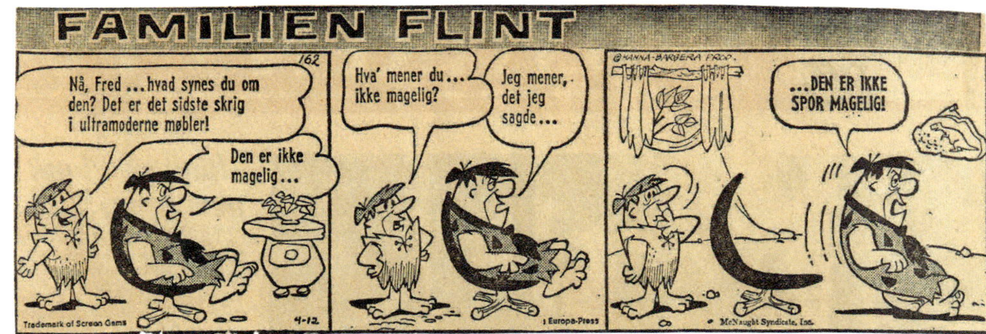

Syndicated internationally, this *Flintstones* strip from 1962 illustrates how Modernism was not always associated with comfort

Photo: *Politiken*, 20.6. 1962, Fritz Hansen's archives

Fjord Jensen's deliberations are interesting in relation to Arne Jacobsen's Kubeflex design for modular holiday homes; the prototype is now on display at the Trapholt museum. The modular system consists of square white cubes, each measuring 3.36 meters x 3.36 meters, which can be combined according to the residents' wishes and needs (Thau & Vindum, 1998, p. 506). Arne Jacobsen developed the house in 1969–70 in collaboration with Høm Typehuse, a company specialising in prefabricated houses. It was first presented at the *Archibo II* exhibition in Ishøj in 1970. Kubeflex was intended as a flexible system where the units could be freely combined, adding or removing modules as required. The system included different façade elements, which could be made entirely of glass, be completely solid, or incorporate aspects of both. The interiors could also be changed, turning a kitchen into a bedroom or antechamber. The idea was that it should be possible to deliver each cube on-site complete with electricity and insulation, ensuring that the construction would also be financially viable. The large expanses of glass mean that you have an unimpeded view of nature no matter where you are in the house.

However, this experimental holiday home never entered production. Indeed, it would seem that it attracted very little attention in its own day. For example, the house was not mentioned in the journal *Arkitekten*'s reviews of the *Archibo* exhibitions. Perhaps it failed to correspond to the general notion of what a holiday home should be like? Was it too far ahead of its time? Could it have been presented in a better, more attractive way?

For many years, the Kubeflex prototype – the only one of its kind – stood at Orøsund beach in South Zealand, where it served as a holiday home for the Jacobsen family. The modules were eventually moved to Trapholt, where they can now be viewed by visitors. Here, their stringent lines interact directly with the white Modernism of the museum building itself.

Many other Modernist experimental holiday homes suffered similar fates, never progressing beyond the page – or with only very few examples actually being built (Dahlkild, 2018). This included Ib Lunding's drawings of small, circular futuristic houses, Verner Panton's semi-cylindrical house and Simon Spies's rather more exotic project known as 'Villa Fjolle' in the Stockholm archipelago. The latter was intended to be the first of a series of houses that would land in an all-new kind of leisure landscape like flying saucers.

Instead of Modernist designs, the holiday homes springing up in 1960s Denmark were mostly brown, wooden holiday cottages made by the many prefab house companies that proved successful at catering to the consumers. Not even Friis and Moltke's award-winning prefabricated house, reminiscent of Mies van der Rohe's Farnsworth House except for being made of wood, was able to compete with the more popular designs.

At the end of the 1960s, *Bo Bedre* ran competitions to find the 'holiday home of the year'. The competing houses were far from identical, but would typically be wooden cottages, stained brown outside and with light wood and light wooden furniture inside. The winning submission in 1967 received its medal because it had good 'holiday' properties. Moreover, it had 'a traditional, but clear and well-proportioned form ... This is neither intriguing nor distinctive architecture ...' (Steen-Andersen, 1967, p. 14). The final selection also included a Skarridsø house, Type 44, which was also a wooden house with a low pitched roof: 'Like the other prefabricated houses made by this company, this house makes an excellent holiday home' (Steen-Andersen, 1967, p. 19). The following year it was on the cover of a *Bo Bedre* book on prefabricated holiday homes (Jepsen, 1968). Obviously, holiday architecture had to be relaxed and traditional.

Let Arne Jacobsen have the last word. He himself was aware of how unpretentious surroundings could be an aid to relaxation. He was fond of cakes and cafés, and his close associate Otto Weitling relates a visit they paid to a real Viennese café and patisserie. Arne Jacobsen leaned back and said: 'Here one can really relax, because here everything is hopeless. Nothing can be changed here' (Tøjner & Vindum, 1996, p. 105).

Endnotes

1. The specifics of the development have been described in greater detail than space permits us to do here in e.g. Kaiser (1992); Hansen (2006); Dybdahl (2017)

Bibliography

Bo, J., Lauridsen, I., Wohlert, V. (1961). Vil vi bo i akvarier?. *Bo Bedre*, 1

Bourdieu, P. (1997). *Af praktiske grunde: Omkring teorien om menneskelig handlen*. København: Hans Reitzlers Forlag

Breunig, M. (2013). Kunstmuseet som totaloplevelse: Louisianas genius. I: Breunig, M., Frank, S., Kortbek, H.B., Moslund, S.P. (Red.). *Stedsvandringer: Analyser af stedet betydning i kunst, kultur og medier*. Odense: Syddansk Universitetsforlag

Dahlkild, N. (2019). From Bauhaus to Bispebjerg – Edvard Heiberg and the Social Avant-Garde. I: Hjartarson, B., Kollnitz, A., Stounbjerg, P., Ørum, T. *A Cultural History of the Avantgarde in the Nordic Countries 1925-1950* (s. 423-440). Leiden og Boston: Bill Rodopi

Dahlkild, N. (Red.) (2018). *Sommerlandets arkitektur: Drømmen om det gode liv*. Charlottenlund: Museum Tusculnums Forlag

Dybdahl, L. (2017). *Det danske møbelboom 1945-1975*. København: Strandberg Publishing

Fritz Hansens arkiv

Hansen, P.H. (2006). *Da danske møbler blev moderne*. Odense: Syddansk Universitetsforlag og Ascheboug

Heiberg, E. (1935). *To Vær. Straks*. København: Mondes Forlag

Hjort, E. (1947). *Bo Rigtigt*. København: Jul. Gjellerups Forlag

Hoffmeyer, E. (Red.) (1962). *Velfærdsteori og velfærdsstat*. København: Berlinske

Hvidberg, E. (Red.). (1989). *Boligform og livsstil. Arv og Eje*. Dansk Kulturhistorisk Museumsforening

Jensen, J.F. (1966). *Homo Manipulatus: Essays omkring Radikalismen*. København: Gyldendal

Jensen, K.W. (1966). *Slaraffenland eller Utopia: Artikler om Velfærdsstatens Kulturpolitik*. København: Gyldendal

Jepsen, H. (1968). *Bo Bedres bog om Typeferiehuse*. København: Fogtdal

Juhl, F. (1954). *Hjemmets indretning*. København: Thaning og Appels Forlag

Jørstian, T. & Nielsen, P.E.M. (1994). *Tænd! PH lampens historie*. København: Gyldendal.

Kaiser, B. (1992). *Den ideologiske funktionalisme*. København: Gad

Kritisk Revy. (1926a). *Kritisk Revy, 1*. Henningsen, P. (Red.)

Kritisk Revy. (1926b). *Kritisk Revy, 3*. Henningsen, P. (Red.)

Littrup, S. (2004). PH5. I: *De industrielle ikoner: Design Danmark*. København: Det Danske Kunstindustrimuseum

Lund. N (1991). *Nordisk Arkitektur*. København: Arkitektens Forlag

Ministeriet for Kulturelle Anliggender (1969). *Betænkning 517: En Kulturpolitisk Redegørelse*. København

Steen-Andersen, Ove. (1967). Vi kårer årets bedste feriehus. *Bo Bedre, 3*

Thau, C. & Vindum, K. (1998). *Arne Jacobsen*. København: Arkitektens forlag

Tiedemann, A. (2013). Bladet, der lærte danskerne at bo bedre. I: Christiansen, J.H. & Møller, V.A. (Red.), *Architectura*, 35, København: Selskabet for Arkitekturhistorie

Tøjner, P.E. & Vindum, K. (1996). *Arne Jacobsen: Arcitect & Designer*. København: Dansk Designcenter

Wendt, F. (1972). Besættelse og Atomtid. I: Danstrup, J. & Koch, H. I., *Danmarks Historie*, 14. København: Politikens Forlag

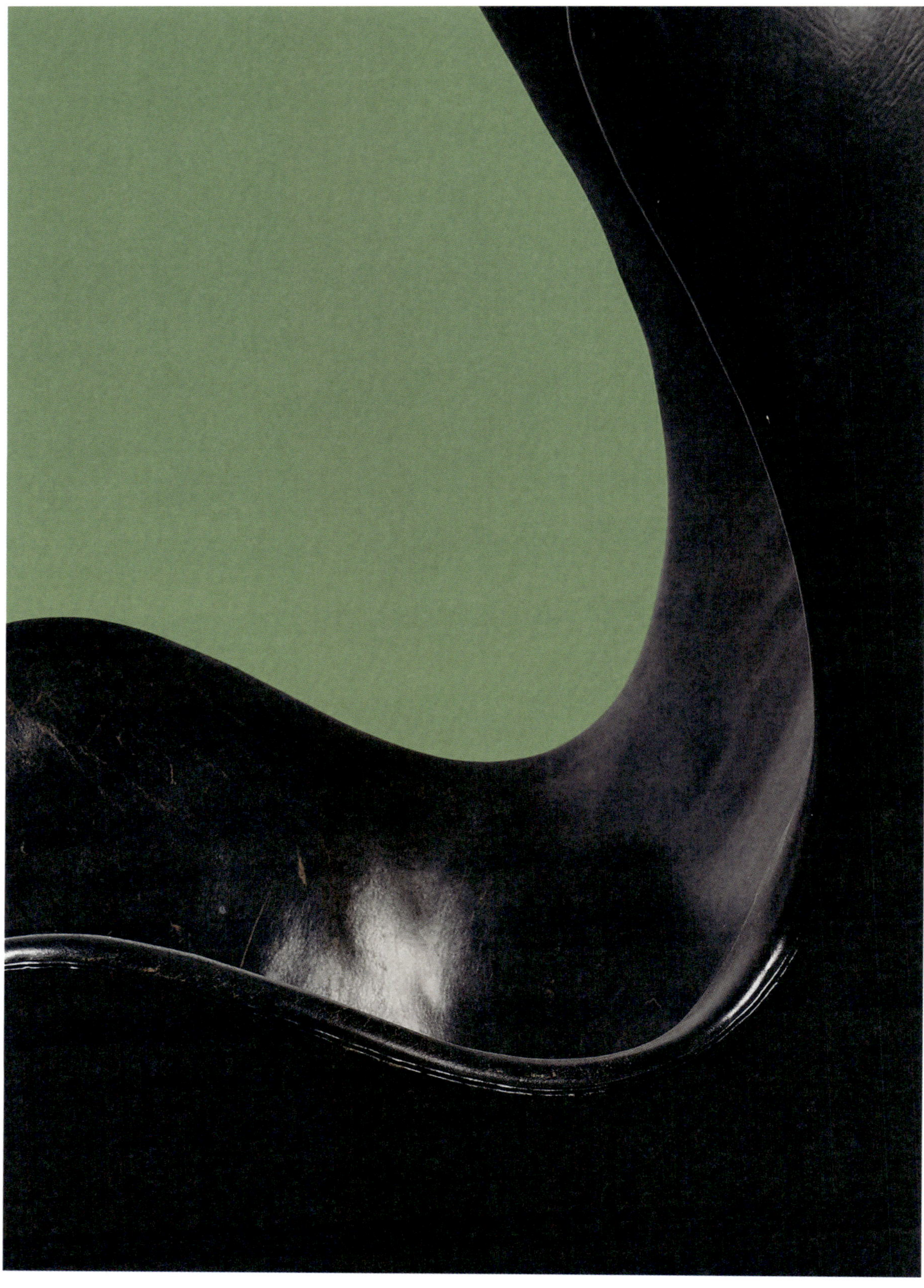

The Egg chair (1958)

Trapholt Collection

Series 7 on a
carpet with one of
Arne Jacobsen's
pattern designs

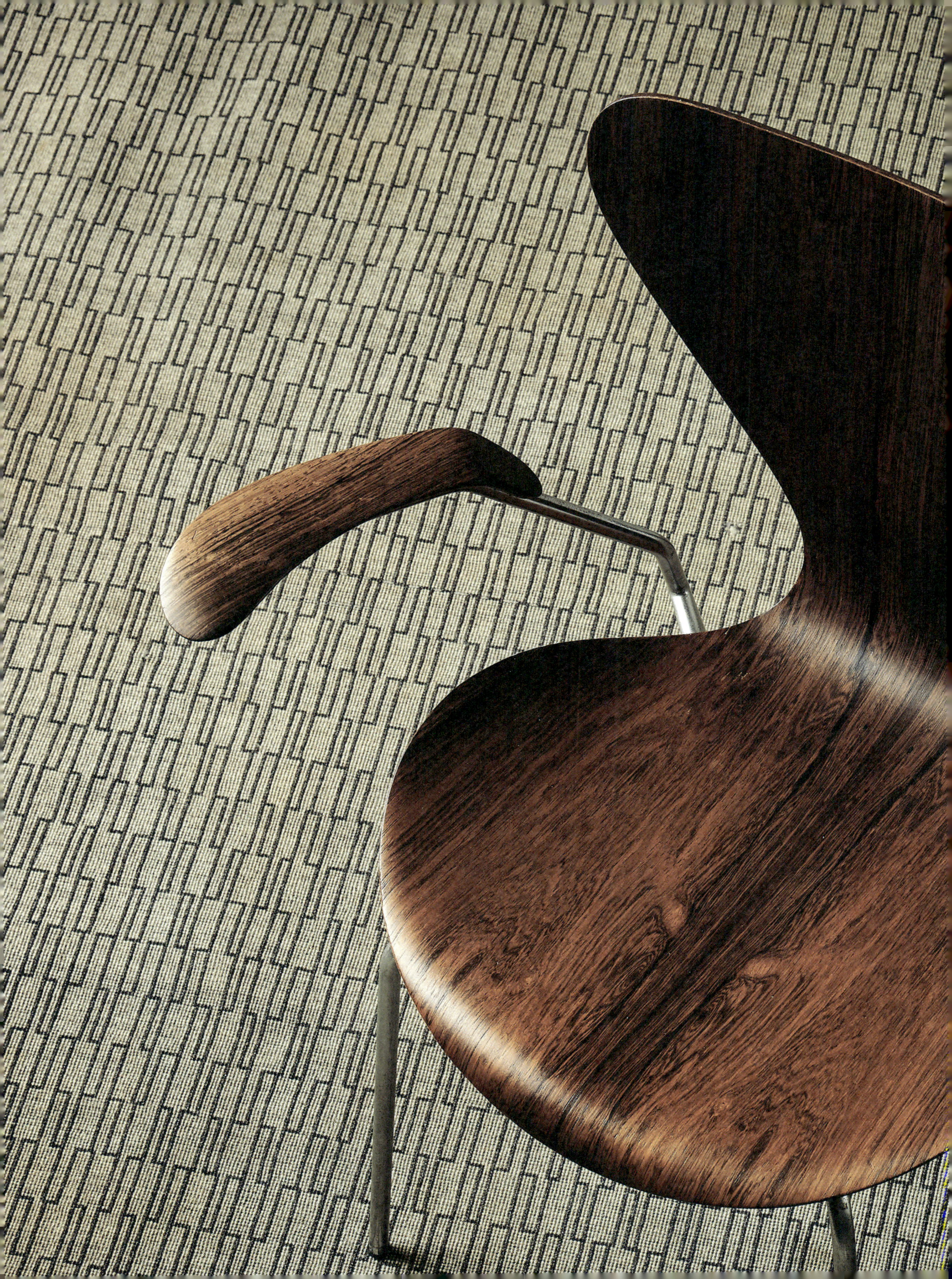

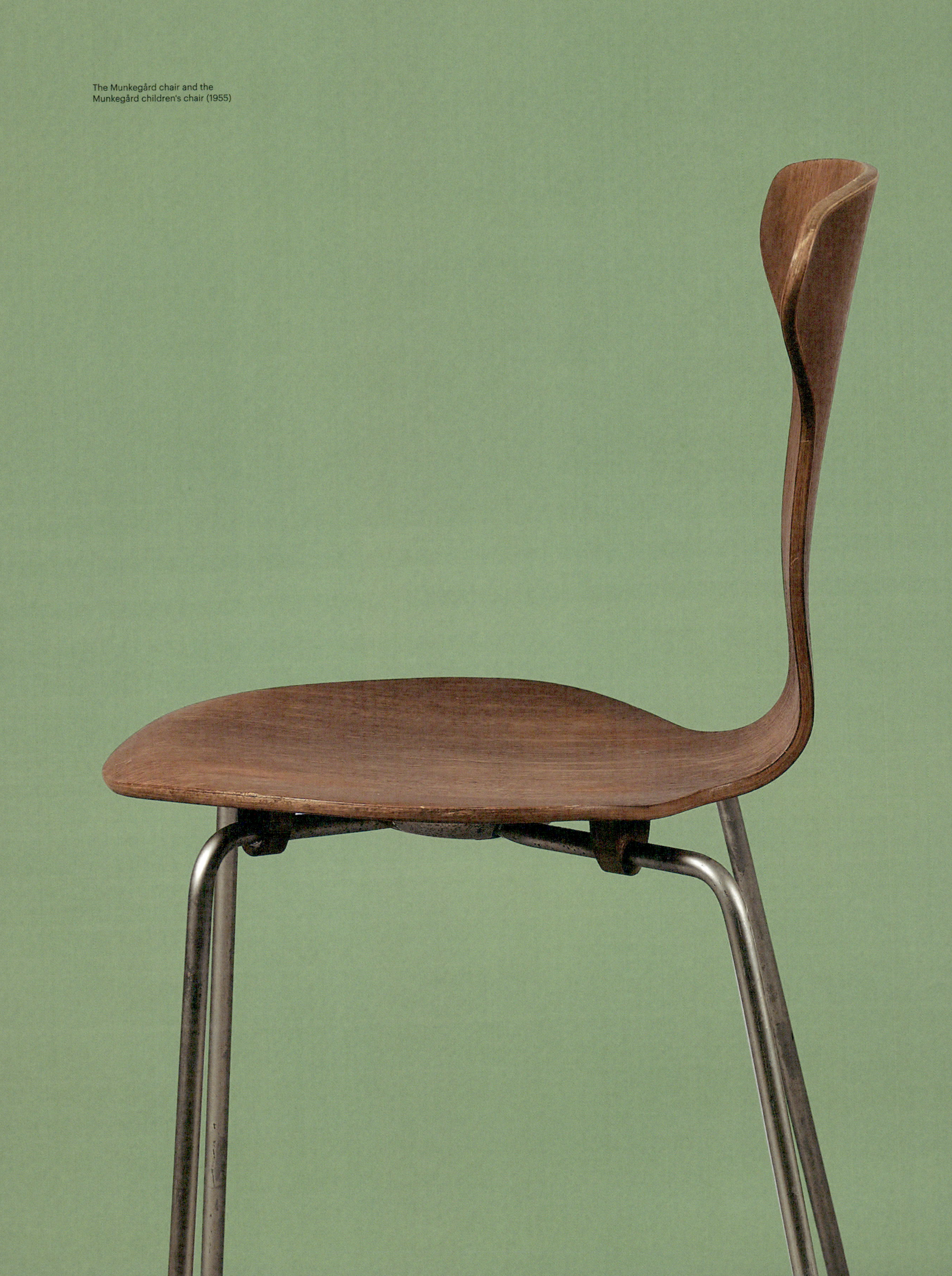

The Munkegård chair and the
Munkegård children's chair (1955)

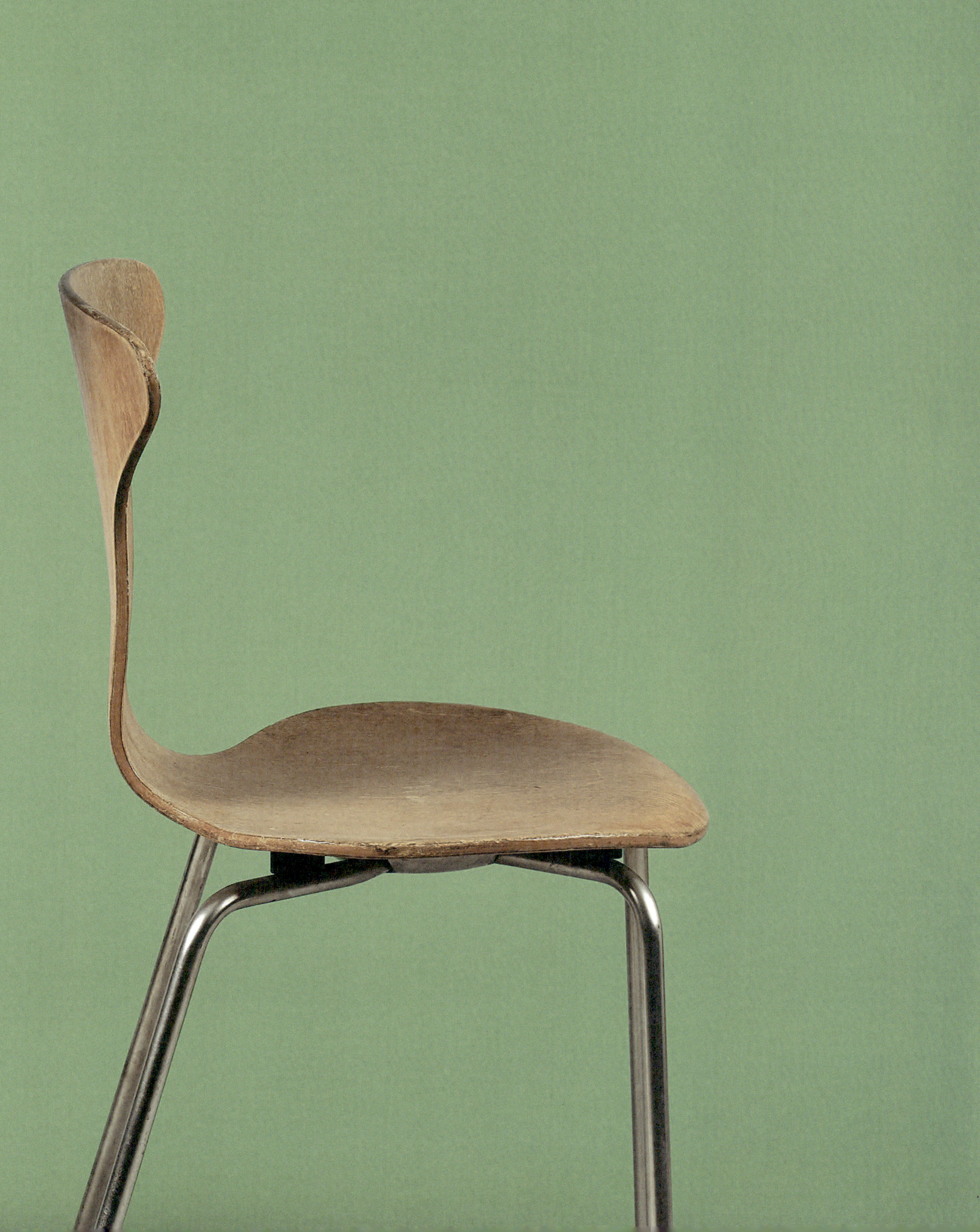

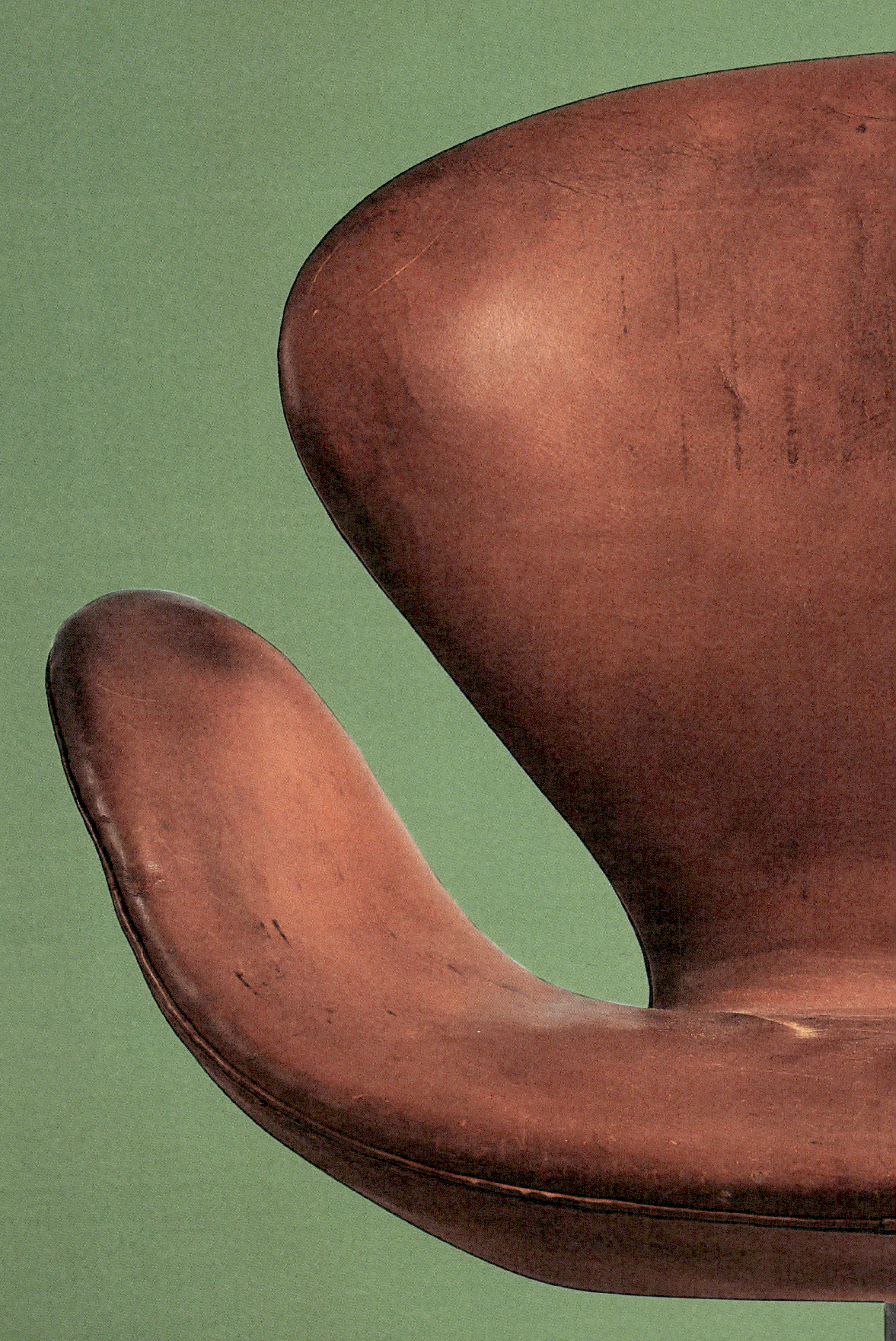

The Swan (1958)

Trapholt Collection

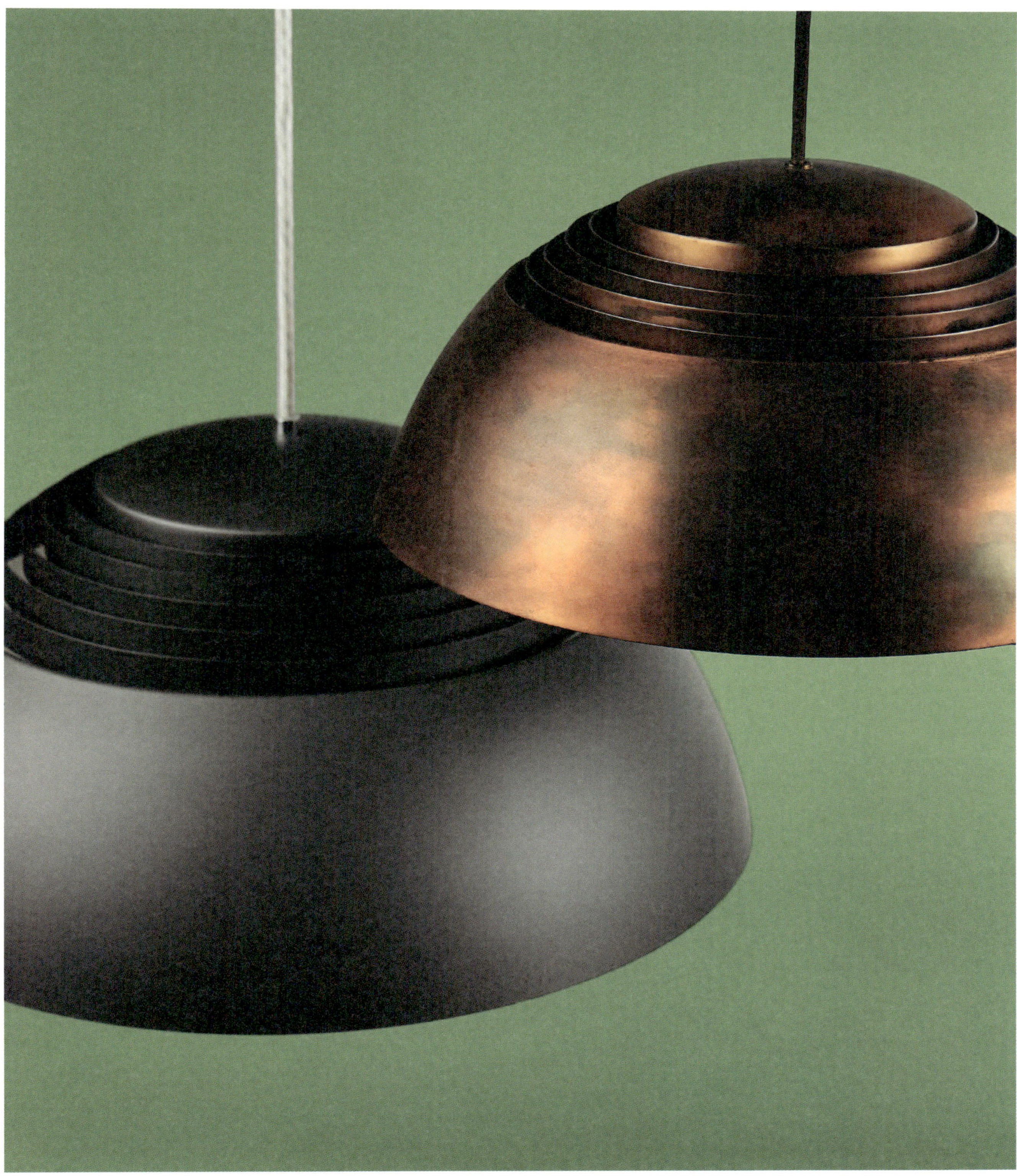

The AJ Royal pendant lamp (1957)

Giraffe chair (1959)

Giraffe chair (1959)

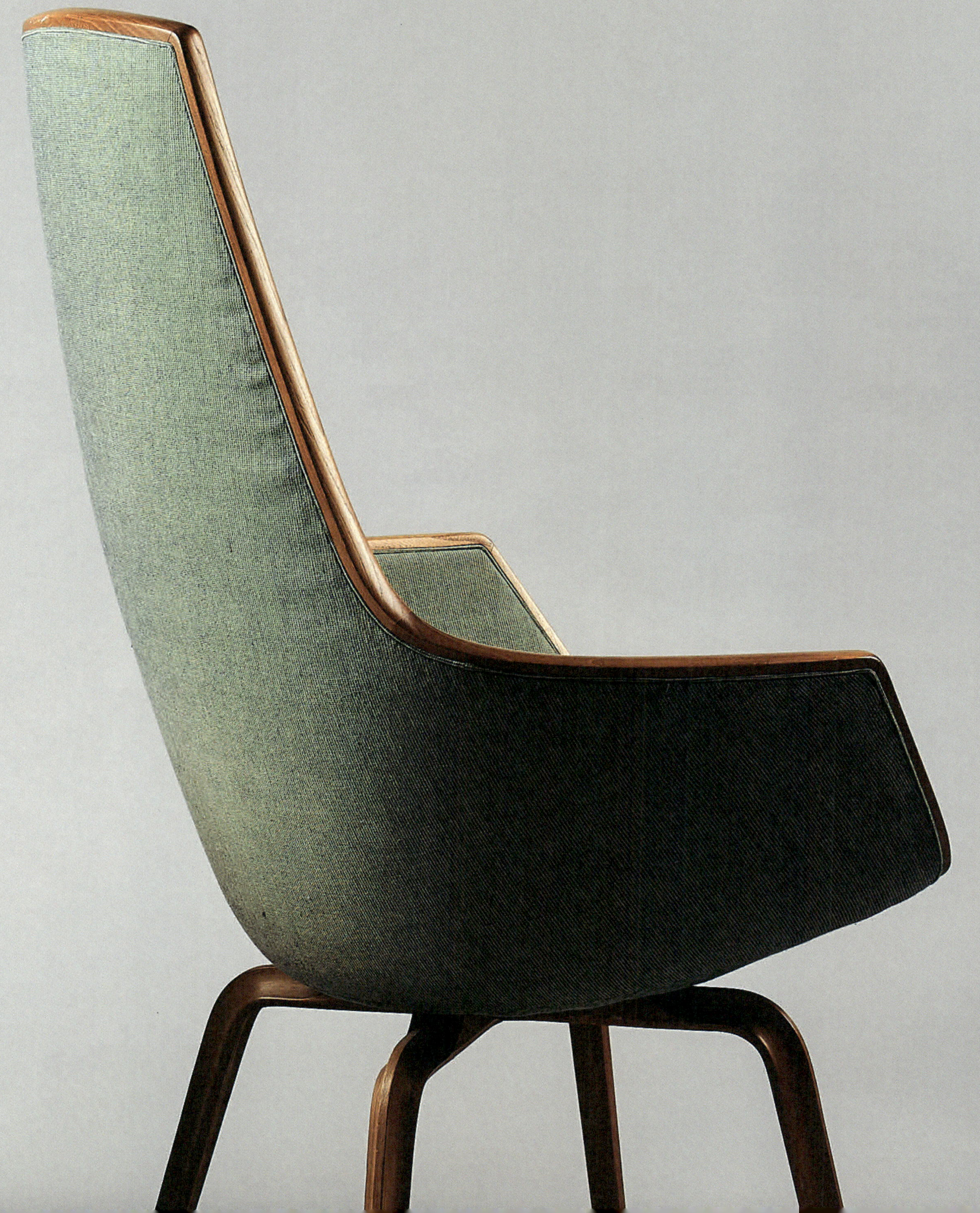

Biographies

Annika Skaarup Larsen

b. 1989. MA in Art History from the University of Copenhagen and studies at the Université Paris Diderot (Paris 7). Since 2017, Annika has worked as an art historian and registrar for Arne Jacobsen Design I/S, cataloguing Arne Jacobsen's work on the digital platform *The Arne Jacobsen Library*. Her research areas include artistic working processes, as exemplified by the article *Bertel Thorvaldsen and Zeuxis: The Assembling Artist* (2017), in which she addresses the connection between imitation and innovation in Neoclassical art theory.

Katrine Stenum Poulsen

b. 1990, MA in Art History and Curating from the University of Birmingham, UK. Katrine is a curator at the Trapholt Museum for Modern Art and Design. At Trapholt, Katrine has curated the exhibitions *Arne Jacobsen – Designs Denmark* (2020) in co-operation with Annika Skaarup Larsen, *Anette Harboe Flensburg – In Company with No-One* (2020), *SENSE ME* (2019) in co-operation with Karen Grøn, *Eske Kath – Fundamental Uncertainty* (2019), and *Michael Geertsen – EKKO* (2019). Her research focuses particularly on the affective potential of art, but she is also interested in the role and significance of art in public spaces. Katrine also acts as a consultant for the Municipality of Kolding on commissions for public art. Major publications include SENSE ME (2019), Trapholt, edited with Karen Grøn; *Anette Harboe Flensburg – In Company With No-one* (2020), Trapholt, and *FLUX 2017*, Room7 Curating.

Nan Dahlkild

b. 1949, associate professor, PhD at the Department of Communication, University of Copenhagen. Nan has written books such as *Biblioteket i tid og rum* (2011) and curated the following exhibitions and edited the catalogues accompanying them: *Huse der har formet os* (2015), *Sommerlandets arkitektur* (2018) and *Danish Architecture and Society* (2020). He has also contributed essays on 'Bauhaus og Danmark' in *Architectura 28* and on 'Velfærdens spydspids' in *Architectura 35. Temanummer om Velfærdssamfundets bygninger*.

Timeline

06

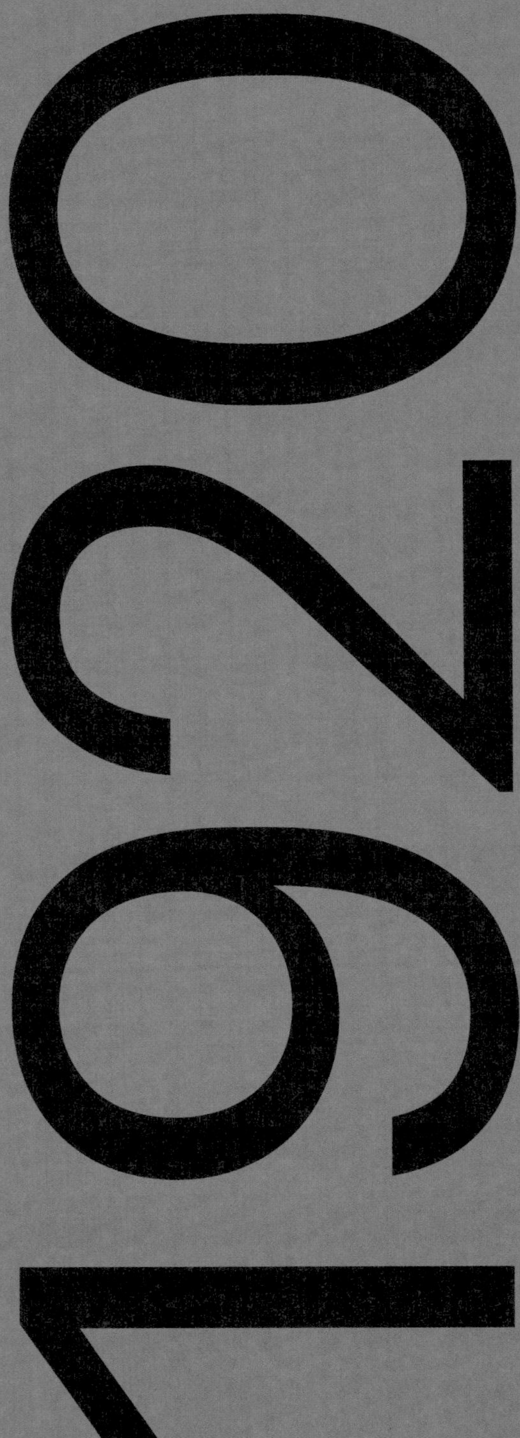

Photo: The Royal Danish Library – The Danish National Art Library

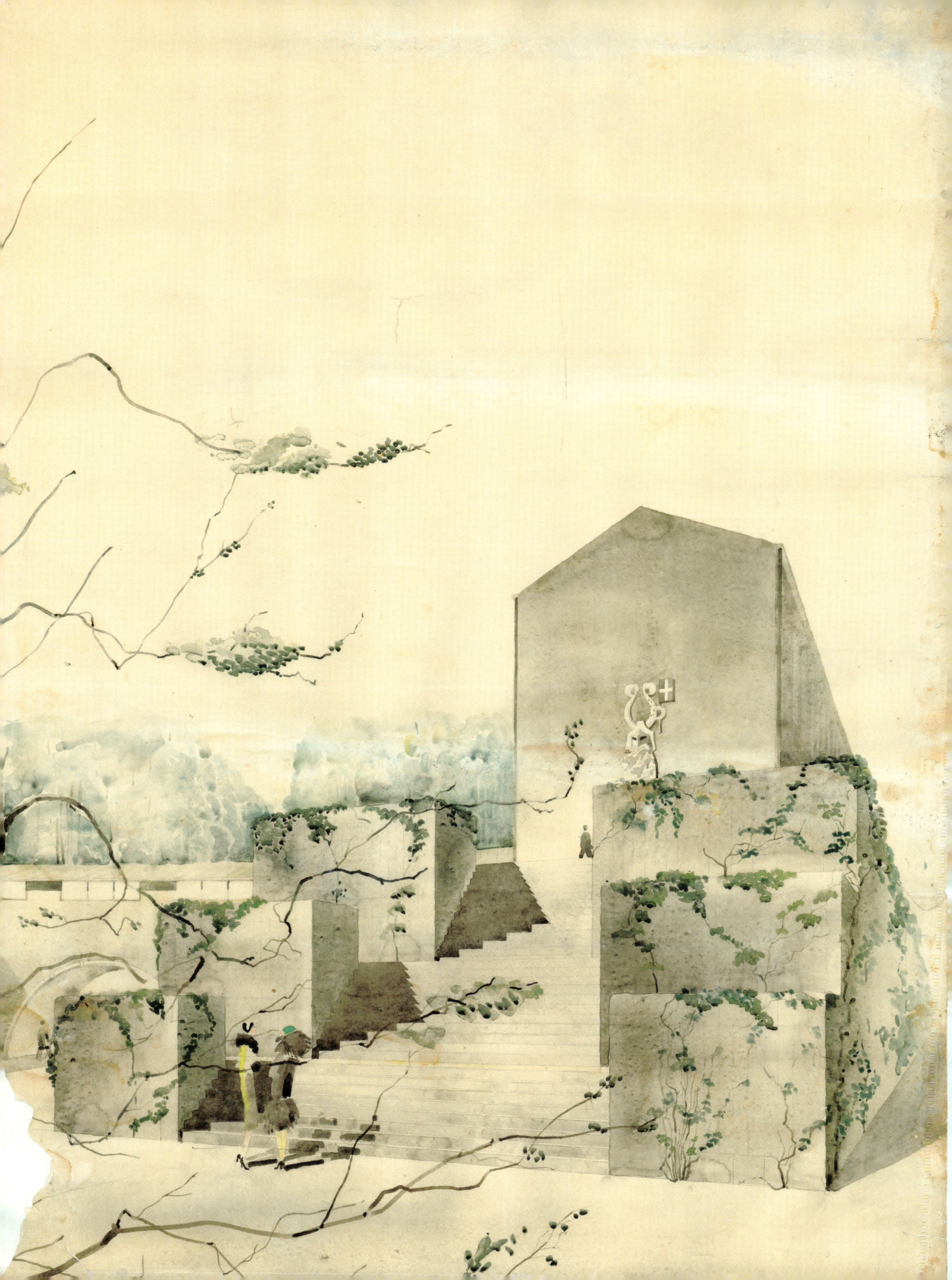

1921

On the passenger ship, the *Frederik VIII* bound for New York etc.

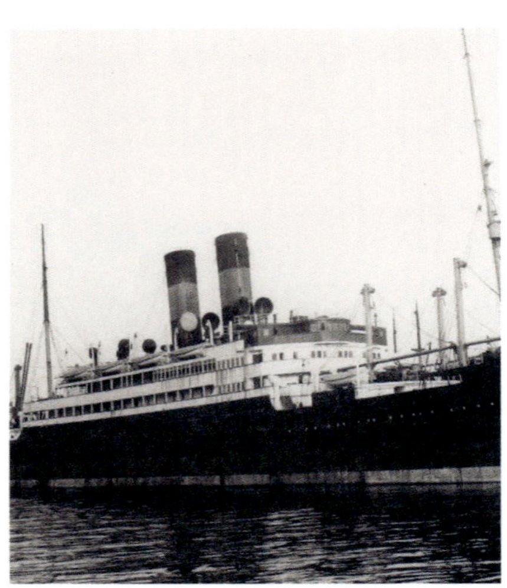

1924

Graduates from the Building programme at the Technical College and admitted to the Royal Danish Academy of Fine Arts, School of Architecture in Copenhagen

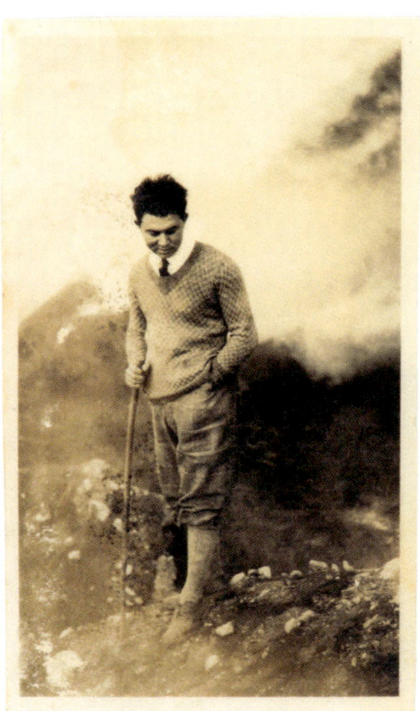

A young Arne Jacobsen
Photo: Private photo

1925

1 |

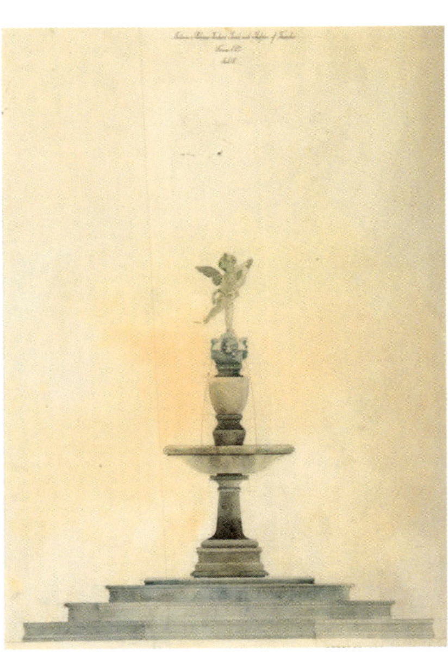

Watercolor from a travel to Florence
Photo: Private photo

Travels in France and Italy | 1

His first-known chair design (unknown today). Awarded a silver medal at the Exposition internationale des arts décoratifs et industriels modernes in Paris

Works for Kay Fisker at the Danish Pavilion of the Exposition internationale des arts décoratifs et industriels modernes in Paris

1927

1 |

Photo: The Royal Danish Library – The Danish National Art Library

2 |

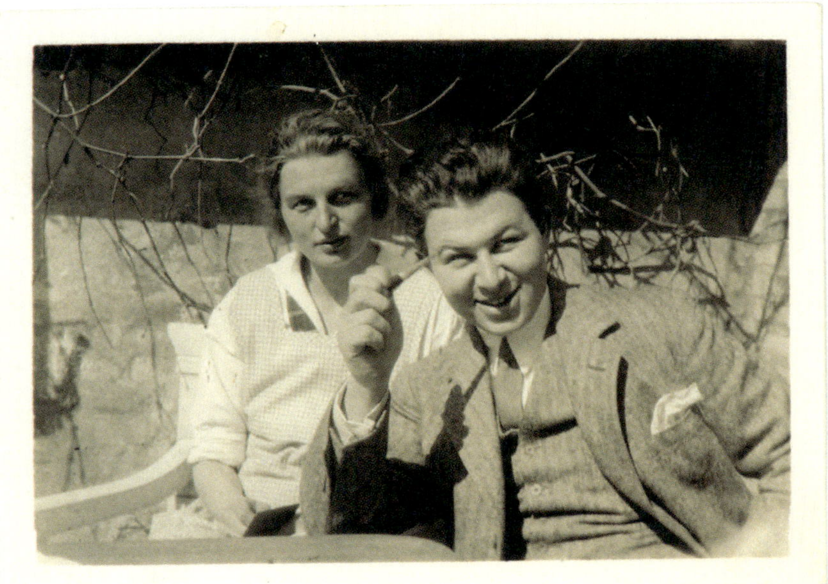

Photo: Private photo

The Library chair | 1

Graduates from the Royal Danish Academy of Fine Arts

Marries Marie Jelstrup Holm | 2

Works at the Copenhagen City Architect practice. Here he designs buildings for Enghaveparken

Designs his first two private homes, including one for Professor Sigurd Wandel in Hellerup

1928

Awarded the Academy's minor gold medal for his proposal for a National Museum in Klampenborg

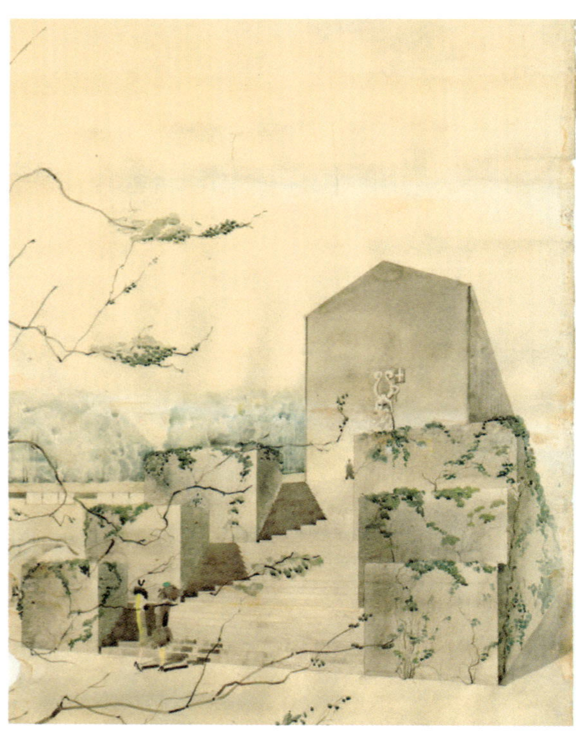

Photo: The Royal Danish Library
– The Danish National Art Library

1929

1 |

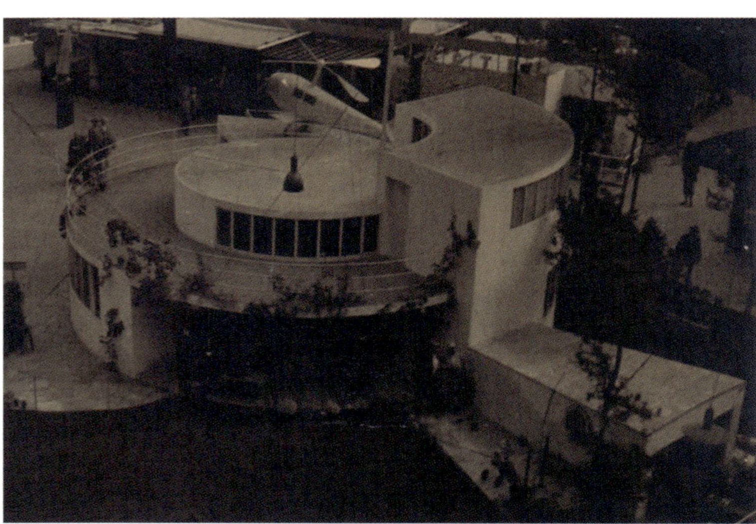

Photo: The Royal Danish Library
– The Danish National Art Library

The Forest Snail easy chair

'House of the Future' with Flemming Lassen | 1

CLOC Bar at the Danish Association of Architects exhibition in Forum | 2

The AJ reading lamp

Sets up his own practice. In the same year, he builds five detached houses, including his own *funkis*-style (Danish functionalist) house in Ordrup

2 |

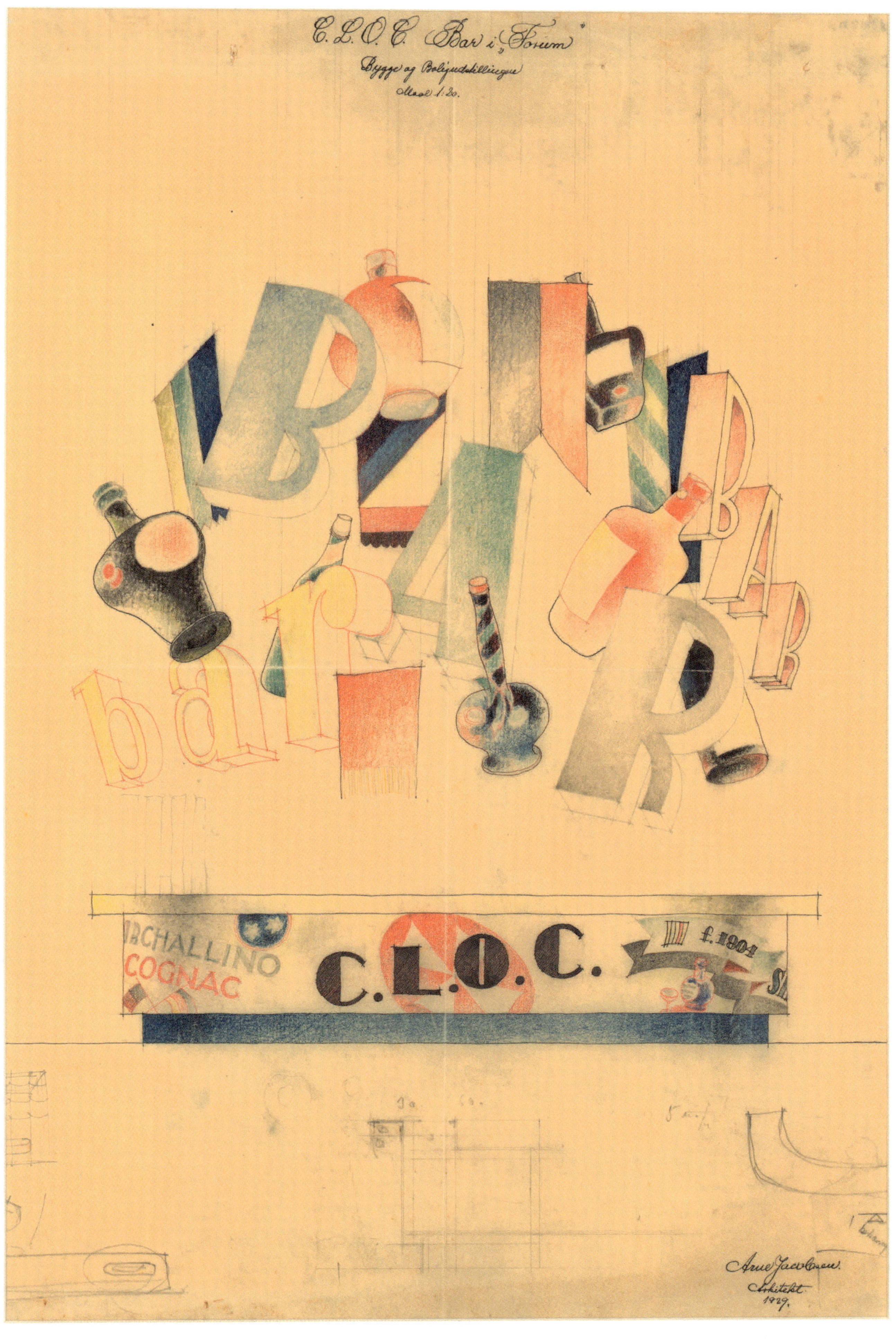

Photo: The Royal Danish Library
– The Danish National Art Library

Photo: The Royal Danish Library – The Danish National Art Library

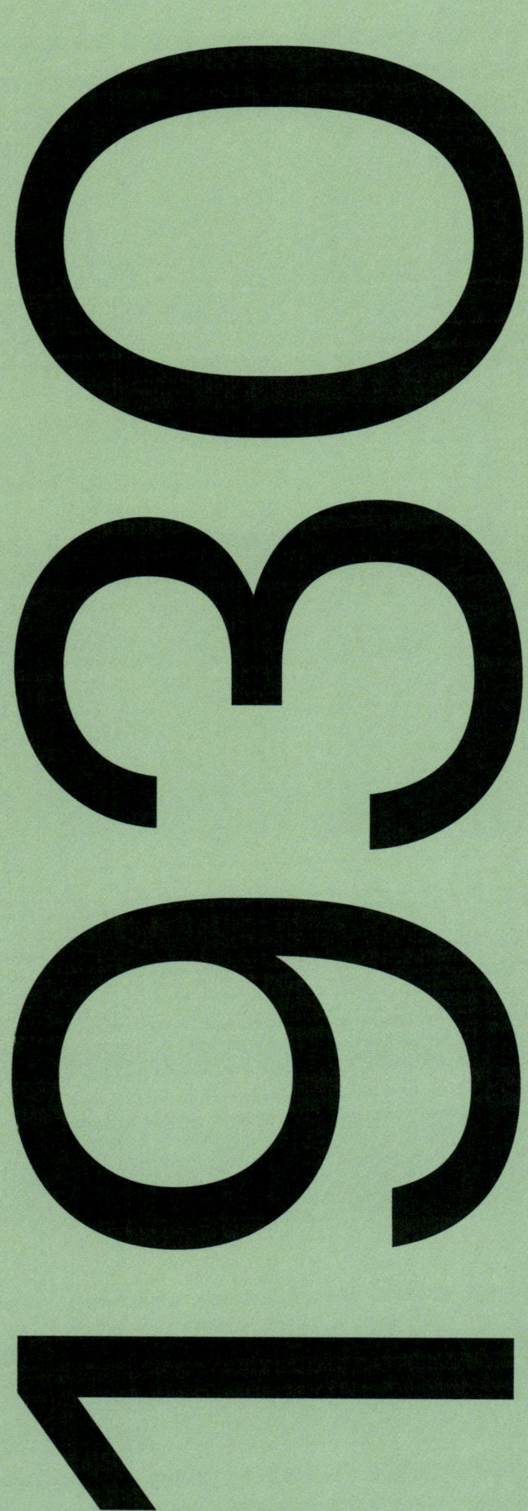

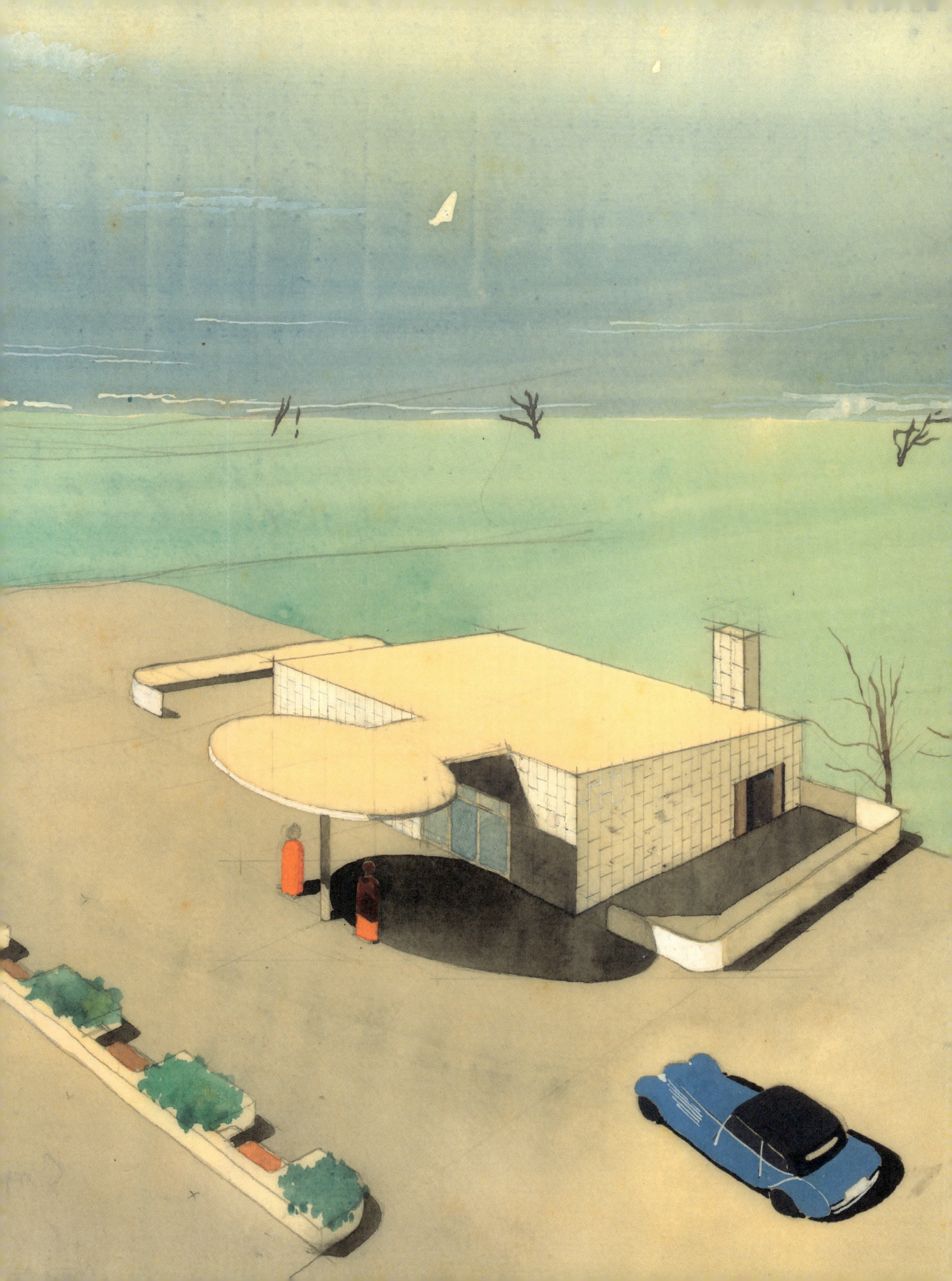

1930

House for the Rothenborg family in Klampenborg

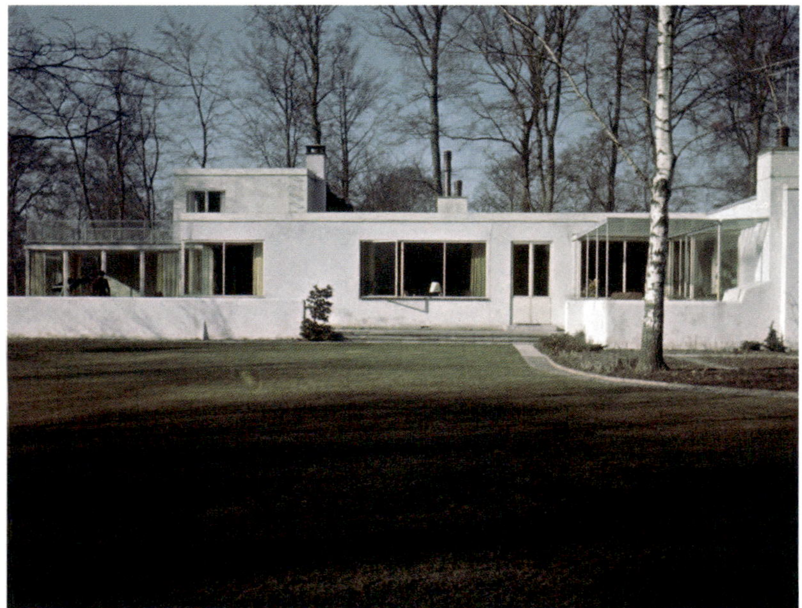

Photo: Arne Jacobsen. The original can be found in: The Royal Danish Library – The Danish National Art Library

1931

Hearse and pall with Flemming Lassen

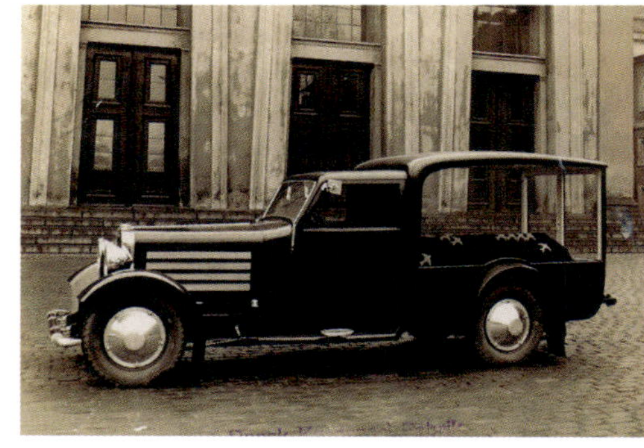

Photo: Private photo

1932

Bellevue Beach, incl. design for tickets and ice cream kiosks | 1

Exhibition design and poster for the Radiofoni Exhibition | 2

Living room for the master carpenter, N.C. Christoffersen, exhibited at the Cabinet-makers' Exhibition with Flemming Lassen

1 |

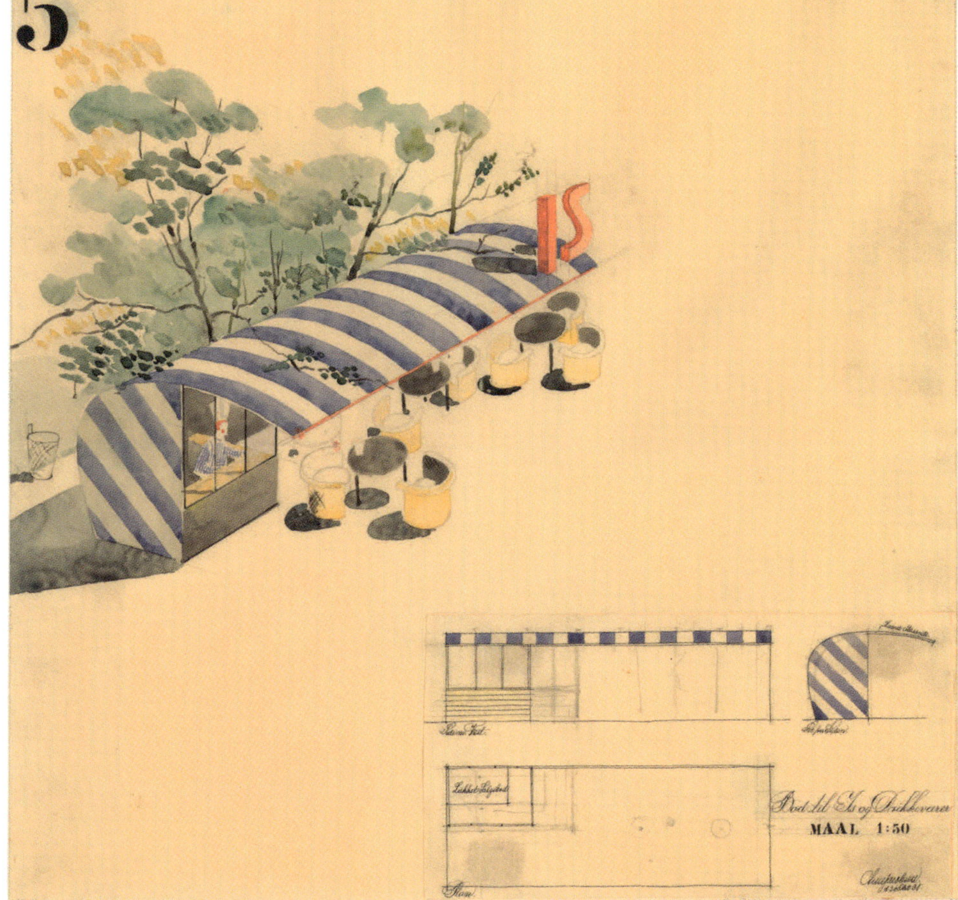

Photo: The Royal Danish Library – The Danish National Art Library

2 |

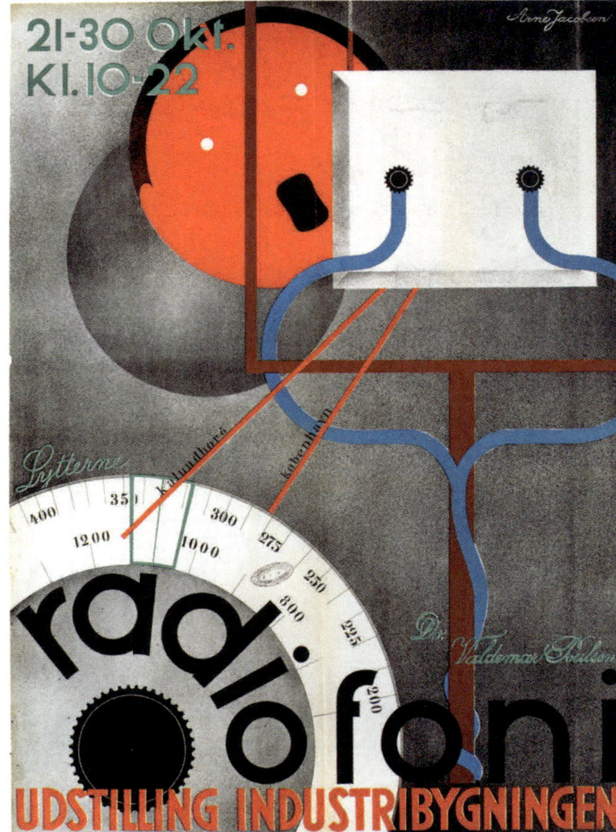

Photo: Pernille Klemp

1933

Dragør Beach
Bathing Facilities

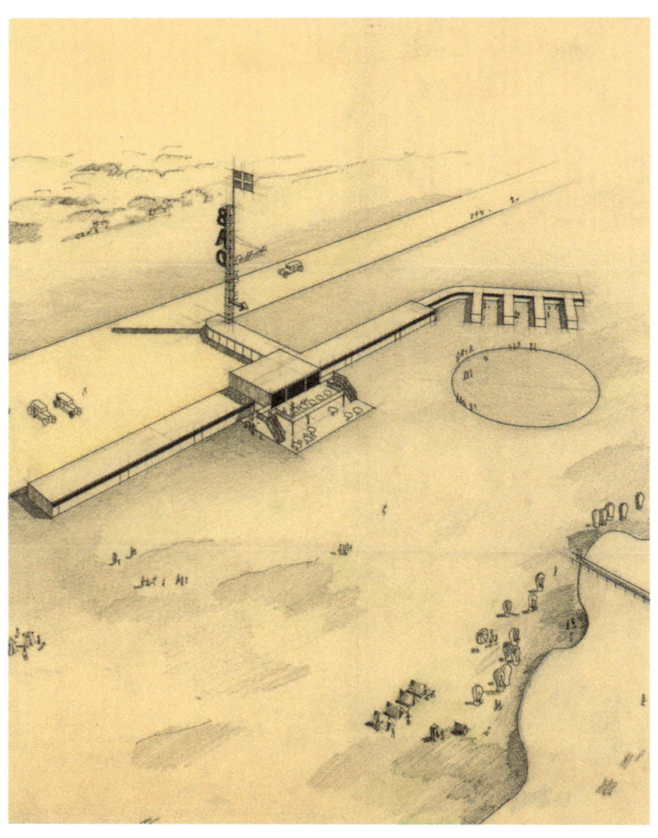

Photo: The Royal Danish Library
– The Danish National Art Library

1934

Bellavista housing estate | 1

Mattson's Riding Stables | 2

Junkershallen

1 |

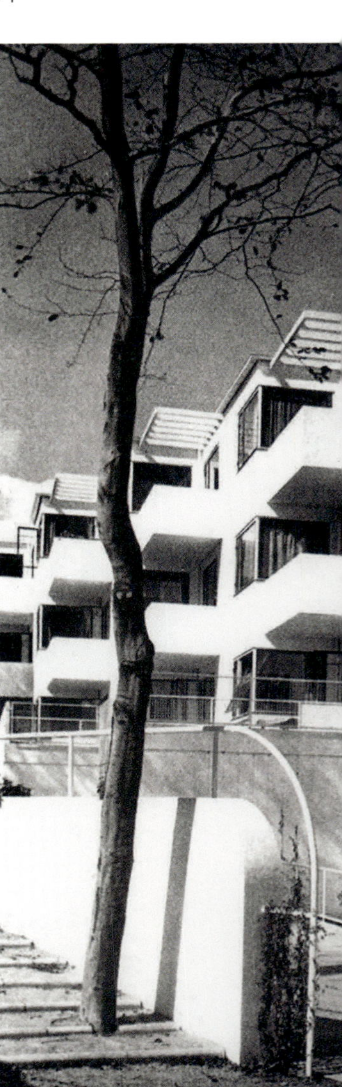

2 |

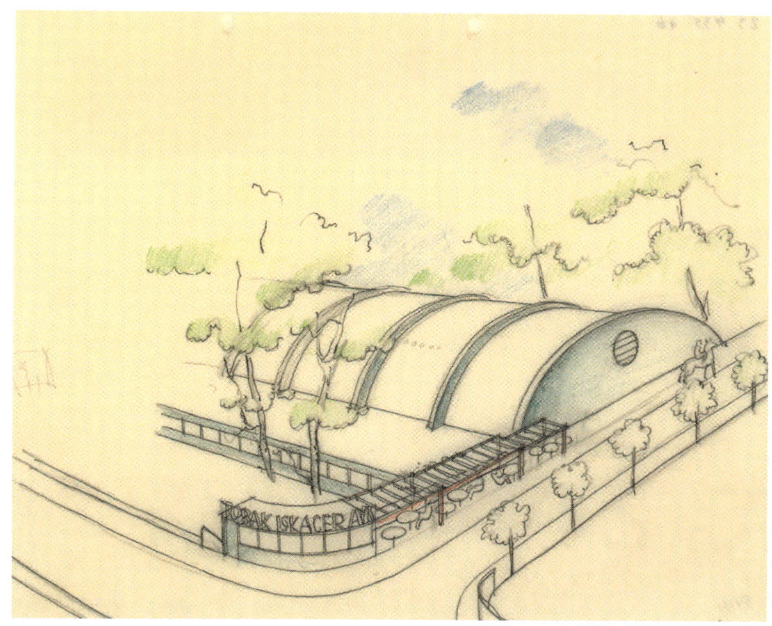

Photo: The Royal Danish Library
– The Danish National Art Library

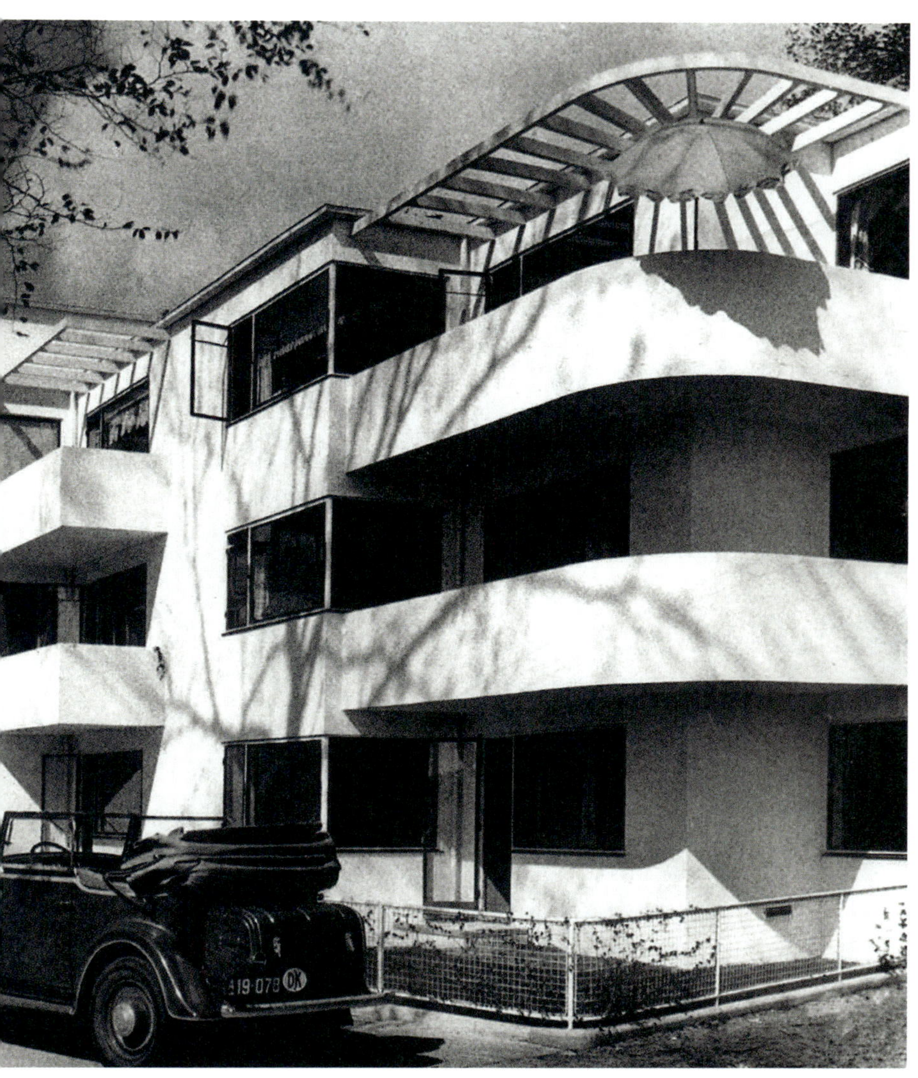

Photo: Aage Strüwing © Jørgen Strüwing

1935

1 |

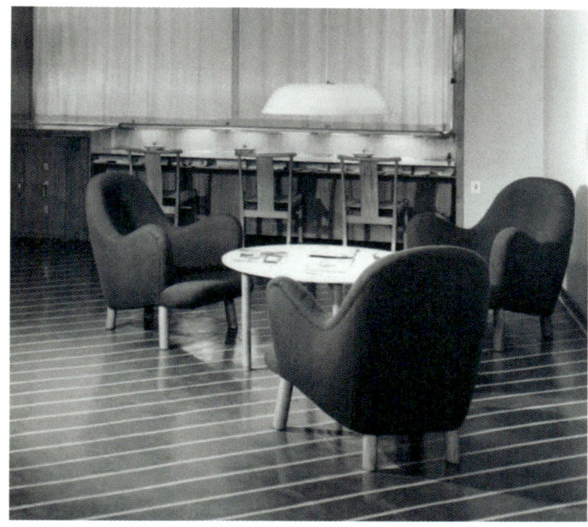

Photo: Aage Strüwing © Strüwing Reklamefoto

Armchair and sofa, part of the interior design for the Danish bank Landmandsbanken | 1

Travels to the Soviet Union for Soviet-Russian Film Week

Novo Terapeutisk Laboratorium (Therapeutic Laboratory). The project includes a range of furniture, for example, a wooden chair for the canteen, a wall lamp and furniture for managers' offices | 2

2 |

Photo: Novo Nordisk History Collection. Aage Strüwing © Jørgen Strüwing

1936

1 |

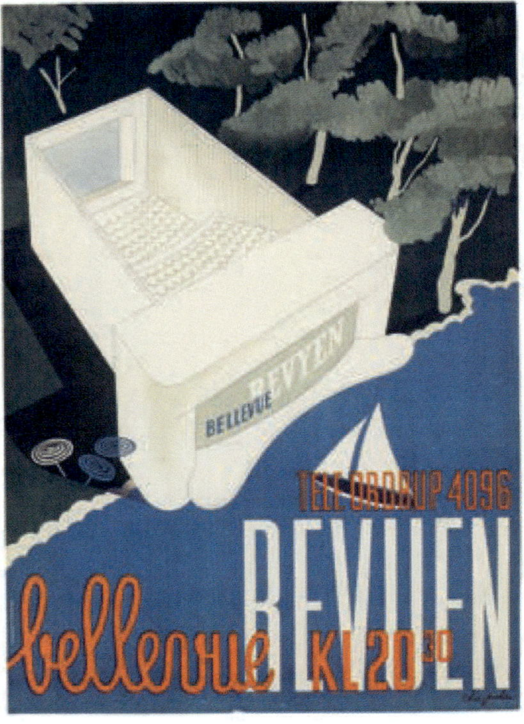

Photo: Pernille Klemp

The Charlottenborg chair

Poster for the
Bellevue Review | 1

Indoor tennis court for
Hellerup Sports Club

The Danish bank Landmandsbanken, Nørrebro branch

Klampenborg chair | 1

Bellevue Theatre and restoration. Entire design by Arne Jacobsen, including the Klampenborg Chair, steel-tube bar furniture and custom-designed theatre seats | 2

Texaco Petrol Station | 3

Stelling pendant lamp | 4

The paint company Stellings Farvehandel head office and flagship store. Entire design by Arne Jacobsen, including the Stelling pendant lamp and steel-tube office chairs | 5

2 |

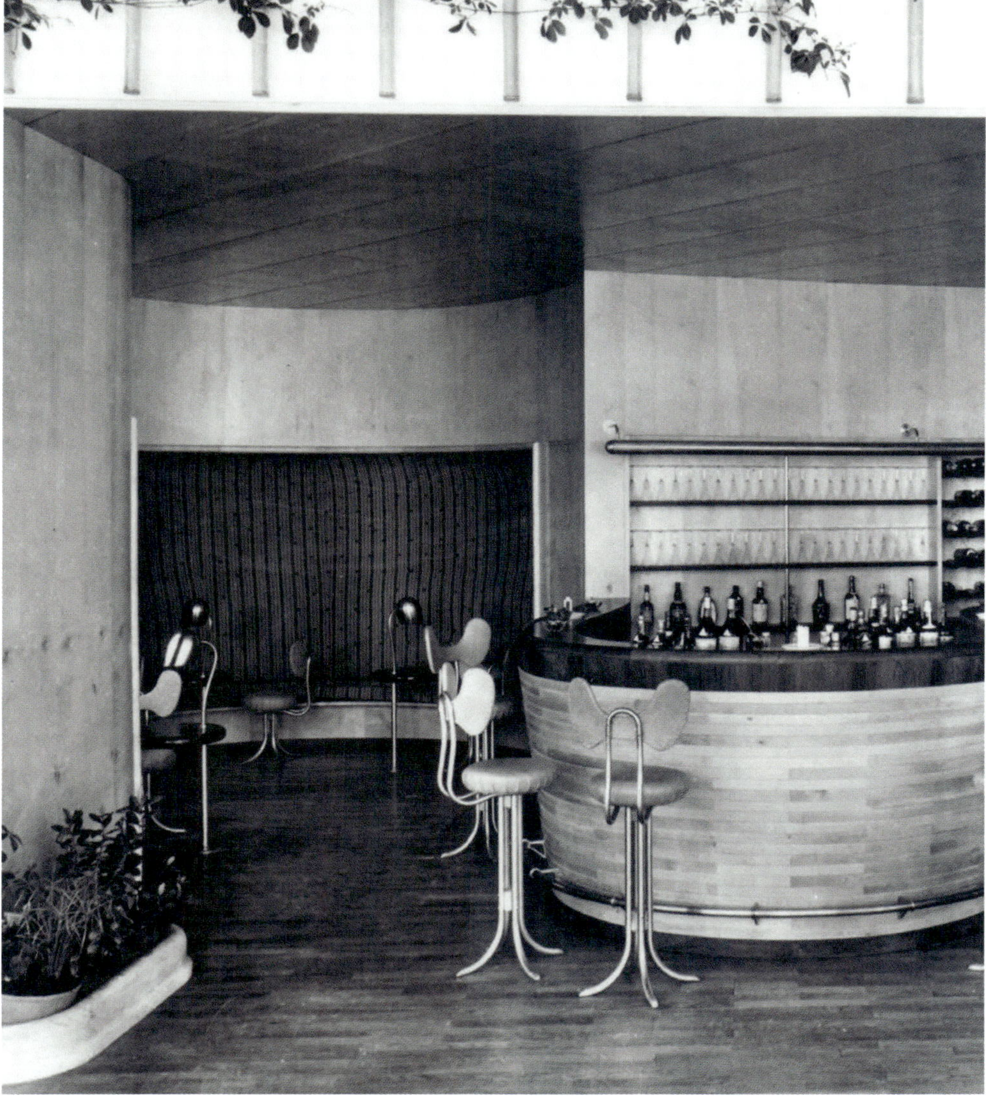

Photo: Aage Strüwing © Jørgen Strüwing

1 |

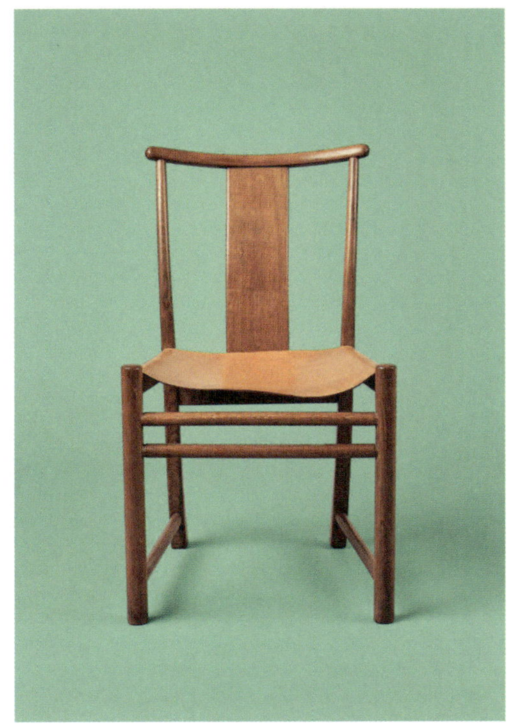

3 |

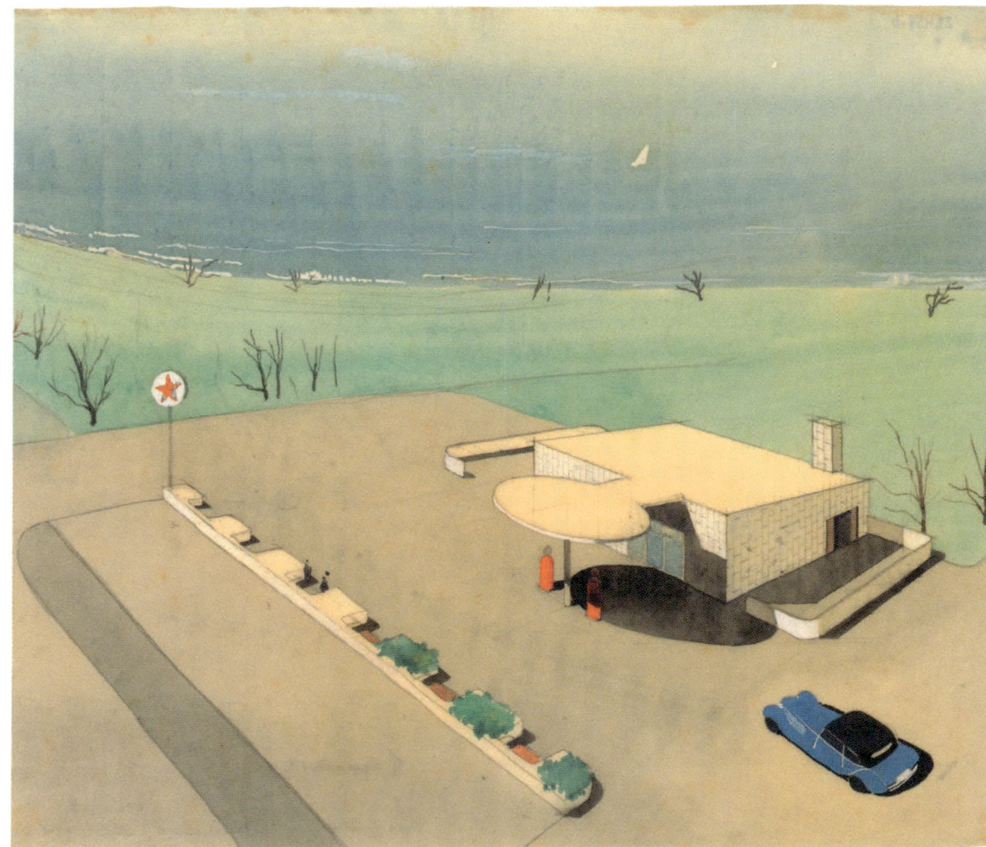

Photo: The Royal Danish Library – The Danish National Art Library

5 |

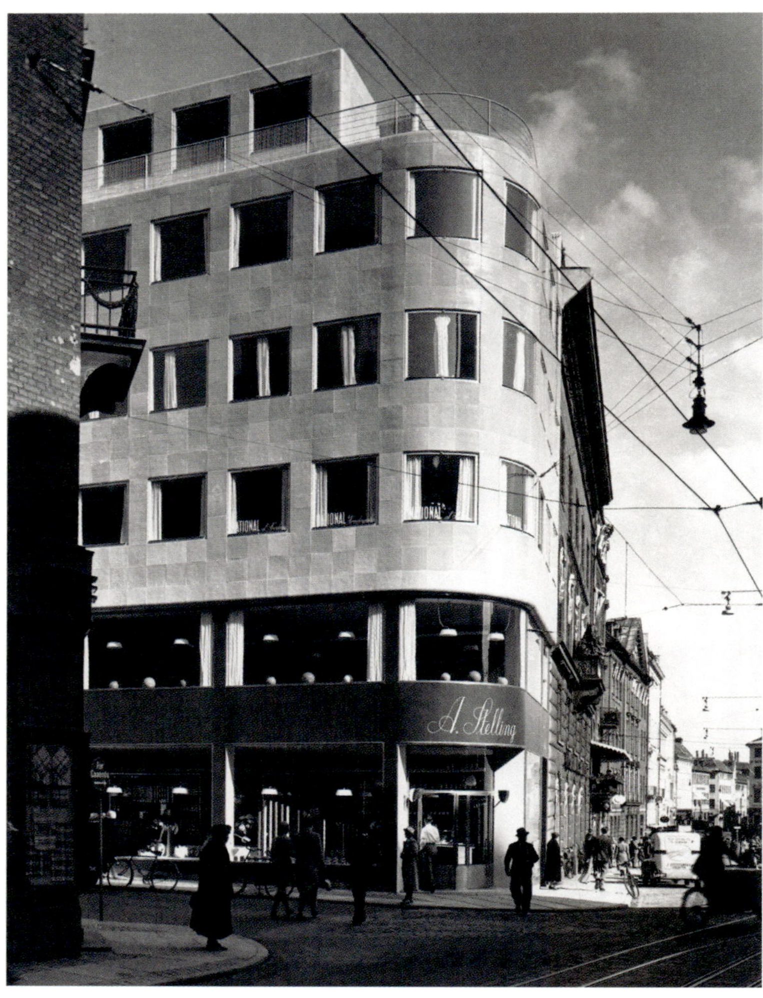

Photo: Aage Strüwing © Jørgen Strüwing

4 |

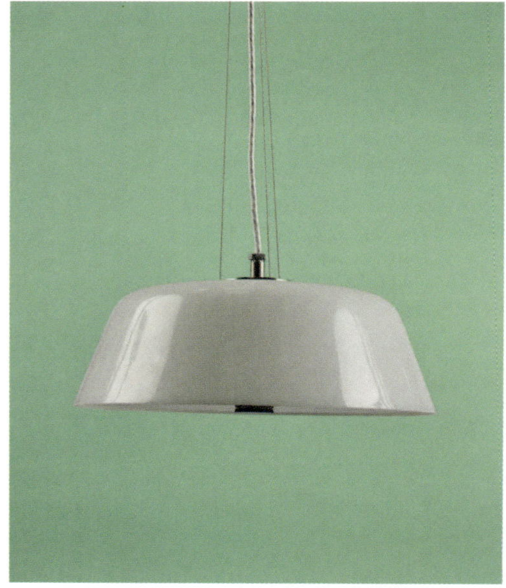

Trapholt Collection

1938

1 |

Photo: Arne Jacobsen. The original can be found in: The Royal Danish Library – The Danish National Art Library

His own holiday home in Gudmindrup Lyng | 1

The Danish bank Landmandsbanken, Vesterbro branch

Kiosk facilities and kayak club at Bellevue South Beach

Design of Hvidøre Diabetes Sanatorium for Novo Terapeutisk Laboratorium

1939

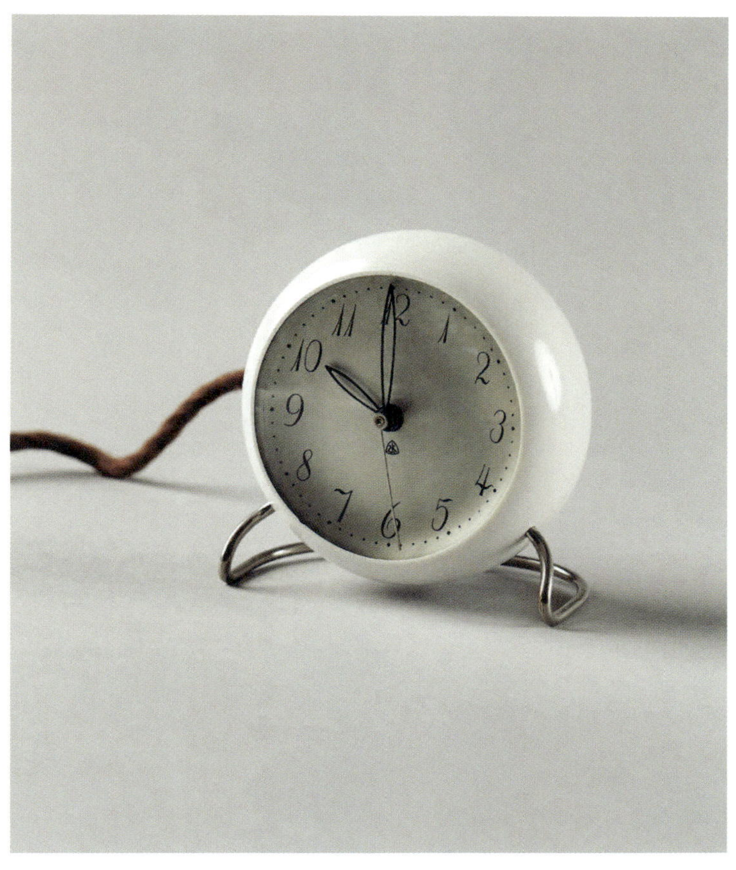

Table clock for Lauritz Knudsen

Photo: The Royal Danish Library – The Danish National Art Library

1940

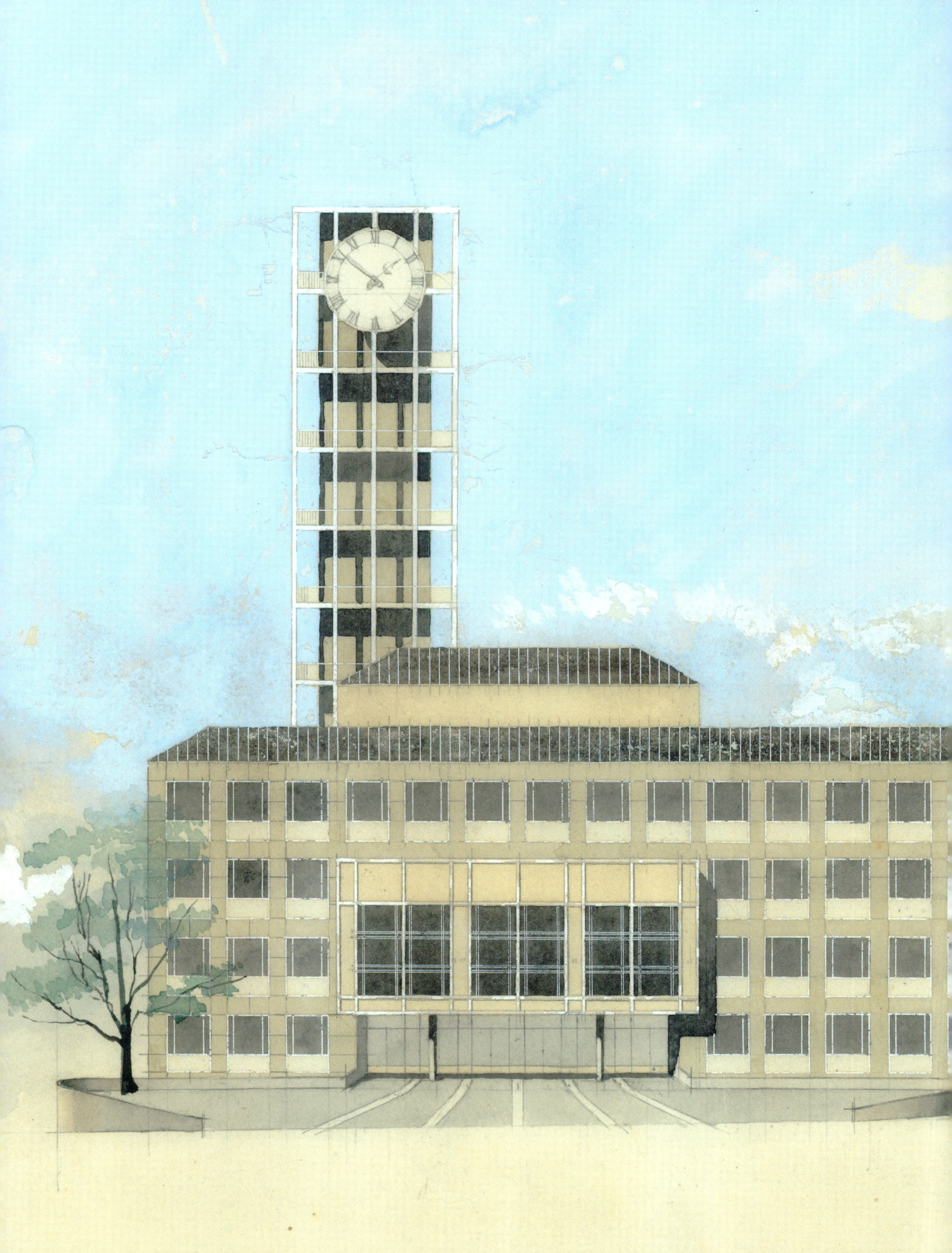

1941

The Ibstruparken I residential development in Gentofte

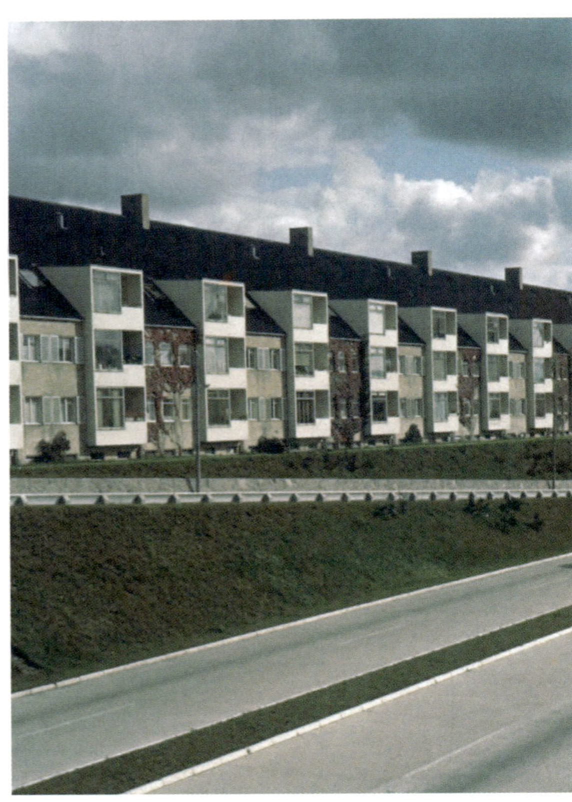

Photo: Arne Jacobsen. The original can be found in: The Royal Danish Library – The Danish National Art Library

1942

Aarhus City Hall with Erik Møller. Entire design by the architects and the young Hans J. Wegner, an employee at the practice | 1

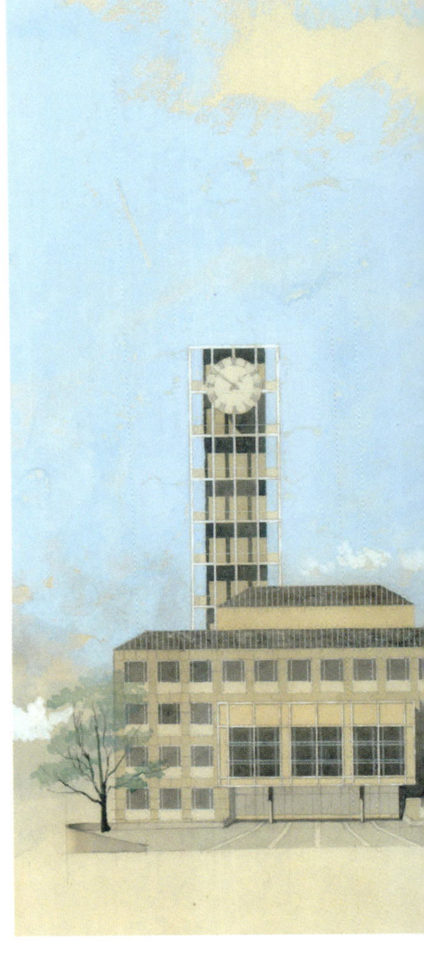

Arne Jacobsen and Erik Møller

Photo: The Royal Danish Library - The Danish National Art Library

Søllerød Town Hall with Flemming Lassen. Entire design by the architects, featuring custom-designed furniture, including the Søllerød pendant lamp, which is then sold by Louis Poulsen | 2

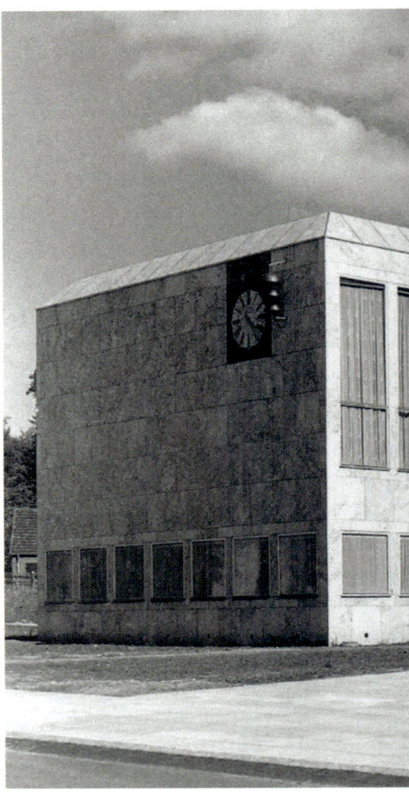

Photo: Aage Strüwing © Jørgen Strüwing

1 |

2 |

1943

1 |

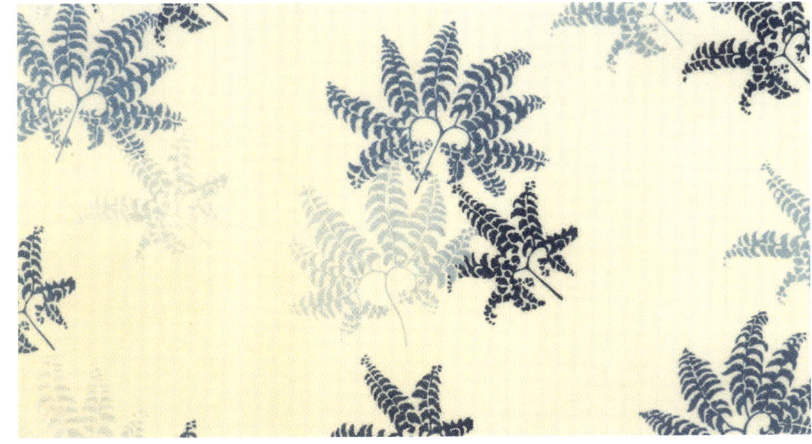

Foto: Arne Jacobsen Design I/S

Exhibits patterned textiles together with Jonna Møller at the Charlottenborg Spring Exhibition | 1

Fish smokehouse at Sjællands Odde

Terraced houses for Novo at Sløjfen in Gentofte

The Chain Houses for A/S Gentofte Rækkehus

Changing room building for YMCA in Emdrup

Flees to Sweden with Jonna Møller. They get married the same year

1944

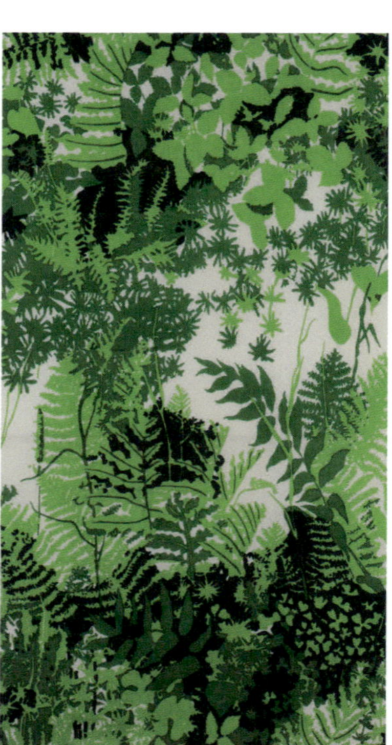

Photo: Arne Jacobsen Design I/S

Patterned fabrics and wallpapers for Nordiska Kompaniet, including Clover, Bamboo, Vegetation

Based in Sweden

1945

Returns to Denmark at the end of the war

Patterned fabrics for Grautex, exported to the United States, and an exhibition in the Lord & Taylor department store in New York

Holiday home for the writer Ebbe Munck in Arild, Sweden

Terraced houses on Ridebanevang in Gentofte

1946

The Ibstruparken II residential development in Gentofte

Roman clock | 1

1 |

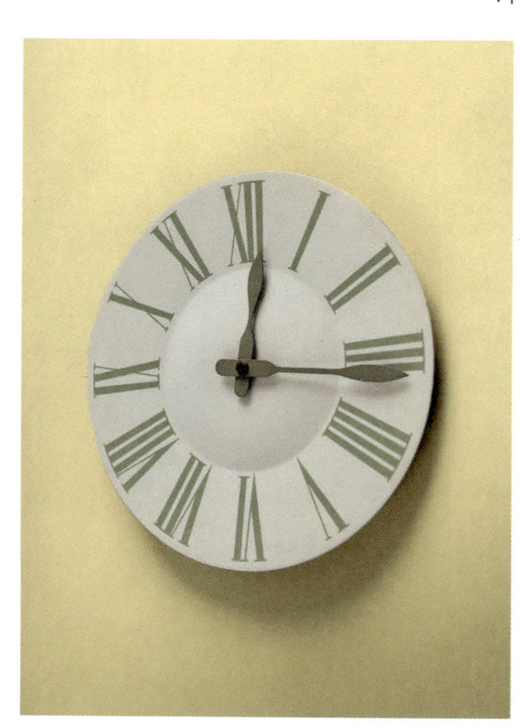

1948

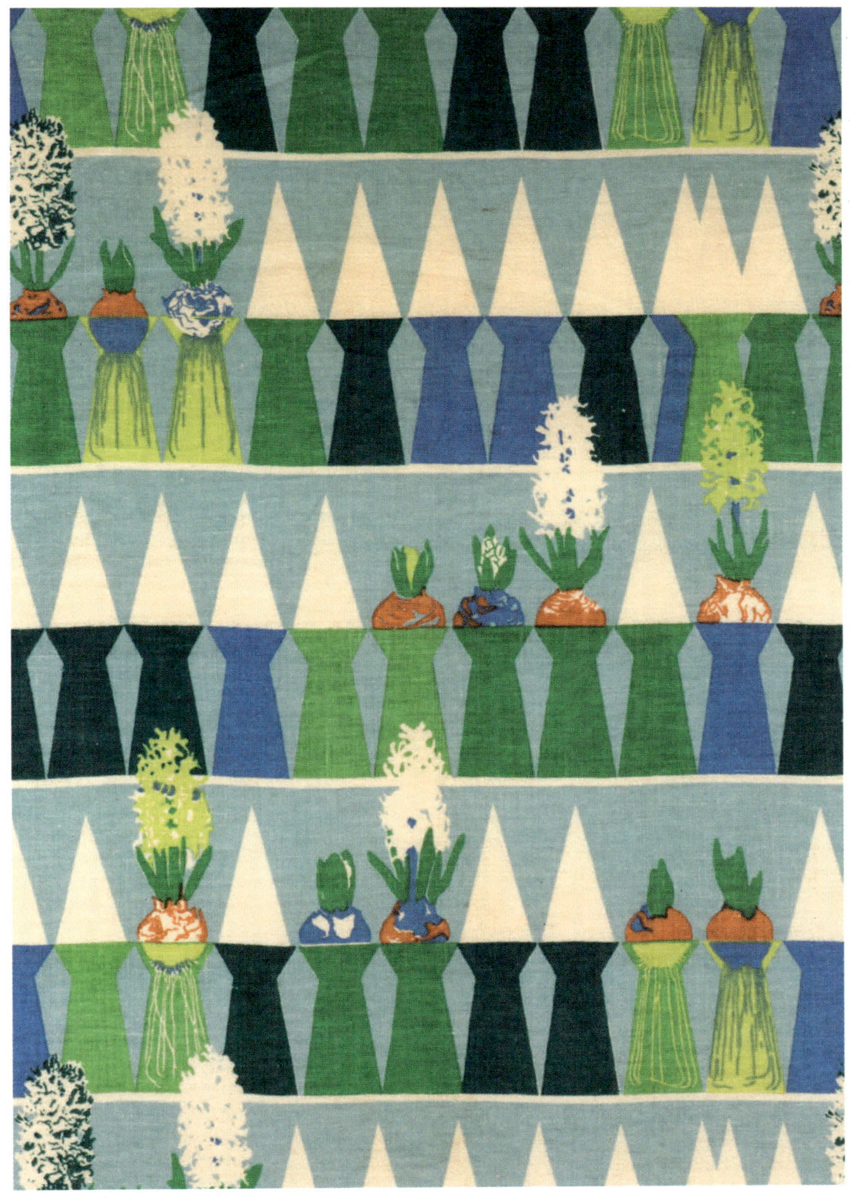

Photo: Arne Jacobsen Design I/S

The Hyacinths fabric pattern

1949

Young people's housing for Gentofte Municipality

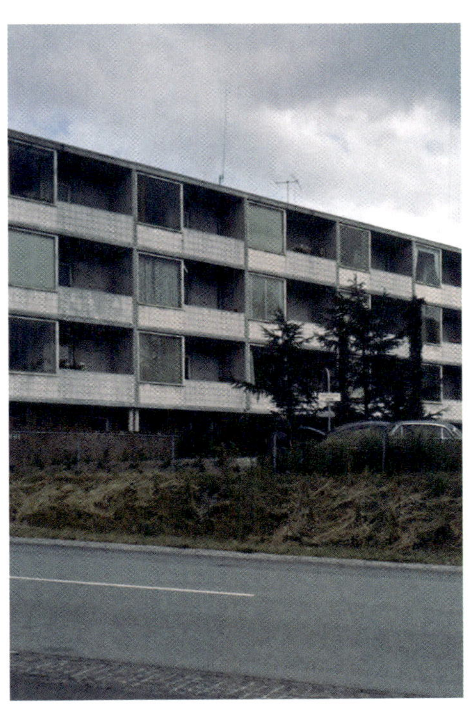

Photo: Arne Jacobsen. The original can be found in: The Royal Danish Library – The Danish National Art Library

Photo: Arne Jacobsen. The original can be found in: The Royal Danish Library – The Danish National Art Library

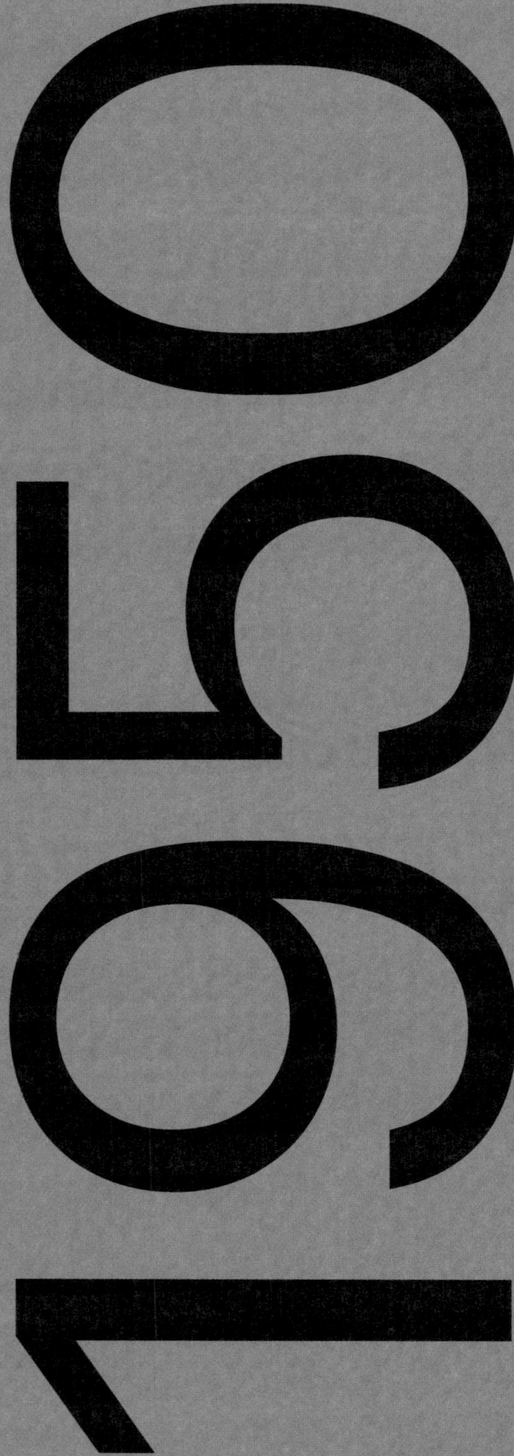

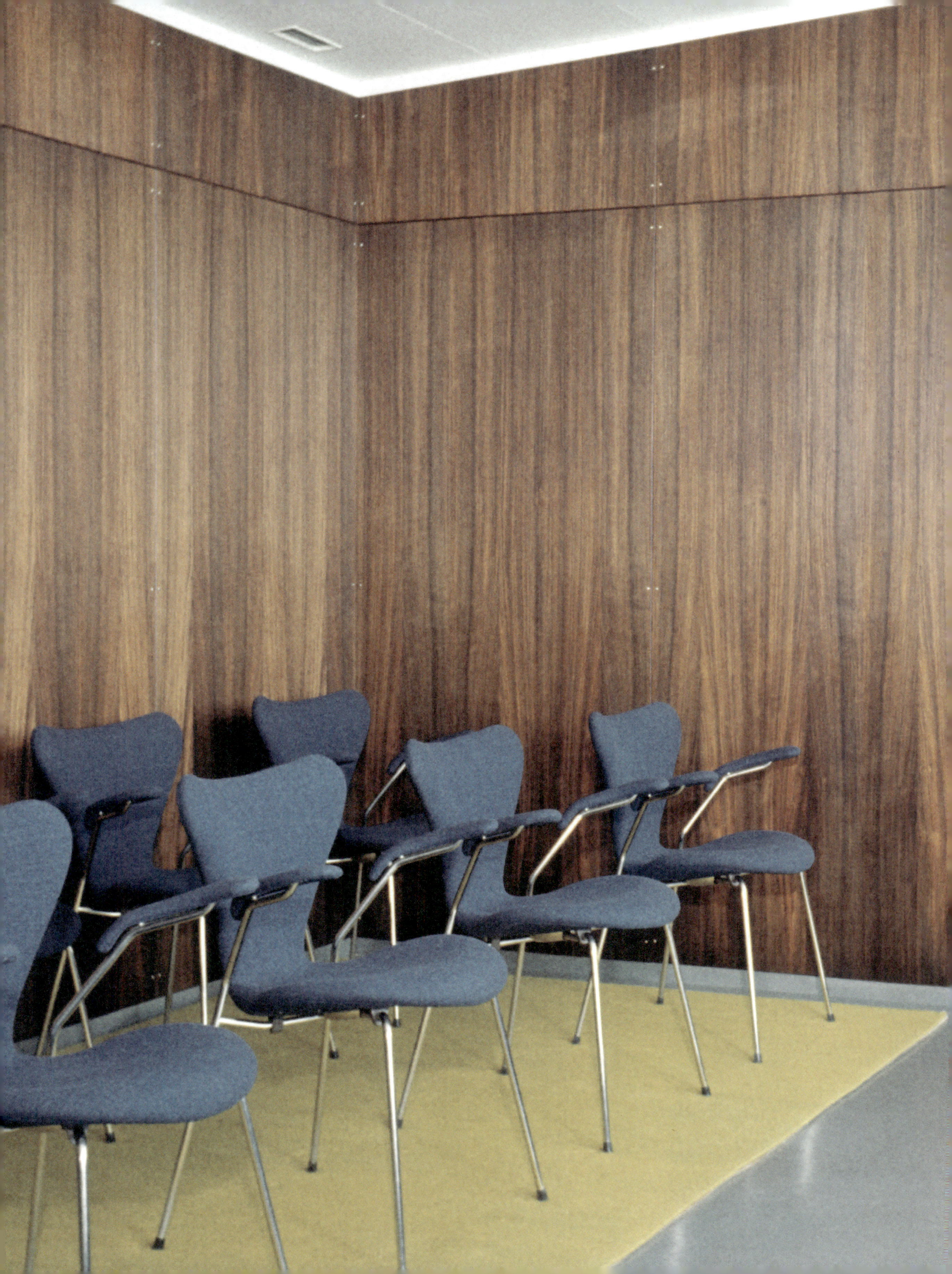

1950

1 |

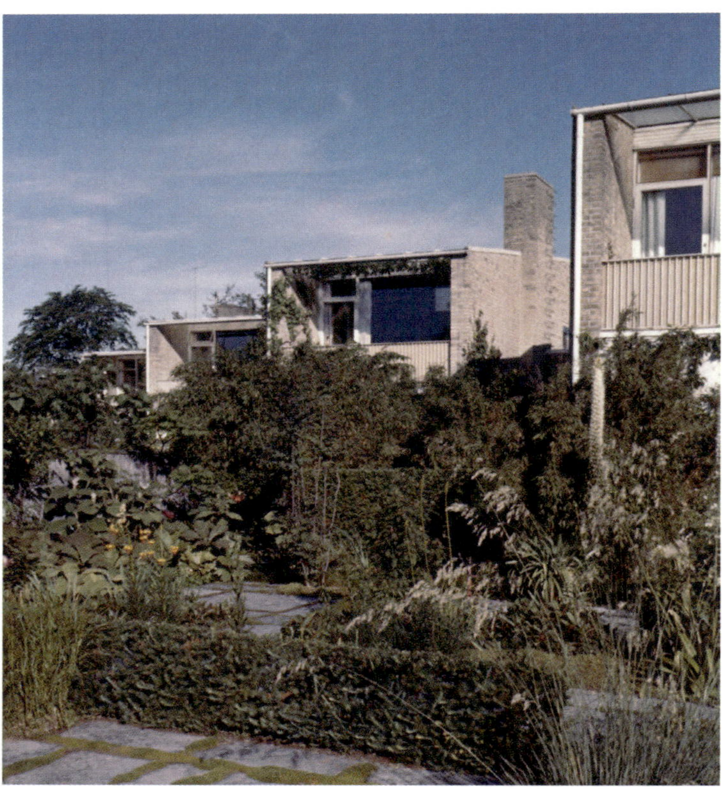

Photo: Arne Jacobsen. The original can be found in: The Royal Danish Library – The Danish National Art Library

The Søholm I and II terraced houses on Strandvejen. Arne Jacobsen moves into Strandvejen 413, where he also runs his studio for many years | 1

Hårby School

1951

Signs the manifesto for Le Groupe Espace in France

Detached house in Vedbæk for C.A. Møller | 1

---

1 |

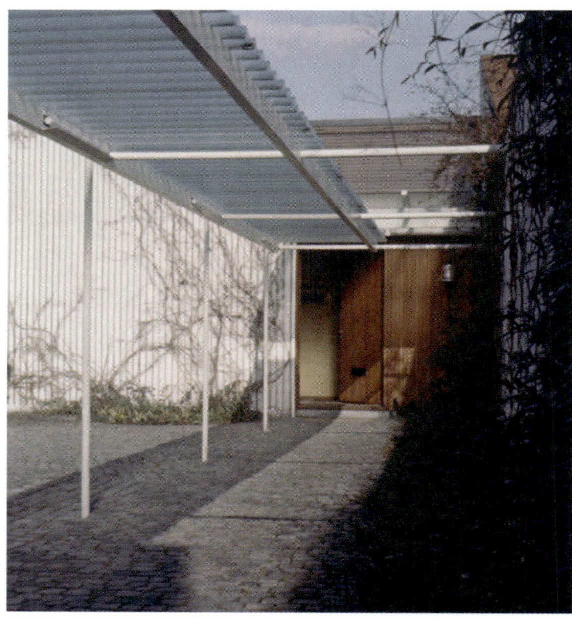

Photo: Arne Jacobsen. The original can be found in: The Royal Danish Library – The Danish National Art Library

1952

2 |

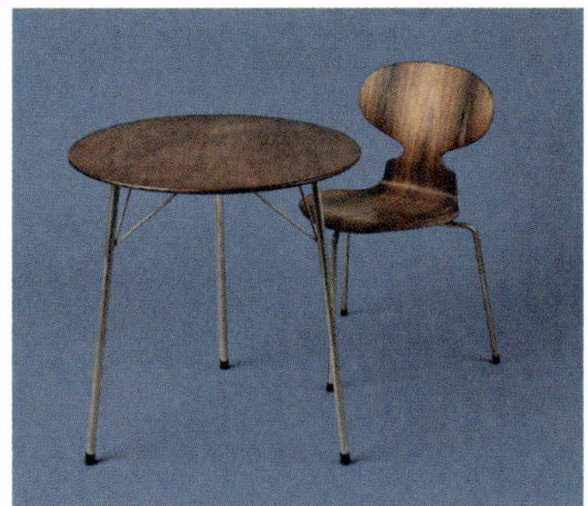

1 |

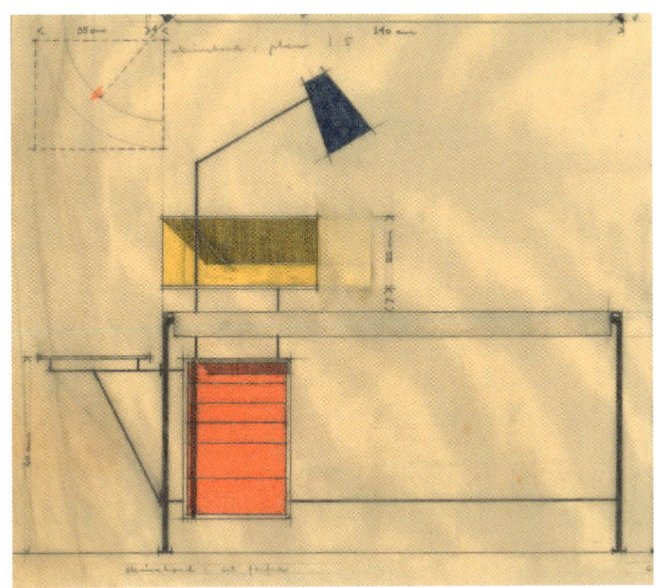

Photo: The Royal Danish Library
– The Danish National Art Library

Chair, desk and tray table for The American Scandinavian Foundation | 1

The Ant chair and table range for the Ant | 2

1953

1 |

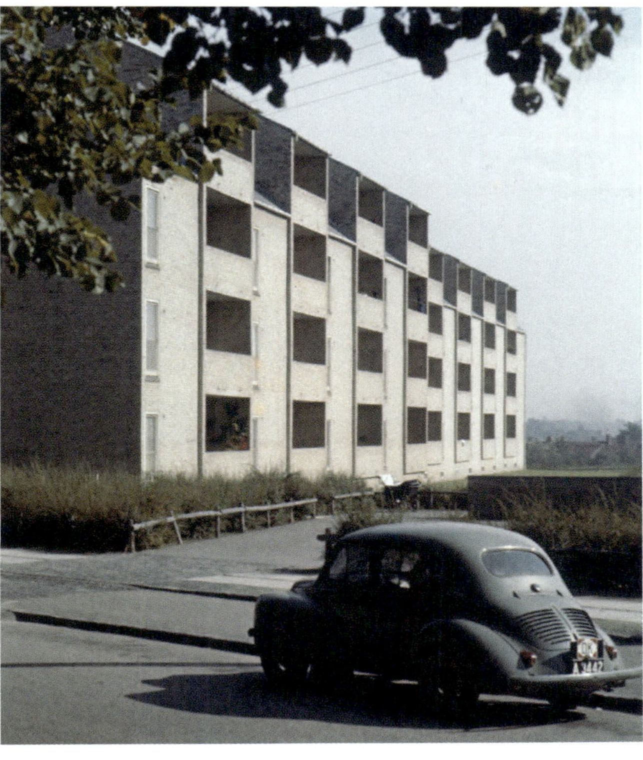

Photo: Arne Jacobsen. The original can be found in: The Royal Danish Library – The Danish National Art Library

Office and showroom for Massey-Harris in Glostrup

The Alléhusene residential development in Gentofte | 1

The Almegård farm complex in Højby

1954

2 |

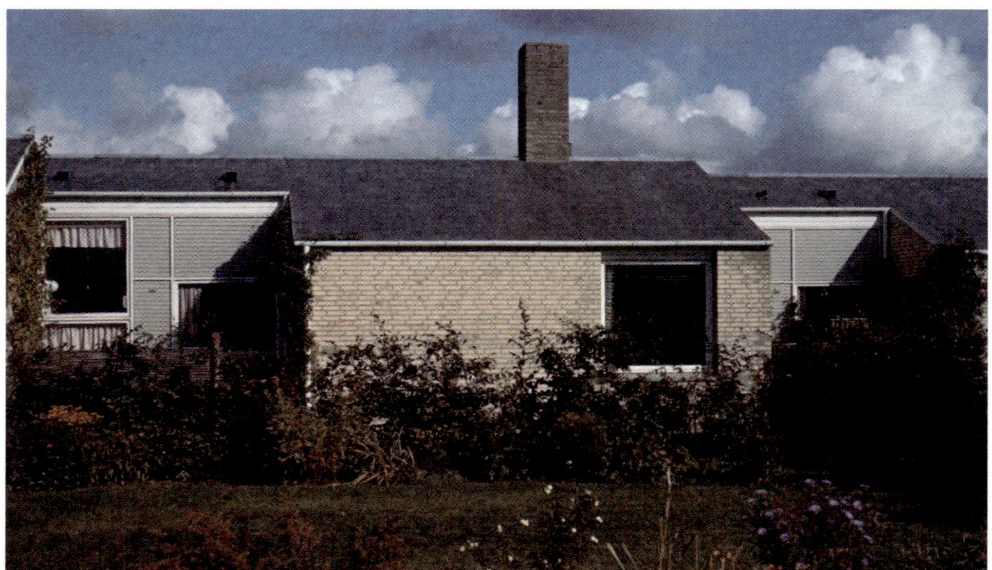

Photo: Arne Jacobsen. The original can be found in: The Royal Danish Library – The Danish National Art Library

Dot | 1

The Islevvænge terraced houses in Rødovre | 2

The Søholm III terraced houses in Klampenborg

1 |

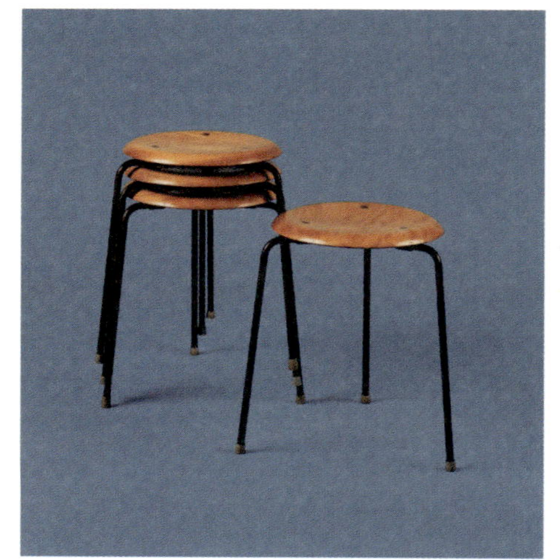

Trapholt Collection

1955

1 |

The Series 7

The Munkegård chair

The Tongue chair

Administration building for H. Jespersen and Son

Member of the Academy Council, Copenhagen

Laboratory building for Novo Terapeutisk Laboratorium, Frederiksberg | 1

The Munkegård lamp

The City Hall clock | 2

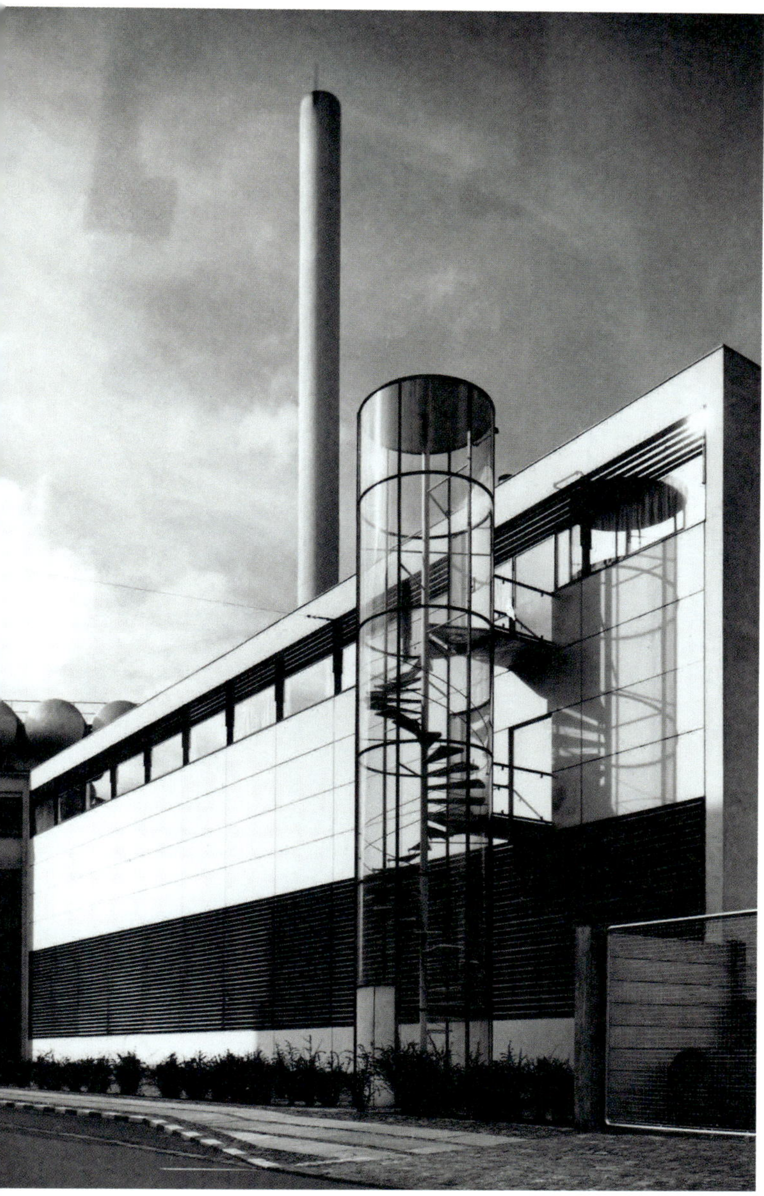

Photo: Aage Strüwing © Jørgen Strüwing

1956

The AJ Eklipta wall lamp | 1

The AJ door handle

The AJ park lamp

Series 3300 | 2

1 |

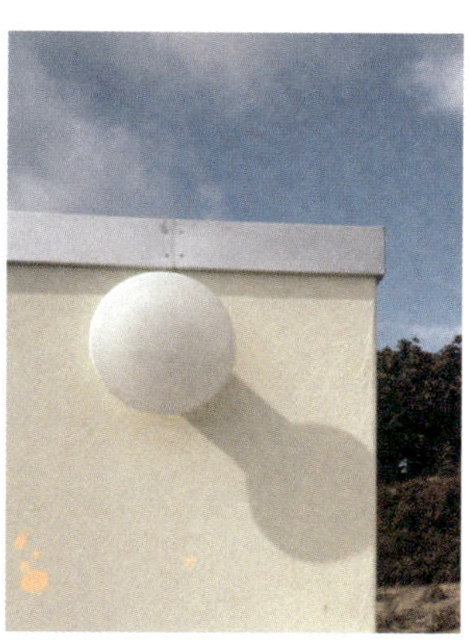

Photo: Arne Jacobsen. The original can be found in: The Royal Danish Library – The Danish National Art Library

2 |

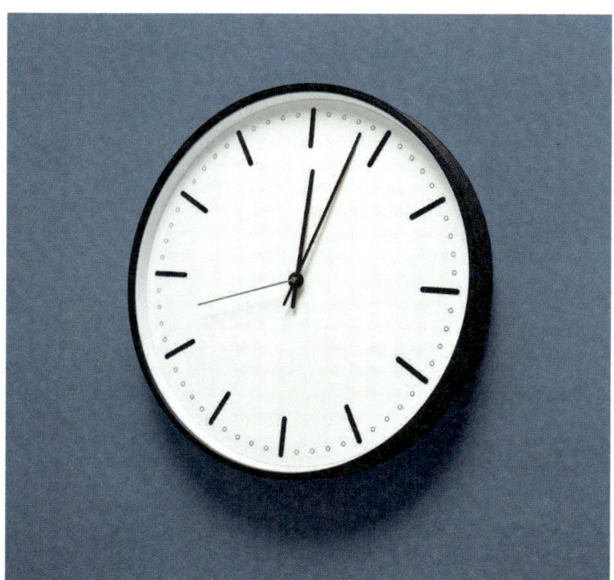

2 |

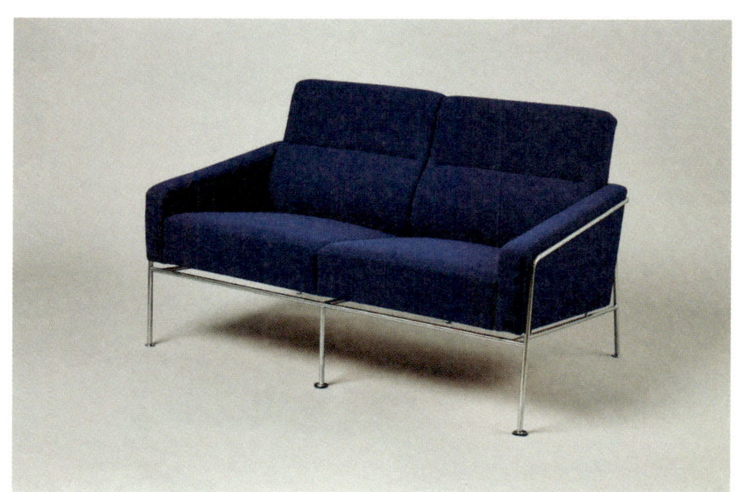

Trapholt Collection

1957

3 |

Photo: Arne Jacobsen. The original can be found in: The Royal Danish Library – The Danish National Art Library

'The Round House' for Leo Henriksen, the owner of Sjællands Odde Fish Smokehouse | 3

Professor at the Royal Danish Academy of Fine Arts in Copenhagen

---

Rødovre Town Hall. The interior design features the Series 7, Series 3300, Dot and custom-designed tables and lamps | 4

Hot-dog stand on Strandvejen in Klampenborg

Factory for CAC Engine Repair Company

---

4 |

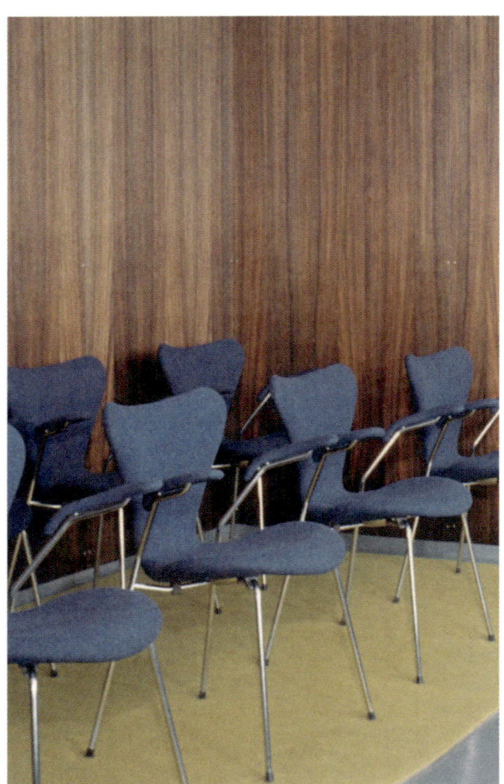

Photo: Arne Jacobsen. The original can be found in: The Royal Danish Library – The Danish National Art Library

Royal floor lamp

The AJ Royal pendant lamp

The AJ lamp

The AJ steel cutlery | 1

---

1 |

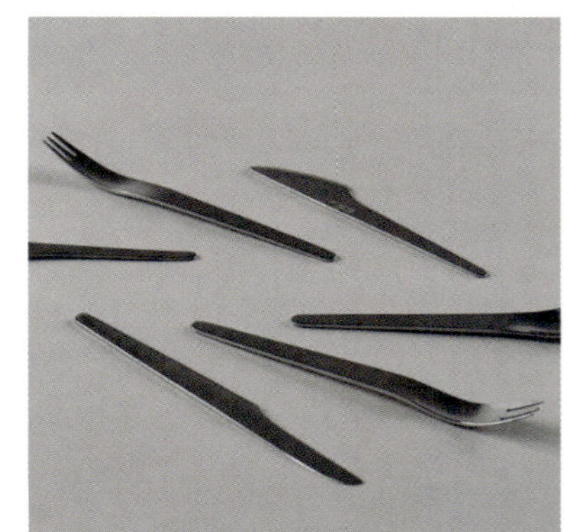

4 |

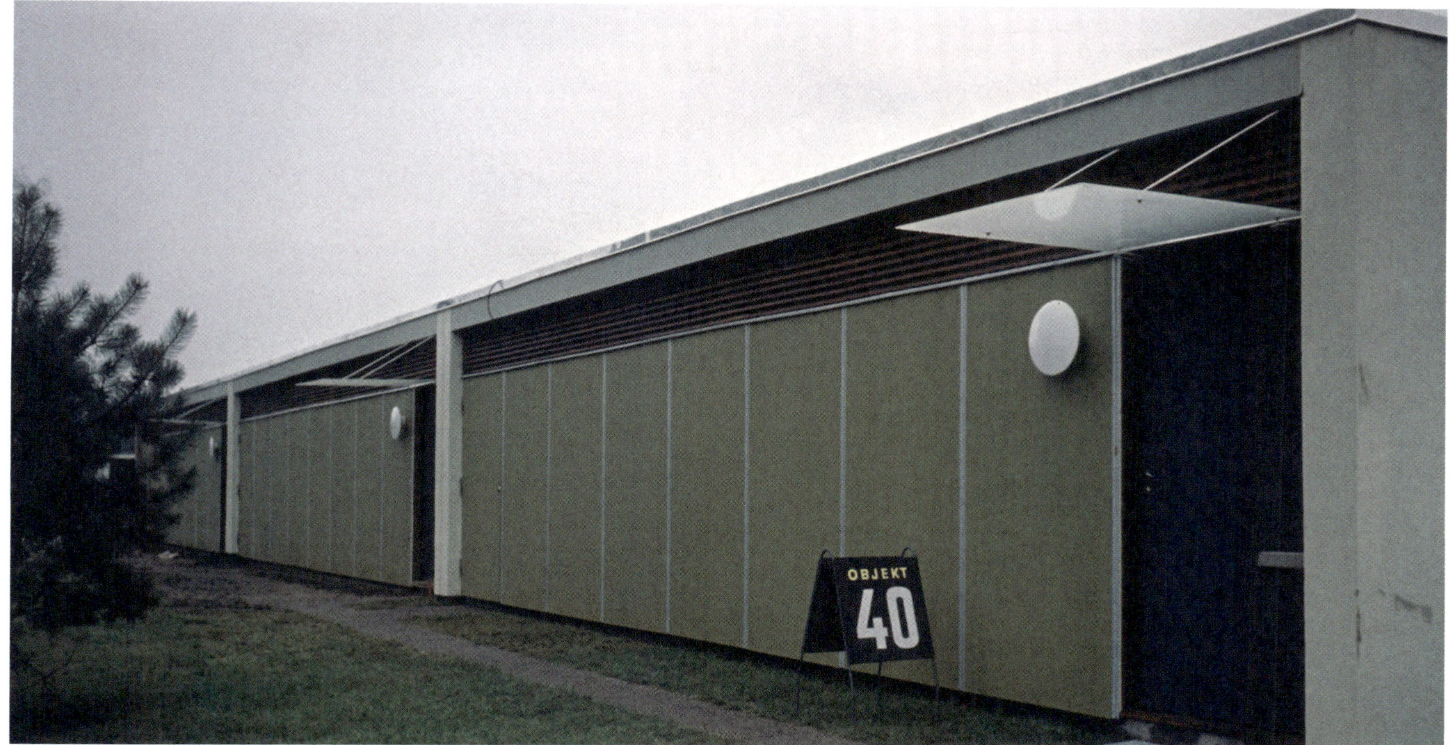

Photo: Arne Jacobsen. The original can be found in: The Royal Danish Library – The Danish National Art Library

Munkegård School. The interior design features the Munkegård chair, the Tongue, the Grand Prix speaker, custom-designed classroom desks and a colourful front curtain for the stage

The Grand Prix chair | 2

The Tasco pattern for Grautex | 3

Four atrium houses in Berlin in the context of the Interbau exhibition. Exhibition of Danish design in one of the atrium houses during the run of the exhibition | 4

2 |

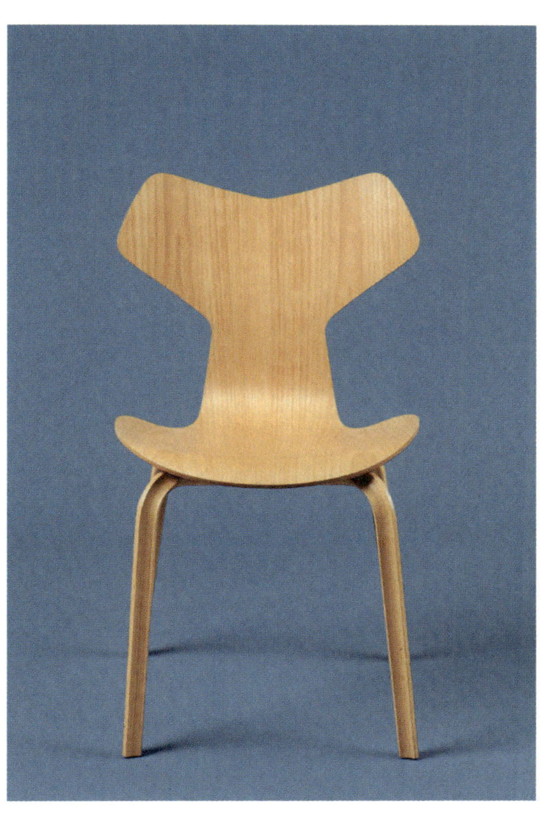

Trapholt Collection

3 |

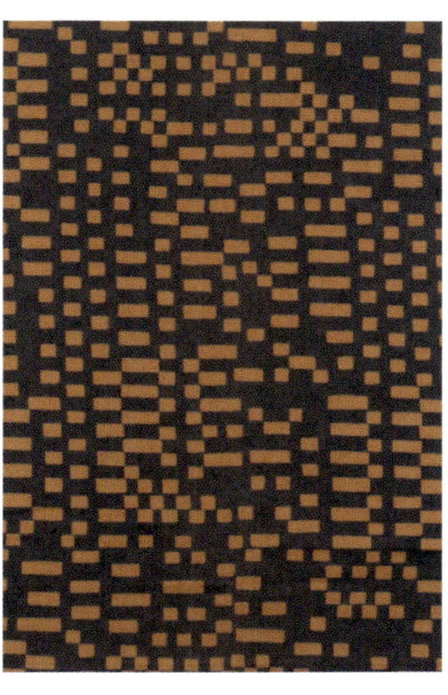

Photo: Arne Jacobsen Design I/S

1958

The Egg | 1

The Swan | 1

Exhibition of the SAS Royal Hotel furniture at the Formes Scandinaves exhibition in Paris | 2

1 |

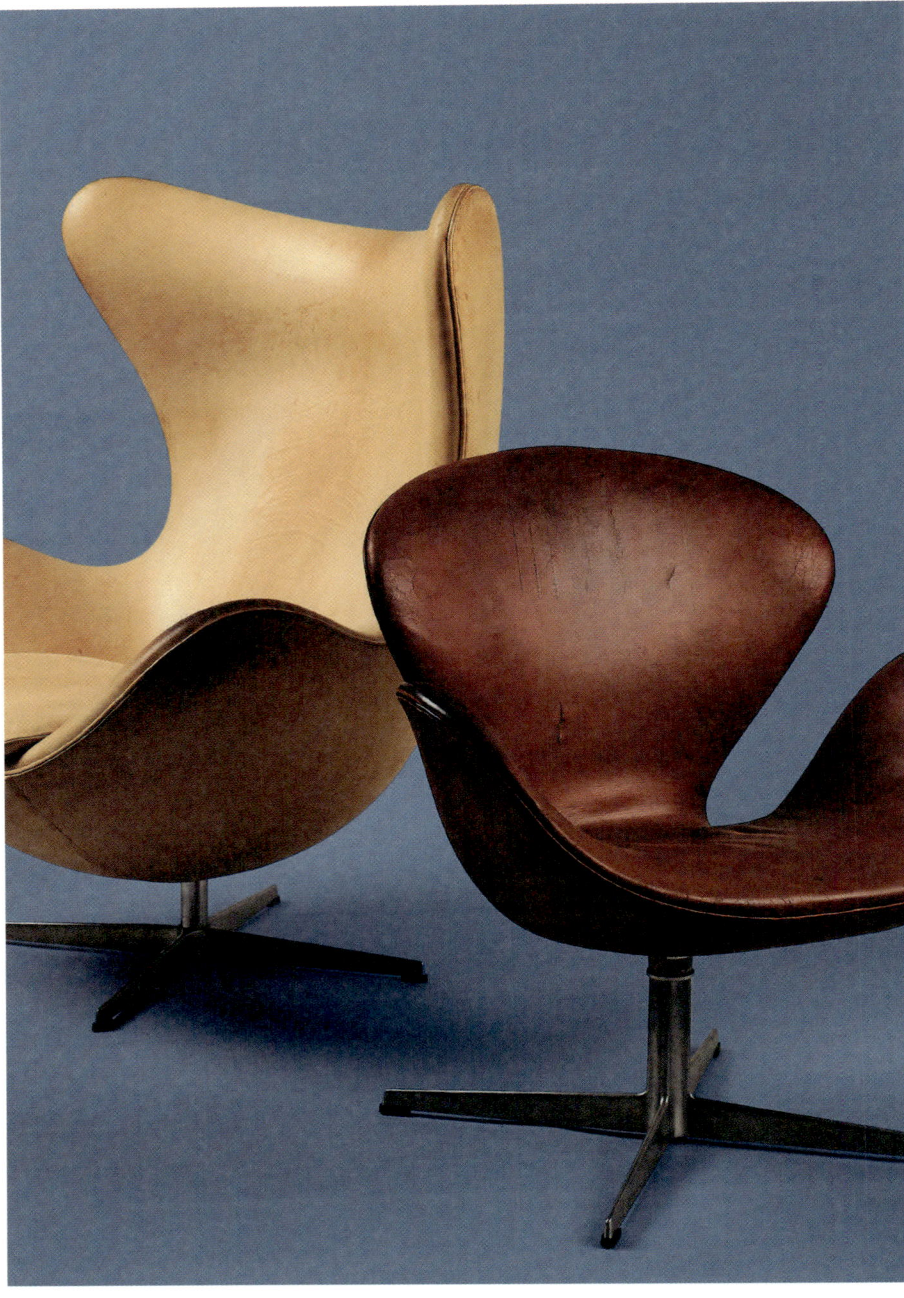

Trapholt Collection

2 |

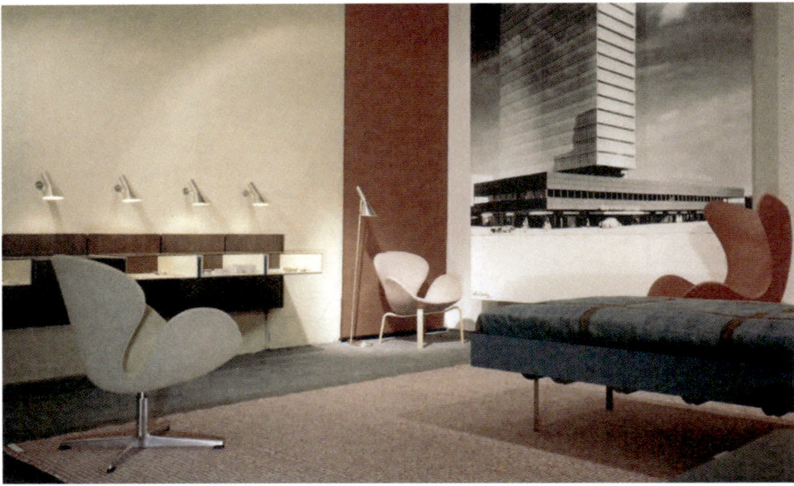

Photo: Arne Jacobsen. The original can be found in: The Royal Danish Library – The Danish National Art Library

1959

Glostrup Town Hall

Opening of the SAS hotel airport terminal in Copenhagen | 1

The Pot chair | 2

Bar pendant lamp

1 |

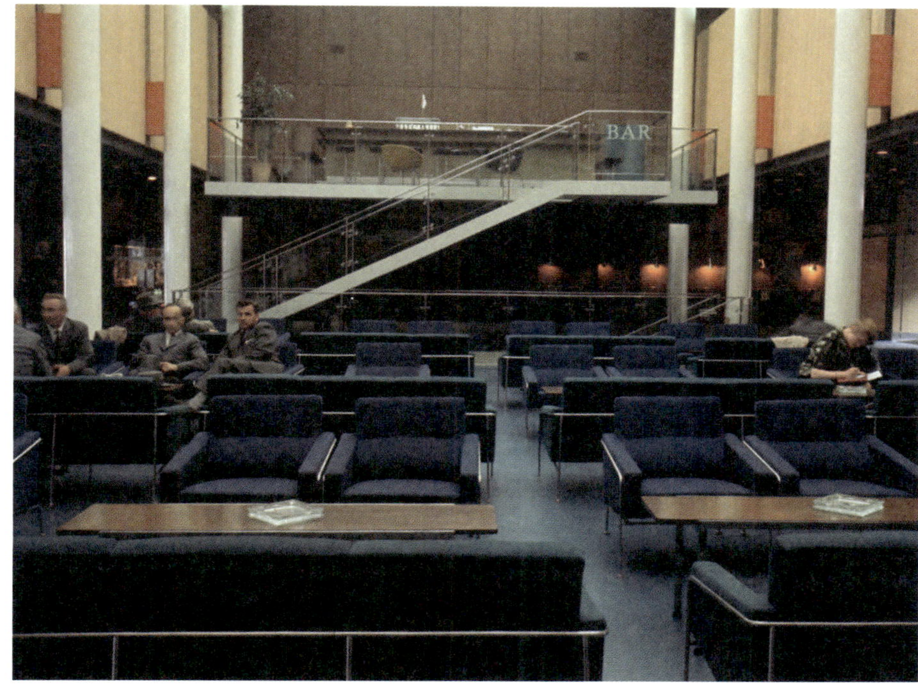

Photo: Arne Jacobsen. The original can be found in: The Royal Danish Library – The Danish National Art Library

2 |

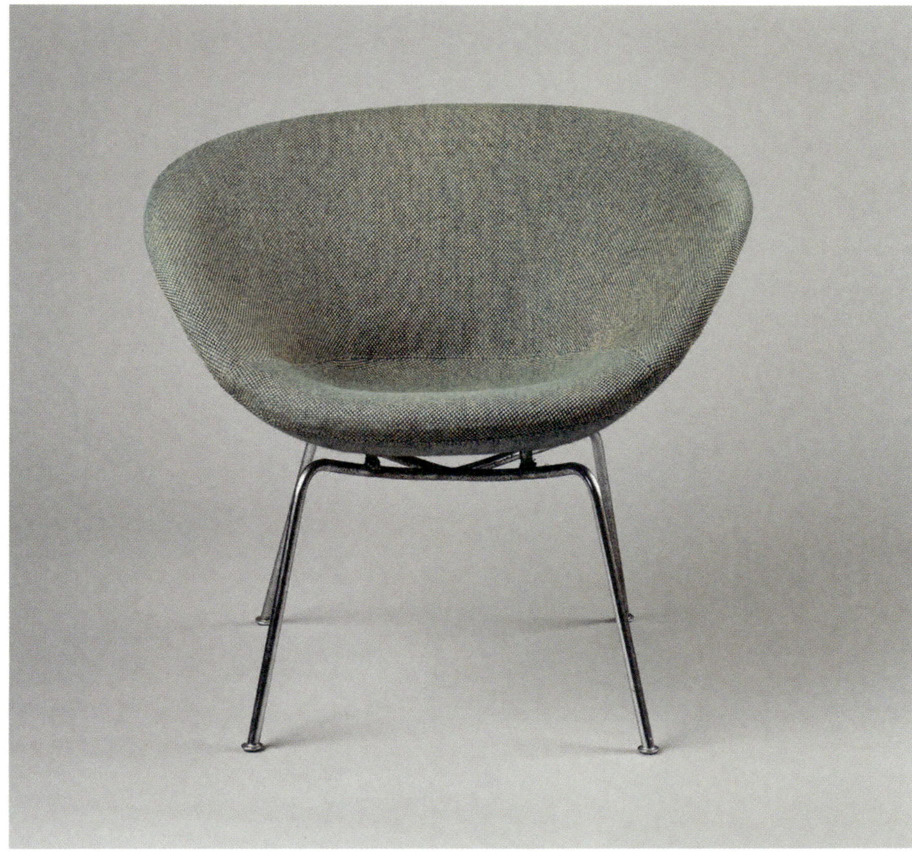

Photo: Arcaid/Universal Images
Group via Getty Images

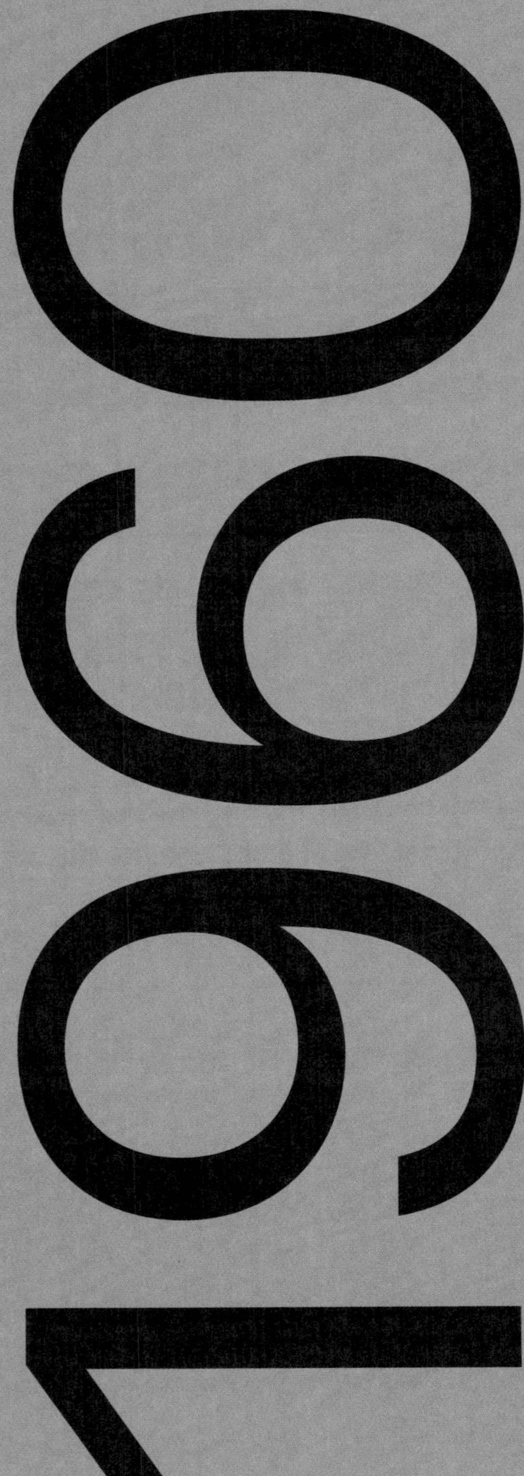

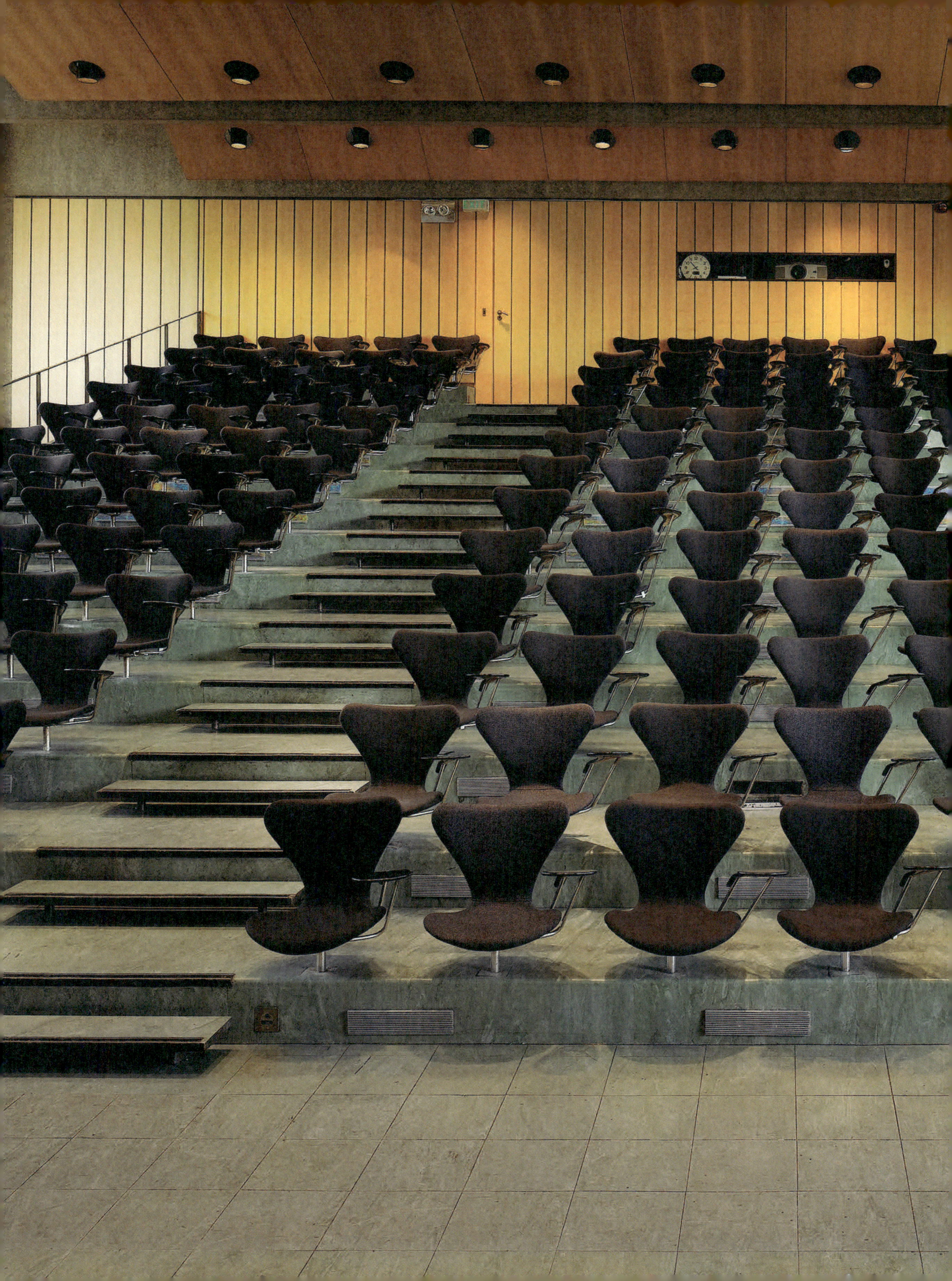

1960

SAS Royal Hotel. In addition to a range of furniture already launched, the project includes the Drop and Giraffe chairs, a custom-designed range of furniture for the rooms, and cutlery, vases, ashtrays and glasses for the restaurant

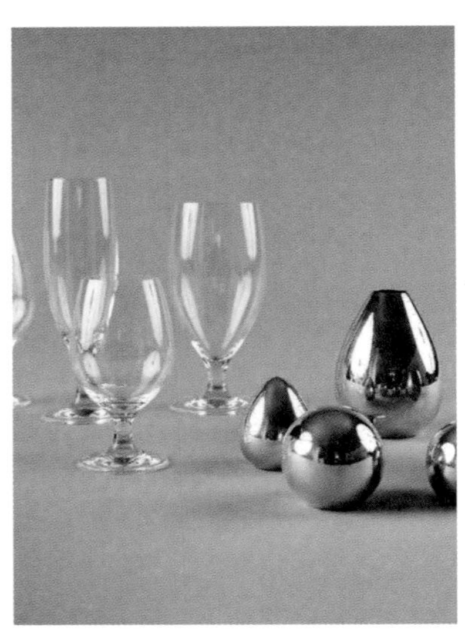

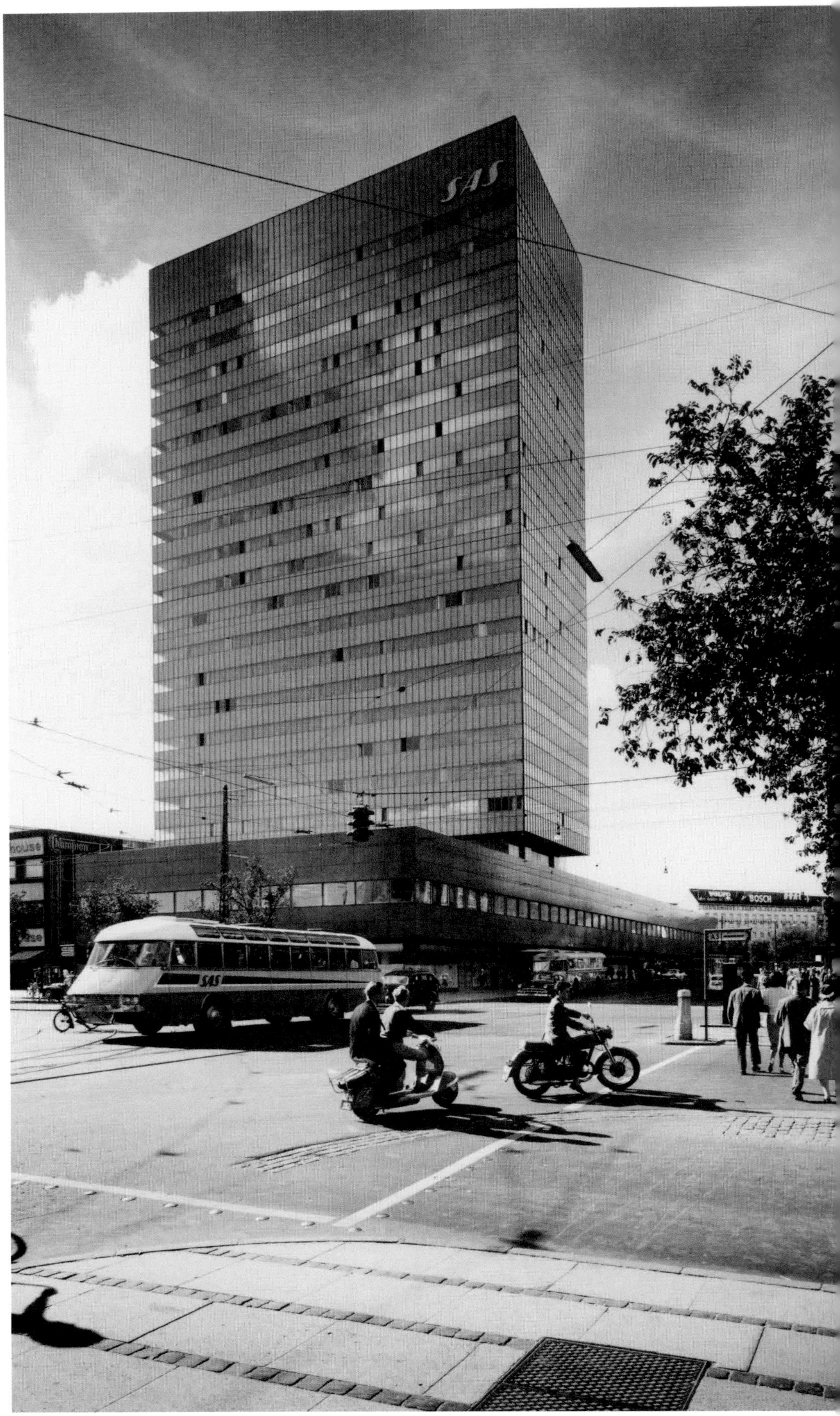

Photo: Aage Strüwing © Jørgen Strüwing

1961

1 |

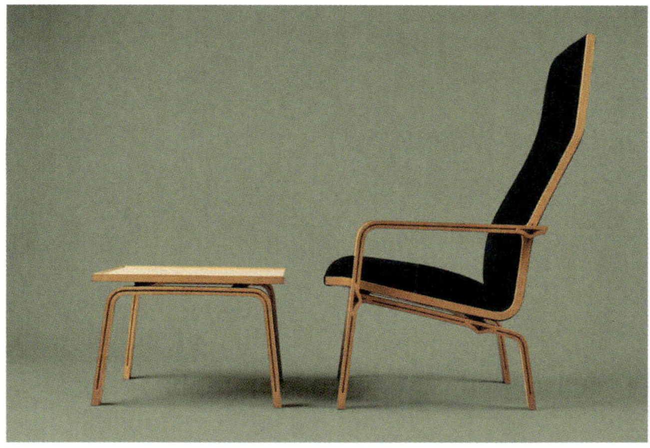

The St. Catherine chair | 1

Etude chair for
St. Catherine's College

The 'Ved Bellevue Bugt'
residential development
in Klampenborg | 2

Detached house for Gertie
Wandel, the last detached house
Arne Jacobsen designs | 3

---

3 |

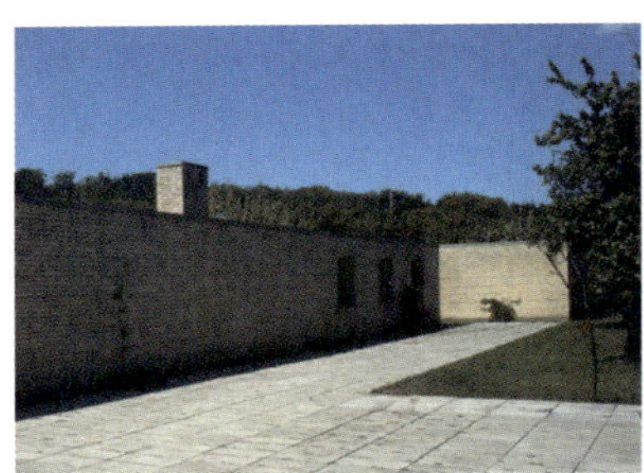

Photo: Arne Jacobsen. The original can be found in The Royal Danish Library – The Danish National Art Library

2 |

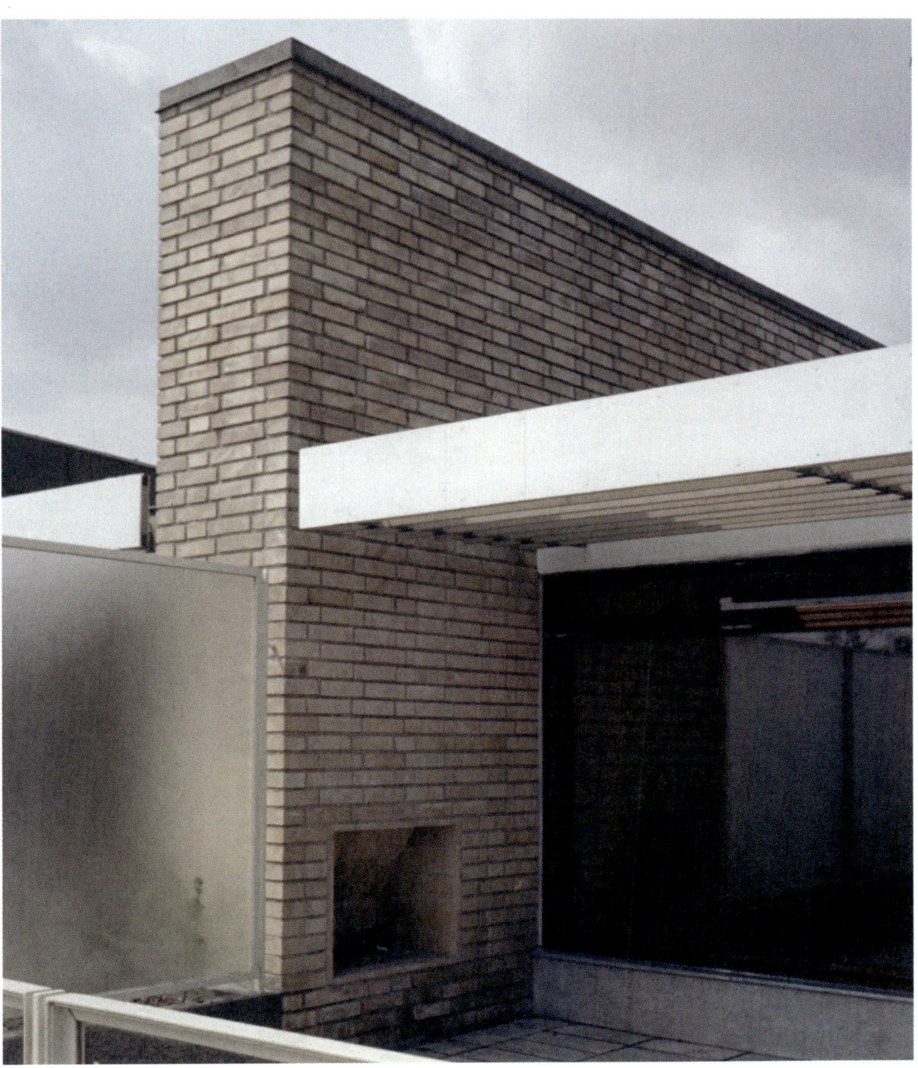

Photo: Arne Jacobsen. The original can be found in The Royal Danish Library – The Danish National Art Library

1962

Member of the American Institute of Architects

Arne Jacobsen turns 60. Students of the Royal Danish Academy of Fine Arts, School of Architecture pay tribute to him with a torchlight procession | 1

1 |

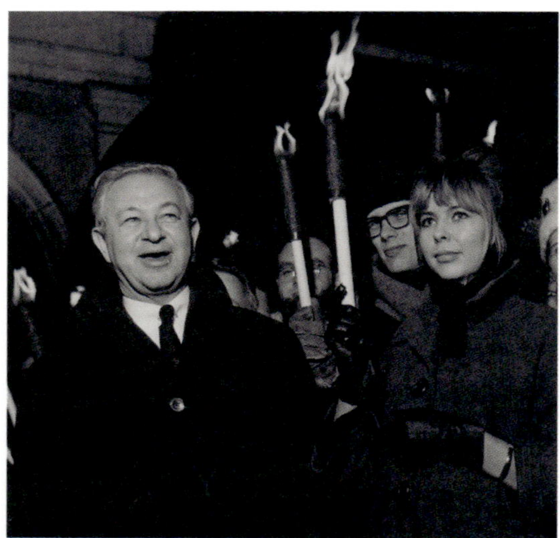

Photo: Polfoto/Ritzau Scanpix

1963

The Oxford lamp | 1

Oxford pendant

Fabric patterns for C. Olesen (Cotil), including Tassen, Forest, Ypsilon and Polygon | 2

1 |

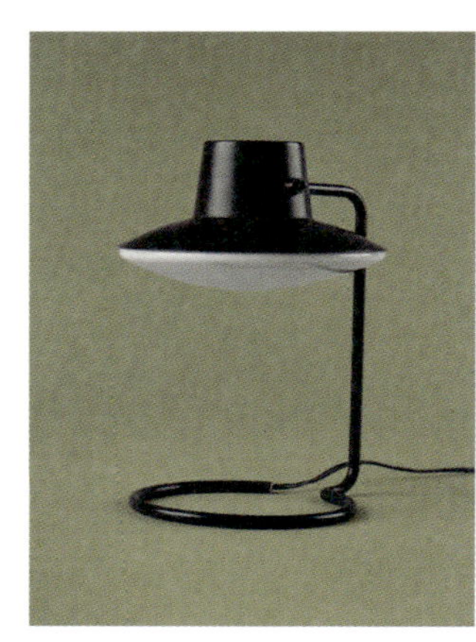

2 |

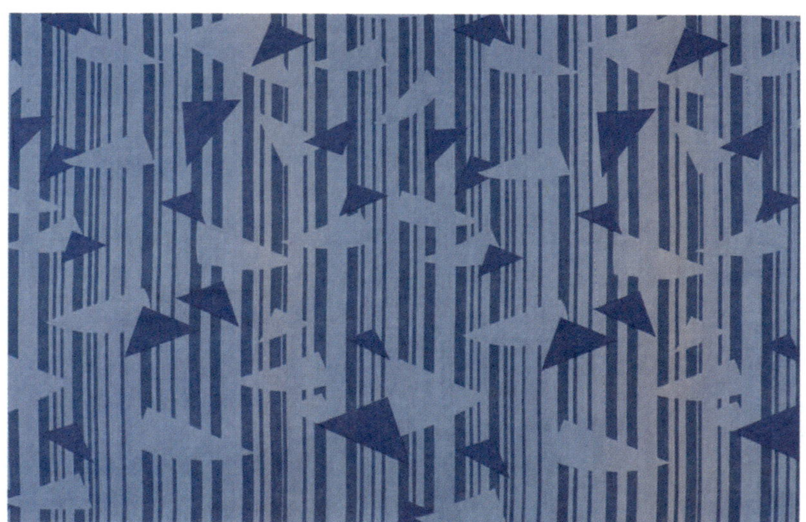

Photo: Arne Jacobsen Design I/S

1964

Nyager School in Rødovre. Interior design features the T chair etc. | 1

Member of the Akademie der Künste, Berlin

St. Catherine's College, Oxford. Interior design features Series 7, the Swan, the Airport sofa, the St. Catherine chair, the Professor chair, the Oxford table lamp and the Oxford pendant lamp etc. | 2

Sports hall for Landskrona City

1 |

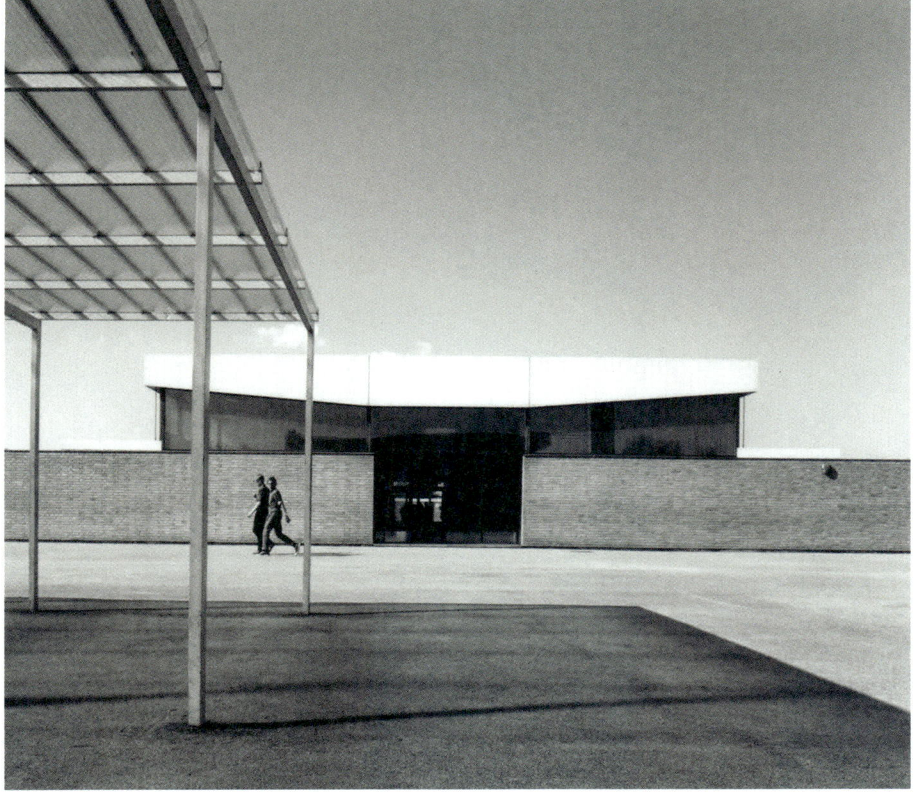

Photo: Aage Strüwing © Jørgen Strüwing

2 |

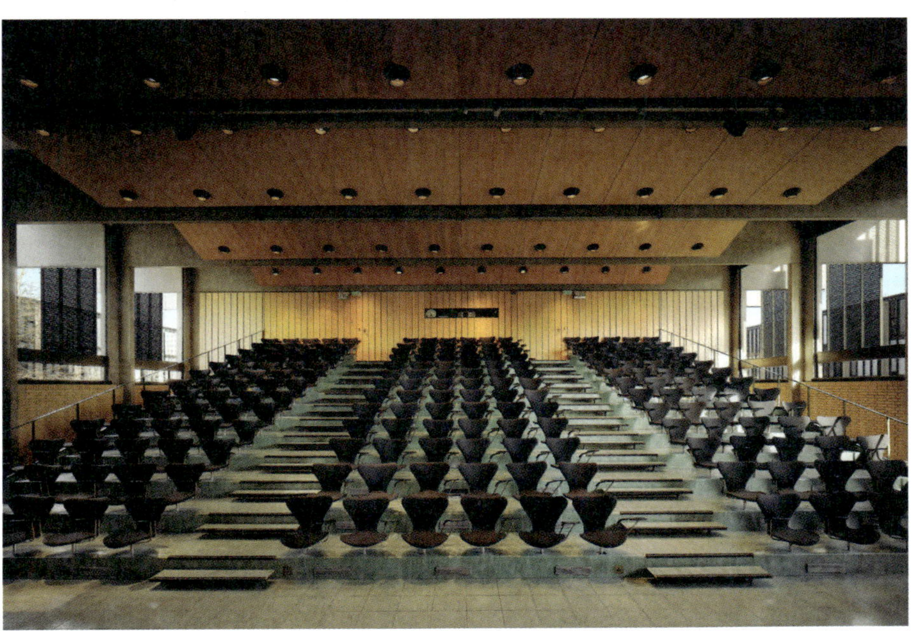

Arne Jacobsen. The original can be found in The Royal Danish Library – The Danish National Art Library

1965

2 |

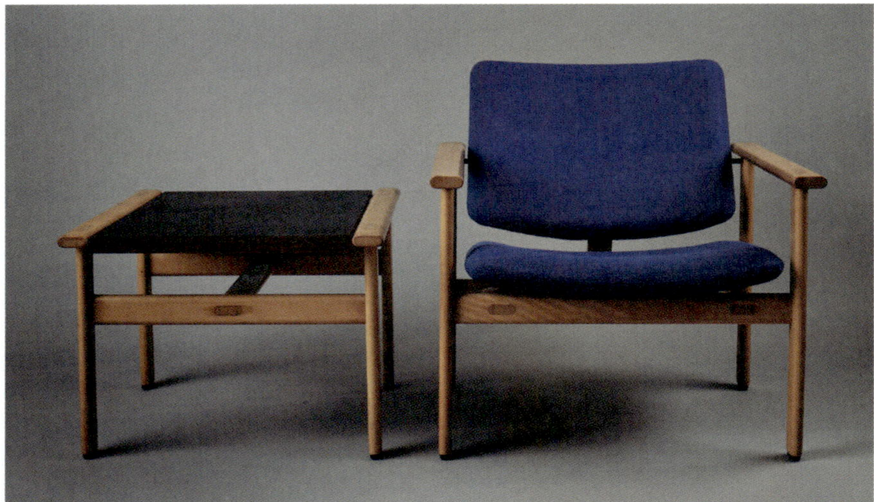

1 |

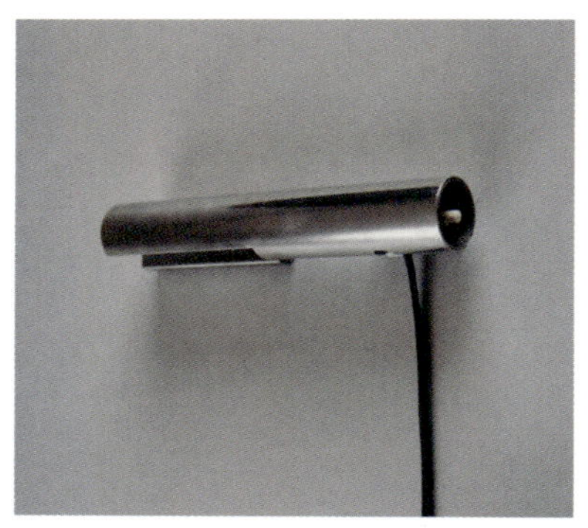

The Oxford chair series

Bedside lamp | 1

Foyer for Herrenhausen Castle Park in Hanover

Armchair with a rocking back and the associated series of office chair, tables and daybed | 2

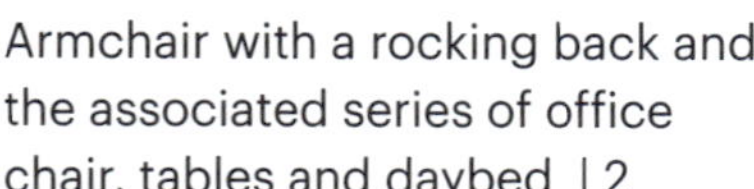

Member of the Accademia Nazionale di San Luca, Rome

1966

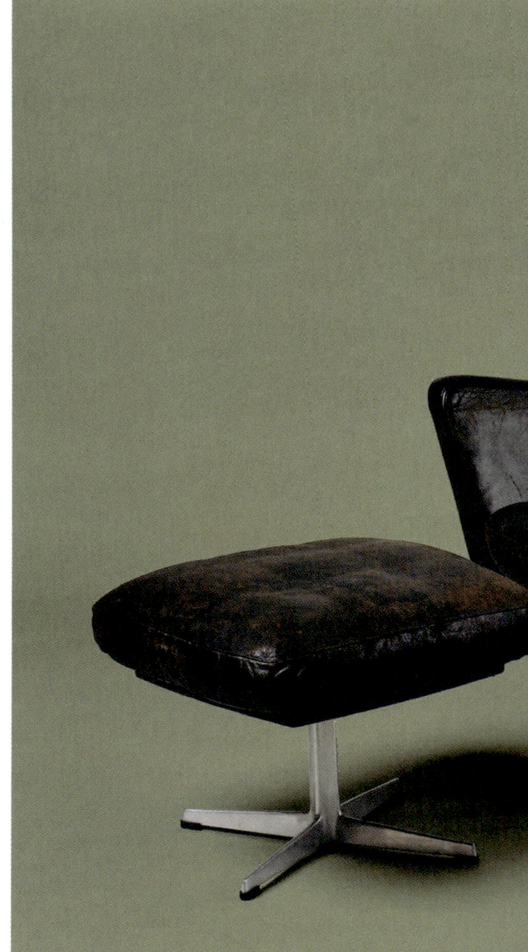

The Ox chair | 1

Honorary doctorate at the University of Oxford

1967

1 |

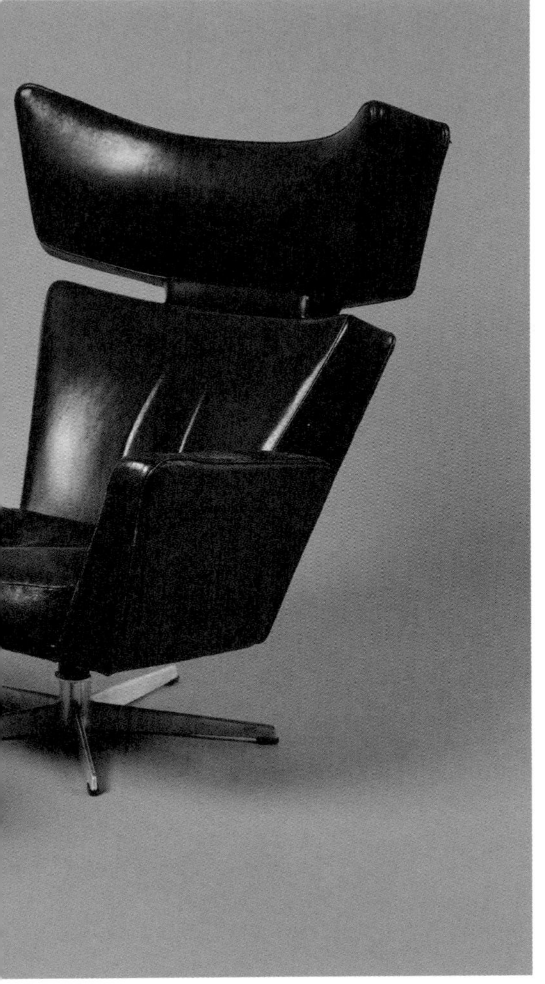

Trapholt Collection

Cylinda Line | 1

Own holiday home at Tissø. A converted 18th-century smallholding

1 |

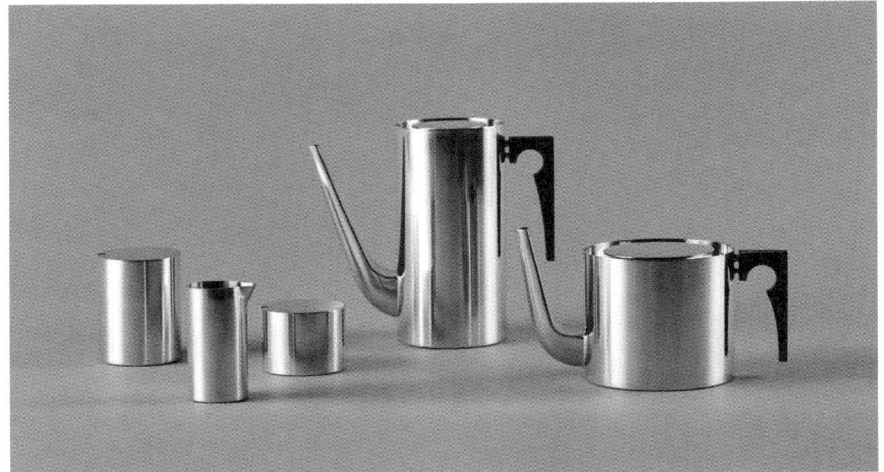

Trapholt Collection

1968

The Rover safari chair

Honorary doctorate (University of Strathclyde, Glasgow)

The 'Pre Pop' chair | 1

The Lily chair | 2

1 |

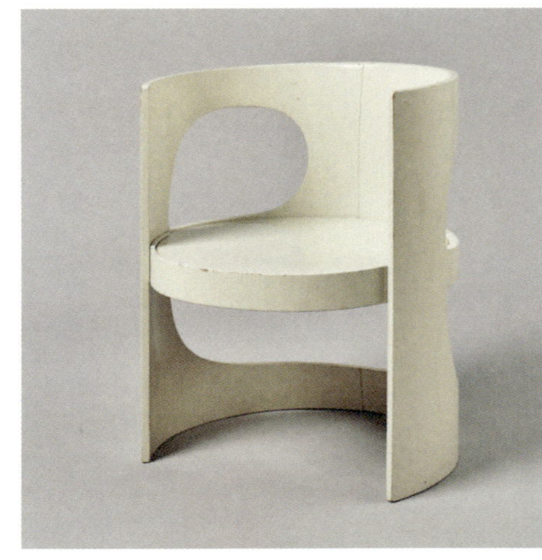

2 |

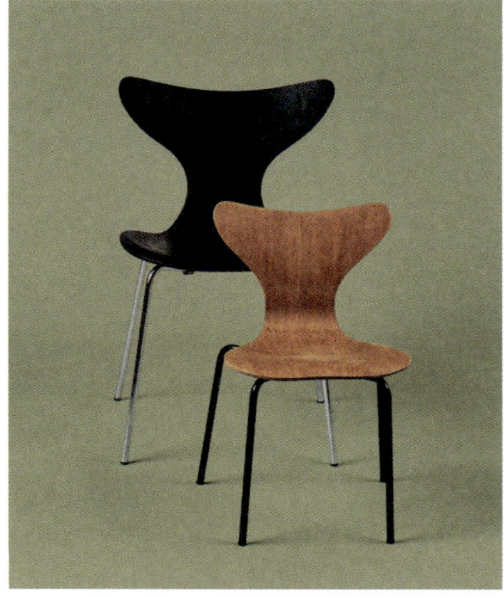

1969

The VOLA faucet series | 1

Administration building for HEW with Otto Weitling, Hamburg | 2

Rødovre Central Library. The interior design features custom-designed furniture and a children's version of the Lily

Three production facilities for Novo Terapeutisk Laboratorium in Nørrebro in Copenhagen, Kalundborg and Bagsværd

2 |

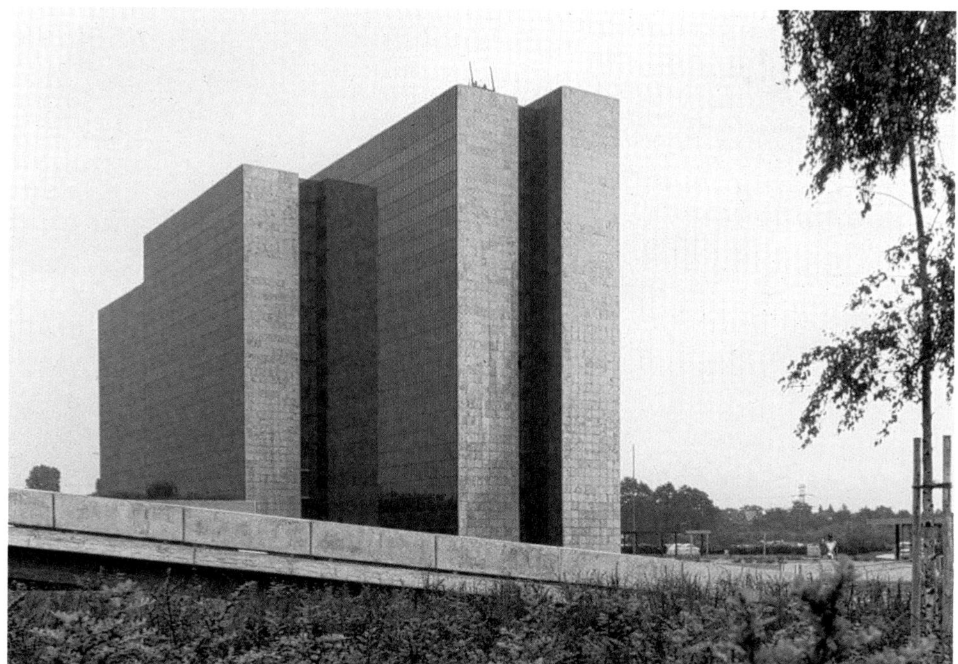

Photo: Dissing+Weitling

1 |

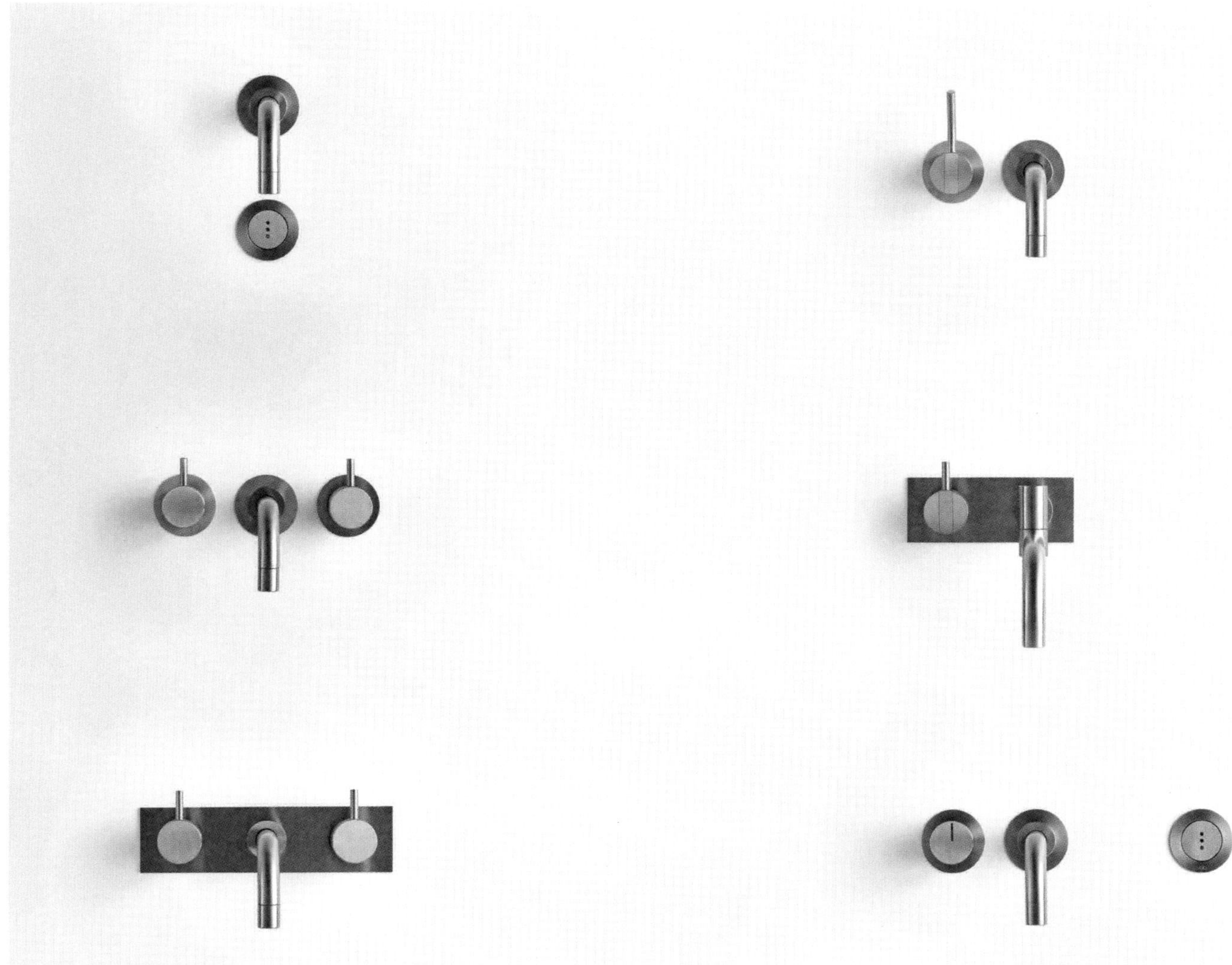

Photo: VOLA

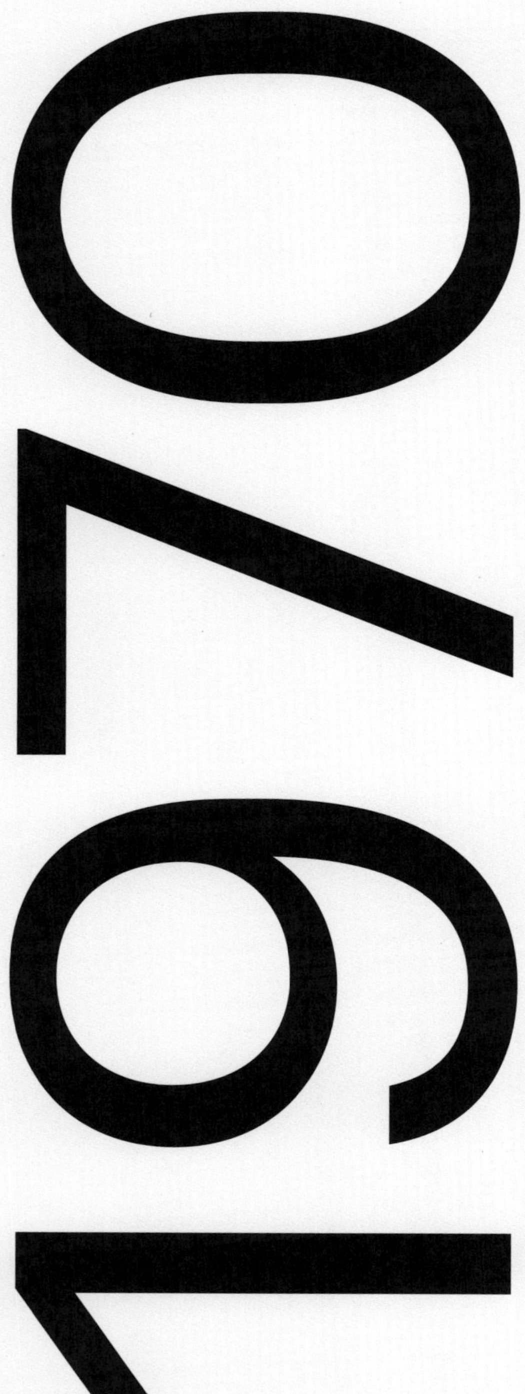
1970

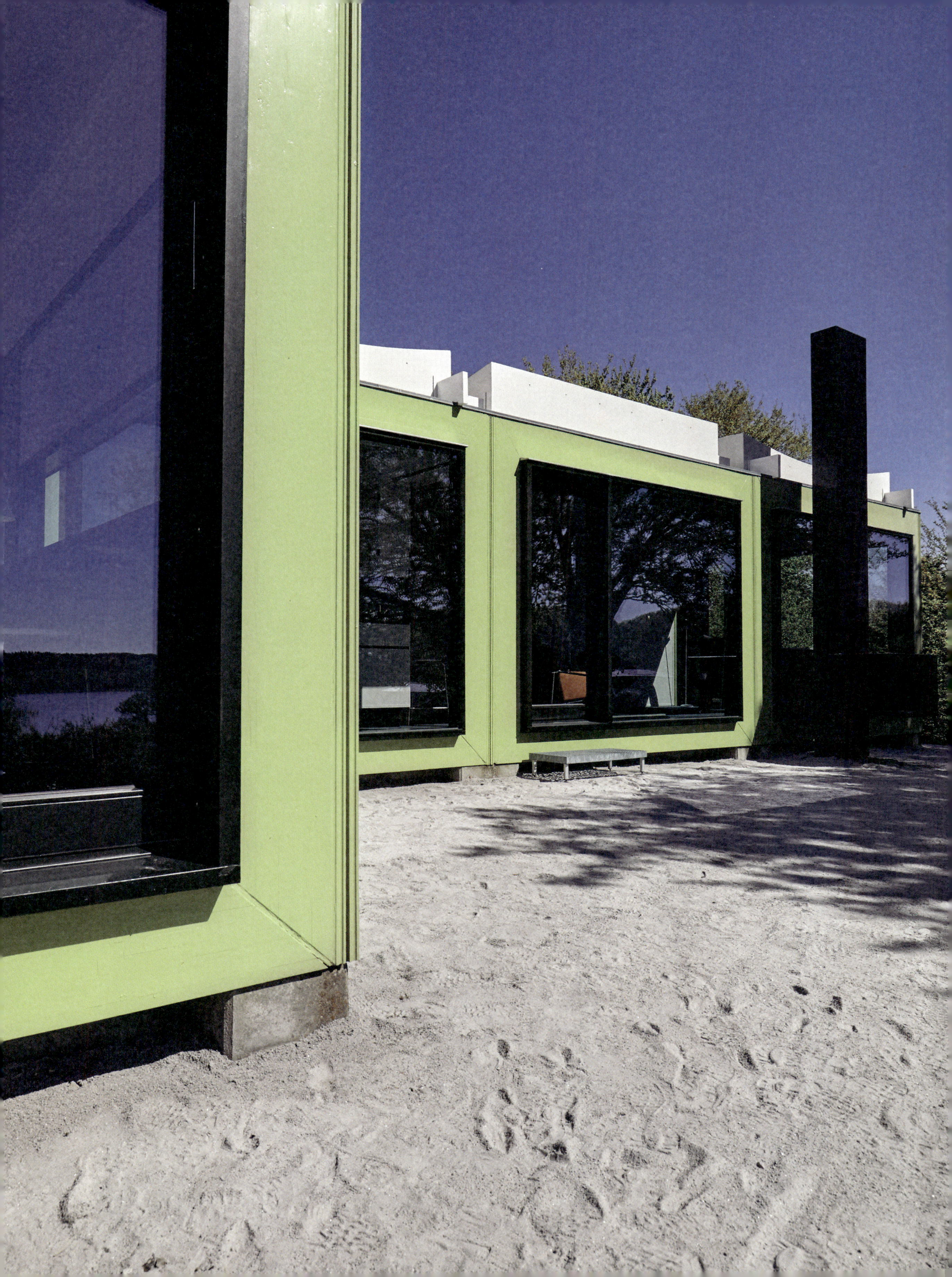

1970

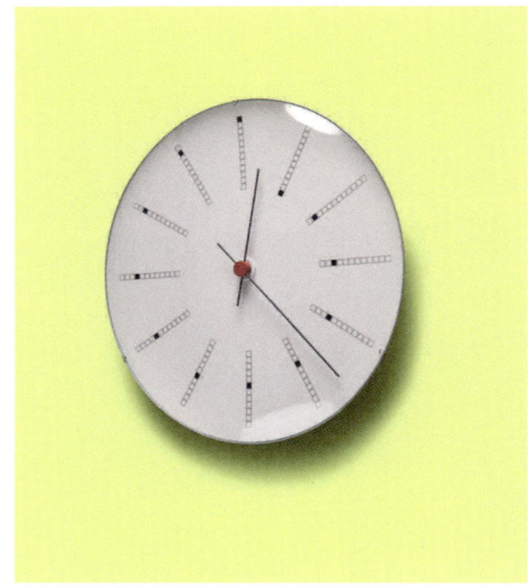

1 |

Bankers clock | 1

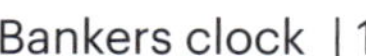

Novo Chemishe Industri, Mainz (with Otto Weitling)

Kubeflex and Kvadraflex are presented at the Archibo II prefabricated standard-house exhibition | 2

The TV chair | 3

2 |

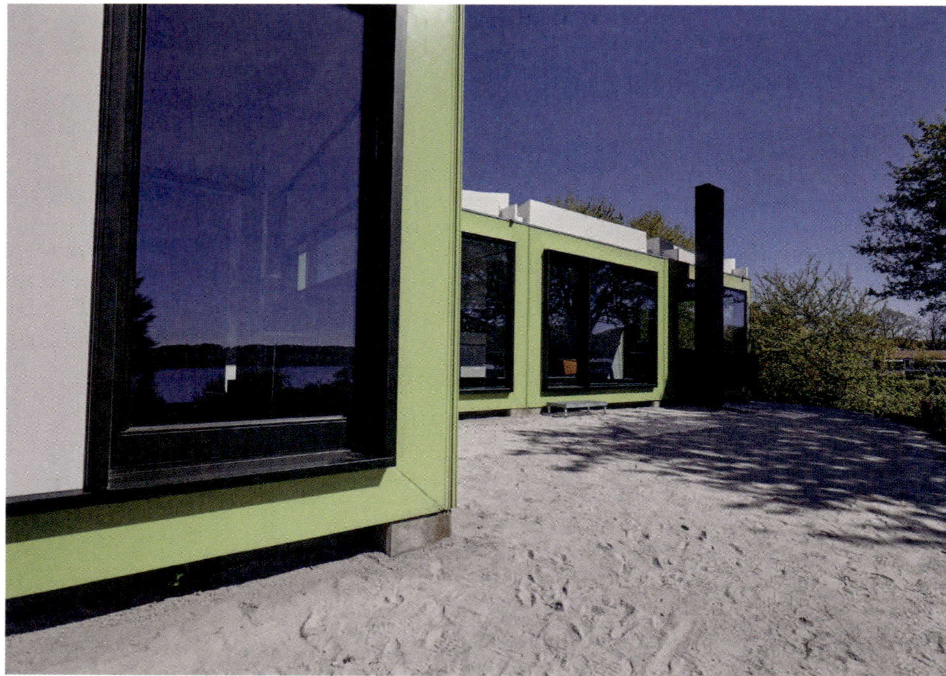

3 |

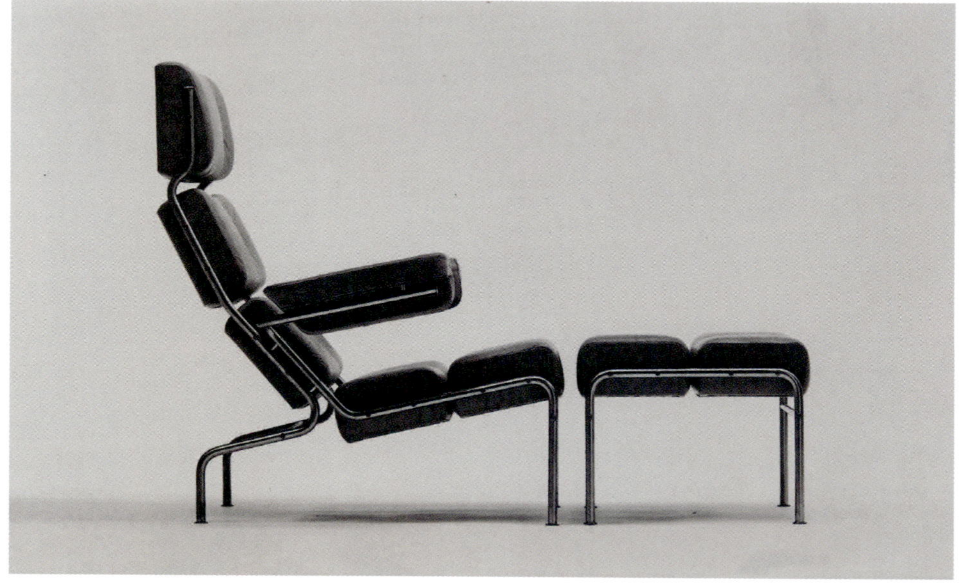

1971

Series 3400 | 1

The DJOB office furniture series

National Bank of Denmark (1st phase). Interior design features the Lily and VOLA | 2

Christianeum High School, Hamburg (with Otto Weitling)

Arne Jacobsen dies at home on 24 March

2 |

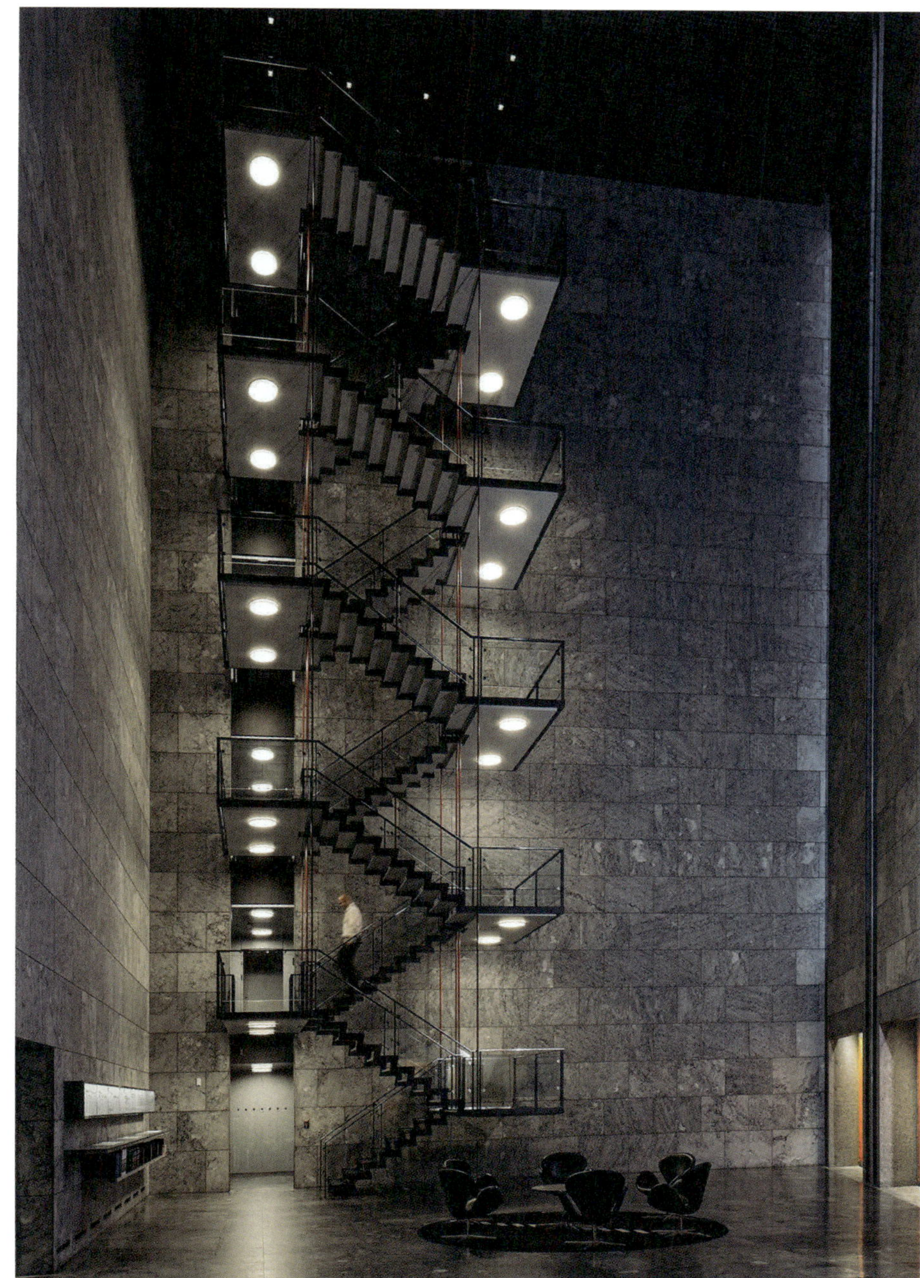

Photo: Nationalbanken

1 |

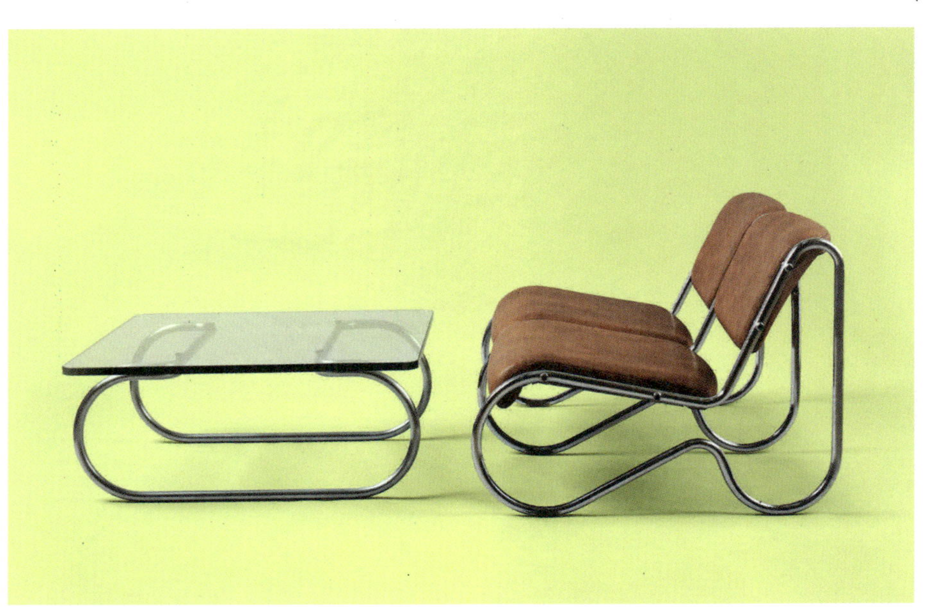

1972

The Østersø holiday centre, indoor swimming pool and spa, Burgtiefe på Fehmarn. Designed in 1965 (with Otto Weitling), built by Dissing+Weitling

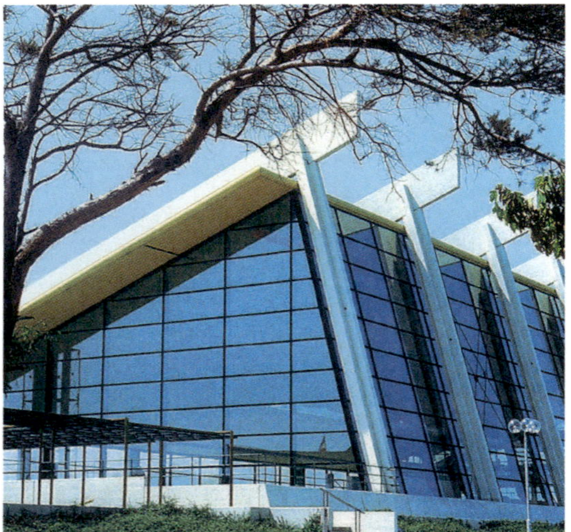

Photo: Dissing+Weitling

1973

Mainz City Hall Designed in 1968 (with Otto Weitling), built by Dissing+Weitling

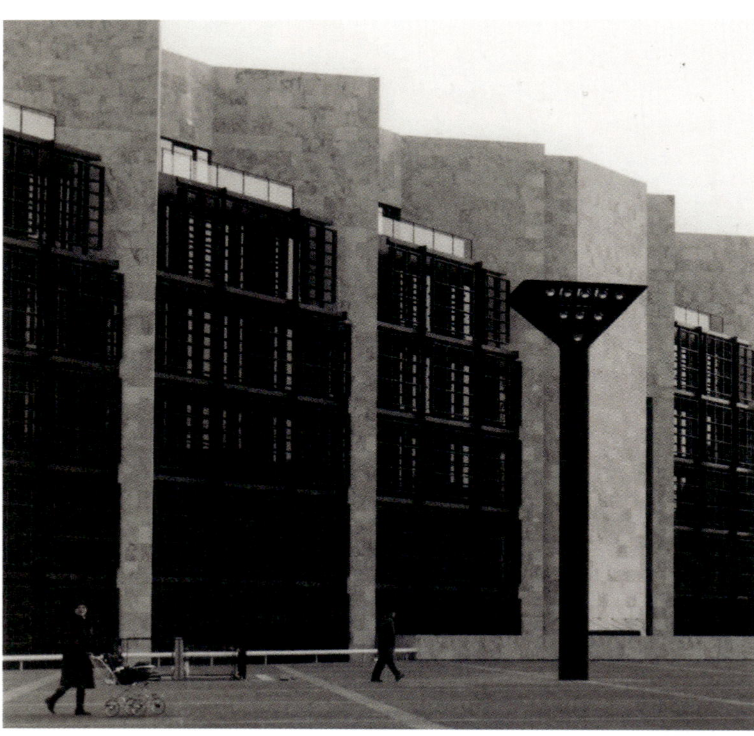

Photo: Dissing+Weitling

1976

1 |

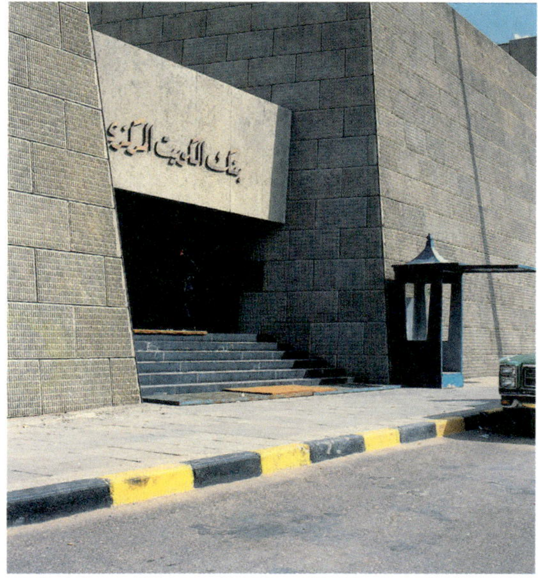

Photo: Dissing+Weitling

Castrop-Rauxel city centre, Germany. Designed in 1966 (with Otto Weitling), built by Dissing+Weitling

Kuwait National Bank. Designed in 1966, built by Dissing+Weitling | 1

1977

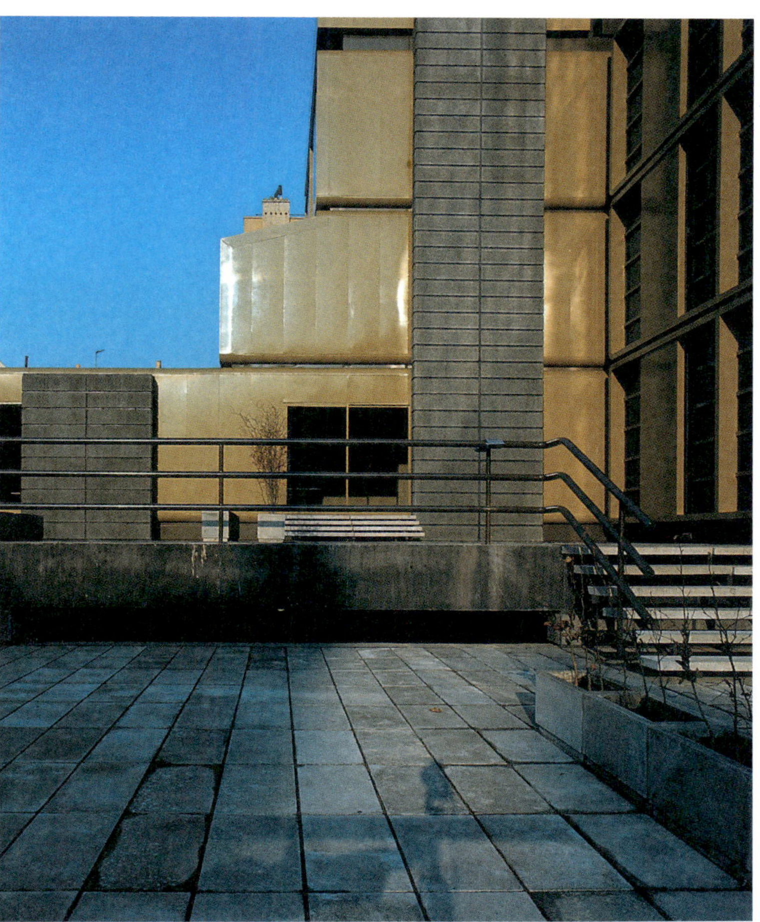

Photo: Dissing+Weitling

The Royal Danish Embassy in London. Designed in 1969, built by Dissing+Weitling

Today, visitors can see the 1970 prototype house at Trapholt, where it has been restored and recreated, featuring its Archibo II interior

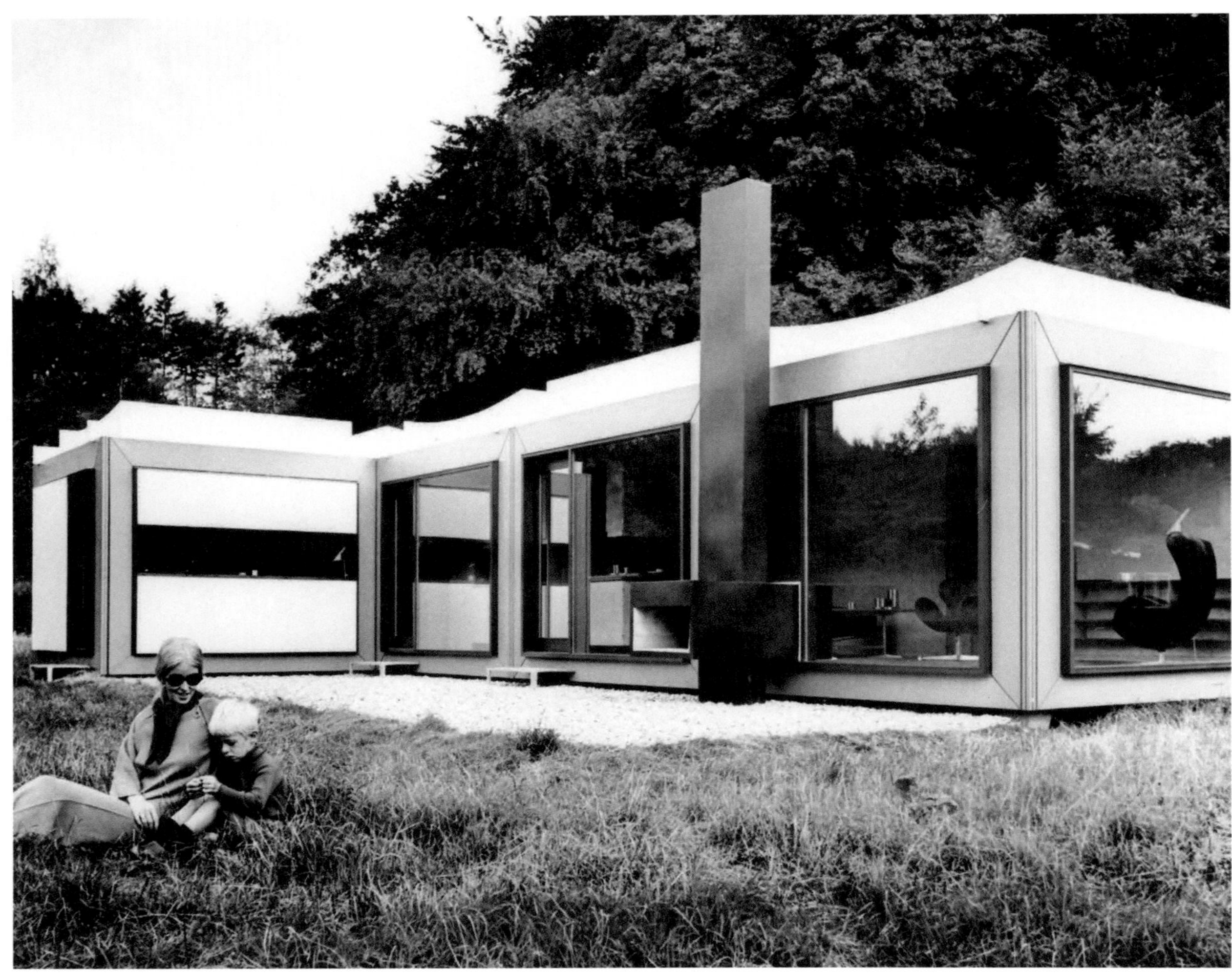

Arne Jacobsen's Kubeflex (1970). Kubeflex was a construction system based on identical, prefabricated, square modules that could be combined in various ways, thereby accommodating individual requirements. In 1970, in cooperation with the company, Høm Huse, Arne Jacobsen built a prototype for Archibo II, a prefabricated standard-house exhibition

Photo: Trapholt's archives

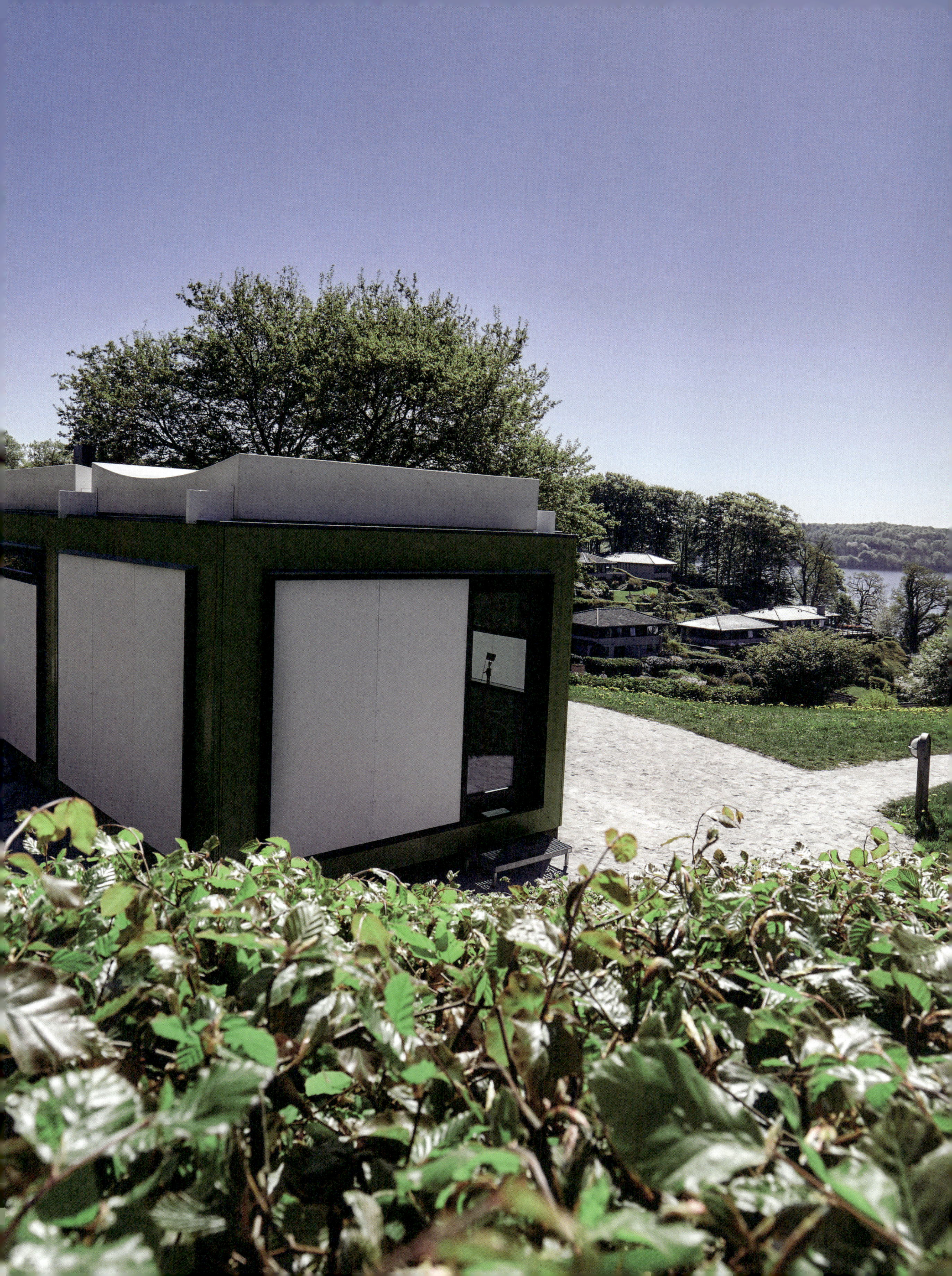

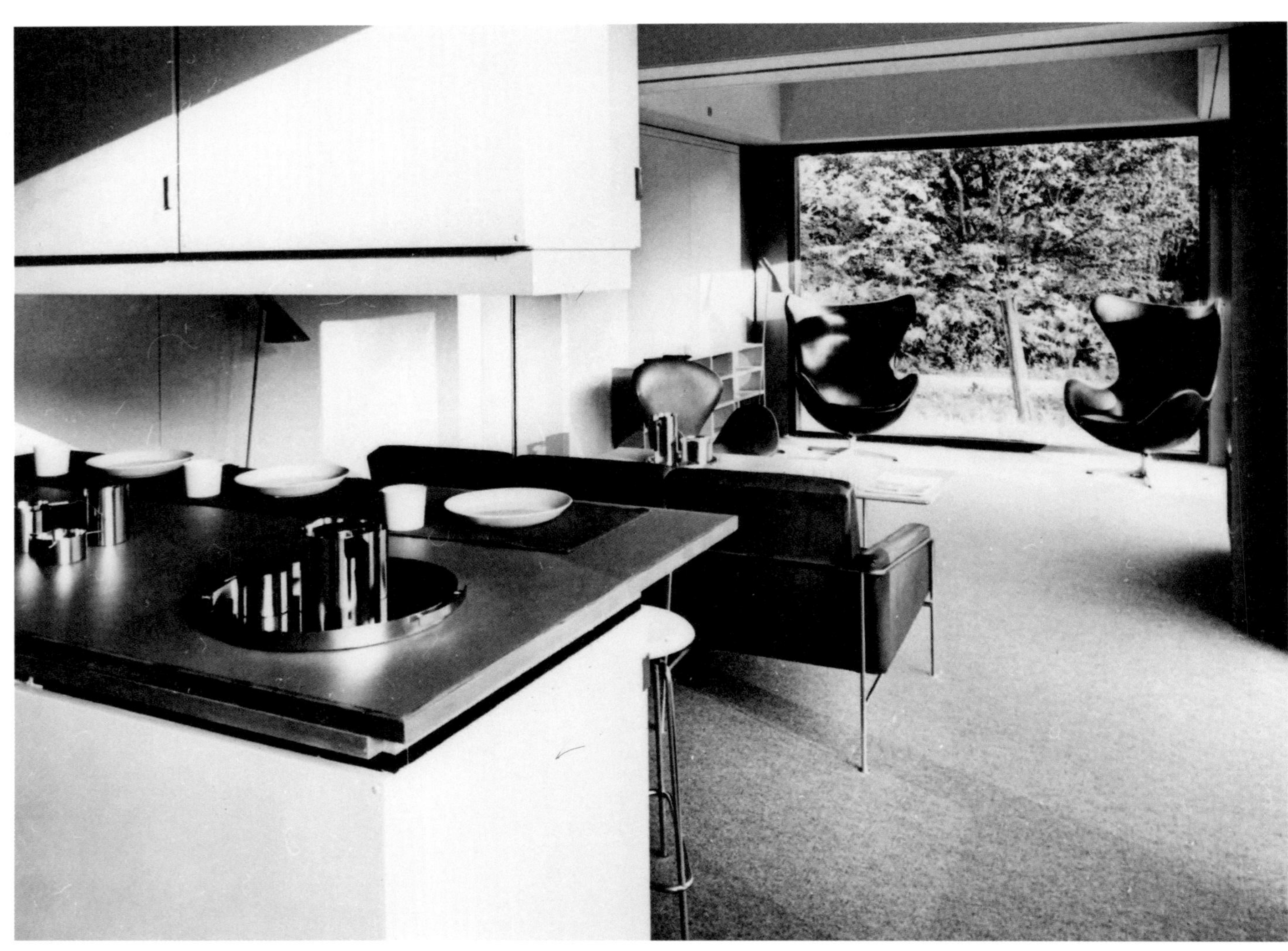

Kubeflex interior (1970). For the Archibo II prefabricated standard-house exhibition, Arne Jacobsen designed all the furniture and fittings for the prototype house

Photo: Trapholt's archives

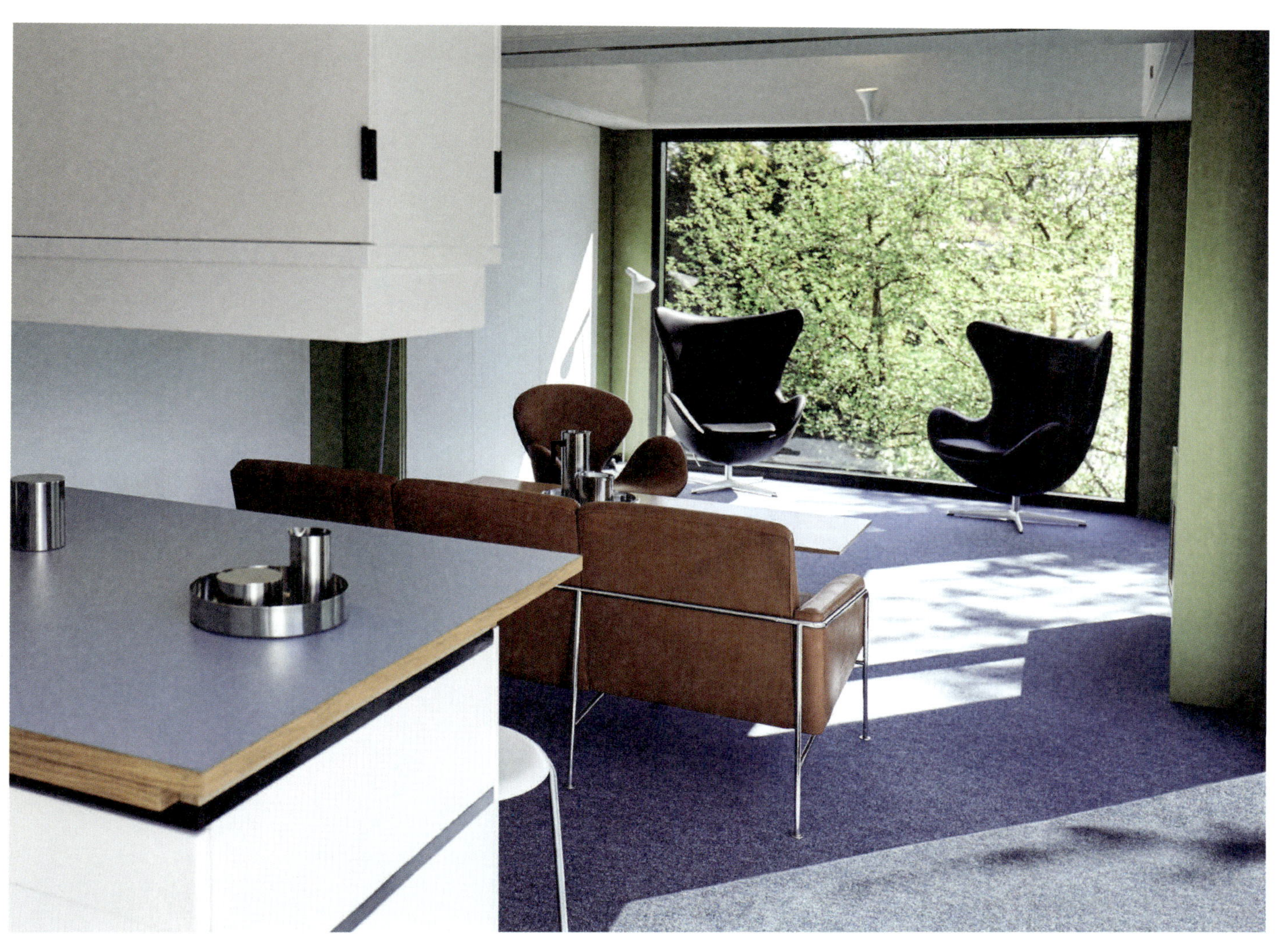

Today, all interior elements of the Kubeflex house at Trapholt are the same as those which Arne Jacobsen designed for the prefabricated standard-house exhibition - furniture, lamps, faucets etc.

Arne Jacobsen – Designing Denmark

Published in connection to the exhibition
Arne Jacobsen – Designing Denmark
Trapholt, September 2020 – May 2021

Cover illustration
Arne Jacobsen: The Ant Chair
Foto: Kenneth Stjernegaard

Executive Editor
Katrine Stenum Poulsen
Curator, Trapholt

Editors
Annika Skaarup Larsen,
Art Historian and registrar
Arne Jacobsen Design I/S
Sara Staunsager
Curator & Head of Collections, Trapholt

Exhibition design and production
Vera Westergaard
Head of Exhibitions, Trapholt

Publishing editor
Cecilie Harrits

Graphic design
Cover: Søren Varming
Layout and typesetting: AM Copenhagen

Translation
René Lauritzen

Photography
Kenneth Stjernegaard
Stjernegaard Fotografi & Film

Proof reading
BERING by Ulla Vitus Bering
Emma Marley
Culturebites

Printed by Clausen Grafisk, Denmark
Printed in Denmark, 2024
2. edition, 2024

ISBN 978-8-775-97290-6
Library of Congress Control Number: 2023949263

Publishers
Trapholt
trapholt.dk

Aarhus University Press
aarhusuniversitypress.dk

Yale University Press
yalebooks.yale.edu

Distributed by Yale University Press
302 Temple Street P.O. Box 209040
New Haven, CT 06520-9040
47 Bedford Square, London WC1B 3DP
yalebooks.com | yalebooks.co.uk

The carbon emission of this book is calculated to be 3,5 kg CO_2 according to ClimateCalc. Cert. no. CC-000157/DK

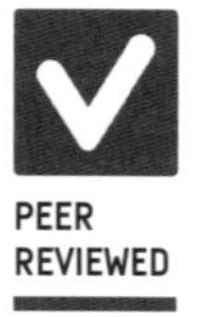

/ In accordance with requirements of the Danish Ministry of Higher Education and Science, the certification means that a PhD level peer has made a written assessment justifying this book's scientific quality.

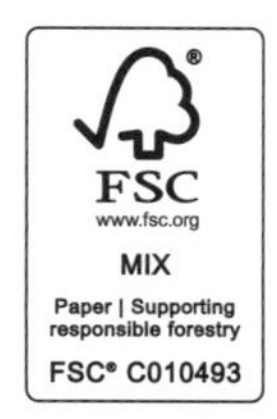

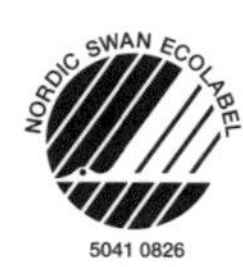

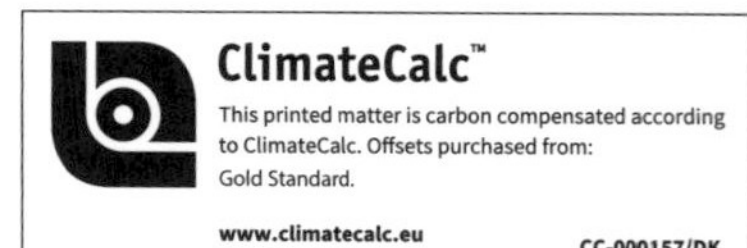

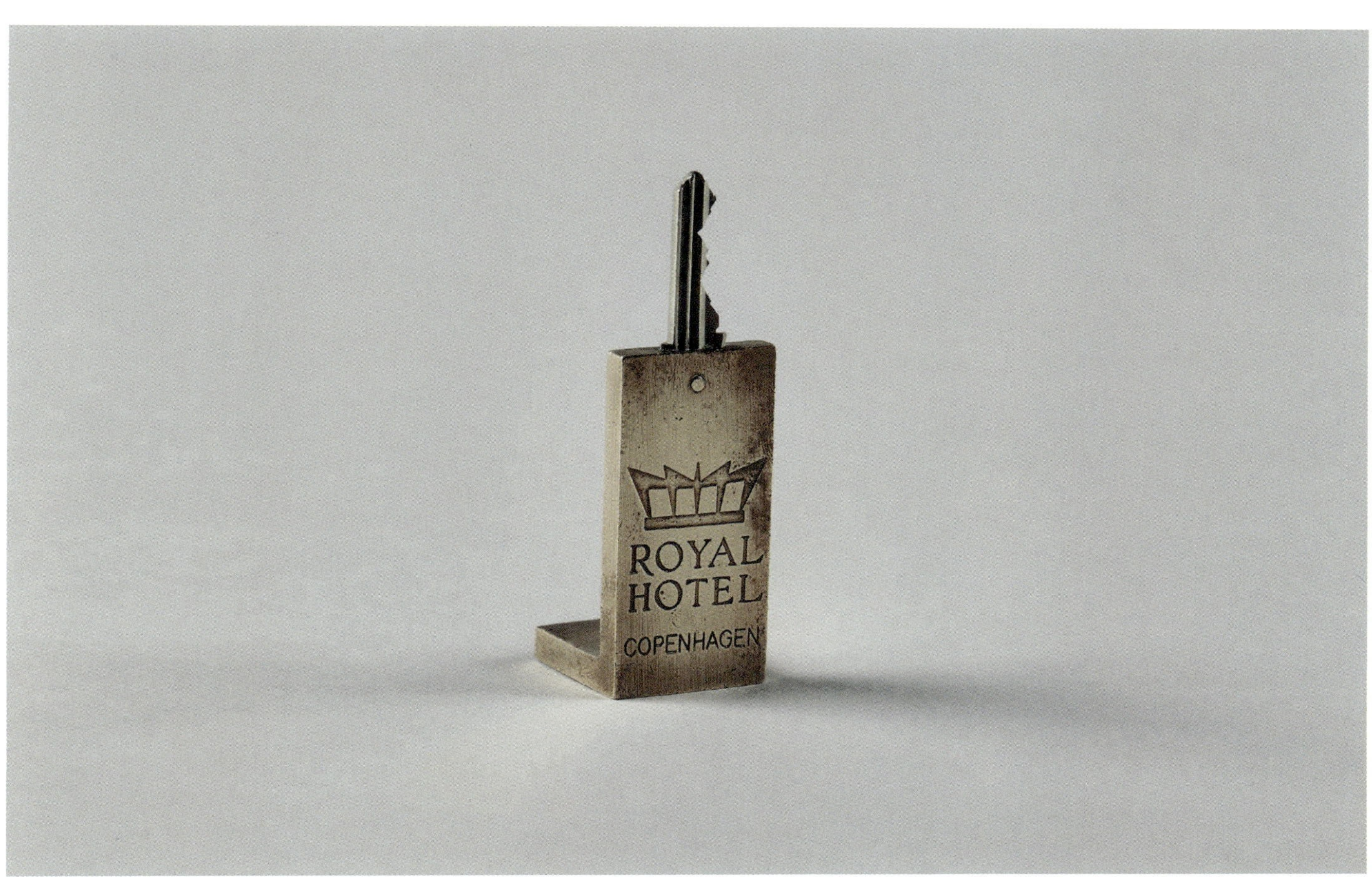

Key for the rooms at the SAS Royal Hotel

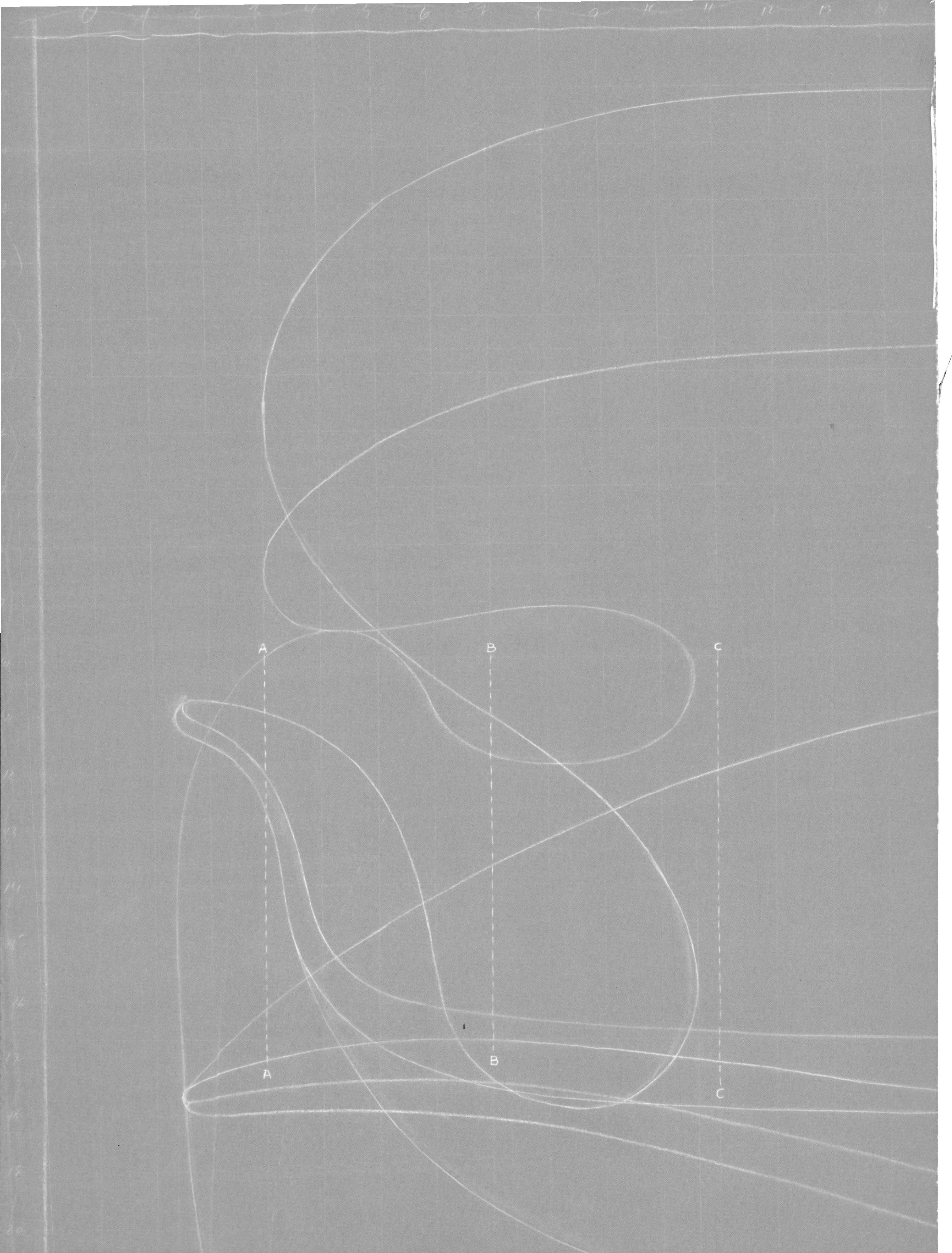
A
B
C
B
A
C